CRITICAL ISSUES IN
FOREIGN LANGUAGE INSTRUCTION

SOURCE BOOKS ON EDUCATION
(VOL. 22)

GARLAND REFERENCE LIBRARY
OF SOCIAL SCIENCE
(VOL. 459)

SOURCE BOOKS ON EDUCATION

CRITICAL ISSUES IN
FOREIGN LANGUAGE INSTRUCTION

edited by
Ellen S. Silber

GARLAND PUBLISHING, INC. • NEW YORK & LONDON
1991

Library of Congress Cataloging-in-Publication Data

Critical issues in foreign language instruction / edited by Ellen S.
Silber
    p.   cm. — (Source books on education ; vol. 22) (Garland
reference library of social science ; vol. 459)
    Includes bibliographical references.
    ISBN 0–8240–4432–0
    1. Languages, Modern—Study and teaching (Elementary)—United
States. 2. Languages, Modern—Study and teaching (Secondary)—
United States. I. Silber, Ellen S. II. Series: Garland reference
library of social science. Source books on education ; vol. 22.
III. Series: Garland reference library of social science ; v. 459.
LB1580.U5C75   1991
418'.0071.273—dc20   90-47987
                                                                     CIP

Printed on acid-free, 250-year-life paper
Manufactured in the United States of America

TO MY MOTHER, NORMA

Foreword

It was hard to imagine in 1957 that the launching of a Soviet rocket would push the United States into its greatest investment ever in foreign language education. As American policy-makers attempted to play catch-up with our brothers and sisters behind the iron curtain, this country infused federal dollars into extensive foreign language teacher training and the creation of new foreign language educational programs. The remainder of the fifties and most of the sixties were thus characterized by unusual support for the field.

As suddenly as federal support was given, however, so was it taken away; and its withdrawal was responsible for one of the darkest periods in the history of foreign language education in America. Hand-in-hand with financial cutbacks in teacher education and curriculum development, we witnessed a dramatic drop in foreign language requirements at all levels of education. When long-standing programs lost federal and administrative support, they lost interested students, and foreign language enrollments dipped to their lowest levels since the days following World War I.

Yet at this low point in the profession, a dramatic reversal occurred. The Report of the President's Commission, released in 1979, pointed the way to a brighter future. *Strength Through Wisdom: A Critique of U.S. Capability* brought to light the economic, diplomatic and military costs that are incurred when we neglect the teaching of foreign languages and cultures in American education. The report called for solutions to this problem which could be implemented without delay.

While very few of the Commission's recommendations were followed in every detail, the report's real impact was in calling attention to some of the nation's most serious educational shortcomings in foreign languages and international studies and in creating a momentum to effect change. Since then, other reports have followed adding their support for a renewal of foreign language learning in our schools and colleges. Almost every major study which has offered prescriptions for improving American public education during the 1950's has singled out the need for foreign language learning by all students.

The impact of these numerous reports and subsequent discussions has been tangible. Whereas during the seventies, very few states had foreign language requirements for high school graduation and/or admission to college, at present thirty-three states have such mandates. Consequently secondary school foreign language enrollments in many states have doubled and the number of foreign language students in colleges and universities is rising.

Politically speaking the study of foreign languages and cultures helps maintain a strong competitive position in an increasingly global marketplace. As the need to remain competitive grows, the United States is faced with a new internal imperative. We are witnessing enormous changes in the composition of our population, as immigrants, including many Asians and Hispanics, continue to come here to build new lives. These Americans challenge us to learn more about their native cultures and to use their languages. In schools, in work places, in governmental agencies, we are learning that cultural diversity increasingly affects us all.

Now with rapidly growing foreign language programs, we can once again explore important stimulating questions about what to teach and how to teach it. With renewed federal support and incentives, foreign language educators have developed numerous methodologies and have published a considerable body of research. Focusing on creative ways to maximize student success, faculty in foreign languages have experienced this decade as a period of curricular innovation.

As a result of heightened activity in foreign language education, we find ourselves again at a critical juncture. The momentum has taken hold; the rationale for foreign language instruction has been clearly and publicly stated; gradually the American people have become more aware of the need for multi-lingualism; curriculum requirements are in place; and students are enrolled in record numbers. Yet these developments do not diminish the challenge. Recent successes demand a critical assessment of our strengths and weaknesses, for we cannot afford to fail in educating future generations. We as a profession still have many questions to answer. From an educator's standpoint and from a state and national perspective, the need for this book is apparent.

Drawing on the expertise of a number of the nation's most experienced and creative foreign language educators, this volume, edited by Ellen S. Silber, addresses some of the crucial problems we face in foreign language education today. With originality and vigor, the contributors to *Critical Issues in Foreign Language Instruction* offer provocative and imaginative views on a sector of the curriculum which has often been neglected but today appears to be gaining the attention it deserves.

GREG DUNCAN
Coordinator of Foreign Languages
Georgia Department of Education

Acknowledgments

An edited volume is wholly dependent on the work of its contributors, and as editor of *Critical Issues in Foreign Language Instruction*, I have been truly blessed. Authors of the articles in this book are all experts in their fields and in addition, they are gracious, considerate people. They have made this editor's work a pleasure.

Special thanks go to Richard Brod of the Modern Language Association whose help at the beginning stages was invaluable. I am grateful to my colleagues, Eileen Burchell for her thoughtful reading of the entire manuscript, and Joseph Servodidio for some particularly good advice. I am also indebted to my dear friend Jerilyn Fisher for her fine editing skills, always so generously offered. Thanks as well to Marie Ellen Larcada, my very kind and understanding editor at Garland, and to Eric Byrnes for his expertise in preparing the manuscript.

Finally, my deeply felt gratitude to Al Silber, whose constant support and encouragement makes it all possible, and to Kenny Silber, whose very existence is a continuing inspiration.

Contents

Author Biographies

David P. Benseler (Ph.D. in German, University of Oregon) is Professor of German at Ohio State University and Editor (since 1980) of *The Modern Language Journal.* During 1987-88, he was Distinguished Visiting Professor at the U.S. Military Academy, West Point. In spring, 1989, he held the same title at New Mexico State University. Chair of the Department of German, Ohio State University from 1977-85, his publications include over fifty books and articles. In 1985 the President of the Federal Republic of Germany conferred on him the *Bundesverdienstkreuz* (Officer's Cross, Order of Merit) for his contributions to German studies. The U.S. Military Academy, West Point awarded him the Army Commendation Medal for Outstanding Civilian Service (1988).

Elizabeth B. Bernhardt (Ph.D., University of Minnesota) is Associate Professor of Foreign and Second Language Education at The Ohio State University. Previously, she was a Lecturer in German at the University of Pittsburgh where she was also the Teaching Assistant Supervisor. In addition, she has taught German at Gustavus Adolphus College, St. Peter, MN, and at Chatham College, Pittsburgh. At Ohio State, Professor Bernhardt teaches in the areas of second language acquisition, language program development, language planning, and second language literacy. She has published in the areas of teacher education and second language reading. In 1984 she received ACTFL's Emma Marie Birkmaier award for doctoral dissertation research.

Eileen Burchell is Associate Professor of French at Marymount College, Tarrytown where she teaches French language, literature, and culture and directs a seminar for Assistant Teachers in the Intensive Language Program. She chaired the Modern Language Department (1987-90) and served as Faculty Coordinator for International Programs (1987-89). She is a member of the Executive Committee of the Westchester Consortium for International Studies, Inc. and was recently elected Vice-President of the New York Conference of the American Association of University Professors. She received her doctorate in French literature from Tulane University in 1983. Her research interests include seventeenth-century theater and contemporary Québécois literature.

Heidi Byrnes (Ph.D., Georgetown University) is Associate Professor of German and chair of the department at Georgetown University. Her publications include: Editor: *Contemporary Perceptions of Language: Interdisciplinary Dimensions* (GURT 1982); with Michael Canale: *Defining and Developing Proficiency: Guidelines, Implementations and Concepts*; coauthor (with Stefan R. Fink) of *Wendepunkt*, an intermediate college German text. She is a frequent presenter at professional meetings and has published numerous articles with an emphasis on incorporating insights from second language acquisition research into teaching practice.

Gerard L. Ervin is Associate Professor of Slavic Languages at The Ohio State University, Columbus. During 1989-90 he was Visiting Professor of Foreign Languages at the U.S. Air Force Academy. He has taught French and Spanish at the secondary school level and Russian, foreign language methods, and ESL at the college level. Formerly assistant dean and founder of the Foreign Language Center at the College of Humanities at Ohio State, he has also served as President of the Ohio Foreign Language Association and Executive Secretary of the Central States Conference on the Teaching of Foreign Languages. He received the Florence Steiner Award for Leadership in Foreign Language Education from the American Council on the Teaching of Foreign Languages in 1986, and the Robert J. Ludwig National Distinguished Leadership Award from the New York State Association of Foreign Language Teachers in 1988. Ervin is the author of *Speak and Read Essential Russian* and numerous articles and book chapters on language teaching, and is co-founder and systems operator of the "Foreign Language Education Forum" on Compuserve.

Elissa Gelfand is Professor of French and former Chair of the Women's Studies Program at Mount Holyoke College. She is the author of a study of women's prison literature, *Imagination in Confinement: Women's Writings from French Prisons* (Cornell University Press, 1983); *French Feminist Criticism: Women, Language, and Literature* (Garland Publishing, 1985); and articles on French women writers, feminist theory, and women in prison. She holds a Ph.D. from Brown University. Her current project is on Jewish women writers in interwar France.

JoAnn Hammadou is currently an Assistant Professor of French at the University of Rhode Island. B.A., American University, M.A., University of New Hampshire, Ph.D., The Ohio State University; areas of specialization—foreign language education and second language acquisition. Publications in *Theory into Practice*, *Foreign Language Annals*, *Modern Language Journal*, and *The French Review*.

L. Kathy Heilenman, currently Associate Professor of French at the University of Iowa, holds a Ph.D. in Foreign Language Education from the

University of Louisville. She has taught at the middle school, high school, and university levels and has been on the faculty at Virginia Polytechnic Institute and State University, Northwestern University, and Louisiana State University. She has lectured and published in the areas of curriculum, materials, testing, and second language acquisition and is the author of the first-year college French text *Voilà!*.

Gilbert A. Jarvis (Ph.D., Purdue University) is Professor of Foreign Language Education and Chairperson of the Department of Educational Studies: Humanities, Science, Technological and Vocational at The Ohio State University. He is an author of more than forty language textbooks and editor of four volumes of the *Foreign Language Education Series*. He has served as a consultant to various agencies and institutions and has made approximately 100 invited presentations at language conferences.

Myriam (Mimi) Met is Coordinator of Foreign Languages for Montgomery County Public Schools in Maryland. The county's foreign language K-12 program includes total and partial immersion programs in French and Spanish, FLES programs in Spanish, Chinese, and Japanese with a content-based emphasis, and eight foreign languages at the secondary level with a foreign language enrollment over 25,000 students. Prior to joining MCPS, she was foreign language supervisor K-12 with Cincinnati Public Schools where she was involved with the planning and implementation of intensive FLES and partial immersion programs. She has developed programs and curriculum, and been involved with teacher training at all levels of instruction in MCPS, Cincinnati, and other school systems.

Howard Lee Nostrand is Professor Emeritus of Romance Languages and Literature at the University of Washington, where he chaired the Romance Language Department for 25 years. His thesis for the Doctorat de l'Université de Paris was in comparative Greek, Latin and French literature, *Le Théâtre antique en France* (Droz, 1934); but after serving as U.S. Cultural Attaché in Peru, 1944-47, he turned to the problem of defining and teaching the cultural context of languages and literature, where his research has been supported by a Guggenheim Fellowship and seven government grants. He was president of the AATF, 1960-62, recently president of the Seattle-Nantes Sister City Association, and is a board member of the Committee for a Community of Democracies/U.S.A.

Sue K. Otto is Director of the University of Iowa Language Media Center, Adjunct Assistant Professor of Spanish, the Executive Director of the International Association for Learning Laboratories, and a Director of PICS (the Project for International Communication Studies).

James P. Pusack is Associate Professor of German and a Director of PICS (the Project for International Communication Studies) at the University of Iowa. His computer software package for foreign language instruction, DASHER, is widely used on both mainframes and microcomputers.

Otto and Pusack have contributed numerous publications and presentations in the area of foreign language instructional technology. They are currently developing interactive videodiscs and software based on authentic television programs from European and Latin American broadcasters.

Ellen S. Silber is Professor of French at Marymount College, Tarrytown where she has been teaching French language and literature for the past twenty years. She was coordinator of women's studies from 1973-1989. Since 1985, she has been the national coordinator of Academic Alliances in Foreign Languages and Literatures, a network of school/college faculty collaboratives, and is executive editor of its newsletter, *Collaborare*. She has given numerous papers on French women writers and school/college collaboration. She has also published articles on these topics.

Diane J. Tedick has been involved with language education for over 12 years. After receiving her BA in Spanish and Secondary Education from Kent State, she moved to Spain where she taught English to adults and children for several years. She returned to the U.S. and received an MA from Ohio State in Early and Middle Childhood/Bilingual Education and afterwards worked for two years as a 3rd/4th grade bilingual teacher with Milwaukee Public Schools. She then returned to Ohio State to pursue a Ph.D. in Foreign Language Education/TESOL. While there, she taught ESL composition to graduate students. After receiving her degree in 1988, she spent two years at Fairfield University in Connecticut, where she coordinated the graduate programs in TESOL, Foreign Language, and Bilingual Education. She is currently assistant professor in Second Languages and Cultures Education at the University of Minnesota. She has published a number of articles on writing and writing assessment. Her other research interests include teacher education and critical pedagogy.

A. Ronald Walton is Professor of Chinese Language and Linguistics at the University of Maryland, College Park, and Deputy Director of the National Foreign Language Center located at The Johns Hopkins School of Advanced International Studies in Washington, D.C. Previously, Professor Walton taught Chinese language and linguistics at Cornell University and the University of Pennsylvania. He served on the committees that developed the ACTFL/ILR revised Generic Proficiency Guidelines and the Chinese Proficiency Guidelines, has been active in working with language study programs in China, and is current President of the National Association of

Self-Instructional Programs. Professor Walton is Vice-Chair of the recently formed National Council of Organizations of Less Commonly Taught Languages (the National Council), and is co-principal investigator of a major Ford grant to the National Council for the improvement of the teaching and learning of the Less Commonly Taught Languages.

Critical Issues in
Foreign Language Instruction

Introduction
Re-visioning Education in Foreign Languages

Ellen S. Silber
Marymount College, Tarrytown

In her 1971 essay, "When We Dead Awaken: Writing as Re-Vision," Adrienne Rich constructs "re-vision" to mean "the act of looking back, of seeing with fresh eyes, of entering an old text from a new critical direction." (35) She reminds us, moreover, that re-vision "is more than a chapter in cultural history: it is an act of survival." (35)

Contributors to this volume have each looked at a critical portion of the "text" of our profession from a new direction, and they have collectively created for us a fresh vision of the whole.

Several writers move the student to the center of foreign language education. They argue that to maximize our effectiveness as teachers, we must understand profoundly the learners and the creative capacities they bring to second language acquisition. Others speak of the foreign language classroom, calling upon us to be bold and innovative in transforming the content we teach, the materials we employ, and the pedagogies we practice. Still others focus on the classroom teacher, often an outsider to research rather than among its subjects and producers. They seek insights from the range of teachers' experience through time--as graduate assistants, teachers-in-training and mature professionals.

As our contributors seek to depart from familiar contexts, they raise some critical issues: Who has formulated the questions which inform our research and practice? How have they chosen those questions? How do they seek answers? What kinds of answers have they found? This process of re-vision and the directions in which it may take us have important implications for the future in all educational areas, and more specifically, at all levels of foreign language instruction.

Heidi Byrnes re-envisions the major issues in foreign language program articulation. In doing so, she questions the emphasis on institutions and their somewhat artificially imposed curricular designs. Byrnes rejects an approach to articulation which is based on a linear model of learning in foreign languages, one that implicitly views foreign language instruction K-12 as a watered down version of the "real thing" students get in college. Looking at the triangle of institution-teacher-student, she moves the student to the center and focuses on his or her cognitive development as the common ground for foreign language program articulation. Such a paradigm modifies traditional concepts of active teacher and passive student by recasting the learner as creator within the instructional process. Discussing foreign language program articulation from the perspective of the student, Byrnes advocates an articulated language curriculum based on the needs of learners at each stage of their development rather than traditionally packaged sequences.

In taking a new look at some of the psychological processes involved in learning a foreign language, Gilbert Jarvis also places the learner at the center. Describing the best pedagogical approaches as those which consider the student capable of integrating all prior experience, Jarvis stresses the learner's knowledge of his/her native language as an important contribution to the acquisition of a second language. He describes concept reformation, not label learning, as the way to understand true building of vocabulary in a foreign language, and he envisions communication as problem-solving behavior, not merely the result of the memorization and repetition of fixed sentences.

The three processes favored by Jarvis assume the learner to be a creative individual. However, if we ask students to memorize vocabulary lists, learn fixed sentences in order to communicate, and erase what is known of a first language, we imply that they are passive, devoid of relevant knowledge and experience. Jarvis re-visions the mind of the student. He persuades us that we must alter our approaches in the classroom to activate the creative capacities of those we teach.

Arguing for research that is particularly sensitive to contextual factors and differentiates clearly among ESL, bi-lingual, immersion and foreign language settings, Elizabeth Bernhardt and Diane Tedick seek to refine research paradigms so that the many different types of learners will be better served by teachers, programs and materials. They point out the limits of university-based research for a field in which most of the practitioners teach in the schools. In a fresh vision that refashions the traditional image of the research scholar at work in the library and the laboratory, these authors propose that studies be done in the foreign language classroom itself. This model suggests a new relationship between research and praxis, one that gives classroom teachers a central role they have not held in the past.

Looking at a particularly crucial (yet often neglected) area of our field, foreign language instruction in the elementary school, Myriam Met reviews the research to determine what it can—and cannot—tell us. As do others in this volume, Met conjectures that experience may provide the answers, not yet found by research, to some of the critical questions facing elementary school foreign language educators. She gives considerable experiential evidence for the effectiveness of foreign language instruction when the language is embedded in the context of children's lives, when it is tied to significant experience, and, as Met says, when "language use is viewed as a quest to construct meaning."

James Pusack and Susan Otto re-vision the classroom environment as they seek to expand it radically. They show how teachers can dramatically alter the traditional context of the classroom with its dynamic of teacher, students and text through the use of instructional technology. When technology puts students directly in touch with another culture, its people and language, Otto and Pusack argue, classroom relationships and roles will be transformed. They ask that the teacher not simply add the new technology but re-vision the concept of the foreign language classroom to use it effectively. Sensitive integration of technology, they agree, will not undermine the relationship of student and teacher through which foreign language learning takes place. The challenge will be to create the educational contexts in which technology can enhance our efforts.

L. Kathy Heilenman's treatment of textbook as "text" seeks to demystify the complex network of relationships surrounding the writing, production and use of the foreign language textbook and to analyze its role as the meeting place of teacher, student and curriculum. Pointing out that researchers, although farthest from the classroom, usually have the greatest influence in materials production, Heilenman signals the importance of the knowledge of the classroom teacher, because it has been developed primarily through experience. As Bernhardt and Tedick find in the foreign language classroom the ideal setting for data gathering, so Heilenman sees it as the locus of research for materials production. She recommends that we reverse the top-down flow of information from the "experts" to teachers and learners and that we count student reaction as a major source of information in the writing and marketing of textbooks.

Howard Nostrand renews the notion and importance of cultural competence by showing its relevance to solving both international and internal problems in the United States today. Characterizing America as a multi-cultural nation, Nostrand insists on an intercultural education that goes beyond the merely academic, which he characterizes as "knowledge about," to one that will encourage a student's identification with the ideas, attitudes and values of a second culture. The education described by Nostrand will foster in the student exceedingly valuable skills: the ability to experience a second culture with the subjectivity necessary for real identification and the capacity to re-vision American culture from the outside. Nostrand reminds us that only a true capability in a foreign language will make such intercultural experience possible.

What most of us consider to be the field of foreign language education is really the research and set of practices that apply to the teaching of three European languages. This is A. Ronald Walton's perspective and he suggests that re-visioning the field from the vantage point of practitioners of the Truly Foreign Languages (TFLs) will mean its radical reconceptualization. This reconceptualization will require new models of teaching, a fresh understanding of the meaning of culture and the realization that most foreign language education in the United States today is drenched in European cultural values. By bringing the TFLs from the margins to the mainstream, the entire field will project a truly global outlook as opposed to its current Eurocentric vision.

Like Walton, David Benseler finds that the traditions of European universities are at the base of much of what we currently teach to American upper level undergraduates. Calling on those of us in the foreign language field to revise our advanced courses, Benseler studies an area which has consistently eluded any critical analysis. He finds the need to create explicit definitions, rationales and objectives for these courses, because at present he sees none. In making explicit what has heretofore been assumed—what we have (and have not) been teaching; how our choices have (and have not) been made; which questions we have (and have not) asked—Benseler shows us that our advanced courses do not recognize what comes before them. We need, therefore, to structure the overall foreign language curriculum in a self-conscious way.

It is in Elissa Gelfand's article on marginality that Adrienne Rich's idea of re-vision is applied to the texts of an entire culture. Deconstructing the whole idea of a French canon, Gelfand shows how reading literature by outsiders undermines the idea of a monolithic national cultural legacy and sensitizes students to point of view in texts, not only to the biases of writers, but to students' own subjectivity as readers. Gelfand demonstrates that a reconstructed curriculum in which works by writers from marginal groups are not simply added but brought to the center will expose the politics of canon formation. As a result, traditional polarities such as insider/outsider and central/marginal will no longer apply, and students will have to re-vision the human relationships under discussion.

In writing about the training and supervising of teaching assistants in foreign language programs, Gerard Ervin touches on one of the most sensitive issues in the profession: the distinct lack of interest on the part of most college and university professors in elementary language instruction. This lack of interest becomes especially critical at a time when we foresee a pressing need for foreign language teachers, particularly in the schools. Ervin's article about teaching assistants' supervisors draws on research expressly conducted for this book. He concludes, with cautious optimism, that college and university foreign language departments are only now beginning to acknowledge the importance of training future teachers (as well as scholars) and so may now give long-deserved recognition to language teaching specialists.

JoAnn Hammadou highlights the Case Study as an important source of knowledge (and mental preparation) for the foreign language teacher-in-training. Hammadou believes that teachers-in-training learn best from the accumulated wisdom of experienced classroom teachers, when links are drawn to their own practice. She emphasizes how important it is for preservice teachers to learn the art of teaching by reflecting upon significant everyday educational processes such as student/teacher relationships and error correction in the foreign language classroom. For Hammadou, teachers need to understand theoretical principles within the context of the real live teaching situations found in case studies, along with opportunities for discussing these situations with peers and seasoned practitioners.

Eileen Burchell and I have chosen to write a personal narrative about our professional development as foreign language faculty. We do so in part to underscore the importance of the too often unheard voices of teachers in the creation and implementation of programs for faculty renewal. Highlighting significant personal relationships and experiences as catalysts for professional growth, we hope to empower our foreign language colleagues to play a strong role in decisions about their own continuing education.

When we consider the views of the contributors to this volume, it is clear that the coming decade will require bold and imaginative answers to crucial issues facing foreign language educators today. In calling for a critical examination of some time-honored dualities—theory/experience, researcher/classroom teacher, commonly taught languages/less commonly taught languages, mainstream/marginal, literature/language—these writers suggest new directions for re-visioning education in foreign languages, literatures and cultures as it is practiced today. Following their lead will require courage and daring, but it may well be the best way to ensure our survival in the 1990s and beyond.

References

Rich, Adrienne. "When We Dead Awaken: Writing As Re-vision." *On Lies, Secrets, and Silence*. New York: Norton, 1979. 33-49.

Issues in Foreign Language Program Articulation

Heidi Byrnes
Georgetown University

Introduction

As we begin the 1990s, foreign language professionals increasingly acknowledge the need for assessing within a larger context the changes that have come about in rapid succession during the last decade. It seems that, if our professional activities are to bear substantive fruit, the heady days of exuberant action, perhaps even of overstated or unfounded positions and hopes, must now be followed by times of sober long-term planning, careful weighing of options, and, most importantly, of rethinking underlying issues.

One topic, perhaps more than others, symbolizes this growing understanding. It is the topic of articulation, at once a prism for shedding light on a diversity of concerns as well as a focal point to which our discussion must necessarily be directed as we look toward implementation of a new language acquisition paradigm within an expanded delivery system for language instruction.

In itself, the topic of articulation is by no means unfamiliar. However, while past treatment primarily addressed internal consistency within the curriculum of a given institution or the unsatisfactory progression between secondary and post-secondary instruction, current calls for a reconsideration of articulation indicate a dramatically broadened scope and, by extension, a distinctly different understanding of the concept of articulation itself. It seems that at the core of articulation we now find a focus on well-motivated long-term sequencing of learning events, understood as being irrevocably tied to the issue of language acquisition, no matter who the learner, no matter what the instructional circumstances for such acquisition. While program-administrative concerns, among them placement testing, awarding of credit, materials selection, or requirements, will all continue to play an important role, our vision of articulation is now sufficiently distinct from that of the past and carries its own distinctive direction. This assures that discussion of articulation is not only a current need but a requirement on our professional agenda for some time to come.

Whatever direction that discussion will take, it is clear that equitable and foresighted measures will not come easily and quickly. In order to address an issue that, in even less turbulent times, steadfastly eluded our efforts toward resolution, we have no choice but to rethink our professional credo with great honesty. We must employ all the theoretical and experiential resources at our command, listen with fairness to the diversity of constituencies within our profession, give recognition to a variety of educational philosophies, and deal creatively with the constraints and possibilities that are inherent in the administering of education in the American context.

Let me preface the body of my remarks with the following observation that applies to my entire line of argumentation: while articulation in the foreign language curriculum is undoubtedly a national issue, its most viable and most expeditiously implemented solutions are likely to occur at the regional and local level. National organizations and national fora should do no more and no less than to establish a well-considered framework, fostering and supporting the kind of informed discussion that is the precursor to successful action. Thus, while there may be reasons for advocating a "centralist" stance, the crucial need for action and for detailed steps that support articulated curricula, not merely general recommendations, is an irrefutable argument in favor of regionally or locally prepared solutions.

Background and Statement of Problem

As mentioned earlier, the topic of articulation is by no means new. Indeed, it is touching if not to say humbling, to read the "Proceedings and Papers of the Panel Discussion: Articulation from High School to College and the Problem of Placement" (1969), held at the 1968 AATG meeting in New York. Lest we think that all our problems or all our solutions are hinged to "proficiency" as it has come to be understood in the 1980's, let me quote from the first paragraph of that summary: "Similarly, a student of German will not pursue a path to proficiency and literary understanding if the course of study is uninviting or frustrating." We can easily substitute students of any other language into that unequivocable and inherently sensible statement and apply it to our current situation. Today's greater interest in language instruction beyond the required sequence in college may give learners a better chance for attaining higher levels of proficiency. But only if instruction attends to a smooth transition between oral and literate language use will they gain the desired understanding of literary works. Even with a pronounced proficiency orientation, perhaps because of it, articulation is once more a primary issue.

More to the point, previous discussion, particularly that in Lange (1982), gives a highly informative overview for some of the major terms that must be defined when one wishes to understand articulation. It also offers a number of proposals for solutions to which I refer the reader. As it is not my intention to restate the authors' major findings nor to add to the recitation about lamentable conditions that abound—most of these are generally rather well known in any case—, I incorporate existing literature primarily in order to lay common terminological ground, and as a way of speaking to those issues that I see as crucial in our ability to address problems of articulation in the near future.

Lange (1982) identifies the following terms in the discussion of articulation: (1) *horizontal articulation*, "a coordination of any curriculum across the many or several classes that are simultaneously attempting to accomplish the same objectives" (115); (2) *vertical articulation*, which "refers to the continuity of a program throughout the length of the program" (115) and (3) *interdisciplinary and multidisciplinary articulation* which addresses the "capability of a second language as a school subject to associate with other disciplines in the curriculum" (116).

Lange argues convincingly for the need to consider horizontal and inter-/multidisciplinary articulation as part of the entire complex. In this context, however, I choose to restrict my discussion to that of vertical articulation, that is, the building of instructional sequencing over a significantly enlarged curricular span. A narrow interpretation of horizontal articulation, namely the coordination of parallel sections of the same course, is so much a local issue that it can be safely disregarded for now. A wider interpretation which targets a certain level of instruction irrespective of learner age, e.g., any beginning language instruction, no longer belongs strictly to horizontal articulation where "the same goals" are envisioned. Rather, different treatment of such courses is called for precisely because different learners are involved. Thus, the problem is more appropriately addressed under vertical articulation. Finally, articulation across the disciplines is, to some extent, outside our most immediate professional concerns and can, therefore, be temporarily set aside without endangering the validity of observations regarding vertical articulation.

While these primary divisions are rather non-controversial, the meaning of other key terms identified and discussed by Lange in conjunction with articulation, such as learner outcomes, performance objectives, teaching strategies, materials, and procedures for the evaluation of outcomes, is far less likely to encounter broad agreement in the profession. This is so since any answer, by design or by default, is grounded in the respondent's understanding of the overall goals of language instruction.

Such a reminder may be perceived as an unnecessary note of caution in today's professional climate where communicatively oriented language teaching seems to be advocated by all influential parties. Nevertheless, I am reluctant to state that we have, in fact, found within communicatively oriented language teaching the desired consensus on a national agenda. Assuming that the steps actually taken toward implementing curriculum, e.g., methods, materials, modes of evaluation, are a better indication of where the profession really stands than are professional journal articles and meeting agendas, then we are far from agreement on our goals. The textbook market, in production and sales, is only one, though a rather powerful and tell-tale manifestation of the existence of a wide variety of persuasions, not to mention the fact that it provides continued evidence for a well-known phenomenon of long standing, the textbook essentially serving as curriculum (Ariew 1982).

So how are we to interpret a professional dialogue that has, for some time now, favored students' language use in comprehension and production as the desirable instructional goal for the end of the century? Certainly, such a pronounced focus cannot be dismissed as negligible information. But it bears a closer look. In general terms, the goal of communicative teaching is contrasted with students' metalinguistic or grammatical knowledge about the language, which presumably characterizes much of past teaching practice. A dichotomy has been established that contrasts communicative language teaching with an emphasis on formal features. However, it is worth reminding ourselves that this is not the only possible opposition, nor is determining its validity or usefulness necessarily the most important question that needs to be resolved. Within the setting of American instructed language learning, the goal of language use in comprehension and production can also be defined in other ways, and these are not altogether renegade or uninformed ways. In choosing to dissociate the discussion of the goals of language instruction from such bipolarities as linguistic vs. strategic competence, or knowing vs. doing, these positions simply do not conform to the currently officially "sanctioned" dialogue.

Let me qualify and expand on this last remark. I do not at all wish to defend conditions that are untenable since they disregard the existence of instructional discontinuities of unpardonable proportion, such as the chasm between minimalist language instruction and the lofty goals of literature courses in many college curricula, or the rift between much middle school language teaching and high school instruction (James 1989; Pesola 1988). These are indefensible conditions precisely because they reveal a totally unarticulated curriculum.

But the problem of an unarticulated curriculum that cannot possibly work to reach a particular program's stated goals is completely distinct from the problem engendered by a diversity of goals throughout American public education, both over the entire curricular span and at different stages within it. Indeed, when we observe that teachers in parallel sections of the same course have obviously divergent expectations of their learners, employ teaching strategies that seem only diffusely related to the stated desired outcomes, work with dramatically different materials and have variant evaluation procedures (see Lange 1982:120-22), we may very well be dealing with a serious problem of curricular articulation. However, we may also have an instance of an unresolved diversity of teaching goals. Or we may be dealing with an irreconcilable divergence of opinions regarding paths to language learning,—not to mention far less desirable reasons, such as inexperience, uncooperativeness, budgetary restrictions, or even incompetence. Which of these analyses comes closest to the truth can be ascertained only when the key actors in the implementation of curriculum have been consulted. For all the well-known reasons, not even consultation of curricular documentation in itself is sufficiently informative!

To illustrate the fact that program discontinuities are played out in real time not only as "simple" problems of articulation along the path toward agreed-upon goals, but can just as easily be deep disagreements about the very goals and the ways and means toward them, let me refer to three recent articles.

Lange's latest discussion of articulation (1988) recognizes the crucial role of the learner in all aspects of curriculum development. Although he is optimistic that the four interconnected syllabuses of the communicative curriculum, —the linguistic, communicative, cultural, and general language learning syllabus—can be successfully linked in the person of the learner, it is clear that, in basing communicative language teaching on the individual learner, we potentially sow the seeds for the very loss of curricular consensus that we need for a well-articulated program. I happen to concur strongly with the proposed instructional shift. But if a turn toward the individual learner is to be useful for curriculum building, we must be able to draw on a framework of characteristics that apply to broad groups of learners, beyond each one's particular characteristics. Such a framework is in dire need of definition.

From a different perspective, Sachs (1989) questions our four skills communicative approach to language teaching. To equate current emphasis on language use with oral language use, as is frequently the case, is fallacious: to him, linguistic and cultural literacy in the foreign language are the goals of our efforts, and these are, first and foremost, literate constructs. Therefore a teaching approach which takes students "from the spoken to the written language, as one must with children," would essentially be "pointless" (74).

Finally, Redfield in an article entitled "The Politics of Language Instruction," observes that academic "prestige attaches, not to the ability to teach, but to the thing taught" (1989:9). Considering the ability to communicate in a language to be a rather ordinary phenomenon and judging foreign language study at the college level to be primarily remedial, he echoes, though for purely administrative reasons, the call for making philology the goal of modern language teaching at the university level. To realize this goal, we should search outside the academy to locate the required means for allowing students to come up with the necessary proficiency.

Disconcerting though these different viewpoints on instructional goals may be, our difficulties in resolving the problem of articulation do not stop here. Even if we can clarify and agree upon some major types of goals, we are far from a blueprint on how each desired goal for language use is to be brought about over time. As we know so well, curricular goals do not directly translate into curricular units and sequences, the backbone of articulation (Galloway 1987). A plethora of methods has sprung up, many with claims of being the "true religion", claims which most teachers regularly dismiss in favor of a happy eclecticism. Indeed, methodological pluralism may be precisely what is called for. But simple common sense also indicates that not everything is right for everyone at all times. We need additional criteria for decision-making.

So where shall we turn for guidance in establishing an articulated curriculum? Does the profession's progress amount to no more than agreement, at long last, that descriptions of instructional goals in terms of seat time are meaningless and the concession that, instead, we must find ways to express language competence, however envisioned, in terms of performance, however defined? Is "proficiency" as a construct powerful enough for young learners who are likely to be taught by a less grammar-centered method, or is it, perhaps, too powerful to be applied to language abilities that have more to do with creative achievement in a use-oriented instructional setting than they do with curriculum-independent proficiency? Are the top-down (not bottom-up!) equations "1 semester of college work equals 1 year of high school instruction (or one credit), and 1 year of secondary instruction equals 2 years of middle school instruction" to be the cornerstones for our edifice of curricular articulation at the secondary and post-secondary level? Are we relegated to the vague notion that we somehow need to rethink the incorporation of "grammar"? Is the rift between a functional use orientation and a humanistic use orientation to be permanently unbridgeable? Finally, and most disturbingly, might not the fact that we have dramatically expanded our view of language, from a *language replication* paradigm to a *language creation* paradigm (Swaffar 1989: 56), move successful articulation forever beyond our reach, precisely because we no longer enjoy the luxury of a firm foundation in steady grammatical norms but must deal with the inconsistencies and insecurities of the individual learner's creative and error-prone approximations of the language to be learned?

Some New Professional Realities

Whatever the answers to these questions, we must consider in the solutions at least the following conditions under which we will be conducting our professional activities. They give current discussion of articulation an unprecedented range of content and an unprecedented range of options, not to mention unprecedented urgency.

1. The Expanded Curriculum

With the rapid expansion of foreign language requirements and foreign language programs at all levels of instruction, from kindergarten through the undergraduate college years, the need for coordinated continuity no longer merely refers to the traditional dilemma of an imperfect transition between high schools and colleges. The call for a well motivated sequencing of instruction now applies to a curriculum that is significantly extended over time and already shows every sign of being disjointed at least at two other instructional junctures: from the elementary to the middle school or junior high school years, and from that level to the high schools.

However, I contend that this rapid expansion of language instruction over the entire curricular sequence is not only a drawback, the proximate and urgent cause for action toward an articulated curriculum. It also has the potential of pointing to a solution, since, for the first time in perhaps three decades, we can take the long view on educational and L2 development, rather than always working with disturbingly reduced sights.

2. The Levels of Proficiency

As instruction is extended, it will encompass levels of language ability that have heretofore not been within the reach of American public education. Much of past curricular, methodological, and instructional discussion has focused on the beginning of language learning, with very little interest and effort having been expended on what it means to become an advanced learner of an L2.

In this context several things seem all too clear already. The younger our learners are at the beginning of instruction, the more holistic, semantically based their language learning is likely to be for a number of years. The range of advantages to be reaped from this development is immeasurable. Among the desired outcomes we can expect to find significantly improved listening comprehension, much more native-like pronunciation, a better feel for the socially motivated and socially derived aspects of language use, a greatly expanded set of communicative strategies tied to enhanced pragmatic awareness, and a deeper appreciation of the culture-specificity of language.

However, the full benefits of early instructional contact for ultimate attainment in a foreign language will not automatically accrue simply due to longer association with that language. They depend crucially on a careful balancing between vastly enriched input over the expanded instructional time, but also on significantly expanded opportunities for output of a much broader range than we have previously been able to target. Essentially, we must find ways in the well articulated curriculum to gradually supplant the intuitive semantic grammar of comprehensible input with the reflected syntactic grammar of comprehensible output (Swain 1985). Furthermore, such metalinguistic competence must be built up over the entire spectrum of language use that marks an adult user of the language.

This means that, once learners' oral language has reached a balance between the two aspects of accuracy and fluency—and I could well imagine this to be the case at the end of secondary schooling—, an articulated curriculum must focus on creatively guiding the learner further to literate use of the foreign language, *both* in oral and written language.

In this context, let me briefly refer to at least two major administrative repercussions of an extended curriculum and the desired attainment of upper levels of proficiency.

a. From the standpoint of college foreign language programs it is imperative that, as more and more states are putting high school foreign language requirements into place, modes of placement are devised, even if, in the past, the need for placement testing was grandly dismissed. Neither the proud assertion that high school foreign language instruction simply does not meet the standards of college work nor the soft-hearted claim that students are the best judges of their language abilities and, furthermore, should not be forced into a language class that might earn them less than the desired A are acceptable if expanded language capabilities are the goal of an expanded language curriculum.

b. Likewise, from the standpoint of high school foreign language program administration, the common practice of having students fulfill a two year language requirement in grades 9 and 10, with a two year hiatus before any college language courses, has questionable merit for enhanced language proficiency, given our knowledge about language loss in relation to attained level of language use prior to the instructional discontinuity.

3. The Expanded Learner Group

The call for articulation has particular urgency now and into the immediate future because our instructional efforts must meet, within a relatively short adjustment time, the needs of a significantly enlarged group of learners, not only the self-selected group that has traditionally opted for foreign language study. Due to our instructional goals and certainly also due to our methodological preferences, these learners have generally been academically oriented. In particular, they were able to handle a high level of abstraction and to apply general rules across a variety of particular phenomena and, in reverse, able to induce from a limited range of phenomena those generalizations that have high predictive value for future applications. For languages, the most immediate indication of this orientation was the generation of language through the application of highly abstract and complex grammatical rules and the ability to infer them almost magically from severely restricted, not to mention inauthentic, linguistic data.

While such learner characteristics may have been legitimately targeted in the past, given past instructional goals as well as teaching design and procedures, they seem considerably less appropriate for our current approaches, and even less motivated with the ever younger second language learners who will enter the instructional sequence. For these younger learners second language acquisition may indeed come to approximate key aspects of first language acquisition, a claim that is difficult to sustain for adult language learning though it is implicit in much of the pedagogical practice that is based on Krashen's theories.

4. The Learning Process

Within the profession, a paradigm shift about what constitutes the essence of language, but even more, about what constitutes the essence of L2 language learning, is taking place. This paradigm shift manifests itself most strikingly in an emphasis on the progression of learning over the end product, in a focus on the significance of the creative contributions of the apprentice learner in relation to the materials taught. It recognizes recursive learning, but also the phenomenon of threshold learning as characterized by a readiness to deal with certain features of language and the concomitant inability to tackle others, much less master them. It observes the learner's individual shaping of the learning progression and contrasts it with a linear, fixed progression that is divorced from the learner (Pienemann 1984; Byrnes 1987b).

Once more the relationships between competence and performance, between content and skills, between process and product, between accuracy and fluency, which seemed to be solved so effectively on the theoretical level, are up for serious debate, this time receiving renewed urgency in conjunction with the profession's attempts to gain a differentiated awareness of the long path to language mastery.

5. The Changed Societal Attitude toward Language Learning

Finally, the societal setting in which we lead our professional lives and perform our professional services lends a certain urgency to our response to a whole host of issues (America in Transition, 1989). While we may view the public's expectations regarding language learning with some suspicion because of their inherent proximity to a surface functionalism, we can ill afford to turn our backs on them entirely. Instead, we must seize the opportunities these expectations entail for our goals by finding ways in which a well articulated curriculum can address both the information transmission quality of a language as well as the deeply educational value of cultural and linguistic competency in a foreign language.

A Framework for Addressing Articulation

With key questions posed and some important parameters identified, it is time to look for a framework within which we might locate answers for an articulated curriculum.

Let me characterize what I am about to propose in two ways. On the one hand, the suggested framework is intended to recognize the pluralism of instructional settings, purposes, goals, and approaches that characterizes the American scene, a pluralism that seems only to be increasing in light of the trends just identified. On the other hand, it is unified by a focus on features of educational development in general, second language learning in an instructed setting, in particular. This progression starts with the young, beginning learner and follows through to the mature adult, advanced learner.

I realize that such a progression is an ideal, since only a very small share of our learners will, in fact, participate in a full course of study. But initially exemplifying the issues in this fashion should clarify the central features of this type of articulation. We will subsequently have to accommodate learners entering into the learning progression at different ages, thereby making an articulated curriculum based on developmental stages not only multidimensional and differentiated but administratively vastly more complex. That very fact is likely to result in compromise solutions. Even so, it is important to have firmly grasped the issues involved before one is required to contemplate and accept curtailments.

As regards educational development, my remarks draw heavily on insights presented by Egan (1979) who sees such development not so much in terms of genetic epistemology, as does Piaget's theoretical work, as in terms of the "educational aspects of development, learning, and motivation" which "directly yields principles for engaging children in learning, for unit and lesson planning, and for curriculum organizing" (6). The distinguishing characteristic of his approach is that it sees development as occurring in four main stages, the mythic, the romantic, the philosophic, and the ironic, which are different ways of making sense of the world that require significantly different ways of organizing the knowledge that is to be learned.

Egan's stance indicates a major departure from received practice in that curricula can take a broader view of what constitutes appropriate content than they have in the past. Indeed, it might not even be appropriate to organize content in terms of the standard progression from the individual outward to ever larger circles of events and phenomena in the world around him, essentially making selections according to personal proximity or relevance, however defined. Instead, we may well find that it is not so much the content that impacts on its learnability as *how* knowledge, wherever it is situated, is organized. This is not to deny the existence of some principles for selecting what content is likely to be more encouraging of the learner's development at a particular stage, but, given the strong force of learners' developmental propensities irrespective of content, content in itself is not the critical concern.

For foreign language learning, a curricular progression in terms of organization of knowledge rather than knowledge per se is an important adjustment. Since it redefines in much broader terms *what* can be learned while recommending closer attention to *how* it is being presented, it allows easier access into the other language and culture. This would seem to be the case even with younger learners, a challenge worth investigating in the foreign language curriculum not only for its obvious advantages on the side of purely factual knowledge about the C2. More importantly, the ability to incorporate input from the C2 into children's and adolescents' construction of the world as they are progressing through the four major developmental stages would seem to hold a promise for overcoming one of the key difficulties for adults' crosslinguistic and crosscultural competence, namely their already being totally steeped in their own culture's parameters and interpretive preferences.

Aside from such general developmental considerations we must, of course, draw on insights from second language acquisition research. But here, too, the task will be less one of transferring results directly to the classroom, than it will be one of identifying the *pedagogical* phenomena to which these findings apply (Byrnes 1987a).

In the following I will sketch out a progression that attempts to intertwine both these strands, the general developmental strand and the language acquisition strand, into an articulated foreign language curriculum. I trust that the goals of this volume allow for the freedom of treating the topic more in terms of numerous educated hunches than as totally corroborated research evidence, more in terms of a holistic framework than as a well spelled out and finely tuned set of recommendations, more as a projection of potential than a summary of tried and true prescriptions. The reader will certainly have no difficulty in finding many research lacunae which remain to be filled. I hope, nevertheless, to be able to present a viable proposal for addressing the problem of articulation, one that recognizes and accepts some of the more recent developments in the profession and that can stimulate fruitful future debate.

Defining the Framework for Curricular Articulation

1. The Elementary School Learner

In terms of general educational development, Egan (1979) characterizes the learner aged 5–10 as being at the mythic stage. During this stage, the child's major categories are not rational and logical but emotional and moral. Consequently, the best way to present knowledge is through myths and stories that address this preoccupation while engaging the children's interests. At the same time, such stories provide learners with intellectual security, respect their inability to deal with the concept of otherness and the world as an autonomous entity, and cater to their propensity to handle the world in terms of binary opposites.

Turning to foreign language learning we find that, the younger the L2 learner, the more L2 language learning is likely to resemble L1 learning, even in the instructed setting. Irrespective of the delivery vehicle, i.e. full immersion, partial immersion, FLES, content-enriched FLES, or FLEX, we are likely to find the following characteristics:

As learners attempt to make "sense of the unknown world without in terms of the known world within" (Egan 1979:14), the story form is likely to best address their needs since it has a clear beginning, middle, and end, and is able to reduce and limit reality. Dealing with such basic concepts as good and evil, fear and hope, love and hate, stories with their strong emotional and moral categories, will foster cognitive, emotional and linguistic growth.

Aside from the story form as a primary vehicle for organizing whatever needs to be learned in the foreign language, instruction benefits as well from the incorporation of games, chants, rhymes, songs, imitative play, magic, and make-believe, all accompanied by a diversity of physical involvement. For the young learner the world is accessed primarily through oral language that is experienced directly and holistically, and not mediately through metalinguistic analysis.

So what kinds of abilities are elementary learners likely to acquire and bring into the middle school years? While time on task will affect the details, their abilities will reflect a heavy emphasis on comprehension, essentially through listening, rather than on production. Less easily ascertainable and assessable in the elementary grades, but likely to positively predispose learners' subsequent relationship to the second language and its culture, is the cognitive, emotional and affective bonding such learning would seem to foster.

From the standpoint of learning the form side of the L2, we should assume important similarities between first and second language acquisition in the elementary grades. Thus, we should expect that children's "working hypotheses" about the units of language will be very different from the logical and economical descriptions of language as they have become codified in scientific grammars (Peters 1983). Instead of treating language as being built up from individual words and morphemes, their perception of language will reflect a top-down approach, working with extended formulas, partly set partly open, that constitute units of meaning in the contexts within which the learner has experienced them. Only over an extended period of time, most likely to set in toward the end of this stage and into the middle and junior high school years, will learners ultimately analyze, from the stream of speech, the operable units of meaning as linguistic analysis of language identifies them. In fact, what Peters states to be the central process for first language acquisition may well apply to early second language acquisition: the central process for the learners is "the extraction of pieces, or 'units,' from the speech stream in which the child is immersed" (5). We shall have to return to this fact subsequently.

For child learners, language will be inextricably bound up with communication in a context, as a way of causing and responding to action within a group. They will respond strongly to the intimate relationship between language sounds in the extended sense of the term and meaning. Their active use of language will be tied to certain content areas, thus limited in breadth, depth, and accuracy due to restricted input provided in the setting and restricted time on task (Rhodes et al. 1990)

2. The Middle School Learner

Described by Egan as being at the romantic stage, the middle school learner, aged approximately 8/9 - 14/15 years, is developing "rudimentary but serviceable concepts of 'otherness'; concepts of historical time, geographical space, physical regularities, logical relationships, and causality" (28). This stage differs qualitatively from the mythic stage in that learners must now "forge a new relationship and connections with the autonomous world and so achieve some method of dealing with its threatening alienness" while developing "a sense of their distinct identity" (29). They do so by allying themselves with the most powerful elements in the world around them, the noble, the courageous, the beautiful, the brave, the powerful and creative. What is real and what is possible is explored through a zest for details, while stressing "those human qualities that lead to a transcendence over the everyday and commonplace world" (33).

On the content side, a "quite sudden fascination with the extremes of what exists and what is known" (Egan 1979:31) would seem to support an early inclusion of some of the stories dealing with the myths and historical and folk heroes central to the culture or cultures to which the language is connected. Beyond that, science fiction or adventure stories respond to adolescents' desire to have reality play a central role while at the same time fashioning their reality in terms of ego-supporting heroes and heroines, struggles against all odds, and the ability to glory in victory along with the hero. Another incorporation in the foreign language classroom of the desire for detail would seem to be a substantial dose of factual knowledge about the other country, a host of geographic facts in the wide sense of the word, or major historical events as seen from the perspective of an individual protagonist.

As for modes of language learning, instruction must now target the learners' ability to segment language more along the lines of the familiar major structural units of the language being acquired. Peters points out that the larger chunks that children have previously extracted and acquired must now be further broken down so as to become functional units for creative, flexible, and situationally appropriate use of language (Peters 1983:109-114). The critical difficulty will be to find the optimal segmentation period for introducing "controlled variation within learned chunks just at the point where they have been well enough learned so that resources are freed for paying attention to structures, but before they have been so well learned as to be automatized" (112).

Given the learners' "ability to memorize and retain massive amounts of detail, with an efficiency apparently much superior to any other stage of one's life" (Egan 1979:36), the use of rote learning and the incorporation of poetry, prose, and short dramatic scenes which allow learners to experience the sounds and rhythms of a language, particularly in relation to their emotional and aesthetic value, seem to be particularly appropriate.

Since we know that this "stage of intellectual wonder and excitement is also the stage of most acute boredom" (Egan 1979:47), I do not at all wish to advocate dull repetition drills and mindless pattern practice. But there seems to be evidence that expansions, reductions, variations, substitutions of language on the basis of memorized materials can help learners construct their own learner grammars, as long as social meaningfulness is not compromised.

3. The Adult Instructed Learner

According to Egan, learners during the philosophic stage, aged approximately 14/15 to 19/20 years, rapidly abandon the self-empowering romantic world view and come to appreciate their limitations within the constraints of their particular position. They learn to establish general laws and truths about a whole range of processes, which allows them to bring order to the seemingly endless particular and unrelated knowledge in which they revelled previously.

For our discussion of articulation I find particularly noteworthy Egan's observation that "having enough knowledge to be able to generate from it some general vision of a complex process, some ideology, or metaphysical scheme, is a prerequisite for moving beyond the romantic stage and into the philosophic stage of educational development" (57). Assuming that our extended progression of L2 learning were to become a reality, we might at last be able to assure that learners would have just that kind of requisite "considerable body of knowledge" without which educational development beyond the romantic stage is essentially thwarted.

As suggested previously, this knowledge base would pertain to the language as well as to the culture side of the process of acquiring cross-cultural competence. Only then could the learners' propensity in the philosophical stage toward developing functional and viable generalizations reach its greatest potential in the goal of attaining upper levels of language ability.

We might at this stage of educational development find one other of the necessary bases for truly upper-level language abilities. This is a different kind of learner processing made possible through higher levels of systematization and generalization. Learners must be able to accomplish a system-wide reorganization of the primary features of their interlanguage grammar in order to be able to move appreciably closer to the actual rule system of the target language (see Bialystok and Sharwood Smith 1985).

Finally, if our articulated sequence could allow learners to have reached advanced levels of language use during this stage, instruction could benefit from rather than be hampered by another developmental characteristic identified by Egan. I am referring to learners' reduced interest in particular knowledge for its own sake with the complementary aspect of a willingness to deal with it only insofar as it fits into and allows the building up of larger organizational structures. If that is indeed the case, then previous stages of language instruction should ideally have provided the bulk of the particular knowledge, leaving the learner at this stage free to engage in the important "dialectical process of interaction between general scheme and particular knowledge" (Egan 1979:64).

4. The Adult Learner at the Ironic stage

For the purposes of articulating a language curriculum one might consider dealing with language instruction during the ironic stage, occurring from age 19/20 to adulthood, to be of only marginal concern. However, given that the age brackets indicated are, of course, only broad approximations that vary with individual learners, we should at least briefly consider some of the characteristics of learners at this stage.

While both learners, those at the philosophical and at the ironic stages, are concerned with the relationship of general knowledge and particular realizations, they differ in so far as learners at the philosophic stage lend more weight to general schemes while those at the ironic stage allow particulars to play a special role.

Again, we could obtain striking support between general educational and L2 development if our learners at the ironic stage could essentially reach toward the "Superior" level of oral proficiency as characterized by the ACTFL scale. Focusing on language development, we have here learners who have consolidated their general rule knowledge to an admirable extent. Thus, their ability to attend effectively to particulars, such as pronunciation would deserve to be interpreted not so much in terms of the traditionally presumed form-centeredness of instructed language learning as in terms of the learners' general educational development and their overall linguistic processing capabilities (compare the analysis in Salo-Lee 1987).

Unresolved Issues and Outlook

Readers familiar with current activities relating to articulation may have concluded that the previous discussion of the topic took an unexpected direction. Others may judge more harshly, observing that I have yet to address a number of crucial issues, among them the fact that students enter the progression at different ages, the need for precise goals definition prior to curriculum construction, the potential role of proficiency testing for outcomes statement or placement purposes, or the need for strong alliances in order to effect any sort of substantive change.

Beyond resorting to the customary remark that one paper cannot possibly treat such a complex topic in an exhaustive fashion, I would like to argue somewhat more strongly for the direction I took. Far from wishing to appear aloof from the reality of educational practice or from seeming to underestimate the invaluable service that local initiatives have provided, I chose to look at what might be a comprehensive way of addressing the issue of curricular sequencing if we had the luxury of building our professional dream house. I realize that no one has come forward yet, offering to foot the bill for this enterprise, nor are we necessarily willing or able to tear down the sand castle that currently shelters us! Even so, enough attempts at laying solid foundations are occurring right now as to make my observations more than idle or idealistic dreaming. It seems to me that the greater danger comes from not taking the extended viewpoint but preoccupying ourselves with highly specific topics, such as awarding of credit, without being able to refer to an enlarged context of language instruction.

As for justification for cooperative enterprises, exemplifying their laudable successes, and pointing out work yet to be accomplished, I refer the reader to a number of reports (Cummins 1987; James 1989; Mosher 1989; Taylor 1987). I conclude with some brief observations regarding different lengths of study, goals statements, and the role of proficiency in our efforts to strengthen curricular articulation.

1. Entering the Progression at Different Ages

The previous observations should have made amply clear that we can no longer take the position that instances of language learning in grades K - 12 are essentially the slow and drawn-out, if not to say deficitary version of the real thing, which takes place at the college level. What is wrong here is not only the characterization of the entire enterprise of foreign language instruction in terms of considerations that might hold true within the highly restricted setting at the end of the continuum, a highly dubious practice in itself. More importantly, this viewpoint entirely disregards that an articulated language curriculum must provide for instruction that is qualitatively different at various stages of the learners' educational as well as their L2 development.

Furthermore, learners beginning instruction at the junior high, at the secondary level, or, finally, at the college level, cannot be placed in the same classroom with learners who have had previous L2 experience. Assuming that enrollment figures would permit separate tracking within each of these settings—certainly not a small matter—then a number of issues arise that did not occur in this form within the ideal extended curriculum. I state them in question form, admitting that the answers have yet to be found, but suggesting that the formulation of the question itself proposes a direction for inquiry.

- Does it continue to be advantageous, as it was with young learners, to have an extended period of time with receptive skills work, —in this case listening *and* reading, thus pushing language production into the later years, or would that invite a situation where speaking skills are likely to be difficult to develop?

- Is it advisable to follow such a route with all beginners, regardless of their general educational development, and, presumably, the number of years of study they might yet undertake? Or does this approach become less and less desirable for more mature adult learners? Or are there other characteristics common to adult learners that, once more, support receptive work, though presumably of a different nature?
- Should one advocate a relatively brief period of comprehension work, followed rather quickly by speaking, frequently the reason learners themselves indicate for wishing to study a language?
- Is such speaking directed toward a purposely restricted repertoire of language chunks which provides some sense of security? Or can we follow a rather open format, likely with a topical base, while trusting in the self-corrective power of extensive negotiated language use to foster *continued* development language abilities, even within the highly restricted settings of most instructed language learning?
- Is it sufficiently important, against the background of an extremely form-centered perception of language learning that exists among much of the American public, to emphasize the communicative, creative aspect of language use at the beginning of language instruction for adolescents, even at the expense of accuracy?
- Within what learning stage can learners be expected to benefit most from something like a tightening of the reins, allowing them to foster and, ultimately, consolidate an awareness of the workings of language through grammatical reflection that emphasizes connections between structure and meaning?

All of these questions are, of course, interrelated, contributing to the complexity of the answers. But, more importantly, they clearly point out a major dilemma. The kinds of curricular goals statements that have recently sprung up under the proficiency banner are not so much supported by detailed knowledge of how language acquisition by different learners at different ages takes place as they are unified by a rejection of what we consider to have been past practice. We are, in general terms, rejecting an emphasis in language instruction on user-independent, invariate norms of language form; we are groping for ways of enhancing teaching for individual apprentice speakers who create meaning with whatever resources are available to them.

2. Testing Learning Outcomes

Let me end with a brief look at outcomes testing which occupies a prominent place in the discussion about articulation (e.g., Taylor 1987). It is very much in the American tradition to use testing to set curricular modifications in motion and also to monitor the extent of their success once they have been put in place. In the case of language teaching we have a particularly striking instance of this connection.

For many, the major instructional shift we are currently experiencing seems best summarized by the concept of proficiency which itself had gained initial prominence as a testing procedure for the assessment of oral language use. Proficiency captured the imagination because it held out the promise that the old indirect performance measurements of years of study, grades, or scores on standardized, form-centered tests could finally be abandoned in favor of a more direct global testing procedure targeted at functional abilities. These abilities could be expressed in terms of a relatively small set of intuitively appealing, hierarchically arranged assessment criteria that essentially echo important aspects of pedagogical experience. Small wonder that both the rating scale and the concept of proficiency testing itself became a rallying point for solutions to the problems of articulation.

However, in the range of abilities which the academic proficiency scale has identified as its primary domain and which has become the cornerstone of curricular work we are not really dealing with proficiency testing in the strong sense of the word: the independence of testing content from acquisitional history must be and is compromised. What really takes place with instructed learners is not proficiency-testing but communicatively-oriented, curriculum-based achievement testing (Byrnes 1989).

Thus, there is a strong danger for the misinterpretation of the Proficiency Guidelines in at least these two related issues that pertain to articulation: (1) as blueprints for curricular sequencing and (2) as ways of assessing learner outcomes. The danger is that both the curricular statements being developed and the assessment to be used for indicating the attainment of curricular goals may be predicated on the assumption that the learner is expected to deal with certain specific content areas. However, content is clearly a feature that is related to curriculum which, in turn, should be guided by considerations arising from the local instructional setting.

Thus, proficiency can become the cornerstone for articulation only if we look at language ability in the broader terms that underlie the Guidelines, not in the Guidelines statements themselves. These might be concepts like grammar, cohesion, and sensitivity to register expressed in terms of degrees of control and range (Bachman and Savignon 1986), or the learner's processing capabilities as measured against features of fluency and accuracy on the word, phrase, sentence, paragraph and discourse levels (Byrnes 1989). Without these adjustments, proficiency is at once too broadly conceived and too narrowly interpreted as to be applicable for articulation. Thus, the immeasurable value of the concept of proficiency has been primarily as a frame of reference within which many of the issues that confront us, including articulation, can become clearer. Even if proficiency itself often cannot provide ready answers it has given us a widely shared set of criteria, and has alerted us to avenues of inquiry which regional or local groups of professionals can then turn into viable solutions.

In planning for the 1990s, we are mindful that efforts toward dialogue, cooperation, and consensus-building have not guaranteed results in the past. However, the build-up of professional momentum over the last ten years and the opportunities for further growth in the near future are such, that the hope for creative solutions, even for issues as intractable as articulation, is not entirely unjustified.

References

America in Transition. Report of the Governors' Task Force on International Education. February 1989.

Ariew, Robert. "The Textbook as Curriculum." in Theodore V. Higgs, ed., Curriculum, Competence, and the Foreign Language Teacher. ACTFL Foreign Language Education Series. Lincolnwood, IL: National Textbook Company, 1982:11-33.

Bachman, Lyle, and Sandra J. Savignon. "The Evaluation of Communicative Language Proficiency: A Critique of the ACTFL Oral Interview." Modern Language Journal 70,4 (1986):380-90.

Bialystok, Ellen, and Michael Sharwood Smith. "Interlanguage is Not a State of Mind: An Evaluation of the Construct of Second-Language-Acquisition." Applied Linguistics 6 (1985):101-17.

Byrnes, Heidi. "Who is in Charge in the Learner-Curriculum-Testing Connection?" in James E. Alatis, ed., Language Teaching, Testing, and Technology: Lessons from the Past with a View toward the Future. Georgetown University Round Table on Languages and Linguistics, 1989.

Byrnes, Heidi. "How Do You Get There from Here? Articulating the Foreign Language Major Program." ADFL Bulletin 20,1 (1988a):35-38.

Byrnes, Heidi. "Whither Foreign Language Pedagogy: Reflections in Textbooks—Reflections on Textbooks." Die Unterrichtspraxis 21,1 (1988b):29-36.

Byrnes, Heidi. "Second-language Acquisition Research: Does it Suggest Program Goals?" ADFL Bulletin 18,3 (1987a):35-38.

Byrnes, Heidi. "Second Language Acquisition: Insights from a Proficiency Orientation," in Heidi Byrnes and Michael Canale, eds., Defining and Developing Proficiency: Guidelines, Implementations and Concepts. ACTFL Foreign Languages Education Series. Lincolnwood, IL: National Textbook Company, (1987b):107-31.

Cummins, Patricia. "School-College Articulation and Proficiency Standards: A Status Report." ADFL Bulletin, 19 (1987):8-15.

Egan, Kieran. Educational Development. New York: Oxford University Press, 1979.

Galloway, Vicki. "From Defining to Developing Proficiency: A Look at the Decisions," in Heidi Byrnes and Michael Canale (eds.), Defining and Developing Proficiency: Guidelines, Implementations, and Concepts. ACTFL Foreign Language Education Series. Lincolnwood, IL: National Textbook Company, 1987:25-73.

Grittner, Frank M. "Toward a Solution of the Articulation Problem between High School and College," in Walter F. W. Lohnes and Valters Nollendorfs, eds., German Studies in the United States: Assessment and Outlook. Madison, WI: University of Wisconsin Press, 1976:199-206.

James, Dorothy. "Reshaping the 'College-level' Curriculum: Problems and Possibilities," in Helen S. Lepke, ed., Shaping the Future. Challenges and Opportunities. Northeast Conference Reports. Middlebury, VT: Northeast Conference, 1989:79-110.

Jeffries, Sophie. "Articulation and Proficiency: A Political View." NYSAFLT Annual Meeting Series. Nov. 5 (1988):17-23.

Lafayette, Robert C. "Toward an Articulated Curriculum," in Thomas H. Geno, ed., Our Profession: Present Status and Future Directions. Northeast Conference Reports. Middlebury, VT: The Northeast Conference, 1980:61-76.

Lange, Dale L. "The Problem of Articulation," in Theodore V. Higgs, ed., Curriculum, Competence, and the Foreign Language Teacher. ACTFL Foreign Language Education Series, vol. 13. Lincolnwood, IL: National Textbook Company, 1982:113-137.

Lange, Dale L. "Articulation: A Resolvable Problem?" in John F. Lalande, II, ed., Shaping the Future of Language Education: FLES, Articulation, and Proficiency. Report of the Central States Conference on the Teaching of Foreign Language. 1988:11-31.

Mosher, Arthur D. "The South Carolina Plan for Improved Curriculum Articulation between High Schools and Colleges." Foreign Language Annals, 22,2 (1989):157-62.

Pesola, Carol Ann. "Articulation for Elementary School Foreign Language Programs: Challenges and Opportunities." In John F. Lalande, II, ed., Shaping the Future of Language Education: FLES, Articulation, and Proficiency. Report of the Central States Conference on the Teaching of Foreign Language. 1988: 1-10.

Peters, Ann M. The Units of Language Acquisition. New York: Cambridge University Press, 1983.

Pienemann, Manfred. "Psychological Constraints on the Teachability of Languages." Studies in Second Language Acquisition 6,2 (1984):186-214.

Proceedings and Papers of the Panel Discussion: Articulation from High School to College and the Problem of Placement. Die Unterrichtspraxis 2,1 (1969):73-87.

Redfield, James. "The Politics of Language Instruction." ADFL Bulletin 20,3 (1989):5-12.

Rhodes, Nancy, Helena Curtain, and Mari Haas. "Child Development and Academic Skills in the Elementary Foreign Language Classroom," in Sally Sieloff Magnan, ed., Shifting the Instructional Focus to the Learner. Northeast Conference Reports. Middlebury, VT: The Northeast Conference, 1990.

Salo-Lee, Sirkka-Liisa. Self-Repairs in Learner Language: Evidence from German at Different Oral Proficiency Levels. Unpublished Ph.D. Dissertation. Georgetown University, 1987.

Sachs, Murray. "The Foreign Language Curriculum and the Orality-Literacy Question." ADFL Bulletin 20,2 (1989):70-75.

Swaffar, Janet K. "Curricular Issues and Language Research: The Shifting Interaction." ADFL Bulletin 20,3 (1989):54-60.

Swain, Merrill. "Communicative Competence: Some Roles of Comprehensible Input and Comprehensible Output in its Development," in Susan M. Gass and Carolyn G. Madden, eds., Input in Second Language Acquisition. Rowley, MA: Newbury House, 1985:235-53.

Taylor, Irmgard. "A Proposed Plan for Secondary/Post Secondary Articulation." Language Association Bulletin (New York State Association of Foreign Language Teachers) 38,3 (1987):1, 3-4.

Annotated Bibliography

From the previous citations, the following sources are selected as dealing more directly with the issues arising in conjunction with articulation. They are here listed with brief comments.

Byrnes, Heidi. "Who is in Charge in the Learner-Curriculum-Testing Connection?" in James E. Alatis, ed., *Language Teaching, Testing, and Technology: Lessons from the Past with a View toward the Future*. Georgetown University Round Table on Languages and Linguistics, (1989):265-75. Emphasizes the importance of clarifying the goals of language instruction. Subsequent to such clarification one can devise specific units of instruction on the basis of learner-related factors which are, perhaps, best summarized in terms of their processing capabilities at different stages of language acquisition.

Byrnes, Heidi. "Second-language Acquisition Research: Does it Suggest Program Goals?" *ADFL Bulletin* 18,3 (1987a):35-38. Looks at the relationship between research and the setting of program goals. At the least, such goals setting would consider the nature of language, the sequencing of skills, the potential level of ultimate attainment, and the reality of language attrition.

Cummins, Patricia. "School-College Articulation and Proficiency Standards: A Status Report." *ADFL Bulletin*, 19 (1987):8-15. Reports on a variety of projects nationwide to work on program articulation in light of the concept of a national measure of proficiency. The attractiveness of the concept is discussed, yet the need for guidance stressed.

Egan, Kieran. *Educational Development*. New York: Oxford University Press, 1979. Presents a theory of educational development, as contrasted with psychological theories, which "focuses on the *educational* aspects of development, learning, and motivation and which directly yields principles for engaging children in learning, for unit and lesson planning, and for curriculum organizing." One result of such an approach is that it is not so much content *per se* that is critical in curriculum building but *how* this content is presented, that is, whether it addresses the developmental predelections of learners for organizing knowledge.

Galloway, Vicki. "From Defining to Developing Proficiency: A Look at the Decisions," in Heidi Byrnes and Michael Canale, eds., *Defining and Developing Proficiency: Guidelines, Implementations, and Concepts*. ACTFL Foreign Language Education Series. Lincolnwood, IL: National Textbook Company, 1987:25-73. Weighs the potential of the Proficiency Guidelines and the structure of the Oral Proficiency Interview for informing instructional and curricular decisions. While the guidelines are inadequate to serve as goals statements, they can help convey a "sense of the ranges of the various factors involved in proficiency," thus contributing to better curriculum building.

Garrett, Nina. "Implications for the Classroom: Research on the Role of Grammar and Accuracy in Classroom-Based Foreign Language Acquisition." Paper presented at the conference "Foreign Language Acquisition Research and the Classroom." The University of Pennsylvania, October 12-15, 1989. Advocates using the student language product as the starting point from which one attempts to infer the process of language acquisition. Central is the acquisition of processing capabilities. By investigating, in detail, how the system of language works in the learners' minds one might ultimately arrive at ways of improving the curriculum.

James, Dorothy. "Reshaping the 'College-level' Curriculum: Problems and Possibilities," in Helen S. Lepke, ed., *Shaping the Future. Challenges and Opportunities*. Northeast Conference Reports. Middlebury, VT: Northeast Conference, 1989:79-110. Describes the disjunctures between the language and literature components of most college language programs and suggests ways of bridging the gap.

Jeffries, Sophie. "Articulation and Proficiency: A Political View." *NYSAFLT Annual Meeting Series*. Nov. 5 (1988):17-23. Discusses "whether a proficiency-oriented curriculum might not hold some promises for the development of fully articulated foreign language instruction from the grades through college." By emphasizing a developmental view of language learning which distinguishes achievement and proficiency and offers varied content, teachers, the key factor in articulation, can effect the major paradigm shift in language instruction currently underway.

Lange, Dale L. "The Problem of Articulation," in Theodore V. Higgs, ed., *Curriculum, Competence, and the Foreign Language Teacher*. ACTFL Foreign Language Education Series, vol. 13. Lincolnwood, IL: National Textbook Company, 1982:113-37. Gives a valuable overview of key concepts and problems encountered in curricular articulation. Advocates discussion of articulation in terms of process, rather than product, and notes that extensive discussion in the profession to determine outcomes of language study and ways of assessing these outcomes would be a significant contribution to our ways of improving language learning.

Lange, Dale L. "Articulation: A Resolvable Problem?" in John F. Lalande, II, ed., *Shaping the Future of Language Education: FLES, Articulation, and Proficiency*. Report of the Central States Conference on the Teaching of Foreign Language. 1988:11-31. Advocates a broader definition of articulation that acknowledges the interconnectedness of content, curriculum, and instruction as they facilitate student learning. It places the focus in language education on the learner for whose benefit all cooperative efforts should be undertaken.

Mosher, Arthur D. "The South Carolina Plan for Improved Curriculum Articulation between High Schools and Colleges." *Foreign Language Annals*, 22,2 (1989):157-62. Describes efforts in the State of South Carolina to address the impact of revised admissions requirements to state colleges on both secondary and postsecondary foreign language curricula. Details the development of placement testing procedures that are intended to relate the two instructional levels to each other.

Pesola, Carol Ann. "Articulation for Elementary School Foreign Language Programs: Challenges and Opportunities," In John F. Lalande, II, ed., *Shaping the Future of*

Language Education: FLES, Articulation, and Proficiency. Report of the Central States Conference on the Teaching of Foreign Language. 1988:1-10. Makes a strong call for considering elementary school foreign language programs part of the total foreign language program, a task that is made even more complex due to the variety of language program models being developed at the elementary level.

Peters, Ann M. *The Units of Language Acquisition.* New York: Cambridge University Press, 1983.

Swain, Merrill and Sharon Lapkin. "Canadian Immersion and Adult Second Language Teaching: What's the Connection?" *Modern Language Journal* 73 (1989):150-59. Generalizes from the experience with immersion programs to any second language instructional setting in terms of the following issues: integration of content and language teaching in order to enhance program efficacy, and learner age and length of "exposure" time in relation to kinds of attainment.

Taylor, Irmgard. "A Proposed Plan for Secondary/Post Secondary Articulation." *Language Association Bulletin* (New York State Association of Foreign Language Teachers) 38,3:1, 3-4. Discusses, from the standpoint of testing content and procedures, the attempts in the State of New York to formalize articulation between high school and college.

Psychological Processes
in Foreign and Second Language Learning

Gilbert A. Jarvis
Ohio State University

Introduction

We do not live in a world of things. Just keeping track of the individual objects and activities of our environment would overwhelm us. We live in a world of concepts—a world of representations. In a world in which there are thousands, perhaps millions, of individual trees that we may have seen, touched, heard, or smelled—each different from all the others in height, girth, configuration of branches, shapes and sizes of leaves, density of foliage, and in many other characteristics—we do not—cannot—remember each of the unique trees in our experience, and we do not name them individually in the way that humans are named. We remember only a relatively small number of individual trees, perhaps a few that we planted or trimmed regularly, the one on which a childhood swing was hung, or the one around which we tied a yellow ribbon at the time of a special occasion. Instead of reacting to each tree as a unique encounter, we place these thousands or millions of trees into the category or concept of "tree."

One of the most striking characteristics of our environment is its enormous diversity and how our behavior is influenced by it. We impose on all that comes to us through our senses and from our stored past experience an extensive set of categories or concepts that give meaning and manageability, guide our thinking, and shape our behavior. We label the concepts with what we call words, and we learn complex sets of rules or principles for showing relationships among them. We then use these rules to solve communication problems—the successful sending of messages or reception of messages. This description reflects, to a large extent, the communication process, a process that is most visible during the childhood years in the development of one's first language. It can also describe the process by which one becomes proficient in a second language.

This description of concept learning is not original. It is an abbreviated description akin to that frequently found in the concept-learning and problem-solving chapters of modern educational psychology textbooks.

What is remarkable is that in this late twentieth century this description has never been applied to the foreign- and second-language learning process. That process is instead typically described in terms of learning vocabulary, grammar, functions, or notions. The intent, therefore, of this chapter is to describe the process by which proficiency in a foreign or second language develops in terms of the basic psychological processes involved and to conjecture what guidance concept-learning and problem-solving models and research can provide for the language educator.

There is a long history of belief and some evidence that learning a new language benefits various kinds of intellectual development. [See, for example, Jarvis (1980).] The history of this assertion dates back to nineteenth-century faculty psychologists who believed that the brain was a muscle to be exercised and that certain kinds of study exercised that brain more fully than other kinds. Foreign languages, particularly Latin, and algebra were often cited as being of special benefit.

Strictly as a metaphor, the brain-as-muscle notion is consistent with modern psychological descriptions. Practice with any skills, psychomotor or intellectual, is likely to enhance one's performance of the skills. Problem-solving behavior is among the most complex within the human repertoire, and if indeed learning and using a new language involves problem-solving behavior, learning to communicate in that new language becomes, in effect, practice in complex intellectual functioning. We know that we learn by doing, by active engagement in an activity. If the activity is sophisticated problem solving, then one should become better at sophisticated problem solving.

The Concept of "Concept"

Each of us possesses many mental categories or concepts. The educated adult probably possesses thousands of them. All of us in American culture have, for example, a concept of "window." We can look at an opening in a wall and say, "Yes, that is a window, but next to it that is non-window; that is a door." Yet, the door and the window may have much in common. In fact, some doors and some windows physically resemble each other more than some windows resemble each other. We are, however, generally able to make reliable decisions about what is an exemplar of a concept and what is not. We know the criterial attributes of the concept—those traits that are essential to it, that in effect define it. Although the criterial attributes that define our concepts may appear arbitrary, they probably have been constructed (or have evolved) in ways that facilitate perception, thought, and action. Certainly, our conceptual structures could have evolved differently. What is important is that they are largely learned and therefore shared by members of the culture in which they occur. It is safe to assume, for example, that most Americans know that a window is an opening in a surface such as a wall. It typically permits light and air to pass through it, but it can be of many different sizes and shapes. There is, however, a lower limit in size: We would not likely see a one-inch square opening in a wall as a window. There is probably also an upper limit to its size: At some point it becomes the absence of a wall, rather than ˙ndow. It also must not permit us to walk through it, or we would ˄ening as door rather than window. Its location matters; a large ᴜ₁ ˄ a counter between a kitchen and dining area would probably not ᴜ ˅indow by many Americans. We would accept many different n. ᴸ–ᴸs and procedures for opening the window (vertical "guillotine" movement, tilting glass, horizontal swinging movement, etc.). We also accept the possibility of windows not being able to be opened, particularly in large modern air-conditioned buildings. We see windows as occurring in virtually any structure in which we find humans. Thus, cars have windows; planes have windows; and even tents may have windows.

We have several "sub-concepts" of window. We recognize a ticket window as a special kind of window. Likewise, we see display windows and church windows as special kinds of windows. We utilize the concept metaphorically as in a "window of opportunity" or a "window on the mind."

Concepts are interrelated and can be viewed as existing in hierarchical relationships. An object can be classified at many different levels. A tree is a plant, a living thing, a source of wood, etc. Recently, considerable research has been carried out to understand relationships among concepts and whether there exists, for example, a hierarchical structure among concepts or whether some might be considered "basic." Such inquiry, at this early stage, is not directly instructive to the foreign- or second-language learning process. What is instructive is the well-established relationship between words and concepts.

The word "window" is a label for the concept. Indeed, *all words are labels for concepts.* Often a single word labels a concept, but a phrase can also do so, particularly for identifying sub-concepts. The criterial attributes for a concept are delineated under the concept's label in a dictionary. What makes for "windowness" is described in the definitions given for the concept.

As complex as the concept of window is, it is in fact a very simple concrete concept compared to many other concepts that we all share. Lurking behind words like "of" or "however" are concepts whose criterial attributes are very difficult to describe. The *Oxford English Dictionary* lists, for example, 120 meanings for the word "of." It is a list of 120 ways that that "of" can link other concepts. There is, moreover, no assurance that these meanings adequately describe the concept "of" represents. Such meanings represent our semantic knowledge of concepts.

Concepts are also an important part of our procedural knowledge. The homeowner spraying weeds with a broad-leaf weed killer must be able to separate flowers from weeds—even if the weed is in bloom and the flower is not. Eysenck (1984) utilizes Wittgenstein's (1958) example to show the complexity of concepts:

> Consider for example the proceedings that we call "games." I mean board-games, card-games, ball-games, Olympic games, and so on. What is common to them all... if you look at them you will not see something that is common to *all*, but similarities, relationships, and a whole series of them at that... Look for example at board-games, with their multifarious relationships. Now pass to card-games; here you will find many correspondences with the first group, but many common features drop out, and others appear. When we pass next to ball-games, much that is common is retained, but much is lost... Is there always winning and losing, or competition between players? ... In ball-games there is winning and losing; but when a child throws his ball at the wall and catches it again, this feature has disappeared (pp. 31-32).

Some have used a notion of "family resemblances" to describe the phenomenon. One must recognize, however, that some members of a category are better members than others. "A robin is a better bird than a chicken is" (Eysenck, p. 316). Sometimes only one characteristic or feature of a concept is necessary in order to classify an exemplar within the concept; at other times, multiple features or criterial attributes are necessary. A baseball strike, for example, occurs when either the ball passes over the plate in a particular area or when the batter swings at and misses the ball. Thus, a concept can be viewed as possessing criterial attributes and rules as to which combinations of attributes must be present to make it an instance of the concept. Such issues are not essential for developing a model that describes second language learning.

In summary, we see the world through lenses that categorize all that comes to us through our senses or that we retrieve from memory. Although the category boundaries are sometimes fuzzy, we largely share these categories within a culture. We further label our categories with words.

How Are Concepts Learned?

Although several models of concept learning have been proposed over the past 30 years, one that fits particularly well with the acquisition of concepts in educational settings is a cognitive model that postulates two different means of acquiring concepts. Ausubel et al (1978) call the processes *concept formation* and *concept assimilation*.

Concept formation is an inductive, discovery approach to concept learning. From encounters with exemplars of the concept, the learner infers its criterial attributes. This approach is the dominant mode by which young children learn concepts. The child is told, "Don't set your milk too close to the edge of the tray." "Be careful; the edge of the table is sharp." "Look at that squirrel at the edge of the roof." Eventually, the child forms the concept of edge. When the child first begins referring to edges, the behavior might be viewed as testing his or her hypothesis about the concept. If he or she is misunderstood or corrected, the feedback indicates that he or she has not induced the criterial attributes that other members of the culture share.

When, for example, the child refers to the edge of the wagon when he or she means the side of the wagon, the parent may inquire, "You mean the side of it?" The child modifies his or her concept on the basis of such feedback. Likewise, the child might refer to the edge of a ball. Such gradual "trial and error" refinement of our concepts occurs in all of us, but it is especially visible in children. (Adults may have learned skills in concealing their "fuzziness" about such matters.)

Concept assimilation, the other concept-learning process, occurs more frequently with adult learners. It is the process by which one is told directly the criterial attributes of a concept: "An edge is the line or point where a material object or area begins or ends." With an adequate cognitive structure and the developmental maturity to understand abstract propositions, a person can acquire a concept very efficiently via this approach. For the child, however, who cannot yet handle abstractions, this approach would be futile.

Concept Learning and Foreign Language Learning

Learning, particularly the kind involved in school settings, is today frequently—and usefully—viewed in modern conceptualizations as extending the cognitive structure of the learner. We use what we know already as an "anchor" for new content. New learnings are subsumed into existing frameworks of knowledge. Via all of our experience, we continually augment our cognitive structures. One's cognitive structure becomes, in effect, the interconnected, hierarchically organized residue from all that we have experienced. Some of this building on or elaborating of the cognitive structure is probably random activity; some of it is through trial-and-error activity; and some of it occurs through planned structured learning experiences. A rich, well-organized cognitive structure becomes synonymous with what the lay person often calls intelligence.

Each learner therefore begins his or her study of a language with a cognitive structure that has developed from previous experience. The nature of that cognitive structure is a powerful variable influencing learning. Ausubel et al. (1978) see it as the most powerful variable of all. "If I had to reduce all of educational psychology to just one principle, I would say this: The most important single factor influencing learning is what the learner already knows. Ascertain this and teach him or her accordingly" (p. iv).

In light of this statement, the important question for a language teacher becomes: What are the most relevant aspects of students' existing knowledge when they are beginning to learn a new language? A major portion of the answer has to be the knowledge, skills, or proficiency that the learner possesses in a first language. Unfortunately, language teachers frequently seem to see this background as a liability rather than an asset. They speak much more frequently of "interference" from the first language rather than of "transfer" from that language. In terms of psychological models of the early twentieth century, transfer of elements was a powerful component. The language educator's use of the notion of interference fits well these old models: It merely restricts the meaning of interference to the transfer of those elements that are judged "undesirable" transfer. Odlin (1989) has from a linguistic perspective reached a similar conclusion.

It is acknowledged that the beginning language learner brings to bear much that he or she knows about communication, interaction, and instruction, but the dominant realm of relevant knowledge has to be that of the learner's first language (or other languages he or she has learned). The preponderance of evidence supporting this view is never more evident to any classroom observer than on the first day of any beginning language course. Students struggle to connect the new language to the familiar language. They want the grammar, the vocabulary, and even the sounds to be as close as possible to what is familiar and comfortable to them. They seem disappointed with each discovery of another instance where the new language does not connect readily to what they know already and does not seem to operate in the way that they want it to operate.

Without yet addressing questions of pedagogical implications, one cannot avoid noting the dramatic differences that one would find between instruction that attempts to capitalize on students' first-language knowledge and skills versus instruction that is premised on the assumption that the most unfortunate characteristic of all learners is that they bring to the foreign or second language learning situation a relatively sophisticated, well-developed first language. How much better off they would be in a *tabula rasa* state, according to this latter view. One can find in our history many instances of both of these views about the first language. Politzer (1970) wrote that "the older you become, the more practice you have had in speaking the native language, the more the rules and system of the native language are likely to interfere with learning the system of the foreign language... The older the person, the more difficult it is to combat the interference coming from the native system, and the more it must be a matter of directed, conscious effort" (p. 10).

One of the best intuitively brilliant examples of capitalizing on what the learner already knows appeared in the Hendrix and Meiden textbook, *Beginning French*, where the very first words in French that the learner encountered were *Paris est la capitale de la France*. By capitalizing on parallels between sentence patterns in French and in English and on the existence of cognate words, the student could relate this first contact with the new language to what was already familiar. The ideal in an English learner's approach to learning French would be a gradual progression from those aspects of French that are most like English to those that differ most from English. At an early stage, the student's French would be a kind of interlanguage—a French that is overrepresented by those aspects of French that have some similarities to elements of English.

This latter approach is consistent in multiple ways with modern learning theory. Instruction must, however, take into account the specific phenomena that are involved. First, at the level of what most language teachers call vocabulary learning, the process must be clearly understood. When a student encounters a new word, he or she relates it to his or her existing knowledge. That usually means a direct association of the new word with the native language word that is closest in meaning. In terms of conceptual functioning, the new word is linked to the label of the native language word. The learner assumes that the existing native concept can merely be re-labelled with the new-language label. What the learner does not understand initially is that this association is merely the point of departure for learning the new word. The learner's native concept may function in a way that is not unlike the role of a prototype in some models of conceptualization.

The most important point to be made in this chapter is that vocabulary learning is not a matter of label learning. It is a matter of *concept reformation*. With each succeeding encounter with the new word—whether in receptive skills or in attempts to produce the new word in a context—the learner gradually infers the criterial attributes of the new target language word and thereby gradually distinguishes it from the native language word that had been the point of departure. The beginning French student assumes initially that *bonjour* is equivalent to "hello" and that *université* is another label for "university." Through each successive encounter with these words, he or she learns that all the contexts and times in which one would say *bonjour* are not the same as the situations in which an American might say hello. The behavior accompanying the greetings will also be seen as different. Likewise, with greater French classroom (or outside-of-classroom) experience and learning more about higher education in French-speaking areas, the student sees that a university is not a single universal entity and that it is not viewed uniformly by peoples of all cultures. Indeed, at a sufficiently advanced level, the student will come to see its variability across French-speaking regions.

The language student is in effect encountering the differences between concepts in different cultures. If viewed in two dimensional space, the similar concepts of any two cultures vary from being largely coextensive, through partial overlap, to lack of any overlap. This last status has always been described by language teachers in terms of there being "no word for that in a particular language." The most frequent situation from culture to culture is one of partial overlap from one to the other. This is especially true among connected cultures such as those within the western world, but there will be less overlap across cultures that differ substantially. The concept of window will be a convenient initial anchor for the student of French who learns *fenêtre*. Gradually, the student will reform the concept labelled by *fenêtre* to understand its physical characteristics (e.g., how a *fenêtre* opens in France) and that ticket windows, stained-glass windows, and store display windows are not at all a part of the concept of *fenêtre* but are entirely independent concepts for the French speaker. With sufficiently advanced study the student may also understand characteristics of windows in francophone Africa and eastern Canada.

Most concepts are not concrete like *fenêtre*. Their criterial attributes are partially delineated in dictionaries but are not fully spelled out anywhere. The criterial attributes must be seen to include elements of appropriate usage, and appropriateness may be determined by structural features or by social factors. A particular preposition may be used in one context but not in another context that seems very similar. A student learning English, for example, must learn that you "look up information" but that you "look into an issue." Only through repeated encounters with the usage will a learner sort what is permitted use from what is not or how the meaning changes with variation in the context.

Pedagogical Implications

Several implications for instruction and instructional materials seem apparent. Certainly, on the one hand, it may be premature to seek applications for a conceptualization that has yet not been examined extensively in a field. Yet, on the other hand, the conceptualization is consistent with an empirical base in psychology. First, quantity of contact with the new concepts and their labels is an important variable but far from a sufficient determining variable. Perhaps much more important is the nature and the variety of the encounters with the label. Ausubel et al. (1978) note the importance of variety in developing transferability and cite Hull's early work (1920) as showing that "familiarity with a concept in a large number of different specific contexts and illustrative forms is more efficacious for generalization than is intensive experience with a few illustrations" (p. 200).

Although Ausubel et al. were not writing specifically about foreign- or second-language learning, it is easy to read their example in vocational education as applying to language learning. They state that transfer is facilitated by providing opportunity for learning in

> ... as wide a variety of situations as possible, by explicitly emphasizing the similarity between training and criterial tasks and by presenting the latter tasks continuously or in close succession. In the case of vocational learning, knowledge and skill become more transferable when they are learned originally in realistic and "real-life" situations that are similar to the settings in which final utilization of the training will take place.
>
> Some tasks are so complex that they cannot be learned directly. The learner must be trained first on a simplified version of the task and then transfer this training to an attempt at mastering the task itself (p. 200).

The argument can be interpreted, first of all, as supporting the maximizing of communicative practice—the realistic and life-like situations in which the language would be used. This assertion has become one of the best documented in the foreign- and second-language education literature (e.g., Jarvis, 1970; Joiner, 1974; Schaeffer, 1979). In light of this fact, it would seem that new vocabulary should be presented as glossed words in contexts—but not just any context. The student should encounter a new word in a context that has three characteristics: (1) the use is the most common or at least one of the most common for the word (or phrase), thereby creating considerable communicative potential, or the use represents the average or central tendency of the concept; (2) the use builds upon what the student knows already, as much as possible; and (3) the use is one in which the context helps as much as possible to clarify the meaning of the word. These three considerations are not necessarily correlated. A use that "demonstrates" the meaning in the clearest way possible may be a relatively rare use of the word, rather than a use that has high communicative potential. Thus, the challenge is to make the student's first encounter with the word one that blends clarity, communicative value, and learning ease.

The notion of a primary or "base" example of a concept is consistent with psychological research on concept learning. Erickson and Jones (1978) have traced research along this line.

> The most promising research programs involve carefully dimensionalized stimuli. The most promising research programs involve natural language or perceptual "prototype" concepts... The common theme is that categories or concepts develop around a prototype or "central" example (or examples) of the category. The prototype can develop even though it is never itself presented as the conceptual class is being learned. It will usually be a class member having strong similarity (measured in a variety of ways) to other class members and little similarity to members of other classes (pp. 74-75).

After the language student has encountered the new word or phrase several times in this first base application (by seeing it used, hearing it used, by using it in speech or writing), the next encounters move it gradually through uses that represent the next best combinations of the three criteria. Each of the uses helps the learner in shaping gradually the criterial attributes of the concept represented by that new word. Thus, vocabulary learning is indeed concept re-formation.

A student learning English as a foreign or second language might first encounter the word "class" as referring to a group of students learning the same subject matter. In the student's head would be the closest concept in his or her native language. Only after multiple instances of reference to different classes in several contexts would the student encounter it with its meaning of a course of instruction. Later, the slightly different meaning relating to the time at which a course meets ("my nine o'clock class") would be encountered. At some later point in developing proficiency the learner might encounter it referring to a society-wide grouping of people who share certain traits. During this gradual shaping and differentiation of the new concept the learner would eventually encounter uses other than as a noun. Early in the process would be uses such as "class schedule" and later would be those in which the meaning changed significantly (e.g., a class act). It should be emphasized that the term "encounter" here refers not only to the instances in reading and listening but also to the learner's attempts to produce the item in speaking or writing. Each such attempt yields feedback that helps the learner in shaping the criterial attributes of the concept. Feedback may come directly as a correction (especially from an instructor), as lack of understanding, or as misunderstanding of the meaning intended.

In a similar way, the student learning English would probably learn the word "catch" by relating to what you do with an object such as a ball. Gradually, the learner will modify the concept so that it is what can be done with fish, a cold, a few winks, or what someone else says. Eventually, there will be recognition that the word can be a label for a noun as well as a verb.

This process does not take place within a day or a week. It happens gradually, usually through several years as the learner moves from a beginning point of no proficiency in a language ultimately to the point of the highest proficiency that a non-native speaker of a language can achieve. It is simultaneously happening with hundreds or thousands of concepts and words in the new language. It is happening at the same time that the language student is learning the rules about how to string words together and to change their forms to show relationships among the concepts and thereby to express complex meanings.

The term "reentry" has long been current in language education; its meaning to most language educators seems to fall far short of the phenomenon described here. The complexity of the process is remarkable, and one can readily understand the reductionist tendencies frequently observed in teachers, authors or instructional materials, and even students themselves. What we do not know is how much reductionism or what forms of reductionism are helpful and which are counterproductive. At any given point in the long development of proficiency, there is an elusive optimal kind of instruction, which likely incorporates the well-established principle of simplifying in early stages and which, at the same time, manages to push the student one small step beyond yesterday's learning.

The complexity of the process makes it extremely difficult for anyone shaping instruction to think on a micro level about how the use of each word or each form relates to previous uses. We have not really identified the instructionally salient aspects of the linguistic and non-linguistic environment. In a practical sense, much of such instructional design has to be intuitive. Just as the student progresses from day to day with only a vague sense of how his or her proficiency is developing, the instructor's intellectual control is only partial and is largely influenced by the skill with which the author of the materials has written. The impact of the materials' author is critical and will likely become more dominant in the future, particularly in light of the growing potential of technology in storing and analyzing data about instructional materials.

One of the most critical facts about language teaching and learning and at the same time one of the most frequently overlooked characteristics of the phenomenon is this very complexity or unpredictability and the far-reaching implications of it. We forget Miller's (1967) reminder that "it would take 100,000,000,000 centuries (one thousand times the estimated age of the earth) to utter all the admissable twenty-word sentences of English" (p. 80). We do not have a discrete body of knowledge to impart to others. Our goal is that students become able to invent... to invent with words. Rarely within educational institutions do we set such lofty goals—and when we do we are content if only an isolated individual occasionally meets them through artistic skills or other ingenuity.

Language learning as a combination of concept re-formation and rule learning is not easily reconciled with the notion of langauge learning as a complex creative process. The process of problem solving provides a model for integrating these conceptualizations.

Language Use as Problem-Solving Behavior

A first reaction of many language educators to the notion of language use or language learning as problem-solving behavior is at best puzzlement and at worst shock. Problem solving is associated with mathematics or perhaps the physical sciences. If imposed on the language class, one might think of classical-language instruction that involved intricate translations or parsing of sentences. Such views do not take into account the nature of problem solving.

Nearly all definitions of problem solving postulate a goal that a person wants to achieve but for which he or she has no ready adequate response. A barrier must be overcome in order to reach the goal. "The cognitive representation of prior experience and the components of a current problem situation are reorganized to achieve a designated objective" (Ausubel et al., p. 566). Rules that interrelate relevant concepts are employed or even are generated in the process. At times, the approach is well described as trial and error, and at other times the goal-seeker seems to make conscious use of rules that have been previously acquired.

Graphically, the process is represented in Figure 1. Blair et al. (1975) describe the process in the following manner:

> Every situation in which a student has a need and a goal, with a barrier between, leads to some kind of learning... As Robert M. Gagné has noted, problem solving is not just an activity in which one applies already known rules or principles in a novel situation. It is true that the learner does that. But there is more. Once the problem is solved the student has likely learned a new rule. He may also have acquired new skills for processing information and developed attitudes of

independence that may carry over into new situations quite unlike the one in which the problem was solved (pp. 248-49).

Figure 1.

INTENT	BARRIER	GOAL
Desire to express (or understand)	What are the words that I need? How do I put them together? What are the cultural considerations?	Expression (or understanding) of intended meaning

Communication readily fits this problem-solving model. The speaker or writer seeks to transmit ideational content to one or more listeners or readers. The goal of those persons receiving the message is to understand this ideational content. The attainment of the goal entails the production of a new utterance or sentence that the learner has probably never before produced in exactly that way before. In routine first language intercourse the process occurs easily and fluidly because of our considerable skill in overcoming the barriers.

We get a more vivid view of the process when someone attempts to explain technical or highly complex content to another person who may have little relevant background knowledge for the explanation. The process resembles one of hypothesizing various ways in which one could encode or decode an idea. The speaker attempts paraphrases and provides related ideas, sometimes gives additional information, sometimes reduces ideas to simpler forms, and usually uses nonverbal means of various sorts. In some ways, the process often resembles trial-and-error efforts to reach the goal of communication. The interlocutor shares the task of solving the problem; he or she will indicate understanding or uncertainty, will ask questions, will prompt the other person, and will also use nonverbal strategies. The process is multiplied when more than two persons are involved in the communication task.

Even more vivid is the problem situation when the sender and perhaps even the receiver are attempting to conduct the transaction in a new language that they are in the process of learning, where their vocabulary is limited in both range and accuracy, where their knowledge of the grammar rules is incomplete, and where their knowledge of social expectations is just beginning to develop.

This conceptualization of communication as problem solving is again consistent with today's emphasis on foreign language learning for development of genuine communicative ability and with various constructs of proficiency, which all imply the ability to solve communication problems. Proficiency becomes, in effect, the ability to solve billions of communication problems. This conceptualization is also consistent with the research evidence that indicates that practice in communication—practice, in fact, in solving communication problems—is essential. Any lesser manipulation of language forms becomes *de facto* questioning that is akin to "if you wanted to use xxxx in an utterance or sentence, how would you form it?" This conceptualization also highlights the problems that will result if an instructor continually asks students to repeat the same behavior. Even the same question asked and answered repeatedly converts what was initially a true communicative exchange into a rehearsal of a formula. It is moreover extremely destructive of the learning process because it creates a misrepresentation of what knowing a language means. Proficiency cannot be achieved by knowing a list of fixed sentences—even if that list were long enough to encircle the globe.

Annotated Bibliography

Ausubel, David P., Joseph D. Novak, and Helen Hanesian. *Educational Psychology: A Cognitive View*, Second Edition. New York: Holt, Rinehart and Winston, 1978. [Reprinted by Werbel and Peck, 1989, ISBN 0-87066-001-2.] A cognitive psychology text that treats the usual topics but also delineates Ausubel's model of meaningful verbal learning. Book is viewed by many as one of the most important of the twentieth century in this field.

Blair, Glenn, R. Stewart Jones, and Ray H. Simpson. *Educational Psychology*, Fourth Edition. New York: Macmillan, 1975. A standard educational psychology textbook.

Erickson, James R., and Mari Reiss Jones. "Thinking." *Annual Review of Psychology* 29 (1978): 61-90. Respected treatment of problem solving and concept learning.

Eysenck, Michael W. *A Handbook of Cognitive Psychology*. London: Lawrence Erlbaum Associates, Ltd., 1984. A thorough treatment of psychological issues from a cognitivist perspective.

Hendrix, William, and Walter Meiden. *Beginning French: A Cultural Approach*. Cambridge, Mass.: Houghton Mifflin, 1948. One of the most widely used French textbooks of the twentieth century.

Hull, C.L. "Quantitative Aspects of the Evolution of Concepts." *Psychological Monographs* 28 (1920): Whole Number 123.

Jarvis, Gilbert A. "A Comparison of Contextualized Practice with Particularized Referents versus Practice with Generic Meaning in the Teaching of Beginning College French." Ph.D. dissertation. Purdue University, 1970. Empirical research report comparing the effects of differential practice upon language skill development and student attitudes.

_____. "The Value of Second-Language Learning." *Learning A Second Language: Seventy-ninth Yearbook of the National Society for the Study of Education*. Edited by Frank M. Grittner. Chicago: The University of Chicago Press, 1980. Delineates benefits from language study that are humanistic, cognitive, and pragmatic.

Joiner, Elizabeth G. "Communicative versus Non-Communicative Language Practice in the Teaching of Beginning College French." Ph.D. Dissertation. The Ohio

State University, 1974. Empirical research report comparing the effects of differential practice upon student language skill development.

Miller, George A. "The Psycholinguists." *The Psychology of Communication: Seven Essays*. Edited by George Miller. New York: Basic Books, 1967.

Odlin, Terence. *Language Transfer: Cross-Linguistic Influence in Language Learning*. Cambridge: Cambridge University Press, 1989. The history and analysis of cross-linguistic influences, written from a perspective of linguistic science.

Politzer, Robert L. *Foreign Language Learning: A Linguistic Introduction*. Englewood Cliffs, New Jersey: Prentice-Hall, 1970. One of the last publications to reflect a "linguistic" view of the language teaching-learning process.

Schaeffer, Reiner H. "Computer-Supplemented Structural Drill Practice versus Computer-Supplemented Semantic Drill Practice by Beginning College German: A Comparative Experiment." Ph.D. dissertation. The Ohio State University, 1979. Report of empirical research comparing the differential effects of two types of computer-mediated practice.

Wittgenstein, L. *Philosopical Investigations*. New York: Macmillan, 1958.

On Paradoxes and Paradigms
in Language Education Research

Elizabeth B. Bernhardt
The Ohio State University
Diane Tedick
Fairfield University

Introduction

The words "context" and "generic" have been used very often in the past decade. "Context" refers to environmental factors that provide clues to the meaning or to the understanding of some event. "Context" is frequently used to explain apparently inexplicable phenomena such as why teenagers attack innocent joggers or why learners appear to make mistakes when they have supposedly "learned" a grammatical feature. During the same period of time that "context" has been used so frequently, the word "generic" has also become a standard part of contemporary vocabulary. "Generic" implies general; i.e., that teenage behavior is the same regardless of who, what, or where, or that the ability to use features of language is transferrable from situation to situation regardless of who is speaking, what he or she is talking about, or where that talking is taking place.

The world view described above, which is simultaneously specific and general, dependent and independent, broad and narrow, is one of the many paradoxes that plague modern life. Language education research, as a subset of the modern world, can also be viewed as a dialectic. It has tried to be generalizable to and useful in a variety of settings; concomitantly, researchers have acknowledged the context dependency of their research and, simultaneously, have broadened its implications.

This paper, which will take a paradigmatic view of language education research, has as its organizing principles the concepts of paradox and paradigm. We hope this approach will help to clarify expectations and uses of particular kinds of research and to conceptualize the ways in which many pieces of research are potentially contradictory, leading to paradoxical findings.

It is important to note that the paper is not intended to provide a detailed review of research findings in language education. A number of excellent sources offer comprehensive reviews of the literature and discussions of the research methodologies used in the field (e.g., Cummins & Swain, 1986; Ellis, 1986, 1987; Faerch & Kasper, 1987; Genesee, 1987; Ringbom, 1987; Woods et al., 1986).

A research-analytic framework

In a review synthesis of comprehension research, Samuels and Kamil (1984) remind readers of "Jenkins' tetrahedron" (1979). They state:

> ...research... is influenced by four interacting factors. These are the age and skill of the experimental subjects, the tasks which the subjects are asked to perform, the materials which are used, and the context (e.g., the classroom, laboratory, type of school, etc.) which surrounds the study. A change in any of these variables can alter the results of a study and the researcher's view of the process (p. 189).

These four interacting factors were described at length by cognitive psychologist Joseph Jenkins, who conceptualized the factors in such a way that they form a geometric design.

Jenkins' tetrahedron provides a useful framework for viewing the paradigm of language education research. The *individual differences* between and among different subject groups in second language programs are enormous. Clearly, second language research has focused on and will continue to focus on learners of all ages, socioeconomic circumstances, and educational levels and settings. Rarely are there educational research endeavors that focus on such complex sets of learner variables as those found in second language settings.

Tasks form another angle in the tetrahedron. Second language research can encompass analyses of speaking, listening, reading, writing, explicit knowledge of grammatical rules, discourse rules, conversational rules, monologic and dialogic performances. The quantity and variety of these tasks coupled with individual difference factors serve to make the picture of second language research enormously complex.

Materials form the third angle. The materials that can influence research are linked certainly to task expectations, but also to individual subject differences. Materials can be written or oral, authentic or contrived; they can be words, sentences, short stories, novels, application forms, or an array of pictures, just to mention several examples.

The final angle of the tetrahedron, which is linked to the other three, is *context*. Context is the variable that makes the situation even more complex: for it can change in implicit and explicit ways the nature and the content of the other variables.

Each of these factors must be understood and accounted for in the development, interpretation, and application of any piece of research. In the following pages we will outline and discuss each one of the four interacting factors in Jenkins' tetrahedron. Tables 1 through 4 list particular factors related to four types of second language program designs: foreign language, second language, bilingual, and immersion. The tables display the *paradigm* of second language education research. As such, they are meant to communicate the more salient, broader features of the landscape of this research area; they are not meant to provide either a complete set of influencing factors or close-up details. What emerges from the discussion of these paradigmatic features is an inevitable set of apparent *paradoxes* about research and research findings in second language.

Individual Differences

Table 1 outlines the array of factors that are potentially involved in any discussion of individual differences between groups in second language programs. It is important to underscore at the outset that this discussion centers on between-group not within-group differences. Individual differences in individual learners are certainly critical variables and must be considered by implication. Table 1 presents group factors such as age differences, mother tongue and target language attitudes, socioeconomic status, status within society, motivational factors, and parental attitudes or what Richterich and Chancerel (1980) consider "user-institution" factors.

Age factors within this discussion are not an attempt to return to a consideration of the "Critical Period Hypothesis" (Scovel 1988). Rather, they need to be considered in terms of the manner in which they affect data generation, analysis, and interpretation. Analyzing the second language development of children, for example, is inherently confounded with the cognitive processes of initial language development. In other words, research findings can never state with great assurance whether language *per se* or cognitive growth is actually affecting language development. In contrast, with the generation of language by adults, it can be stated with some confidence that cognitive growth is not a major variable, but rather experience with the language to be learned. Adolescents make the situation even more complicated: cognitive development within adolescent groups can be so variable that statements about language development can be speculative at best.

Table 1 lists two sets of attitudinal factors that must also be considered in the analysis, generation, and interpretation of data. In general, attitudes toward the learners' native cultures are positive in most program types. The most variable set of factors, however, is found in a second language setting, into which learners may bring low self-esteem. On the other hand, much greater variability is found across all groups in attitudes toward the target language and culture. Again, the greatest variability is found in a second language setting.

Table 1. Individual differences.

	Age	SES	Attitudes towards native language & culture	Societal Status	Attitudes towards target language & culture	Motivation	Parental or user-institution support (literacy)
FL							
Traditional	Adolescents & adults	Variable	Generally positive	Majority group	Variable	Generally extrinsic/ instrumental	Generally neutral (most literate in L1)
FLES	Children (K-6)	"	"	"	Variable, but generally positive	"	Generally supportive (most literate in L1)
Intensive LSP	Adults	Mid-high	"	"	Variable	"	Generally supportive
Hearing Impaired	All ages	Variable	"	"	Variable, but generally positive	Intrinsic/ integrative	Supportive (most literate in L1)
ESL							
Pull-out	Children & adolescents	Variable (dependent upon L1, SES may be low in U.S. but not in native country)	Variable-dependent upon L1, length of residence, SES, societal attitudes, politics, etc.	Minority group	Variable, dependent upon length of residence, SES, social status, societal attitudes, religion, etc.	Intrinsic/ extrinsic and integrative/ instrumental	Generally supportive (variable literacy)
Intensive (self-contained, content-area based)	"	"	"	"	"	"	"
Intensive (university)	Adults	Mid-high	Generally positive	"	Variable	Generally extrinsic/ instrumental	Generally supportive
Competency-Based	"	Generally low	Generally positive, but self-esteem may be low	"	Variable, may tend toward negative side	"	"
ESP	"	Variable; Generally mid-high	Generally positive	"	Variable	"	"

	Age	SES	Societal Status	Attitudes towards native language & culture	Attitudes towards target language & culture	Motivation	Parental or user-institution support (literacy)
BE							
Transitional	Children & adolescents	Variable (dependent upon L1)	Minority group	Variable	Variable	Intrinsic/extrinsic and integrative/instrumental	Generally supportive (variable literacy)
Maintenance	"	"	"	Generally positive	"	"	"
Two-way	Children	Variable	Minority and majority group	Generally positive	Variable, generally positive	"	"
ESL							
Canada							
Early Total	Children	Mid-high	Majority group	Generally positive	Variable	Generally extrinsic/instrumental	Generally supportive (literate)
Early Partial	"	"	"	"	"	"	"
Delayed	"	"	"	"	"	"	"
Late	Children & adolescents	"	"	"	"	"	"
Double (early and delayed)	"	"	"	"	"	Intrinsic/extrinsic and integrative/instrumental	"
Heritage-Language	"	"	"	"	"	"	"
US							
Educational Enrichment	Children	Generally mid-high	Majority group	Generally positive	Variable	Intrinsic/extrinsic	Generally supportive (literate)
Magnet	"	Variable (generally mid-low)	"	"	"	Generally extrinsic/instrumental	Generally supportive (variable literacy)
Two-way	"	Variable	Minority and majority group	"	Variable, generally positive	Intrinsic/extrinsic and integrative/instrumental	"

✓   Economic and social status constitute another set of individual factors that influence research. Table 1 indicates that immersion and foreign language settings tend to include majority group individuals from middle to high socioeconomic backgrounds. In contrast, bilingual programs tend to contain minority group members who are frequently also of lower socioeconomic status. Parallel to age differences above, a second language setting has the greatest variability. Depending on the program type and goals, individuals may be of virtually any socioeconomic level.

Motivation to be in the educational setting is another complicated factor to be considered under the rubric of individual differences. Table 1 indicates that none of the settings seems to foster exclusively instrumental or exclusively integrative motivation. Perhaps motivation is so person-based rather than group-based that it is practically impossible to make a general assessment of its role in any of the settings.

Parental support, in contrast, is a factor that varies considerably from setting to setting. In foreign language and immersion curricula, parental support is positively correlated with socioeconomic status as well as with educational and literacy levels. Similarly, parental support is generally positive in bilingual settings, yet frequently colored by variable literacy levels. As noted above, in many second language settings, the concept of external support, frequently although not exclusively parental, is complicated. With adult learners, for example, outside agencies such as governments or companies often send individuals into the second language learning environment. These outside agencies may provide variable degrees of support.

An additional group difference is unique to second language situations—language. In foreign language, bilingual, and immersion settings, the norm is a native *lingua franca* shared by the vast majority of the students and the teacher. In many second language situations, however, the student body is frequently multilingual—indeed, some groups of learners may consist of students from ten or fifteen different language backgrounds with a teacher who may know one or none of these mother tongues.

Finally, differences in cultural backgrounds will undoubtedly influence research in second language settings. When learners share cultural knowledge and expectations with the teacher and other learners, communication and learning are likely to be facilitated. In contrast, when there is a cultural "mis-match" between and among learners and teachers, problems in communication are likely to arise. This latter situation more often than not results in differential treatment and/or low expectations of minority group students, which, in turn, lead to low achievement on their part.

The implications for research of this array of individual group differences are profound. These differences practically render the generalizability of findings impossible. That is, in order for findings to be valid from one subject group to another, groups have to "match" at some level. It is a rare published research study that offers appropriate subject descriptions; it is a rare consumer of research who recognizes the impact of these differences on the usability of research.

Tasks and Materials

Tables 2 and 3 outline factors related to both the types of materials that second language learners encounter and the types of tasks that they are expected to perform with those materials. Because of the inextricable links between tasks and materials in second language settings, they will be discussed together. Like learner differences, tasks and materials must be considered in light of the impact they have on research findings and implications. It is not uncommon for a second language study to give learners tasks to perform that they have never done previously. Data generated in such a situation may measure anxiety toward a new task rather than an actual language behavior. In like manner, materials, can be alien; they may present values and concepts that the learner does not hold. They may focus on topics about which a learner has no knowledge. They may be uninteresting or targeted toward an inappropriate age group. In other words, the learners may interact with the materials in such a way as to generate measures of affect or prior knowledge rather than language development. Clearly, much second language literacy research speaks to this issue.

Second language learners throughout the world are given materials that differ radically from setting to setting and that generate different outcomes. Foreign language learners in school and university programs are generally given grammatically sequenced materials and, after a period of time, great works of the target language literature. Such materials may be characterized as basically non-functional except for those students who wish, ultimately, to become literary historians. Other types of second language programs present materials that are more functional. Both bilingual and immersion contexts tend to give learners materials that are authentic or nearly authentic school-based curricular materials. The majority of second language programs, too, although providing some grammar support, ultimately have students engaged with authentic forms of written and oral discourse because of a focus on language for "real" purposes.

Categories of tasks in Table 3 are parallel to many of the types of materials listed in Table 2. A critical factor is that bilingual, immersion, and second language settings focus almost exclusively on school-based, academic tasks that concentrate on content and literacy in some specific context. Foreign language tasks are generally demonstration tasks that indicate that the learner has knowledge of the language *per se*, but not necessarily the skills to do something *with* the language.

50 / Critical Issues in Foreign Language Education

Table 2. Materials.

	Type	Focus	Function	Access to Authentic Materials
FL				
Traditional	Literary/Cultural texts, often contrived and/or glossed texts, grammar exercises, vocabulary lists, textbooks, computer grammar drills, movies, interactive video.	Language & Culture	Non-Functional	Limited
FLES	Games, songs, storybooks	"	"	"
Intensive LSP	Materials specific to purpose (some contrived, some authentic)	"	"	"
Hearing Impaired	Textbooks used in regular curriculum, materials designed for hearing impaired	"	"	Easily obtained
ESL				
Pull-out	Contrived grammar exercises, ESL readers, workbooks, games	Language (some academics)	Functional	Easily obtained
Intensive (self-contained, content-area based)	Textbooks used in regular curriculum, workbooks, some contrived ESL materials for grammar, basal readers, skills books, spelling books	Academics (less focus on language)	"	"
Intensive (university)	Often contrived texts, grammar exercises, vocabulary lists	Language	"	"
Competency-Based	Often contrived, though some authentic texts, samples of forms, applications; grammar exercises	Language/ survival skills	"	"
ESP	Materials specific to purpose (some contrived, some authentic)	Language/ special purpose	"	"
BE				
Transitional	Textbooks used in regular curriculum, some texts (not basals) may be translations of English	Language & academics	Functional	Easily obtained in English, not necessarily in L2
Maintenance	textbooks due to curricular constraints, ESL grammar books, workbooks, games, skills books, spelling and vocabulary exercises	Academics (some language)		
Two-way		"		
IM				
Canada				
Early Total		Academics (some language)	Functional	Easily obtained
Early Partial				
Delayed				
Late				
Double (early & delayed)	Textbooks used in regular curriculum, often textbooks in L2 have been translated from			
Heritage-Language	English texts due to curricular constraints, workbooks, games, skills books, spelling and			
US	vocabulary books, possibly some L2 literary			
Educational	works depending upon program of school	Academics and language	Functional	Access may be limited depending upon geographical setting
Enrichment				
Magnet		"		
Two-way		Academics (some language		

Table 3. Tasks.

	Type	Focus	Function
FL			
Traditional	Oral presentations, pronunciation drills, tests on language use, grammar drills, translation exercises, small group/pair dialogues, read literary and cultural texts, write to demonstrate language use	Language & Culture	Non-Functional
FLES	Games, songs, repetition, listening to stories	"	"
Intensive LSP	Dependent upon purpose of training, reading/writing, telephone skills, listening comprehension drills	"	"
Hearing Impaired	Tell stories in sign, demonstrate comprehension, exhibit general communication skills in sign	"	"
ESL			
Pull-out	Oral presentations, pronunciation drills, tests on language use, grammar drills, small group/pair dialogues, reading/writing to demonstrate language use	Language (some academics)	Functional
Intensive (self-contained, content-area based)	Academic tasks, reading groups, small group work, filling in workbooks, writing to demonstrate learning, tests on content	Academics (less focus on language)	"
Intensive (university)	Grammar drills, tests on language use, listening comprehension exercises, reading of academic texts, writing	Language	"
Competency-Based	Survival skills, listening comprehension and pronunciation drills, literacy skills for a specific job	Language/survival skills	"
ESP	Dependent upon purpose of training (see LSP)	Language/special purpose	"
BE			
Early Total		Academics (some language)	Functional
Early Partial			
Delayed			
Late			
Double (early & delayed)			
Heritage-Language	Academics tasks, reading groups, small group work, filling in workbooks, tests on content, writing to demonstrate learning, some translation possible		
US			
Educational Enrichment		Academics and language	Functional
Magnet		"	
Two-way		Academics (some language	

Context

The final table addresses some of the more salient factors that describe the various contexts in which language education occurs. We focus on the language education that takes place in school settings, not in natural settings. The latter brings forth yet further differences that influence language learning. For a review of these differences and a discussion of the effects they have on research see, for example, Ellis (1986).

Table 4 presents essentially two sets of group factors: those related to the context of the school setting and those related to the larger, more encompassing societal context. The first set includes the nature and underlying purpose of the various program models, general estimates with regard to the amount of time spent on language instruction, the make-up of the classrooms in the various settings, and teacher variables. The second set contains such factors as the geographical setting and political climate of a particular area, in addition to those that stem directly from these variables: the amount of exposure to the target language that is available to the learners and the attitudes of members of the society toward the them.

The Context of Schooling

The nature and underlying purpose of the distinct program model(s) directly influence the kinds of tasks and materials used, as noted above, as well as the classroom make-up and the amount of time spent on the target language(s). Foreign language programs represent perhaps the least variable of the program models. On the other hand, second language, bilingual, and immersion programs are exceedingly diverse.

Ovando and Collier (1985) point out that "researchers, politicians, journalists, and school administrators have used a wide variety of sometimes conflicting terms to refer to [bilingual] program differentiation, with little sense of continuity or clarity" (p. 37). In fact, Genessee (1987) points out that no one clear model is in operation (p. 147). The three major models listed in the table—traditional, maintenance, and two-way—are represented by any number of program types. That is, within each general model exists a plethora of varieties that differ in terms of methodology, materials, and time spent in the two languages.

Similarly, immersion programs are defined broadly. In Canada, the distinction is made primarily on the basis of the total amount of exposure to the target language(s). In contrast, in the United States, all of the immersion programs in operation thus far are classified as "early" (Genesee, 1987) and differ instead with respect to their underlying purpose, and, consequently, to geographic area. For example, programs designed for linguistic, cultural, and general educational enrichment tend to be in suburban areas that are more socioeconomically fortunate. Programs designed for magnet schools, on the other hand, exist in inner-cities, because their primary purpose is to create racial and ethnolinguistic balance. Two-way immersion (or bilingual) programs, although few in number, are found in inner-cities because they rely on large numbers of both minority and majority group students. Second language settings represent programs of greatest variability. They are often implemented quickly in response to an unexpected influx of non-native speakers of English into a community, be it urban or suburban. Consequently, facilities, materials, and instructional time are often limited, particularly for pull-out (one hour per day) programs. It is not uncommon for a second language teacher to have to cart around her materials and set up temporary working space in any number of schools that often contain an entire continuum of grade levels, not to mention proficiency levels among the learners. The effect these differences have on research is staggering.

Directly influenced by the nature of the program model is the amount of time spent on language instruction in any particular setting. Traditional foreign language programs typically devote 50 minutes a day, five days per week to language instruction, while the instruction time in FLES programs tends to vary. Immersion programs are well-defined with respect to instruction time. Second language and bilingual programs, however, differ greatly. The broadest variability in the amount of time spent on language instruction exists both among and within second language programs (see Table 4). Ironically, the highest performance expectations (in terms of language acquisition) appear to be directed toward second language learners.

Although bilingual programs are usually characterized by self-contained classrooms where instruction occurs throughout the day, their variability lies in the balance in use of the two languages. Ovando and Collier (1985) specify a number of methodologies that reflect differences in balance: concurrent, alternate, preview-review, team-teaching, and grouping. Often the language use is determined by the native language background of the teacher and her level of proficiency in the second language. It is rare for bilingual teachers to be truly bilingual and bicultural. They usually feel more comfortable in their native tongue, be it English or another language; consequently, their instruction tends to favor one language over the other. This fact alone makes generalizable research in bilingual settings difficult.

As Table 4 clearly shows, foreign language, bilingual, and immersion programs, with the exception of two-way programs (i.e., programs that teach two native languages as second languages), have largely homogeneous student bodies, whereas the second language programs have heterogeneous ones. It should be noted that even though two-way programs are characterized by heterogeneity, in that they include students from both minority and majority groups, they are not nearly as heterogeneous as second language groups, because minority students in two-way programs tend to represent just one group, as defined by native language background (e.g., Hispanics).

Table 4. Context.

	Underlying Purpose	Time	Classroom Make-Up	Teacher Preparation	Teachers' L1 and Attitudes Toward Learners	Geographical Setting	Exposure to Target Language & Culture	Political climate	Societal Attitudes Toward Learners
FL									
Traditional	To enable learners to communicate with native speakers of target language; curriculum requirement	50 min. day, every day, 2 years minimum	Homogeneous	Relatively controlled, much known of preparation	May be either native speaker of English or of TL; attitudes generally positive	Generally monolingual, though it depends on geographic area	Limited amount	Subtle & obvious influences (e.g., recent pressure to demonstrate success)	Generally positive
FLES	To provide linguistic, cultural enrichment	variable; e.g., ½ hour, 3 times/week, years vary	Homogeneous	Not controlled; little known	"	"	"	Subtle influence	"
Intensive LSP	To enable learners to communicate in the target language in a particular job setting	variable; all day, 1 week-several months	"	"	"	"	Limited amount	"	"
Hearing Impaired	To enable learners to communicate fluently in sign language	variable; usually all day for several years	"	Relatively well controlled	May or may not be hearing impaired; attitudes positive	"	A potentially great amount	"	"
ESL									
Pull-out	To create "native-like" speakers; To provide language teaching for students who are mainstreamed in regular classes	variable; 20 min., 3 times/week; 2-3 years	Heterogeneous	Little known of preparation	Often does not know L2 — cannot know L2 of all learners; attitudes variable	Generally monolingual	Great amount	Obvious influence	Possibly negative
Intensive (self-contained, content-area based)	To integrate language and academic teaching; to create "native-like" speakers	half day/all day; 1-2 years	"	"	"	"	"	"	"
Intensive (university)	To prepare students for college-level course work	half day/all day; 3 months-year	"	"	"	"	"	"	"
Competency-Based	To provide survival skills and job training	variable; 1 hour, 3 times/week; several months	"	"	"	"	"	"	"
ESP	To provide learners with enough language ability to be able to succeed in a certain job	variable; half day/all day; 1 week-several months	"	"	"	"	"	"	"

	Underlying Purpose	Time	Classroom Make-Up	Teacher Preparation	Teachers' L1 and Attitudes Toward Learners	Geographical Setting	Exposure to Target Language & Culture	Political Climate	Societal Attitudes Toward Learners
BE									
Transitional	To provide instruction in L1 so that students don't fall behind academically; to mainstream students as soon as possible	all day; 1-2 years	Homogeneous	Little/some known of preparation depending upon when educated	May be either native speaker of English or of TL; attitudes generally positive	Generally monolingual	Great amount	Obvious influence (e.g., "English only" movement)	Possible negative
Maintenance	To provide a balance of content-area instruction in both L1 and L2 throughout school, or in as many grades as possible	all day; 4-6 years (sometimes K-12)	"	"		"	"	"	"
Two-way	To promote bilingual proficiency in English and non-English language among both native English-speakers and LEP students	all day; 4-6 years	Heterogeneous (two groups)	"		"	Great amount for LEP students; limited amount for native speakers of English	Possible obvious influence	Negative/Positive
ESL									
Canada									
Early Total	To promote Canada's two official languages while providing academic instruction as specified by the curriculum	all day; 4-6 years	Homogeneous	Little known of preparation	May be either native speaker of English or of TL; attitudes generally positive	Bilingual or monolingual	May be a limited or a great amount	Obvious influence (e.g., Quebec-French vs. English)	Generally positive
Early Partial	"	"	"	"	"	"	"	"	"
Delayed	"	all day; 3-4 years	"	"	"	"	"	"	"
Late	"	all day; 4-6 years	"	"	"	"	"	"	"
Double (early and delayed)	To use two non-native languages (e.g., French and Hebrew) for curricular instruction	"	"	"	"	"	"	"	"
Heritage-Language	To revitalize/develop heritage langauge; to provide academic instruction through the use of the two languages		"	"	"	Generally monolingual	"	Subtle influence	"
US									
Educational Enrichment	To provide linguistic, cultural, general educational enrichment; to integrate language and academic teaching	all day; 4-6 years	Homogeneous	Little known of preparation		Generally monolingual	Limited amount	Subtle influence	Generally positive
Magnet	To create a balanced ratio of ethnolinguistic groups in a certain area; to integrate language and academic teaching	all day; 4-6 years	"	"		"	"	"	"
Two-way	To promote bilingual proficiency in English and non-English language among both native English-speakers and LEP students	all day; 4-6 years	Heterogeneous (two groups)	"		"	Great amount for LEP students; limited amount for native speakers of English	Possible obvious influence	Possibly negative and positive

The heterogeneity of second language programs leads to innumerable confounding variables that unavoidably cloud research findings.

The final factors related to the school context are teacher characteristics. As mentioned earlier, the teacher's native language and culture will have a direct effect on instruction and on the student-teacher relationships established in the classroom. As noted in the discussion of individual differences, second language teachers are often faced with students representing any number of native language backgrounds; the teachers may or may not have knowledge of any one of these languages/cultures. To further complicate the issue, in some settings the learners have two or more teachers. In second language pull-out programs, for example, the learners have a second language teacher and a regular classroom teacher. It is often in the regular classroom that discrimination occurs, due to the teachers' unfamiliarity with and/or negative attitudes toward minority group students (see, for example, Schinke-Llano, 1983; Trueba, 1987).

An additional factor related to teachers is their prior preparation. Among the four major models, foreign language programs are the most predictable with respect to teacher preparation, by virtue of their long history. The education of teachers for second language, bilingual, and immersion programs is ill-defined. Many state departments of education have yet to implement teacher certification requirements for the various programs, although the programs have been in operation for years. Connecticut, for example, began certification requirements for bilingual teachers in July 1989 after having bilingual education programs in the state for well over a decade; second language certification has yet to be implemented in this state, despite the variety of second language programs that have been in operation here for years. In fact, across this nation, little is known about the preparation (or qualifications) of second language teachers. In the past, many regular classroom teachers were encouraged to take second language positions when districts were faced with school closings caused by student shortages.

Similarly, little is known about the preparation of immersion teachers. Genesee (1987, citing Lapkin & Cummins, 1984) states, "it is still rare in Canada to find teachers trained specially for immersion even though the program has been in existence for some 20 years now" (p. 18). In addition, language teachers in general, with the exception of those teaching second language classes, are expected to demonstrate proficiency in the language(s) they teach, yet it is unclear how, or even whether, the teachers' proficiency is indeed assessed.

The Societal Context

Geographical setting affects language education in several ways. One involves the degree to which learners in an area are exposed to the target language outside of the school environment. Foreign language learners have limited access to the target language. In fact, they have to seek contact through movies, radio, travel, and interaction with native speakers of that language. In contrast, second language learners are surrounded by target language input. Similarly, immersion students who live in bilingual areas of Canada such as Montreal have high degrees of exposure to the second language. It is important to note, however, that although access to the target language is readily available in a particular area, there is no guarantee that learners will take advantage of their surroundings. For example, in some communities in the United States such as Miami, New York City, and Los Angeles, Hispanics have no immediate "need" to communicate in English because virtually all the information and facilities they need are available in Spanish. Similarly, immersion students (who are primarily native speakers of English) in bilingual communities display limited use of French despite the fact that they have ample opportunity to do so (Genesee, 1987). This lack of interaction between cultural groups is partially a direct result of both political issues and societal attitudes.

Education is never neutral; rather, it reflects the hidden agenda of those in power (Apple 1979; Freire, 1970; Shor, 1986; Shor & Freire, 1987, among many others). Educational factors are in some way influenced by the larger, sociopolitical context of a setting. Shor (1986) provides a brilliant account of how the political changes that have occurred in the United States since the late 1960s have had a direct and profound impact on educational policy, curricula, materials, and practice. The sociopolitical influences on language education can be either obvious or subtle, often depending upon the geographical setting.

In Canada, the general sociopolitical climate, particularly in the region of Quebec, has been one of conflict and animosity. These feelings have carried over into school settings where anglophone and francophone teachers often avoid interaction (Genesee, 1987). The obvious negative feelings between the two groups certainly affect the language learning and social attitudes of the immersion students.

Political movements that have had an obvious influence on language education in the United States include the "English Only" movement, bilingual education controversies, increased emphasis on testing, and the recent proficiency movement in foreign language education. Foreign language curricula and testing issues have been affected by strong statements about the lack of proficiency among foreign language learners (e.g., Lambert, 1986).

Covert sociopolitical forces also affect language education, particularly involving minority group students. Auerbach and Burgess (1987) present sound evidence to show that the curricula and materials for competency-based second language programs are written so as to disempower the learners in subtle ways. They state:

Survival on the job is often equated with being submissive; students are taught the language associated with being on the bottom of the power hierarchy. This can be seen in the often expressed position that prevocational ESL students be taught to *understand* the imperative but not to *produce* it because they must obey orders but not give them. Language functions in most survival texts include asking for approval, clarification, reassurance, permission, and so on, but not praising, criticizing, complaining, refusing, or disagreeing (Auerbach & Burgess, 1987, pp. 158-159, their emphasis).

Contextual factors clearly have a critical impact on the results of language education research. In addition, they have the power to change the nature and the content of the other three variables: individual differences, tasks, and materials.

Conclusion

This discussion of the paradigms of language education research has revealed a number of paradoxes. When research findings generated within one paradigm are applied to a setting that does not fit that first paradigm, serious misuse of the research findings is the result. A classic example is applying Canadian research findings to U. S. contexts.

The vast majority of language education research in the United States is conducted in second language settings. It is often characterized by serious methodological limitations due, in part, to the variability that characterizes these settings. Researchers seldom provide explicit descriptions of subject groups, of their linguistic, cultural, and educational backgrounds, and of the research context—all factors critical to sound research. One reason for the failure of researchers to provide details about their subject groups may be their inability to cope with a multitude of languages. As Ferguson and Huebner (1988) point out:

> The TESOL profession has been an important locus of American research in second language acquisition, a fact largely responsible for the existence of a generation of American SLA specialists who do not themselves speak a second language. One can point to outstanding exceptions of Americans with extensive overseas experience or with outstanding FL specialization, but the majority of contributors to the active American scene of SLA research still belong to this English-oriented group (p. 4).

This statement underscores just one of the limitations facing research in second language settings. The above discussion has revealed more of the many variables that affect second language research. The irony of the situation lies in the fact that the setting where researchers need to be most sensitive to the four interacting factors of Jenkins' (1979) tetrahedron is precisely the setting where researchers are least sensitive. In fact, the profession appears to be searching for "truth" about second language acquisition in the setting that is the least revealing. This argument leads to a realization of the foreign language classroom as an excellent forum for data collection. As noted above, many of the confounding variables in second language research are eliminated in foreign language settings where groups are largely homogeneous, where researchers generally have intimate knowledge of the subjects' native language and culture as well as the target language and culture, and where variables such as instructional time, exposure to the target language and culture, and teacher preparation are well-controlled. Ultimately, these advantages can facilitate the development of a more coherent, valid, and reliable research base. Paradoxically, despite the advantages it has to offer, the foreign language setting receives perhaps the least amount of attention in the United States as a legitimate research environment.

At the present time, conclusions that can be made about second language acquisition are limited at best, because researchers do not have a clear understanding of how all of the paradigmatic features outlined above interact. Researchers in this profession would be wise to begin collecting data in settings where they can exercise more control over the variables, such as in foreign language and immersion settings. This approach would lead to a more legitimate, organized research program. In addition, the knowledge gained from research in such settings would prepare researchers to conduct studies in contexts where fewer variables need to be controlled.

Annotated Bibliography

Apple, M. W. (1979). *Ideology of Curriculum*. London: Routledge & Kegan Paul. In this book the author discusses the content of educational policy and curricula. He argues that current curricula reflect the conservative ideology of those in power.

Auerbach, E., & Burgess, D. (1987). "The hidden curriculum of survival ESL." In I. Shor (Ed.), *Freire for the Classroom*. Portsmouth, NH: Boynton Cook. The authors provide examples of an array of ESL texts designed for adult competency-based programs to reveal racial and class bias in these presumably helpful materials. They offer an alternative approach to adult ESL education based on Freirian principals.

Cummins, J. & Swain, M. (1986). *Bilingualism in Education: Aspects of Theory, Research and Practice*. London: Longman. This book reviews recent theoretical and research work relating to the educational development of bilingual children. The impact of bilingual education on the linguistic, cognitive, and academic growth of majority and minority language students is investigated. The book also outlines various ways of operationalizing the construct of bilingual proficiency, of assessing it, and of recognizing the educational and policy implications involved in the different conceptualizations.

Ellis, R. (Ed.). (1987). *Second Language Acquisition in Context*. Englewood Cliffs, NJ: Prentice-Hall. This collection of articles explores the effect of contextual variability on second language use and development. The theoretical and methodological concerns involved in researching interlanguage (IL) variability are treated in one section. Subsequent articles investigate the impact of linguistic, situational, and social contexts on IL variability. A final section examines the pedagogical contributions of IL variability studies with regard to second language teaching and testing.

Ellis, R. (1986). *Understanding Second Language Acquisition*. Oxford: Oxford University Press. This book provides a comprehensive synthesis of recent research work in second language acquisition (SLA). SLA is characterized as a complex process, involving many interconnected factors, such as the role of the first language, learner strategies, and input. The theoretical and research base of each factor is treated in depth in separate chapters. The author concludes by summarizing the contributions and explanatory power of current theories of SLA.

Faerch, C., & Kasper, G. (Eds.). (1987). *Introspection in Second Language Research*. Clenedon, England: Multilingual Matters. This book is a collection of articles, outlining the use of introspective methods (verbal accounts by learners of their thought processes) in second language research. The introductory chapters delineate the historical background, theoretical foundations, and methodological concerns of various introspective techniques. Subsequent chapters report on ten empirical studies, employing introspective methods for data collection purposes.

Ferguson, C., & Huebner, T. (January, 1989). *Foreign Language Instruction and Second Language Acquisition Research in the United States*. Washington, D.C.: National Foreign Language Center. This contribution to the NFLC occasional papers series is an overview of the ways in which foreign language and second language acquisition are related and comprehensible within the context of the United States educational system.

Freire, P. (1970). *Pedagogy of the Oppressed*. NY: Continuum. This classic work presents the first description of the literacy program Freire set up in Brazil to educate and empower the illiterate peasants. In his discussion of the "dialogic" method of teaching, Freire explains the fundamental principles underlying his philosophy.

Genesee, F. (1987). *Learning Through Two Languages: Studies in Immersion and Bilingual Education*. Cambridge: Newbury House. This book takes an in-depth look at second language immersion and bilingual programs. The first chapter provides an historical framework, while subsequent sections describe various Canadian immersion programs—their theoretical base, research findings, and evaluation procedures. Additional chapters discuss immersion programs and bilingual education programs for minority language children in the U.S. A concluding chapter delineates the relationship between language proficiency and academic achievement in immersion and bilingual programs.

Jenkins, J. J. (1979). Four parts to remember: A tetrahedral model of memory experiments. In L.S. Cermak & F.I.M. Craik (Eds.), *Levels of Processing in Human Memory*. Hillsdale, NY: Erlbaum. In this article, Jenkins explains how four interacting factors—context, tasks, materials, and individual differences—affect experiments in cognition. His geometric conceptualization of the interaction of these factors is illustrated in a tetrahedral model.

Lambert, R. D. (1986). *Points of Leverage: An Agenda for a National Foundation for International Studies*. NY: Social Science Research Council. This report, sponsored by several foundations, presents a rationale for a National Foundation for Foreign Languages and International Studies. It provides a series of recommendations for improving foreign language education in order to meet increasing political and corporate needs.

Lapkin, S., & Cummins, J. (1984). Canadian French immersion education: current administrative and instructional practices. In *Studies on Immersion Education: A Collection for United States Educators.* (pp. 87-112). Sacramento: California State Department of Education. This book provides a comprehensive review of policy issues in immersion education in Canada.

Ovando, C. J., & Collier, V. (1985). *Bilingual and ESL classrooms: Teaching in multicultural contexts.* NY: McGraw-Hill. Designed for bilingual and ESL teachers, this volume combines theory and research with practical applications. Its eight chapters provide an in-depth look at important issues including student characteristics; politics, programs and resources; language acquisition; culture; assessment; school and community relations; and methodologies related to various content areas.

Richterich, R., & Chancerel, J. L. (1980). *Identifying the needs of adults learning a foreign language* (2nd Ed.), NY: Pergamon Press. This book presents a synthesis of the research that resulted from the Council of Europe Modern Languages Project. It includes a detailed discussion of the types of information required to conduct needs analyses for the purpose of preparing communicative syllabi for adult language learners. In addition, it outlines a variety of methods of collection, such as needs surveys, attitude scales, language tests, and content analyses.

Ringbom, H. (1987). *The Role of the First Language in Foreign Language Learning.* Clenedon, England: Multilingual Matters. This book investigates the role of the first language (L1) in second language (L2) learning by comparing two groups of learners, who are culturally and educationally homogeneous but have different L1's, as they learn the same L2, i.e., Finnish-speaking and Swedish-speaking Finns learning English. The book addresses how learners' knowledge of their L1 impacts their L2 acquisition, emphasizing the importance of similarities between the L1 and L2 and their effect on the acquisition process.

Samuels, J., & Kamil, M. (1984). Models of the reading process. In P. D. Pearson (Ed.). *Handbook of reading research.* NY: Longman. This article, part of a volume that covers a wide spectrum of research related to reading in a first language, provides a synthesis of models of the reading process. The authors include discussion of the historical background of the models, the problems with model evaluation, and the construction of models. In-depth analyses of several models are presented.

Schinke-Llano, L. A. (1983). Foreigner talk in content classrooms. In H. W. Seliger & M. H. Long (Eds.), *Classroom oriented research in second language acquisition.* Rowley, MA: Newbury House. The article by Schinke-Llano is just one of a series of papers in this book that deal with five major areas of research pertaining to language acquisition in the classroom environment. The five areas include methodological issues, learner strategies and variables, teacher speech, teacher and learner feedback, and input, interaction, and acquisition. Schinke-Llano presents the results of a study conducted during content instruction in 12 fifth and sixth grade classrooms, each of which contained a small number of limited English proficiency (LEP) students. She found significant differences in the teachers' treatment of LEP and non-LEP students.

Scovel, T. (1988). *A time to speak*. Rowley, MA: Newbury House. This volume synthesizes the research data reflecting age differences in second language acquisition.

Shor, I. (1986). *Culture Wars*. Boston, MA: Routledge and Kegan Paul. In this volume Shor explains how three major periods of conservative school reform (Career Education, 1971-5; the Literacy Crisis and back-to-basics 1975-82; and the war for "excellence," 1982-84) helped to displace the protest culture of the 1960s. He argues that each was a political effort to restore order after the 1960s. The book also provides a critique of the current war for so-called "excellence" in education.

Shor, I. (Ed.). (1987). *Freire for the Classroom*. Portsmouth, NH: Boynton/Cook. The edited volume is a sourcebook for teachers who are interested in liberatory pedagogy. The chapters describe practical application of Freirian philosophy in a variety of settings, including teacher education, women's studies, language arts, second language education, and mathematics.

Shor, I., & Freire, P. (1987). *A pedagogy for liberation*. South Hadley, MA: Bergin & Garvey. Engaging in dialogue, the authors illuminate the problems of the educational system in relation to those of the larger society and argue for the need to transform the classroom. They illustrate the possibilities of transformation by describing their own experiences in liberating the classroom from its traditional constraints.

Trueba, H. T. (Ed.). (1987). *Success or Failure: Learning and the Language Minority Student*. Cambridge: Newbury House. This collection of research articles addresses the specific needs of language minority students. The contributers have used ethnographic and anthropological techniques to tap the relationships between culture, language, and learning in both home and school environments. These cross-cultural perspectives examine why school learning is often difficult for minority students and what can be done to make minority education more successful.

Woods, A., Fletcher, P., & Hughes, A. (1986). *Statistics in Language Studies*. Cambridge: Cambridge University Press. This book describes what researchers in linguistics and related fields need to know in order to use statistics effectively in their research work. The first chapters deal with basic statistical concepts, probability, and inferential statistics. Later chapters cover chi-square, analysis of variance, and multivariate techniques. The book serves as a valuable resource tool for researchers and students.

Elementary School Foreign Languages: What Research Can and Cannot Tell Us

Myriam Met
Montgomery County (Maryland) Public Schools

The number of elementary school foreign language programs has sharply increased since the 1970s, due in part to the recognition that American students simply begin too late to learn other languages, and to the awareness that a language-competent America is in the national interest. The growth of such programs at the elementary school level has been accompanied by a number of critical issues facing program planners. These include, among others, questions about who should take a foreign language and the grades in which foreign languages should be introduced, the design of elementary school programs, which languages students should study, who should teach them and where teachers can be found, and articulation with middle- and high-school level programs. In recent decades increasing attention has been paid to research on second-language acquisition by children. Some of the results bear direct implications for foreign-language instruction in elementary schools; some have indirect implications.

This paper will examine some of the critical issues in elementary school foreign language instruction and what research can or cannot tell us about them. This paper addresses:

- When should students begin to learn a foreign language?
- What should students learn?
- How should they learn it?
- How can we measure what they've learned?

When should students begin to learn a foreign language?

Age and language proficiency

Folk wisdom has long held that young children learn languages more quickly and more effectively than older children or adults, This has been the primary rationale for introducing foreign languages in the elementary school and, if possible, as early as kindergarten. While research on the optimal age to begin studying another language may not unequivocally support an early (or for that matter, later) start, there are other significant benefits to beginning in childhood.

Several works have reviewed the research on the optimum age question (Harley, 1986; Collier, 1989; Krashen, Scarcella, and Long, 1982). Harley's review of the literature examines both the theoretical arguments and the empirical data. Harley contrasts hypotheses positing a biological advantage (e.g. Lenneberg, 1967; Penfield, 1959) or cognitively-based advantage for younger learners (Krashen, 1975; Rosansky, 1975; Felix, 1981) with hypotheses that children and adults acquire language by similar processes (McLaughlin, 1978), and also with hypotheses that hold that older learners may benefit from their more fully developed experiences, background knowledge, and cognitive maturity (e.g., Cummins, 1981). Summarizing these theoretical perspectives, Harley concludes

> ... it is clear that although most theorists would agree that there is at least some potential advantage to an early start in childhood, there is little consensus on the precise nature of such advantage, or its fundamental causes, and some would even deny that it exists. (p. 22)

Empirical research comparing the relationship between age and learning is difficult to design. Experimental studies should insure that the context in which language is learned be equally advantageous to both the younger and older learner. Further, the cognitive and linguistic demands of the assessment measure should not favor either group. Such research is obviously difficult to design and implement since instructional approaches appropriate to adults are usually inappropriate for children. In the same vein, testing adults and testing children may require markedly different approaches and instruments. Thus, Harley commenting on the empirical data, observes that

> ... a persistent problem in relating theory to empirical findings has been one of interpretation, since it is generally impossible within the context of a single study to isolate the variable "age" from the setting in which the L2 is learned and the way in which L2 progress is assessed. (p. 23)

Harley's review of the empirical data shows that attainment of second language proficiency varies with the setting in which language is learned and the tasks which learners are asked to perform in the language. In natural language learning settings, younger learners appear to outperform older learners in the long run on measures of interpersonal communication skills. The converse is often true in school settings, where language use tends to be decontextualized and tasks are relatively cognitively demanding. Older learners may be more efficient learners simply because they have more tools for learning in school at their disposal. They have knowledge of the world, a knowledge which means that they are acquiring new vocabulary for concepts they have already mastered; in contrast, younger learners must both develop concepts and learn related vocabulary. The cognitive maturity of older learners also allows them to bring into play a wider range of learning tools and strategies.

In reviewing a series of papers on child-adult differences in second-language acquisition, Krashen et al. conclude that while adults may outpace children, and older children outpace younger children in the early development of control of the syntactic and morphological system of the language, children are superior language learners to adults in the long-term development of language proficiency. Thus, older may be better than younger in *rate* of language development, but younger is better than older in ultimate level of attainment (p. 161).

Several well-known studies have compared younger and older students in a school setting. Burstall (1974) reported higher attainment for older students. Other studies cited by Harley (Dunkel and Pillet, 1962; Oller and Nagato, 1974; Genesee, 1979) all showed similar results. Yet the results of each of these studies are questionable. In the Burstall study, teachers in the elementary school may have been underqualified; there was poor articulation from the elementary to the secondary level and eventually, students from both groups were mixed in classes. In the other studies, poor articulation, again, from the elementary to the secondary level did not allow students to maintain or continue to develop their foreign language skills.

In Canada, students may elect to enter immersion programs early (grades K-1) or late (e.g., grade 7). Studies comparing early and late immersion students shown an advantage for the early immersion students (Harley, 1986; Swain and Lapkin, 1988), although this advantage has not always been highly significant. Early immersion students tend to score somewhat better than do late immersion students on aural/oral measures, but their performance is not better on literacy-related tasks. Early immersion students, however, are more confident of their abilities to use French.

It is important not to quickly infer from these results that a later entry point into immersion programs is advantageous for most students. While students in early immersion programs are there because their parents believe immersion is an educational advantage, students in late immersion have selected this option for themselves. Most often, late immersion students are academically able; less able learners are likely to be daunted by the challenge of mastering school subjects in a language they don't know. Clearly, the range of academic abilities and interests of students in late immersion programs may be limited by the self-selected nature of this population. Further, late immersion students are not true beginners—they have participated in core French instruction (the Canadian equivalent of FLES) for at least one year, and often several years, prior to immersion. Obviously, they, too, may have had something of an early start in learning language. Nonetheless, the results of research comparing the foreign-language attainment of early and late entry immersion students raises questions as to why early immersion students do not significantly outperform late-entry students. Researchers in Canada continue to explore this question. The question of which age is best to begin immersion also continues to be debated in Canada.

In a 1989 summary of research on academic achievement and second-language skills, Collier also reviews of the literature on age and second language acquisition. Citing some of the same studies as Harley and Krashen et al., as well as other studies focused on language-minority students in the United States, Collier concludes that the optimum age for acquiring school language is between 8 and 12.

Cognitive benefits of early language learning

Several studies have examined the relationship between cognitive development and bilingualism or between cognition and foreign language study in childhood. A landmark study by Peal and Lambert (1962) showed that balanced bilinguals achieved higher scores on measures of verbal intelligence than did monolinguals. More recently, studies by Ben Zeev (1977) and Hakuta (1984) have shown that bilingual children demonstrate greater metalinguistic awareness and mental flexibility than do monolingual children. Hakuta also reports a positive relationship between bilingualism and non-verbal reasoning ability. Hakuta's research is particularly interesting, since his study also showed that even children who were at low levels of proficiency in their second language demonstrated benefits from their incipient bilingualism. For foreign language educators this finding is significant, since it implies that children do not have to achieve equal proficiency in both languages (i.e., full bilingualism) in order to accrue any cognitive benefits.

Research has also found that when children learn a second/foreign language in school, there are measurable cognitive and academic benefits. Bamford and Mizokana's 1989 paper reporting on a study of Spanish immersion students includes a review of the literature, citing numerous studies which have demonstrated that students acquiring a second/foreign language in school settings significantly outperform controls on measures of cognitive functioning. They note Bruck, Lambert, and Tucker's study (1974) of seventh-grade French immersion students who outperformed controls on measures of cognitive flexibility, as well as reporting their own findings of significant differences favoring Spanish immersion students on a measure of non-verbal problem-solving skills.

Cognitive benefits have been demonstrated by Landry (1974), who found that sixth-grade students who had taken a foreign language since first grade scored higher on a measure of divergent thinking (which includes fluency, flexibility, and originality of thought) than did a comparable group of students who had not. A recent study in Louisiana found that higher levels of cognitive and metacognitive processing were directly and positively associated with the number of years of elementary school foreign-language instruction (Foster, 1989).

Academic benefits of early language learning

A similar pattern begins to emerge over the course of many years when Canadian immersion students are compared with their counterparts in English-only programs. The data have shown that there is a strong positive relationship between participation in an immersion program and higher scores on measures of intelligence and academic achievement. A recent analysis of longitudinal data on the academic achievement of early immersion students and that of comparable non-immersion students provides strong support for the positive long-term benefits of immersion. Swain (1989) reports that longitudinal data on the English achievement of students in early immersion programs shows they outperform comparable peers educated in English-only settings. Even more encouraging is Swain's finding that within the immersion student population, higher scores on measures of French achievement were positively correlated with higher scores on measures of English achievement.

Similar support for the improved academic performance of foreign-language students comes from several recent studies in the United States which have involved students participating in FLES programs.[1] An extensive study of more than 13,000 third, fourth, and fifth graders in Louisiana showed that students who had taken a foreign language significantly outperformed those who had not on standardized tests of reading and mathematics (Rafferty, 1986). Researchers at Purdue University studied the relationship between elementary school foreign language in grades four through six (Garfinkel and Tabor, 1987). Again, these results support improved academic performance for the foreign-language group. Even more interesting was their finding that students of average academic ability showed greater gains on a standardized reading test than did those of above average ability. One clear implication of this finding is that the opportunity for foreign language study should not be restricted to the academically elite.

While a few other studies have shown that students who take a foreign language in elementary school perform no better academically than those who do not, the foreign language group is still at an advantage: they have gained knowledge, skills, and attitudes that their classmates have not.

Attitudinal benefits of early language learning

Indeed, development of positive cross-cultural attitudes is a goal of foreign language programs most likely and most effectively reached when foreign language instruction begins in the elementary school. Research on the cross-cultural attitudes of the developing child and emerging adolescent seems to indicate that younger children are more receptive to learning about and accepting other peoples and cultures (Lambert and Klineberg, 1967; Carpenter and Torney, 1973; Torney, 1979). Emerging adolescents place great value on belonging to a group and on conformity to within-group norms. This makes them less likely to be accepting of differences between themselves and others and also less likely to identify in a positive way with those of different cultures. Gardner and Lambert's work (1972) on integrative motivation (the desire to identify/integrate with a target group) indicates that integrative motivation is positively related to foreign language learning. Thus, the diminishing receptivity of adolescents to those outside their group may undermine the effectiveness of foreign-language programs introduced in the early teen years.

When should FL instruction begin? — Conclusion

Clearly, elementary schools deciding at which grade to initiate an elementary school foreign-language program may want to consider the research to date. The research evidence on foreign-language proficiency attainment might suggest the program begin at grade three, four, or five. The clear positive cognitive and academic benefits of foreign language study, however, might suggest that the earlier the language is introduced, the sooner children have the opportunity to accrue the benefits to be derived. If cross-cultural goals are important, an early start has the advantage of allowing students a longer opportunity to develop positive attitudes, and particularly, at a time when the cross-cultural goals of the foreign language curriculum can be easily achieved through integration with the social studies curriculum of the primary grades.[2]

Other factors such as resources available, curriculum, and program model may also impact such decisions. Limited funds may constrain the number of teachers to be hired for a FLES program. To insure uninterrupted development of skills from elementary through middle level through high school, it may be better to start in third grade than in kindergarten. Curriculum for the foreign language program must be developed for each level of the program. If students begin in grade one, a K-6 elementary school must commit itself to developing a six-year articulated sequence of study. In contrast, programs which begin in grade four only require a three-year curriculum. Curriculum developers must also insure that students who begin in grade one are not placed at the same point in the secondary foreign language sequence as those who begin in grade four or seven. It is very hard to justify significant expenditures for elementary school foreign-language programs if students do not advance beyond the point at which others arrive who begin much later.

Lastly, program model also impacts decisions about when students should begin. Short-term programs which are neither sequenced nor articulated and which have limited language objectives (i.e., FLEX[3]) are most appropriate when they can lead into a sequenced, articulated program of study. Thus, FLEX at grade one or two is appropriate when it is followed by FLES the next year; in contrast, FLEX at grade one is inappropriate when the next opportunity for serious foreign language study is at grade six or seven. Many schools find FLEX at grade five or six a good foundation for the traditional foreign-language program in the middle or junior high school.

What should students learn?

Like all difficult questions, this one requires complex answers. And, answers may depend, in part, on the model of elementary school foreign-language instruction. Immersion students learn the content of the elementary school curriculum through the medium of the foreign language. Concurrently, they acquire native-like proficiency in the receptive skills (i.e., listening and reading) but rarely approach native norms in the productive skills of speaking and writing (Genesee, 1987). Although part of what students learn in immersion programs is determined by the school's subject curriculum, there is little agreement on what the language curriculum (if any) ought to be. Hammerly (1987) for example, has suggested that the poor productive skills of immersion graduates result from the lack of a concerted approach to grammar instruction and recommends abandoning early immersion in favor of an approach that combines a sequenced grammar curriculum beginning in grade five with late partial immersion. Others (Snow, Met and Genesee, 1989; Obadia, personal communication, 1985) are developing approaches to grammatical remediation which are incorporated into subject matter instruction. One of the questions which remains for research to answer with clarity is when grammar should be taught to immersion students, and how.

FLES programs, too, would benefit from research related to the question of how, when, and how much grammar should be taught. Research is needed to address the question of how syntactic skills evolve when children learn a foreign language in a school setting (Met and Rhodes, 1990). For FLES teachers and students, the issue of grammar is even more pressing, since articulation between elementary school foreign language programs and those at the secondary level has often been undermined by the mismatch between the emphasis in elementary school curricula on vocabulary development and the secondary emphasis on grammar. Indeed, the predominant syllabus of the secondary program for over forty years has been grammar based. A cursory review of recently published secondary textbooks reveals that despite practice activities which are contextualized (mostly) and communicative (occasionally), the determination of what students should learn and the order in which they are expected to learn it remains remarkably unchanged. Students still learn definite articles, number and gender agreement, and the present tense early, almost in a fixed order, regardless of the textbook program followed. It is hard to discern in which ways the communicative needs of the learner, purportedly an important feature of communicative syllabi, have determined what is taught, when, or how.

In contrast, the FLES curriculum pays little attention to the sequential development of grammatical skills. In large part this is due to the recognition that younger learners lack the cognitive maturity to deal with abstract syntactic rules. As a result, the typical FLES curriculum is thematic, developing vocabulary related to such topics as the family, colors, numbers, clothing, the house. In order to use vocabulary meaningfully, students acquire some rudimentary grammar skills as incidental to the vocabulary. For example, students will learn forms of the verb "to be" and "to have" in order to describe their families. Fortuitously, much of the vocabulary taught in FLES programs coincides with topics of interest to younger learners and often with curriculum from other areas of the elementary school curriculum. Kindergartners learn about colors in their native language; learning this vocabulary in the FLES class is a plus. First graders learning concepts of numeration and arithmetic will find learning the numbers in a foreign language and related practice activities of interest. Similarly, the curriculum of the elementary grades deals with the family, shelters (housing), transportation, clothing appropriate to the weather, and nutrition. Each of these has obvious potential connections to the vocabulary taught in most FLES programs.

In contrast, older learners have progressed beyond the stage where counting to ten is a challenge. Their cognitive development is appropriate to dealing with abstract grammar. Here, then, lies the challenge: how can FLES programs design a sequence of learning objectives which will allow students to enter the secondary program beyond Level I? Conversely, is it possible to alter the secondary curriculum, and thus related expectations of FLES achievement, in order to allow a smooth flow of learning objectives from the elementary to the secondary level?

Defining the content of the FLEX curriculum is an even greater challenge. This is due, in large part, to the wide variety of program models which fall under this designation. While approximately 41% of elementary schools which offer foreign language have a FLEX program (Rhodes and Oxford, 1988), the objectives of the curriculum, grade levels at which the program operates, and duration of the foreign language experience range across an enormously broad spectrum. Some programs aim for exposure to language and culture with an emphasis on the latter.[4] However, the definition of exposure is imprecise and may not be clearly distinguishable from programs which provide a foreign language "experience." In some schools, FLEX involves experiences with one language and its culture(s); in other schools FLEX may involve opportunities to experience several languages and cultures. At the middle/junior high school, it is also common to find exploratory language programs which teach *about* language. These programs allow students to develop an understanding about language as a uniquely human form of communication (both verbal and non-verbal) as well as lay the foundation for success in future study in a more traditional, grammar-based secondary program by exposing students to concepts such as "verb conjugation" and "adjective agreement."

Given the fact that most FLEX programs are of relatively short duration (a few weeks to one year), it is difficult to determine what the curriculum of such programs should be. Should students learn about language? Or, should they acquire a smattering of vocabulary on a few chosen topics? If the latter, what are the short-term and long-term benefits to be derived from such limited language exposure? And, how do these benefits compare to the cost of the program? The research related to the cognitive and academic benefits of early foreign language instruction has been conducted in immersion, FLES and ESL settings. Research is needed to provide data on the long-term benefits derived from short-term foreign language programs with limited language objectives.

As noted above, many FLEX programs emphasize the development of cultural knowledge and positive cross-cultural attitudes. What is the appropriate culture content of FLEX programs? Because both FLEX programs and FLEX classes tend to be of short duration teachers may not have sufficient opportunity to develop in-depth understanding of the target culture. The temptation may be great to deal merely with surface culture (e.g., the proverbial 3F's: food, festivals, and famous people). As a result, it is difficult to know how effective FLEX programs are, or can be, in promoting long lasting positive cross-cultural attitudes. Research in this area is critically needed to assist FLEX program planners.

How should students be taught?

Current trends in foreign language instruction today aim toward developing student's ability to use language to perform a variety of communication tasks involving various topics in diverse contexts with ever-increasing accuracy. This orientation has characterized elementary school foreign language curricula for the last decade.

By the very nature of the subjects they must deal with in the foreign language, immersion students acquire the skills to use language for diverse purposes and to discuss a variety of topics. Language functions such as asking/answering questions, describing, and explaining occur naturally in the day-to-day tasks of learning science, mathematics, social studies, and of course, reading and writing. Through social discourse with peers, immersion students also develop proficiency in language functions such as making suggestions, persuading, complaining, and expressing preferences. Similarly, they develop the vocabulary related to a wide range of topics and contexts. Although the language proficiency of immersion students is well developed, accuracy is an area in which their skills can bear considerable refinement. Thus, *how* immersion students are taught relates directly to *what* they learn.

Successful FLES teachers discovered long ago that only those language practice activities which were communicative would result in classes where students remained on-task and engaged. Since most FLES objectives are vocabulary oriented, finding activities which are of interest to children and also provide meaningful practice is not difficult. Guessing games where students are asked to identify a hidden object or person provide a context for practice of language functions such as requesting/giving information, describing, or explaining. Further, guessing games are not only fun for children, they also provide the "information gap" necessary for real communication to occur. Listening comprehension skills can be refined through story-telling and dramatizations of culturally authentic folktales (Met, 1984).

Recent methodologies such as Total Physical Response (TPR) (Asher, 1951) and the Natural Approach (Krashen and Terrell, 1985) have been embraced with enthusiasm by FLES teachers. They fit well with what FLES teachers have known instinctively for a long time: children learn best when they are physically engaged; children learn language when it is tied to their background knowledge and experience, when language is viewed holistically, and when learning experiences are set in a meaningful context. These approaches are also consistent with current thinking about children's development of skills in their first language.

Much of the recent literature in first language development (both oral skills and literacy) advocates a "whole language" approach (Goodman, 1986). In this approach, language skills are not taught in isolation; rather language is seen as a whole and language use is viewed as a quest for constructing meaning. To this end, language must be tied to its context and to its communicative functions. Language is related to children's experiences and background knowledge.

The growing recognition by FLEX teachers of the important relationship between language learning and other learning experiences, coupled with the success of immersion programs in developing both academic and linguistic skills, has resulted in a growing enthusiasm for content-based instruction.[5] Content-based foreign-language instruction draws objectives and language practice activities from the subjects of the elementary school curriculum. In so doing, foreign-language instruction enriches and reinforces what students learn in other classes and ties language to meaningful experience. Moreover, by using language practice activities drawn from the content areas, students can be challenged to perform at higher levels of thinking when engaged in using their foreign language. For example, students learning to describe daily activities (to sleep, to eat, to dress, to study, to watch television) can calculate the percent of time they spend each day on these activities. Having calculated these percentages, they can then make and describe in the foreign language a pie graph which illustrates this information. Calculating percentages and making pie graphs are intellectually challenging activities drawn from the sixth grade mathematics curriculum. Students in the foreign-language classroom thus engage in meaningful, cognitively engaging language practice tied to their background knowledge and to related experiences in the school.

Almost every topic included in the FLES curriculum can be practiced through content-based activities. When learning classroom vocabulary, students can estimate and then measure distances between places in the classroom using standard or non-standard units of measure. They can predict the appropriate sequence of a set of classroom objects according to the objects' length or weight and then test their predictions by actual measurement. A foreign-language unit on foods can include the calculation by upper-grade students of their daily caloric intake; younger children can sort foods by those that are nutritious and those that are not, or those eaten cooked vs. those eaten raw. A foreign-language unit on clothing may include developing picture graphs (primary grades) or a ratio to express the probability of occurrence of a given item of clothing in the class (upper grades).

It is hoped that this increasing interest in content-based instruction will yield several positive results; students will achieve higher levels of foreign-language proficiency, because language practice will be communicative and meaningful; students will accrue even greater cognitive benefits from foreign-language study, because language practice will be cognitively demanding; administrators will be less fearful about "taking time out of the school day" for foreign language, because language and content will be integrated with, rather than separate from, one another.

How can we measure what students have learned?

Until recently we knew very little about how much foreign language FLES and immersion students in U.S. schools learned, and we had few valid means of finding out.

As noted earlier, research on the foreign-language proficiency of immersion students in Canada has been extensive. Numerous studies of various immersion program models have revealed important information about the receptive and productive skills of participating students and have provided data which allows us to compare the relative efficacy of early vs. late immersion, as well as total vs. partial immersion (Genesee, 1987; Swain and Lapkin, 1985). Similar studies have evaluated the effectiveness of core French (i.e., the Canadian term for FLES) and extended French (a program which teaches one or more subjects in French) (Stern, et al., 1976). While assumptions about appropriate foreign-language practices may be generalized from this data to applications in the United States, there are differences in the U.S. context that may also limit the generalizability of the data. The nature and extent of the urban school population in the United

States may be significantly different from that of Canada; further, Canada is a bilingual nation by law, with all the social and political ramifications thereof.

Unfortunately, research data on the foreign-language proficiency of immersion and FLES students in the United States is limited, and most information is primarily anecdotal. There are two major reasons for this lack of hard data: good research costs money and thus far, foreign language has been too low on most funding agencies' list of priorities to provide funds for this endeavor. In contrast, most of the major evaluations of second-language programs in Canada have been underwritten by the government. Such support has included the opportunity to develop appropriate testing instruments. For example, Lapkin and Swain have recently developed an oral-proficiency measure which assesses immersion students' French skills in a paired situation (Lapkin, personal communication, 1985). In contrast, lack of funding in the United States has resulted in just a handful of controlled studies and, until recently, an over-reliance on inappropriate assessment tools.

One important study compared the Spanish skills of students in FLES, partial, and total immersion programs (Campbell et al., 1985) It showed, not surprisingly, that total immersion students outperformed partial immersion students, who in turn outperformed FLES students. Other results of this study provide additional important data and suggestions for further research. Although not highlighted in the report, the data reveal that within group variations (e.g., scores of the different students within the total immersion group) were greater than the variations between program models (e.g., between total and partial immersion). This suggests that research is needed to identify the variables within a given program model which are related to student achievement of foreign-language proficiency. Second, the measure used to assess students' skill was the MLA Cooperative Test, normed on students who had completed at least two years of high-school foreign-language study. Both immersion groups—total and partial—performed at or above the 98th percentile on the speaking portion of the test. Because these students "topped out," it was clear that a more sensitive measure was needed to determine students' oral proficiency accurately. Lastly, it should be noted that the reading and writing portions of the test, which was developed in the 1960s, do not reflect current thinking about what "reading" is (i.e., the process of constructing meaning from text) nor what "writing" is (i.e., the ability to communicate information, one's feelings, or intentions to a specific audience). These limitations of the testing instrument place constraints on the appropriate interpretation of test results.

Other efforts to assess the foreign-language proficiency of younger learners have been made using an adaptation of the ACTFL oral proficiency guidelines. Phillips and Liskin-Gasparro tested students in Pittsburgh with a modified version of the ACTFL oral proficiency test (Phillips, personal communication, 1987). While they found the oral interview provided information about the growing skills of the students tested, they believe the assessment may not have been an accurate measure. Students may have been less comfortable in face-to-face communication with a stranger and may not have produced the quantity or quality of discourse of which they were capable. Nonetheless, the assessment provided valuable data for program modifications. Phillips believes the modification of the ACTFL scale was more valuable in providing data for formative program assessment than for assessing the skills of any individual student.

In response to a request from the New Brunswick Department of Education in Canada, the Educational Testing Service (ETS) modified the ACTFL scale for use in testing students in grades seven through nine (Rabiteau and Taft, 1985). The test was used to compare the skills of students who had participated in elementary school immersion and core French programs. ETS termed the modified novice level "junior." The researchers report that the modified scale was useful in describing the skills of these younger students and in discriminating among degrees of language proficiency.

While modifications in the ACTFL rating scales may hold promise for assessing the skills of early language learners, some cautions are in order. First, there is as yet no research base to support the validity or reliability of the ACTFL scale. Although there is no doubt that these guidelines provide an invaluable common metric for assessing where learners are in their language development, research that supports the reliability and validity of the ACTFL rating scales is needed to insure that we are actually measuring what we think we're measuring and that we're doing it in a valid and consistent way.

Another caution regarding the use of the ACTFL scales with young children is that the standard of comparison is the educated adult native speaker. Research is needed to ascertain what kinds of modifications in these scales are appropriate to insure that we measure the language proficiency of young foreign-language learners and not their cognitive maturity. In addition, the ACTFL ratings are hierarchical and assume that the skills needed to discuss more abstract or technical matters subsume social/survival language skills. It is unknown whether immersion students, who learn to deal with technical information in the foreign language, and have more limited opportunities to use language for social/survival purposes, would demonstrate a similar performance pattern.

In the 1980s, the Center for Applied Linguistics (CAL) has taken leadership in addressing a variety of issues related to early-language learning. Several projects have allowed CAL to ascertain the current extent of foreign-language instruction in elementary schools, to compile lists of programs, and to facilitate networking among professionals active in this field. CAL has developed two instruments for evaluating the Spanish oral proficiency of immersion students and FLES students respectively (Wang, Richardson, and Rhodes, 1988; Thompson, Richardson and Rhodes, 1988).

The Clear Oral Proficiency Exam (COPE) is patterned after the ACTFL/ETS oral proficiency interview and assesses students' receptive and productive oral skills within the school context. Pairs of students role-play conversation focusing on cognitive-academic language use (ability to discuss subject matter) and social language. Subjects are evaluated on fluency, vocabulary, grammar, and comprehension. The FLES test is an achievement test designed to measure the skills of students who have had from one to three hours per week of Spanish instruction over the course of two to six years. The test measures listening and reading skills only in the domains most frequently covered in FLES curricula (e.g., greetings, family, classroom objects, parts of the body).

In a recent study, the COPE and FLES test were administered to students in immersion and FLES programs (Rhodes, Thompson, and Snow, 1989). Like the Campbell et al. study earlier, the results showed that the immersion group significantly outperformed other students in all measured language skills. Both immersion and FLES students were strongest in comprehension, followed by fluency and vocabulary; both were weakest in grammar. Interestingly, as in the Campbell et al. study, within group variation among the students from different immersion programs was significant. In contrast, the difference in scores of FLES students from different schools was not.

Immersion and FLES programs are proliferating rapidly. The availability of these two instruments may provide the necessary tools required for the long overdue research to be conducted on both veteran and newly initiated programs. The viability of such programs will depend in part on their ability to demonstrate that they do, indeed, live up to their promise.

Conclusion

This paper has sought to examine what research tells us in answer to some of the critical questions related to foreign language in the elementary school: when students should begin to learn a foreign language, what they should learn, how they should learn it, and how we can measure what they have learned. These issues have significance for those who must plan, implement, and evaluate early-language programs. Research has told us a great deal about how children acquire second or foreign languages. It can inform decisions about the appropriate time and place to introduce foreign language in the curriculum; it can inform decisions about how children should be taught language and what we can reasonably expect as outcomes.

Unfortunately, the research to date can provide only limited answers to some of the critical questions facing elementary school foreign-language educators. Some answers may be found more readily in experiential rather than research data. While experiential data has been valuable in providing guidance to program planners and implementers, there remain many opportunities for further research to provide direction for continued expansion of and improvements in elementary school foreign-language programs.

Notes

1. FLES (foreign language in the elementary school) is a model of foreign-language instruction which may begin anywhere between kindergarten and sixth grade, has a language curriculum with clearly stated linguistic objectives (primarily aural/oral) and develops cultural knowledge as well.
2. For examples of the integration of culture with social studies instruction see Met, Anderson, Brega and Rhodes, 1983 and Met, *Learning Language Through Content: Learning Content Through Language*, 1989.
3. FLEX (foreign language experience/exploratory) is a model of foreign-language instruction which is usually short-term, providing exposure to another language or several languages. Learning objectives include limited language skills, with more emphasis given to cultural knowledge.
4. For a fuller discussion of exploratory foreign-language programs, see Kennedy and DeLorenzo, 1985.
5. For a fuller discussion of content-based instruction see Met, *Learning Language Through Content: Learning Content Through Language*, and Curtain and Peseola, 1988.

References

Asher, James J. *Learning Another Language Through Actions: The Complete Teacher's Guidebook*. Los Gatos, CA: Sky Oaks Publications, 1981.

Bamford, K.W., and D.T. Mizokawa. "Cognitive and Attitudinal Outcomes of an Additive-Bilingual Program." Paper presented at the annual meeting of the American Educational Research Association, San Francisco. March, 1989.

Ben-Zeev, S. "Mechanism by Which Childhood Bilingualism Affects Understanding of Language and Cognitive Structures." *Bilingualism: Psychological, Social and Education Implications*. Edited by P.A. Hornby. New York: Academic Press, 1977.

Bruck, M., W.E. Lambert, and G.R. Tucker. "Bilingual Schooling Through the Elementary Grades: The St. Lambert Project at Grade Seven," *Language Learning*. v. 24, p. 183-204, 1974.

Burstall, C., J. Jamieson, S. Cohen, and M. Hargreaves. *Primary French in the Balance*. Windsor, England: NFER Publishing, 1974.

Campbell, R.N., T.C. Gray, N.C. Rhodes, and M.S. Snow. "Foreign Language Learning in the Elementary Schools: A Comparison of Three Language Programs." *Modern Language Journal*. vol. 69, no. 1, 1985.

Carpenter, J., and J. Torney. "Beyond the Melting Pot," in *Children and Intercultural Education*, edited by P.N. Markum and J.L. Land. Washington, D.C.: Association for Childhood Education International, 1973.

Collier, Virginia P. "How Long: A Synthesis of Research on Academic Achievement in Second Language." *TESOL Quarterly*, vol. 23 (September 1989).

Curtain, Helena, and Carol Ann Pesola. *Languages and Children: Making the Match*. Reading, Mass., Addison-Wesley Publishing Co., 1988.

Foster, Karen M., and Carolyn K. Reeves. "FLES Improves Cognitive Skills," *FLESNEWS*, vol. 2, no. 3 (Spring 1989), p. 4.

Gardner, R.C., and W.E. Lambert. *Attitudes and Motivation in Second Language Learning*. Rowley, MA: Newbury House, 1972.

Garfinkel, Alan, and Kenneth E. Tabor. "Elementary School Foreign Languages and English Reading Achievement: A New View of the Relationship." Purdue University, unpublished manuscript, 1987.

Genessee, Fred. *Learning Through Two Languages*. Rowley, MA: Newbury House, 1987.

Goodman, Ken. *What's Whole in Whole Language?* Portsmouth, NH: Heinemann Educational Books, 1986.

Hakuta, Kenji. "The Causal Relationship Between the Development of Bilingualism, Cognitive Flexibility, and Social-Cognitive Skills in Hispanic Elementary School Children." Rosslyn, VA: National Clearinghouse for Bilingual Education, 1984.

Hammerly, Hector, "The Immersion Approach: Litmus Test of Second Language Acquisition through Classroom Communication." *Modern Language Journal*, vol. 71, no. iv (1987), pp. 395-401.

Harley, Birgit. *Age in Second Language Acquisition*. San Diego, CA: College-Hill Press, 1986.

Kennedy, Dora, and William De Lorenzo. *Complete Guide to Exploratory Foreign Language Programs*. Lincolnwood, IL: National Textbook Co., 1985.

Krashen, Stephen D., Robin C. Scarcella, and Michael H. Long, eds. *Child-Adult Differences in Second Language Acquisition*. Rowley, MA: Newbury House, 1982.

Krashen, Stephen D., and Tracy Terrell. *The Natural Approach. Language Acquisition in the Classroom*. San Francisco, CA: Alemany Press, 1983.

Lambert, Wallace E., and O. Klineberg. *Children's Views of Foreign People*. New York: Appleton-Century-Crofts, 1967.

Landry, Richard G. "A Comparison of Second Language Learners and Monolinguals on Divergent Thinking Tasks at the Elementary School Level." *Modern Language Journal*, vol. 58, no. 1-2 (Jan.-Feb. 1974), pp. 10-15.

Met, Myriam, Helena Anderson, Evelyn Brega, and Nancy Rhodes. "Elementary School Foreign Language: Key Links in the Chain of Learning." In Robert G. Mead, ed., *Foreign Languages: Key Links in the Chain of Learning*. Middlebury, VT: Northeast Conference on the Teaching of Foreign Languages, 1983.

Met, Myriam. "Listening Comprehension and the Young Second Language Learner." *Foreign Language Annals* 17:5, Oct. 1984.

Met, Myriam. "Learning Language Through Content: Learning Content Through Language." In Kurt E. Muller, ed. *Languages in Elementary Schools*. New York: American Forum, 1989.

Met, Myriam, and Nancy Rhodes. "Elementary School Foreign Language Instruction: Priorities for the 1990's." In press.

Peal, Elizabeth, and Lambert, Wallace. "The Relation of Bilingualism to Intelligence," *Psychological Monographs*, vol. 76 (27), no. 546, 1962.

Rabiteau, Kathleen, and Hessy Taft. "Provisional Modified ACTFL/ETS Oral Proficiency Scale for Junior High School Students." Paper presented at the annual meeting of the American Council on the Teaching of Foreign Languages, New York, 1985.

Rafferty, Eileen A. "Second Language Study and Basic Skills in Louisiana." Baton Rouge: Louisiana Department of Education, 1986.

Rhodes, Nancy C., and Rebecca L. Oxford. "Foreign Languages in Elementary and Secondary Schools: Results of a National Survey." *Foreign Language Annals*, vol. 21, no. 1, p. 51-69, 1988.

Rhodes, Nancy Lynn Thompson, and Marguerite Ann Snow. *A Comparison of FLES and Immersion Programs*. Washington, D.C.: Center for Applied Linguistics, May 1989.

Snow, Ann, Myriam Met, and Fred Genessee. "A Conceptual Framework for the Integration of Language and Content in Second/Foreign Language Programs." *TESOL Quarterly*, 1989.

Stern, H.H., Merrill Swain, L.D. McLean, R.J. Friedman, Birgit Harley, and Sharon Lapkin. *Three Approaches to Teaching French*. Toronto, Ontario: Ontario Institute for Studies in Education, 1976.

Swain, Merrill, and Sharon Lapkin. *Evaluating Bilingual Education: A Canadian Case Study*. Clevedon, England: Multilingual Matters, 1985.

Swain, Merrill. "Additive Bilingualism and French Immersion Education: The Roles of Language Proficiency and Literacy." Paper presented at McGill Conference on Bilingualism, Multiculturalism, & Second Language Learning. L'Esterel, Canada, May 1989.

Swain, Merrill, and Sharon Lapkin. "Canadian Immersion and Adult Second Language Teaching: What's the Connection?" *Modern Language Journal*, vol. 73, no. 2 (Summer 1989), pp. 150-159.

Thompson, Lynn, Gina Richardson, Lih-Shing Wang, and Nancy Rhodes. *The Development of the FLES Test—Spanish*. Washington, D.C.: Center for Applied Linguistics, 1988.

Torney, Judith V. "Psychological and Institutional Obstacles in the Global Perspective in Education," in *Schooling For a Global Age*, edited by James M. Becker. New York: McGraw-Hill Pub. Co., 1979.

Wan, Lih-Shing, Gina Richardson, and Nancy Rhodes. *The CLEAR Oral Proficiency Exam (COPE)*. Project Report Addendum: Clinical Testing and Validity and Dimensionality Studies. Washington, D.C.: Center for Applied Linguistics, 1988.

Dear Wilga, Dear Alice, Dear Tracy, Dear Earl: Four Letters on Methodology and Technology

James P. Pusack and Sue K. Otto
University of Iowa

Introduction

Language teaching methodology and instructional technology often talk at cross purposes. In the following four letters we attempt to speak directly to four recognized methodologists in our field and to identify the areas where method and machine can find common ground. While many theorists and practitioners of language instruction could have been chosen, we feel that these four represent a cross-section of the field and are most familiar to many of our colleagues. The letters are addressed to Wilga Rivers, author of countless books and articles on language teaching and one of the few methodologists to deal directly with the implications of technology; to Alice Omaggio, whose publications have made her a leading advocate of proficiency-oriented teaching methods; to Tracy Terrell, a champion of the Natural Approach—a method which has inspired both enthusiasm and controversy on a national scale; and to Earl Stevick, who has done so much to foster widespread awareness of how various unconventional methodologies can contribute to the way we teach and learn languages.

I

Re: *Teaching Foreign-Language Skills*, "Interaction and Communication in the Language Class in an Age of Technology" and *Ten Principles of Interactive Language Learning and Teaching* (Rivers, 1981, 1989a and 1989b)

Dear Wilga,
Throughout your career you have consistently met the challenges of developing a methodology of interactive language teaching and learning that includes the thoughtful integration of technology. Among our four correspondents, you alone have grappled directly with the implications that technology has for our field. While your colleagues pass over the role of

technology in fleeting phrases, you have dedicated whole chapters to the sensible application of technology to language learning. The practical philosophy you have recorded has guided us (and will continue to do so) as we encounter the latest technological wonders. Among the awards that have been presented to you for your contributions to language pedagogy, one merits special mention here, since it was given to you only recently by the International Association for Learning Laboratories (IALL) in recognition of your life-long support of language labs and technology. We hope you will forgive us if our response to your words describing the interactive language learning and teaching is more echo than elaboration.

In the chapter "Technology and Language Learning Centers" in your book *Teaching Foreign-Language Skills* (Rivers 1981), you list three assumptions that must overarch our thinking about technology:

1. "The Language Learning Laboratory is not a Method... A tape recorder, a film projector, or a video player are tools, like the textbook or the chalkboard." (Rivers 1981, 398).
2. "The Language Learning Laboratory Is a Patient Helper" (Rivers 1981, 399).
3. "Laboratory Work Must Be Designed As a Significant Part of the Language Program" (Rivers 1981, 400).

These fundamental and indisputable observations have too often been forgotten in past efforts to exploit technology. We will make real progress in applying technology only when we establish that the technology is a neutral element that can be used in ways that suit our goals, that it is not a replacement for the teacher or the printed page, and that its careful integration into the curriculum is essential to its success.

Countering the indictments often brought against technology is definitely one of your strong points. Your voice of reason speaks convincingly to the unconverted in support of technology, while bringing back to reality those of us who see the world through rose-colored videodiscs. In your recent keynote address at the Georgetown University Language Round Table, you synthesized your views on methodology and technology. Perusing the text of that speech (Rivers 1989a), we find your remarks uniquely suited to introduce this epistolary encounter of language-teaching methodology with foreign-language instructional technology. You rightfully admonish us to beware of the glitz of the machines and to recognize the opportunities the technology presents in a realistic, pedagogically sound way:

> We have come so far in language teaching, with the emphasis on communication, aspects of discourse, and analysis of language functions, as well as the creative aspects of reading and writing, that we must now be watchful. The entry on the scene of the computer and laserdisc leads to great expectations and great opportunities. If the expectations are too high to be realized we may miss out on the opportunities, drifting into a repeat cycle of boom-bust. It is easy to be naively dazzled by technology—with fantastic graphics and moving targets we can zap to make them disappear. Meanwhile inexpert programmers with few notions

of what constitutes language learning design inappropriate courseware in an effort to compensate for the absence of language teaching specialists left behind in the forward surge. There is a real danger of a return to much drill and grammatical practice, with long explanations, which are relatively easy to program. (Rivers 1989a, 189)

Having voiced this caveat, you then discuss the opportunities provided by today's technologies. In this discussion you answer four questions frequently raised about technology and teaching, couching the responses in your Ten Principles of Interactive Learning and Teaching.

The first of these questions arises from the important issue of the pedagogical suitability of technology: "In what ways will the programs for use with the new technologies fit in with the aims, content, and approaches of the courses they will accompany?" You answer that, because of the current emphasis on developing good communication in all the skills, computer-assisted language instruction must move beyond grammar tutorials and drill and practice and must emphasize activities that encourage the student to use the language creatively:

[T]he most pedagogically sophisticated courseware producers have turned their attention to creative and exploratory interaction with the computer, which seizes students' attention and involves them with reception and production of language because of the intrinsic interest of the evolving situation, as in Brigham Young's Montevidisco, MIT's Athena project, the BBC's Domesday Project and the Cambridge Micro Software Granville package. (Rivers 1989a, 191)

While we agree with the importance of software that invites creativity and exploration, we would not limit the list of examples to simulations, as you have. Though such simulations are motivational for students, they have yet to progress far enough in natural language processing to encourage creative use of language. As you concede later, it is overstating the point to say that these seminal projects allow students very much creative latitude in expressing themselves in the language. You observe that in the case of computer/videodisc games and simulations the "combining of live interaction with the interactive program, either at the workstation or in the class group" (Rivers 1989a, 193) can go a long way in making up for the inadequacies of the program alone.

Speaking of current initiatives, we like to highlight efforts such as Harvard's Perseus Project or even Iowa's Interactive Reading Project, which allow students to learn dynamically through exploration and tap the enormous resources of text, video, and graphic images that are accessible at their workstation. Students' minds are engaged not by a game or plot situation but by using the resources to solve a problem that has been assigned to them or that they have discovered through their own curiosity.

The next question you tackle is "What can technology-based courseware accomplish as an aid to learning that cannot be achieved at lower cost (monetarily and in time and energy) in some other way?" (Rivers 1989a, 191). Your answer is the traditional but convincing one associated with the strength of computers:

> The major advantage of technology-assisted language learning is indubitably its potential to meet the needs of individual learners, giving students time and the opportunity to repeat or not repeat material at will, providing immediate access to the desired information, illustration, correction, modeling, or guidance, or the right to ignore such aids. The student may choose more or less practice, exploration, advice, or evaluation. (Rivers 1989a, 191-2)

While individualization of instruction is a major benefit of technology, the representational power of the media should not be overlooked. Consider an analogy: the scribe is to the photocopier as audio recordings are to the modern multi-media workstation. The latter—combining computer, audio, and video components—is much more efficient at accomplishing the desired goal. Today we strive to provide programming for students that allows them to experience authentic language vicariously in culturally authentic settings and to encourage communicative interactivity with those materials. Such experiences simply cannot be delivered satisfactorily by a single, linear medium.

You answer the third question, "How can we ensure that teachers wholeheartedly and advisedly cooperate in the incorporation of the latest technology into the language program?" by stressing the importance of in-depth teacher training in the technology and ways to integrate technology into the curriculum. You say that the success of computer-assisted language learning (CALL) depends not only on its integration into the course materials, but on the ability of the language teacher to incorporate CALL programs into classroom activities to maximum benefit (Rivers 1989a, 193). We also feel that too many teachers view the technology as a tool for the individual learner outside of class and do not give sufficient consideration to it as an in-class resource. Presentation software using interactive videodisc can be a lively, flexible tool for in-class use: presenting vocabulary and concepts, stimulating conversations, illustrating lectures, managing video-based tests.

Your final question is one that remains largely unanswered: "Do we have research evidence that incorporation of the latest technological adjuncts leads to more efficient language learning and language use?" (Rivers 1989a, 191). Not enough studies have been conducted about the effectiveness of technology. We must attempt to evaluate technology-based materials by more thorough and scientific means than impressions and intuition.

We turn now to your *Ten Principles of Interactive Language Learning and Teaching* (Rivers 1989b) in order to complete our introduction to the topic of methodology and technology. Although the word "technology" nowhere appears in the text of the principles and accompanying corollaries, they provide a firm foundation for us to build on in summarizing the way technology figures in our field. Here, then, is a palimpsest in which we venture to superimpose our own ten principles of technology upon your ten principles of interactive language learning and teaching:

1. The language learner must control the technology, not the converse. Corollary 1: Student motivation can be sparked by technology that presents the target culture in authentic but accessible forms.
2. Individual student needs and objectives can be met via technology that incorporates the expert knowledge of experienced teachers. Corollary 2: Technology will diversify language teaching and course design.
3. The breadth of real language usage cannot be adequately presented by instructors who fail to use technology.
4. Machines need not interfere with the non-threatening atmosphere of cooperative learning in the language classroom; they can extend it.
5. Technology can mediate both language knowledge and language control in ways that complement the instructor and the textbook.
6. Authentic video, in particular, can stimulate creativity and provide a vehicle for interactive, participatory activities.
7. There are infinite ways to apply technology as an aid to learning.
8. Computer-adaptive testing can streamline our curricula.
9. Computer-interactive reading, viewing, and listening activities will encourage learners to penetrate another culture without trepidation.
10. Technology is part of a learning continuum that leads from the classroom through the lab to the real world and back.

If teachers and materials developers continue to hold your principles—not necessarily our palimpsest—in mind, we see an exciting future for technology in our field. Thanks for launching us on the right trajectory.

Yours interactively,

Sue and Jim

P.S.

In *Teaching Foreign-Language Skills* and in your practical guides to teaching language, e.g., *Teaching Spanish: A Practical Guide* (Rivers 1988), you comment extensively on audio tape techniques for interactive language learning: aural discrimination exercises, pronunciation drills, situation tapes with conversations to be completed by the students, listening comprehension exercises, and the like. There are only passing references to the other media. We hope that when you and your co-authors prepare the next editions of these manuals, you will incorporate the perspectives you expressed at Georgetown, expanding your practical advice, and including some concrete strategies for exploiting video, computers, and interactive media.

II

Re: *Teaching Language in Context* (Omaggio 1986)

Dear Alice,

Your 1986 book, *Teaching Language in Context: Proficiency-Oriented Instruction*, has become something of a bible for those of our colleagues—especially teacher-trainers—who are attracted to proficiency as an organizing principle. Even those who do not contemplate full-scale implementation of a proficiency-based curriculum can still rely on your extensive recommendations for contextualized practice and testing. We have chosen your book for consideration here because it synthesizes much previous work in the field and yet speaks from a more consistent perspective than earlier anthologies of articles on proficiency-related issues.

Have you ever noticed that the cover of your book has a background design that repeats the words "French·Spanish·German·Italian·ESL· Software·Video" several hundred times? We suspect the inclusion of software and video was an inspiration on the part of the publisher, since these are not topics you address very directly in your otherwise thorough treatment of instructional topics. In order to anticipate the way technology might fit into any proficiency-oriented approach to language teaching, we have built upon the "Preliminary Hypotheses" for proficiency-oriented instruction that you set forth in your first chapter (Omaggio 34–36). We therefore offer five corresponding hypotheses about technology within a proficiency framework:

Hypothesis 1. Instructional technology can significantly expand the number and type of opportunities available to our students to practice using language.

Corollary 1. Technology is still at a disadvantage at responding to written and oral production, but can diversify the range of situations that can be used to stimulate the productive skills.

Corollary 2. Active communication among students can be fostered, in particular, by showing students video documents that provoke discussion.

Corollary 3. Creative language practice can be stressed in the classroom if manipulative or convergent practice can be handled via the individualized feedback mechanisms of the computer.

Corollary 4. Individualized work with authentic readings and video features can be made more efficient and less intimidating when computers provide appropriate tasks and assistance in comprehending difficult language.

Hypothesis 2. Computer-based simulations and computer-assisted comprehension can help prepare students to carry out a wide range of functions needed in the target culture.

Hypothesis 3. Linguistic accuracy can be developed most efficiently by the use of sophisticated computer-based analysis and diagnosis of students' writing; while today's courseware deals best with convergent practice, great strides are being made in dealing with more open-ended written production.

Hypothesis 4. Technology can respond to the affective needs of students by providing a non-threatening, individualized environment for practice and by delivering highly motivating video and reading texts that correspond to students' own ability levels and interests.

Hypothesis 5. Cultural understanding can be promoted by allowing students to study and discuss up-to-date broadcast video features originally intended to communicate viewpoints and information to audiences in the target culture.

The common thread among these hypotheses is that instructional technology cannot stand alone—it is not in itself a methodology—but it can significantly enhance the opportunities for leaning in a proficiency-based classroom. When you ask (Omaggio 1986, 1) "What characterizes a classroom environment in which opportunities to become proficient are maximized?" we must respond that instructional technology radically redefines the very definition of "classroom environment." Technology can deliver unique glimpses into the target culture and can structure the individual student's efforts in the interest of more efficient and rewarding learning.

Your book is comprehensive and deals with all language skills. For each skill you treat, we could suggest some ways that computers, video, audio, and interactive video could be brought to bear on the teaching/learning process. For the sake of better focus, we prefer to concentrate on three issues where the match between our view of technology and your proficiency-oriented methodology appears most striking: context, accuracy, and testing.

Context and Video

In the development of effective teaching materials, "context" is your leitmotiv. In fact, you include video technology explicitly in a longer list of teaching aids: "Videotapes of authentic or simulated exchanges between native speakers, radio and television broadcasts, films, songs, and the like have long been advocated by foreign language educators as stimulating pedagogical aids. The proficiency-oriented classroom will incorporate such material frequently and effectively into instruction at all levels" (Omaggio 1986, 47). We believe that the potential of video goes far beyond that of radio, films, songs, and the like. In particular, we are concerned that the further examples in your book slant the use of this technology too far in the direction of camcorder video as a means of recording role-plays and skits as stimuli for various classroom activities (Omaggio 1986, 132-5, 208, 216, 380). You clearly state your justification for this emphasis in your chapter entitled "A Proficiency-Oriented Approach to Listening and Reading":

> [U]sing only unedited, nonpedagogical materials in the classroom would seem to create more problems than it would solve, since such materials are often difficult to select, obtain, or sequence for learners at lower proficiency levels. Unmodified authentic discourse is often random in respect to vocabulary, structure, functions, content, situation, and length, making much of it impractical for classroom teachers to integrate into the curriculum on a frequent basis. (Omaggio 1986, 128)

Fortunately, you do provide a hint at the solution: "If teachers do choose to use unmodified authentic discourse for listening practice, short segments of recorded broadcasts... or live or taped interviews with native speakers on familiar topics seem best for students at the lower proficiency ranges." What is missing here is an effort to distinguish between authentic discourse via video and other forms of recorded or acted speech that lack a rich and reinforcing visual context. Your conclusion as reflected in the remainder of the chapter leads teachers toward *simulated* authentic discourse. By this approach you seriously underrate the extent to which the visual context of video, combined with the same sort of prelistening, viewing, and postviewing activities you recommend, can overcome the drawbacks of authenticity. This is especially true when video segments are carefully chosen and supported by detailed suggestions for classroom use. The advent of the VCR with remote control enables the classroom teacher or the individual learner to exercise a high degree of control over the flow of words and images to an extent not possible with the earlier 16mm film technology. Lively in-class viewing activities that rely on freeze-frame and rewind mechanisms to simplify the task, rather than the text, make it reasonable to use video in short segments on an almost daily basis, even at the lowest levels of language learning.

As a counterbalance to your emphasis, therefore, we would encourage proficiency-oriented teachers to explore the rich and varied universe of authentic broadcast video, which is becoming more and more available every day. In contrast to simulated situations, which are often filmed in inauthentic environments and with pedagogical axes to grind, broadcast television retains all the advantages of a true communicative act. Television features that portray human-interest situations via on-camera, on-the-scene interviews provide a fertile ground for cultural study and listening practice. Detective programs and other entertaining dramatic forms of programming supply a longer continuous context which can direct students' attention to plot elements and away from the urge to engage in word-for-word translation as a substitute for comprehension. Video should not be limited to serving as a vehicle for listening practice, however. It can also function in a fully integrated series of activities that move gradually from recognition of familiar material through acquisition of new lexicon and structures to active production of written and spoken language, all within a valid cultural context established by the original video document.

Computers and Accuracy

Your book takes great pains to overcome the prejudice that proficiency is somehow synonymous with "survival" language training. In fact, it is the research studies based on oral interviews that bring home the ever-present danger that students who are never exposed to grammar may wind up terminally talkative but not highly proficient. Your chapter "The Accuracy Issue" therefore provides a rationale "for providing corrective feedback from the beginning of language instruction" (Omaggio 1986, 291). You also squarely confront the communication/correction dichotomy: "Communicative activities should be encouraged from the beginning of instruction, but there is no reason to believe that such activities should be carefully planned so that they are within the range of the students' competence" (Omaggio 1986, 304). Despite your strong endorsement of both communicative activities and helpful correction of error under conditions that foster creativity, we feel that in practice it is difficult to reconcile the two, especially for the novice teacher. Teacher trainers intent on fostering a communicative classroom environment, furthermore, may assume that inexperienced teachers will tend toward over-correction; their rule-of-thumb may therefore stress avoidance of correction under many conditions.

We propose a partial solution to this quandary, at least at the elementary level, in the form of computer-based practice. But before you look ahead to see what we wrote to Tracy in this regard, let us hasten to admit that drills came early and badly to computers. Some software was rightly scorned in epithets like "electronic flashcards"; programmed learning was often converted unimaginatively to machines, making it even more mechanical; the power of computing was often wasted on hangman-like vocabulary practice. Even some of the most ardent foreign language computer enthusiasts still lump this whole genre of technology together under the dismissive term "drill and kill." We don't.

Jointly, we represent both the language lab perspective and the faculty perspective on technology and we are incurably pragmatic. We believe that written practice can prepare, reinforce, and recapitulate the learning of the classroom and replace more mechanical in-class activities. High-quality practice that immediately diagnoses students' errors transforms the printed workbook into a dynamic learning experience, one that significantly complements the more passive experience of audio tapes. Since most teachers have far too little time in class and far too many students to deal with, any technology that can make precious classroom time more productive must be taken seriously. We therefore recommend extensive use of computer-based drill materials that meet the following criteria:

1. They must follow the textbook closely, so that students are motivated to use them.
2. They must provide helpful corrective feedback without inundating the student with additional grammatical terminology.
3. They must offer efficient coverage of lesson materials in a relatively short period of time.
4. Students' work must be recorded and reported to the instructor.
5. Exercise formats must not conflict with the principles and practice formats of the textbook.

In contrast to the modest investment required for a teacher to use video in the classroom, the delivery of computer-based practice to individual students in a laboratory setting will require a significant investment in equipment, usually microcomputers. On large university campuses, mainframe computers linked to terminals may still be more cost-effective and simpler than working with diskettes. At the University of Iowa, practice of this sort has largely replaced teacher-graded homework assignments; this year we project that our students will engage in over 30,000 hours of computer-based practice in French, German, and Spanish. Thus, benefits can be identified not only in the use of classroom time, but also in teacher preparation time, to the extent that paper-and-pencil grading time can be applied to better lesson design.

Testing via Technology

As a final note related to proficiency, we would like to call attention to the role of technology in testing. You mention the fact that "ACFTL is working with other agencies and institutions to develop prototypes of computer-adaptive tests of reading and listing proficiency, which should greatly expand our proficiency-testing capabilities, in terms of both skill areas and numbers of students tested" (Omaggio 1986, 309). Computer-based tests of language skills can help place our students much more efficiently by adjusting the questions to the student during the course of test administration. A reading of the ACTFL guidelines for listening and reading reveals a plethora of specific subskills at each proficiency level. Paper-and-pencil tests could never hope to test such abilities thoroughly without exhausting the attention and time of the student. An adaptive test will therefore be required. Such tests will emulate the Oral Proficiency Interview by passing through the stages of warm-up, level check, probes, and wind-up. Despite the cost of developing such tests and the expense of delivering the tests by computer (including random-access video and audio devices for listening), we can be certain that these technology-based tests will at least be more cost-effective than the Oral Interview, which demands extensive training and retraining of the interviewers at a cost bordering on the prohibitive for most institutions. Parenthetically, we see a clear opportunity for interactive video to play a role in training oral interviewers, in full or in part, at a comparatively low cost.

Even without the demands of full-scale proficiency testing to justify the effort and expense, the development of more specialized computer-adaptive tests for placing large numbers of students within the typical required undergraduate course sequence could prove of great value to many institutions.

These last examples, like much of what we have suggested above, call attention to the fact that the concept of proficiency is impoverished when it is limited to oral production. While media such as video can be used to stimulate conversation, technology as a whole still remains a long way from simulating conversation. It is precisely in the other areas of language learning—reading, listening, and writing—that computers, video, and audio can play an effective role today.

Yours contextually,

Jim and Sue

III

Re: *Dos mundos* (Terrell et al. 1986) and *The Natural Approach* (Krashen and Terrell 1983)

Dear Tracy,

What a pleasure it is for us to write to a methodologist who has systematically put his ideas to the acid test in a textbook! And what could be more natural than to explore in some depth just what role the media—which are first and foremost objects for comprehension—might play under optimum conditions in an approach that stresses comprehension? To anticipate what we will say below, we believe that three major topics or tenets of the Natural Approach dictate a radical extension of the classroom via technology, particularly video and interactive video: the input hypothesis, binding, and the affective filter.

We will draw most of our insight into your work from the *Dos mundos Instructor's Manual* (Terrell et al. 1986), since this is where your ideas are formulated most succinctly and most directly from the perspective of the practicing teacher. Permit us also to draw upon *The Natural Approach* (Krashen and Terrell 1983), where you join with Stephen Krashen in presenting the same ideas in greater depth. You do have co-authors for both of these volumes and we must ask their forgiveness for addressing only you in this letter.

The Input Hypothesis

Let's dive in where the pool is the deepest: "The Input Hypothesis describes the conditions under which acquisition will take place. According to the Input Hypothesis, acquisition occurs when the acquirer comprehends utterances in a communicative context" (Terrell et al. 1986, 6). What seems to narrow the value of this dictum is your insistence on the centrality of the teacher's voice: "Since second-language acquisition theory posits that input plays the major role in acquisition, the most important part of [Natural Approach] instruction is the input you supply to your students in the form of 'teacher talk'" (Terrell et al. 1986, 15). In creating your elementary Spanish textbook *Dos mundos*, you apply this principle in developing a wide range of oral activities and comprehension activities which are "designed to introduce most new vocabulary and grammatical forms and structures in communicative contexts *before* students are expected to produce them in speech or writing" (Terrell et al. 1986, 7). What is missing here is any compelling reason to assume that the teacher is the prime and best originator of the necessary communicative context.

We propose that technology can provide helpful alternatives and supplements to teacher talk, especially for teachers who believe, with you, that comprehension precedes production. If any single element of your approach has been widely accepted as most intuitively "natural," it is the precedence that listening takes over speaking. Yet we see a high risk emanating from this emphasis—the risk that students will largely be exposed to pedagogical language, often about the all-too-familiar situations that lend themselves most readily to classroom activity. Another risk may lie in the fact that many college-level instructors (such as teaching assistants) are non-native speakers with relatively limited experience abroad.

Employed as a corrective to this tendency, video offers vast opportunities for comprehension from the very beginning stages of language learning. The curriculum has room for both authentic broadcast television and pedagogically prepared videotapes to provide additional comprehensible input. Simple activities based on video can focus students on identification of easy words and phrases, gestures, and the like. A resource collection consisting of a variety of short video clips on topics specifically designed to fit with the book/tape curriculum will significantly complement the repertoire of activities based on teacher talk and audio tapes.

Such materials can provide new speaking models, stimulate class discussion at any level, and broaden the lexical scope beyond the typical classroom. Given carefully structured learner tasks, students can use videotapes both in and out of class time to build comprehension skills and vocabulary without depending on the instructor. In fact, the activities you recommend for reading (Terrell et al. 1986, 25) can readily be adapted for listening: scanning, skimming, intensive and extensive listening. Either as individuals or in small groups, students can be provided with input in a clear context via video. Group involvement with a video stimulus further reduces excessive reliance on teacher talk and control. In sum, video is ideal for learning language in context. It mediates the most complete experience of a foreign reality short of life in the target culture.

Your concept of input—be it through teacher-choreographed activities or video-stimulated ones—clearly dictates that the class hour should be reserved for communicative activities. Since classroom interaction is ideal for acquisition, it follows that anything that can be exported to the language laboratory or private study time should be banned from precious class moments:

> In most foreign-language classes in the United States, the class hour is the only time students have to interact in Spanish. For this reason, this hour should be reserved almost entirely for communication activities. Other activities that take more time, such as long readings, listening to recorded materials, written exercises, and reading explanations of grammar, should be done outside of class whenever possible. (Terrell et al. 1986, 12)

While this viewpoint is unassailable, substantial interaction in Spanish can be provided outside the class hour in areas where full-fledged conversational communication is not required. By using effective practice forms such as computer-based drill (equivalent to the "blue pages" in which such exercises are quarantined in *Dos mundos*), instructors can make conscious learning of grammar principles available without sacrificing class time. Tutorials and immediate drill feedback can prepare students quite efficiently for acquisition activities. Contrary to popular opinion, you have not excluded this opportunity to let learners meet differing needs and paces:

> The goal of the Natural Approach is to produce optimal Monitor users, performers who put conscious grammar in its proper place. An over-emphasis on conscious grammar has the undesirable result of encouraging over-use of the Monitor. But completely eliminating grammar robs our students of the chance to use conscious learning as a supplement to acquisition. If our observations about individual variation are correct, they imply that formal grammar instruction does not have a central place in the curriculum, but it does have an important role to play. (Terrell et al. 1986, 45)

As a new generation of foreign language courseware becomes available in the 1990s, the individualization and diagnostic help now possible for low-level grammar practice will be extended to reading practice, listening via interactive video/audio, and even limited forms of open-ended composition.

Binding

It is difficult to argue with your contention that words are bound to meaning as learners hear them used in context: "We use the term 'binding' to refer to this process of linking a meaning to a form... We bind words to meaning by hearing them used in contexts. The vividness of the experience and the context in which a word has been used will determine both the rapidity and strength of the binding process" (Terrell et al. 1986, 10). You recommend a variety of techniques for the teacher to use in class, including: using visuals in a picture file; manipulating real objects; evoking affective factors (humor, unusualness, student interest); engaging in movement; and highlighting cultural factors (Terrell et al. 1986, 10-11).

Most of these techniques come naturally through the video medium. Video can serve as full-context stimulus not just for overt skill development—the listening and speaking activities described above—but also for the more indirect forms of exposure to lexical and cultural materials. The ideal technology for organizing short video clips and especially images for systematic retrieval is the videodisc under computer control. Many thousands of useful images or image sequences can be classified not only by their obvious lexical components, but also by precise language function. The accessibility of such a visual database offers a profound improvement over a print or slide picture file. Such image-retrieval discs are already available for work in foreign language teaching.

The Affective Filter

We like your very succinct formulation of the Affective Filter Hypothesis in *Dos mundos*: "If a student does not attend to the input, for whatever reason, acquisition will not take place" (Terrell et al. 1986, 7). Among the many suggestions you make, we will single out one based on media: "Appeal to the student's desire to 'learn.' ... Show slides, movies, videotapes of Spanish-language TV" (Terrell et al. 1986, 17). Once again, however, we believe you have under-represented the power of the video medium and the situations where it can be effective. The text, images, and sounds of carefully selected authentic materials, in particular, can lower affective filters by constantly drawing students into the foreign reality they are studying. Video constantly reminds students of the world outside the textbook—the world they are preparing to encounter. In *The Natural Approach* you come closer to acknowledging the artificial dichotomy between between "country" and "classroom":

> The reason affective factors are hypothesized to be directly related to acquisition is that, in general, they appear to relate strongly to second language achievement when communicative-type tests are used, tests that involve the acquired rather than the learned system, and when the students taking the test have encountered

the language in "acquisition-rich" situations, i.e., second language acquisition in the country rather than foreign language learning exclusively in a traditional classroom. (Krashen and Terrell 1983, 38)

To the extent that use of video can put the country in the classroom, the richness of the acquisition environment is guaranteed.

At first glance, the major affective impact of video would appear to lie in making the class or course enjoyable, particularly via a familiar medium of entertainment that appeals to the TV generation. We contend that in the affective domain, the very fact that video programs are authentic artifacts of the target culture and originated as communication among speakers of the target language makes them inherently motivating acquisition sources. When students know that they are looking in on reality, that in the act of watching TV they are replicating the actions of native listener/speakers, they feel challenged to engage in highly active and interactive listening sessions. This may suggest that the profession's investment of large sums to produce pedagogical video could well be redirected toward selection and preparation of broadcast materials for lower levels of language study.

Nowhere in the two sources of your work cited here do we find sufficient explanation for your neglect of authentic materials. In your sixth chapter of *The Natural Approach*, "Additional Sources of Input for Acquisition and Learning," you do devote several paragraphs to television and radio as input sources, noting that "Broadcasts completely in the target language are difficult for beginners, but not impossible." It is clear that randomly selected, chance programs lifted directly from TV, satellite, or even casually pirated cassettes cannot be catapulted into a Natural Approach classroom (or any other classroom) with any prospect of success beyond satisfying a moment's curiosity about foreign TV. Two factors prohibit this: comprehensibility and the affective filter. The answer to this dilemma is to prepare listening materials with the same care and attention to the acquisition process that you recommend for reading, as encapsulated in your formula:

Text + Goal —> Reading Comprehension —> Language Acquisition
(Krashen and Terrell 1983, 132)

Unfortunately, your recommendations for *listening* to authentic materials fall short of this standard. You advocate "short meaningful intervals," key word lists, and content questions for individual student use. We therefore recommend to all who can benefit from your approach that they simply re-read Chapter 6 of *The Natural Approach*, substituting "listening" for "reading" wherever it occurs. With some additional reflection on the role of the image in listening via video, teachers will find this chapter an excellent introduction to the ways they can make video both comprehensible and affectively viable.

In the best of all possible worlds, the individual student would also develop listening skills on an independent basis using a computer-controlled multi-media workstation. While much work with video can be accomplished in the classroom under teacher direction or in the language laboratory through the use of task-oriented print materials, the comprehensibility of many authentic programs may still cause problems. By employing a computer to manage work with the video, the learner can exercise fingertip control over the text down to the sentence or phrase level, obtain needed assistance with difficult cultural or lexical materials, and engage in listening/viewing tasks that focus attention on the comprehensible aspects of authentic broadcasts. Described in the terms that you establish for the Natural Approach, interactive video can give students access to a large pool of television programming that will:

1. focus on a narrow topic with specific vocabulary;
2. spiral vocabulary and grammar through successive stages of acquisition;
3. challenge learners through tasks that do not overwhelm them; and
4. present a range of materials broad enough to interest any student.

Everything we have seen in your work demonstrates the affinity between the Natural Approach and instructional technology. Moreover, the concrete pointers you already offer toward the use of images, realia, and recorded media reassure us that you have begun to explore such possibilities. We hope our friendly exegesis here will encourage you and other colleagues to realize more of these opportunities.

Yours naturally,

Sue and Jim

IV

Re: *Teaching Languages: A Way and Ways* (Stevick 1980)

Dear Earl,
    When you published *Teaching Languages: A Way and Ways* in 1980, the diverse methodologies you described there may still have been "unconventional and relatively obscure" (Stevick 1980, 4). In the intervening years they have become less so; in fact, more and more language teachers express curiosity about these alternative approaches. For many of us, your book has made you the most balanced and articulate spokesman—albeit a critical one—for non-traditional, humanistic, non-authoritarian, and experimental methods. Many of our colleagues, no doubt, may feel that these people-oriented approaches have little or no relevance to the inhuman world of

computer screens, remote controls, magnetic tape, and spinning disks. We find hints and clues in your book that refute that view.

In the letters we have addressed to other methodologists, we have attempted to highlight the role technology could play in amplifying, strengthening, extending their approaches. In contrast, this letter will point up insights concerning what you might call the "psychodynamic" dimensions of learning via technology. Rest assured: we will not attempt to show how robotic arms will manipulate rods following the Silent Way; no computer screen with tinny voice will join the circle of learners engaged in Community Language Learning; and finally, no music video will be enlisted in support of learning under the spell of Suggestopedia. Instead, we will try to explore several of your intuitions and observations about the psychological situation of language learners. Such insights can help explain why a given technology may appeal to certain students and can guide us in the development of new forms and applications of instructional technology.

Control vs. Initiative

Rather than looking directly at computers or video or other technologies, let's first listen to what you have to say about the situation of the language learner:

> Any student can arrive at a correct response in either of two ways: by using his own power, or by complying with the teacher's skillful lesson plan. If he does what he does on his own, and in conformity with his own timing and his own purposes, then he knows where he is, and why, and how he got there. If he merely lets himself be carried along by the lesson plan, then what he does will not be truly a part of him, and it may be lost all too quickly. (Stevick 1980, 13)

This predicament cries out for solutions that take into account the skills, goals, learning style, pace, attitudes, and previous experiences of the individual learner. In the lock-step of the traditional classroom, such concerns are beyond the reach of the instructor, as you have observed:

> What is unfortunate is that many lesson plans are based on the belief that we should get the turtle to the destination we have chosen for him as expeditiously as possible, even if we have to take him off his feet. Equally unfortunate, though less common, is the opposite extreme: "humanistic" techniques that place a premium on student initiative and student contributions sometimes fall flat. (Stevick 1980, 13-14)

Early generations of computer software for language learning merely substituted the computer for the traditional teacher in lifting your turtle off his feet. There was little conscious attempt to "reconcile the centrality of the teacher with the centrality of the learner" (Stevick 1980, 17). In dealing with this issue, you introduce the helpful dichotomy of "control" and "initiative" and address approaches "which will allow the teacher to keep nearly 100 percent of the 'control' while at the same time the learner is exercising nearly 100 percent of the 'initiative'" (Stevick 1980, 17). This distinction is an extremely fruitful one not only for teachers, but also for those who design instructional computing, because this medium is the one learning environment where control and initiative can remain completely fluid, changing in response to *each* learner's needs. The teacher, as you candidly observe, is hard-pressed to meet this standard in the classroom:

> What so often happens, of course, is that the teacher, in the name of "exercising control," also monopolizes initiative, telling the student which line of the drill to produce, which question to ask (or how to answer it), whom to talk with, and so on. The student knows that he has perhaps 3 to 5 seconds in which to respond, before the teacher reasserts initiative by repeating the question, giving a hint, prompting, or calling on someone else. To avoid this requires skill, and balance, and maturity on the part of the teacher. (Stevick 1980, 20)

Later in the book, you revisit this topic and raise a number of questions about the extent to which teachers may dare to surrender initiative; you hasten to add that "to the hard-working and overworked classroom teacher, they may also be alarming questions" (Stevick 1980, 120). Computer courseware, on the other hand, can be designed to incorporate this valuable expertise in an ideal fashion. A language student exploring an anthology of videodisc-based news reports, for example, can browse through the video segments to her heart's content, listen intensively, ask for cultural or lexical notes, open up a database of exercises on the passive voice (with contextualized sentences from the news) and then return at will or upon advice from the computer to her original exploratory environment. Software designed to provide this setting is already becoming available.

Naturally, there are large gaps in our knowledge about how to devise courseware that accounts adequately for individual learner characteristics. A major bone of contention is whether learner control can be efficient. Can we trust learners to invoke the help they need when they need it? How slowly can we let the turtle crawl? In a recent examination of research on this issue, Steinberg finds confirmation for earlier findings that question stress on learner control: "Students with little knowledge of the subject matter do not perform as well under learner as under computer control" (Steinberg 1989, 120). New directions in this area include advising the learners about possible sequences and amounts of study while allowing them to accept or reject this advice. Future research directions involve changes in the degree to which the student can dictate the course of a learning session:

> In the past we have thought of the locus of control as fixed, as either learner or computer control. But learning is a dynamic process. Not only are there differences between learners in their ability to take control, but there are

> differences in each individual's needs as learning progresses. The locus of control within a lesson should change accordingly, shifting from computer control to learner control to the greatest viable extent. (Steinberg 1989, 121)

Unfortunately, most of the research into these questions has been performed in subject-matter areas other than language learning. It is extremely difficult to state with confidence that such studies conclusively apply to our field. Your description of the trade-offs between control and initiative in language learning should reinforce our determination to resolve these dilemmas.

The Silent Way

Your observations on the Silent Way elevate concern for the learner to an existential plane. We believe it is worthwhile to listen to this more profound formulation of the learner's situation:

> If the essence of the Silent Way is to affirm the individual learner in his self-contained independence—one might almost say, in his aloneness—and to guide him through work that he must do on himself, then whatever dulls that awareness of self-contained independence may distract, delay, or even defeat the deeper kinds of learning. An atmosphere of too much support and solicitude may therefore be inappropriate from this point of view, even if it does, in the short run at least, produce more right answers more comfortably. (Stevick 1980, 59)

Given your larger context of humanistic learning environments, it is striking that you question the value of emphasizing personal empathy between teacher and student. What seems to be needed is individualization without personalization. This corresponds extremely well to our observation that students find even the most impersonal forms of computer-based drill and practice to be "friendly." In a survey of over 200 students using his elementary French program FRELEM, Hope found that more than 80% of the students agreed with the statements "I was motivated to do work beyond minimum requirements" and "Instructor [the computer] helped me develop confidence in my own abilities" (Hope 1982, 252-53). Hope further notes: "It is significant that the most common reaction of the first-time user of FRELEM is to laugh. Unsolicited verbal reactions to the program are almost all positive. Many praise its motivating qualities; a number of students refer to it as 'comforting'" (Hope 1982, 350).

This aspect of computer-assisted feedback is strongly reminiscent of error correction in the Silent Way as you describe it: "Mistakes are dealt with in a way calculated to allow the student to do as much of the work as possible without disrupting the shared sense of moving ahead together in a way that gives learning in exchange for the time spent. ... The purpose here is to convey the necessary information with minimal emotional impact" (Stevick 1980, 59). Our point here is that the computer's ability to deliver individualized feedback with the requisite "minimal emotional impact" has not been fully understood or exploited. Software developers may be well advised to reflect on these issues early in the design stages of their work.

Community Language Learning

Until now, we have focused on the potential for computer-based technologies to meet the needs of individual learners. In exploring Community Language Learning we would like to turn to another technology—video—in its relationship to groups of students. Your chapters on Community Language Learning return to the issues of control and initiative from a new perspective:

> The word "community" means that power is more evenly distributed between knower and learner than it is in a conventional classroom. But in a community, "power" is itself subordinated to "responsibility." Both knower and learner are responsible for bringing to the task the resources that they alone possess. This is a relationship with constantly shifting equilibrium, not a relationship of fixed roles. (Stevick 1980, 115)

Within this context, you introduce the concept of the Whole Learner in order to focus on issues of materials development:

> First for me, chronologically, was the fact that learning is something that the learner does, and that he does it best when the teacher does not stand over him, breathe down his neck, jiggle his elbow, and chatter into his ear. The second fact is that the so-called physical, emotional, and cognitive aspects of the learner cannot in practice be isolated from one another: what is going on in one of these areas inexorably affects what is possible in the other areas. In the same way, and this is the third point, the people in the classroom are not separable from one another: they inevitably make up a more or less successful community. Fourth, the needs of the whole learner go beyond the need for achievement and approval, which are central in the minds of most writers of textbooks. They also include needs for security, predictability, group membership, and the feeling that what one is doing makes sense in terms of an overall and deeply satisfying life pattern. (Stevick 1980, 197)

We regard television, in contrast to print, as an inherently small-group experience. With printed text, it is not possible under normal conditions to know precisely what words are being comprehended at what moment; nor is it possible to synchronize and compare the reactions of a group to a given textual stimulus. By presenting video in the classroom or by assigning small groups to view video together in a laboratory, an instructor can create and build upon a temporary community of viewers. Members of a group of learners centered upon video not only react together; they can also see and hear each others' reactions. Small-group video thus enhances the setting for comprehension.

The instructor can exploit this added dimension quite effectively. In fact, many of the best techniques for teaching with video in the classroom or the lab correspond surprisingly well to the five desiderata in your "materials for the whole learner" (Stevick 1980, 200-201). Allow us to reformulate your principles with video in the foreground:

1. Authentic foreign video provides something for the emotions, as well as for the intellect.
2. Video materials provide occasions for students to interact with one another.
3. Properly selected video materials allow students to draw on present realities, as well as on their distant future goals.
4. Classroom activities focused on video provide for students to make self-committing choices in the areas covered by 1 to 3 above.
5. Well-designed video tasks contribute to students' sense of security.

We believe that both teachers and materials developers who keep these principles in mind cannot fail to exploit authentic foreign video in creative and productive ways. One of the most useful of these techniques is to assign students to small groups, either within the larger classroom setting or for out-of-class work in the language laboratory. Your observations on small groups make a strong case for extensive use of this teaching strategy:

> Sometimes authors do not mention small groups at all. When they do include them, they often treat the group merely as an expedient for giving each student more air time at the cost of having his mistakes less dependably corrected. They almost always ignore at least five important features of groups: (1) A group of even three or four people is likely to be more reliable than any one of its members when it comes to recognizing which of a set of alternatives is the correct one. (2) A correction from a peer is more telling because it comes from someone who has had the same amount of exposure to the language, and not from someone with professional qualifications. (3) At the same time, a correction from a peer is generally less threatening, both because the one doing the correcting is not the person who gives out the grades, and because the correction is less likely to come in a reproachful or other judgmental tone of voice. (4) Competition between groups is less threatening to individuals than competition between individuals is. At the same time, it can be just as exhilarating. (5) Working, risking, and suffering together for even a short time can produce noticeable feelings of mutual loyalty. (Stevick 1980, 202)

All five of these points can be directly translated to the development of innovative methods for presenting foreign language video in the classroom.

Suggestopedia

Let's complete this tour of experimental methodologies by taking the potential and value of video one step further. Among the twelve points you use to outline Suggestopedia, the first one seems most relevant: "Learning involves the unconscious functions of the learner, as well as the conscious functions" (Stevick 1980, 230). Authentic video—originally intended as a communication in the target culture—consists of a multi-channeled bundle of inputs too complex for full comprehension by most viewers, especially language learners. When we attempt to enumerate the benefits and techniques of exposing students to material with this level of complexity, we often dwell on ways of simplifying the message, reducing to the student's level. This is no doubt appropriate, but it may only articulate a small part of the benefit of this technology:

> Lozanov's point, as I understand it at least, is this: that whenever a student is consciously dealing with the overt content of a lesson—the part that he and the teacher are focusing their attention on—he is at the same time dealing unconsciously with other things which lie just outside, or far outside, the center of his awareness; and that what happens on the unconscious level affects what can happen on the conscious level. (Stevick 1980, 230)

We contend that authentic video can window the target culture better than any other medium. What we do not fully understand today is the way both conscious and unconscious learning interact within this window. We do know that work with video makes it possible to focus attention on content while allowing the experience of linguistic structures without the learner's conscious reflection. Even when the facts and lexicon of content occupy the foreground of attention, complex cultural information of a more evanescent nature is constantly transmitted via the audio and visual channels of the medium.

More than anyone else, you write about human relationships and the way methodology must account for them. If technology is to heed methodology, it must do likewise and your book has helped us bring that home.

Yours wholly,

Jim and Sue

References

Hope, Geoffrey R. 1982. "Elementary French Computer-Assisted Instruction," *Foreign Language Annals* 15:347-353.

Krashen, Stephen D. and Tracy D. Terrell. 1983. *The Natural Approach: Language Acquisition in the classroom.* New York: Pergamon Press.

Omaggio, Alice C. 1986. *Teaching Language in Context: Proficiency-Oriented Instruction.* Boston: Heinle & Heinle.

Rivers, Wilga M. 1981. *Teaching Foreign-Language Skills.* 2nd Edition. Chicago: University of Chicago Press.

_____. 1988. *Teaching Spanish: A Practical Guide.* Lincolnwood, IL: National Textbook Company.

_____. 1989a. "Interaction and Communication in the Language Class in an Age of Technology." *Georgetown University Round Table on Languages and Linguistics 1989. Language Teaching, Testing, and Technology: Lessons from the Past with a View Toward the Future.* Edited by James E. Alatis. Washington, D.C.: Georgetown University Press, pp. 186-197.

_____. 1989b. *Ten Principles of Interactive Language Learning and Teaching. NFLC Occasional Papers, February 1989.* Washington, D.C.: National Foreign Language Center.

Steinberg, Esther R. 1989. "Cognition and Learner Control: A Literature Review, 1977-88," *Journal of Computer-Based Instruction* 16,4:117-21

Stevick, Earl W. 1980. *Teaching Languages: A Way and Ways.* Rowley, Massachusetts: Newbury House.

Terrell, Tracy D., Magdalena Andrade, Jeanne Egasse, and Elías Miguel Muñoz. 1986. *Dos mundos: A Communicative Approach.* New York: Random House.

Annotated Bibliography

Alessi, Stephen M. and Stanley R. Trollip. *Computer-Based Instruction: Methods and Development.* Englewood Cliffs, New Jersey: Prentice-Hall, 1985. Provides a comprehensive overview of computer-assisted instruction, including types of courseware, models for development of materials, and lesson evaluation.

Altman, Rick. *The Video Connection: Integrating Video into Language Teaching.* Boston: Houghton Mifflin, 1989. Breaks new ground in defining the application of video to language teaching. Shows how to integrate video throughout the curriculum via practical learning activities. Includes suggestions for selecting and using video equipment, extensive lists of distributors of video materials, legal guidelines for off-air recording and copying, and a selected bibliography.

Hope, Geoffrey R., Heimy F. Taylor, and James P. Pusack. *Using Computers in Foreign Language Teaching.* Washington, D.C.: Center for Applied Linguistics and Harcourt Brace International, 1984. Introduces language teachers to the computer-assisted language instruction. Discusses the advantages of various forms of CALL for teaching and course management. Outlines how computers relate to each of the foreign language skills. Includes an extensive annotated bibliography.

Otto, Sue E. K. "The Language Laboratory in the Computer Age," in: Smith, no. 6, pp. 13-41. Focuses on the expanded role of the language laboratory in an era when new hardware, improved materials, and new confidence in media among language teachers have redefined the lab's purpose and function.

Knight, Denise Bourassa, ed. "Emerging Technologies and Foreign Language Instruction," *ADFL Bulletin*, vol. 19, no. 3, April, 1988, pages 4-31. Comprises five articles devoted to technology in the profession covering the following topics:

language acquisition research, hypermedia, administrative issues, launching CAI on the campus, and satellite distribution of video.

Pusack, James P. "Problems and Prospects in Foreign Language Computing," pages 13-39 in Smith, no. 5. Defines and describes basic concepts in foreign language computing. Elucidates common typologies and terms used to characterize the medium and its hardware and software. Sketches in order of increasing complexity three levels of projects—implementation, development, and research—that teachers might undertake as they become familiar with CALL.

Smith, Wm. Flint, ed. *Modern Media in Foreign Language Education: Theory and Implementation.* Lincolnwood, Illinois: National Textbook Company, 1987. Contains ten articles dealing primarily with CALL. Provides comprehensive and up-to-date information to language teachers at all levels, as well as to administrators, authors, and researchers on the interaction between computer technology and second-language learning.

_____, ed. *Modern Technology in Foreign Language Education: Applications and Projects.* Lincolnwood, Illinois: National Textbook Company, 1989. A companion volume to no. 5, above. Part I contains seven chapter-length essays such topics as the language laboratory, television, interactive video, and pedagogical research on CAI. Part II is a collection of 18 reports on developmental efforts and prototypical course in second-language learning.

Underwood, John H. *Linguistics, Computers, and the Language Teacher: A Communicative Approach.* Rowley, Massachusetts: Newbury House, 1984. Relates the use of computers in language learning to current linguistic theory and methodology. Measures the potential for CALL against the ideals of communicative competence. Offers a general introduction to the field as well as a basis for deciding how to utilize computers most effectively in the classroom.

Material Concerns: Textbooks and Teachers

L. Kathy Heilenman
Louisiana State University

Textbooks, and by extension other published material, occupy a unique niche in second language teaching and learning. Textbooks are the place where teacher, student, and curriculum meet, and everyone—teachers, methodologists, researchers, curriculum developers, and even students—uses them and has opinions about them. This is particularly so at beginning levels. As Kramsch (1988) has put it: "It [the textbook] may be used or abused, followed religiously or humorously, memorized with piety or abandoned with spite—the text remains the bedrock of syllabus design and lesson planning... (63)."

At best, textbooks are seen as compilations of material that help compensate for inadequate teaching (Allwright 1981) or that save teachers the time and trouble of developing material of their own. At worst, textbooks are seen as a hodgepodge of poorly integrated activities (Moody 1988), as "masses of rubbish skillfully marketed" (Brumfit 1985, p. 100), or as "the tainted end-product of an author's or a publisher's desire for a quick profit" (Sheldon 1988, p. 239). Still, no one has seriously suggested, or at least no suggestion to that effect has ever been taken very seriously, that teachers abandon their textbooks in favor of producing their own materials. And, in fact, a closer look at the underlying dynamics of the ties between publishers, authors, textbooks, teachers, and students uncovers an intricate, frequently uneasy, at times even acrimonious relationship. Ultimately, however, this relationship is best viewed as a symbiotic one, a mutually advantageous association, that has had a centuries-long history and shows every sign of a continuing future.

In what follows, I look first at the second language textbook as a sociological phenomenon.[1] Then, with this as background, I explore various issues in textbook and materials development. One caveat however. My experience with second language teaching has been largely within the context of medium to large university programs of French. My experience with textbook publication consists of writing a workbook-lab manual and of collaborating on a first-year, college-level French book. Thus, although the ideas I present here may well have implications for people at other levels and in other settings, I leave it to those individuals to arrive at their own conclusions and draw their own inferences.

The role of the textbook

Although textbooks have been a part of education for more than 500 years (McMurry and Cronbach 1955, 9), we really know very little about how teachers and learners use them. As Cronbach pointed out in 1955 and Walker reiterated in 1981, "the sheer absence of trustworthy fact regarding the text-in-use is amazing" (Cronbach 1955, 216; Walker 1981, 3). How do students and teachers use textbooks? What textbook features affect long-term outcomes? What are the variables underlying how teachers introduce and use the material in textbooks? What kind of reciprocal influence does the experience of teachers and learners have on the form of the textbook? (Walker 1981, 3). Although answers to these questions must remain both highly speculative and beyond the scope of this article, it is important to realize that much of the controversy surrounding the development, use, and misuse of textbooks is, to paraphrase Cronbach (1955, 216), "vacuous," and to the extent that the textbook *per se* has *not* been the subject of principled investigation, represents opinion and speculation.[2]

Perhaps the best way to begin an investigation into textbooks as a critical issue for the foreign language classroom is to avoid the polemical and, instead, to explore the nature of the textbook as part of a complex social system, a system that involves students, teachers, authors, researchers, curriculum developers, and publishers in an intricate pattern of conflicting and converging motivations and convictions.

The textbook as social artifact

The textbook, as we know it today, has evolved over the past several centuries into a tool that both teachers and students appear to find, if not satisfactory, at least necessary. As the textbook has evolved, it has been accompanied by a constellation of individuals who find themselves dedicated to conserving the old while promulgating the new (McMurray and Cronbach 1955) as well as being caught between what Coser, Kadushin, and Powell (1982, 7) have called "the tensions between the claims of commerce and culture." That is, textbooks are charged simultaneously with transmitting the knowledge a culture feels to be basic, while introducing new insights and promoting new ideas, seeking to encompass both the archival (Olson 1980) and the progressive. Further, given that publishing houses have never voluntarily existed as non-commercial ventures, textbooks must also turn a profit. In essence, the situation is one of checks and balances where the interests of all concerned act to ensure that no one constituency has complete control of the process. A closer look at the various constituencies —textbook-users (teachers and students) and textbook-producers (authors and publishers)—illustrates the essentially ecological nature of the textbook-in-development-and-in-use.

The textbook and its users

Sticht (1981) speaks of the "text-teacher-student trilogy" as an ecological system where students learning from textbooks become teachers teaching from textbooks, who, then in turn, become authors responsible for the content of textbooks. In this sense, teachers are experienced students who have implicit assumptions about student needs. Textbook authors, having been both students and teachers, come equipped with an implicit understanding of the needs of those who will use their texts. Sticht goes on to point out that the place to start improving textbooks, is through description of this "eco-system" (1981, 32). By making explicit what is subsumed under 'the way it's always been done' or 'the way that's natural, that seems right' we stand a chance of making informed rather than simply intuitive choices.

An example of the kind of thing I mean is the traditional sequence in which verb tenses are presented in a structural syllabus. Why does present tense always seem to precede past, and past precede future?[3] Why, in French, does it seem 'more rational' to most teachers to present the passé composé before the imparfait, to have the conditional follow the future or to teach the subjunctive somewhere after the passé composé/imparfait but before the compound tenses?[2] Does it have to do with frequency or perhaps cognitive prerequisites, or maybe usefulness? Is it some kind of intuitive evaluation of complexity or is it just 'what we're used to'? I do not wish to imply that this type of question will be easily resolved. I simply mean to emphasize that it should be asked. It may well be that the 'traditional way of doing things' has advantages that are not immediately obvious. On the other hand, a closer look at some of our 'ways of doing things' may reveal places for improvement.

First, however, we need to examine the components of this eco-system in more detail. When considered separately, it may appear that the individuals involved are rather single-mindedly pursuing their own interests. I will argue, however, that the ecological niche represented by the text-student-teacher trilogy, although at times turbulent, is actually functioning rather well.

Teachers

First, it should be made very clear that the real purchasers of textbooks are teachers[4] and not students. Students use the textbooks that their teachers choose. And, in general, teachers choose the familiar and resist the unfamiliar (Tibbetts and Tibbetts 1982), a fact that publishers have been quick to note. As Squires (1981, 28) has pointed out, "distinguished failures" on publishing lists tend to have been "programs of quality which introduced innovations different from those most schools were ready to accept." Why this resistance to change on the part of teachers? I think there are several, very good, but sometimes contradictory reasons. As has already been pointed out in the context of the teaching of composition at the college level, the majority of people currently teaching came to the job as literary student-scholars with little or no explicit knowledge of the subject they were to teach (language). Thrown to the students, so to speak, with only their textbook to protect them, the understandable happened. As Connors (1986, 190) puts it:

> Most teachers assumed that the wisdom of the text was the wisdom of the world. They read their texts, they studied their handbooks, and they taught their tools. Composition was the only college-level course consistently carried on by people whose only real training came from the rules and tenets found in the textbooks they asked their students to buy.

Essentially the same set of circumstances has been the case in departments of foreign languages at the college level. Novice teachers have been handed textbooks, given a few words of general advice, and let loose. Unlike their counterparts in, say, history or psychology whose prior study has involved the field they will teach, novice teachers in foreign languages have been students of literature, not language. Thus, they have had no theoretical, discipline-based background against which to compare the material found in the texts they were teaching. Moreover, for novice teachers, the knowledge represented by the textbook has the aura of accepted wisdom. It will not be until they have acquired sufficient experience and personal expertise to consider themselves the peers of those who write textbooks, that teachers will feel qualified to question and critique them (Olson 1980).

Finally, it has only been within the past 30 to 40 years that both composition and foreign/second language learning/teaching have developed the rudiments of an academic discipline in their own rights. Before then, as Connors (1986) points out for composition, textbooks served to provide whatever definition there was to the field. In other words, knowledge, instead of being forged and debated in journals, was mandated in textbooks. Thus, for teachers, the textbooks as they found them, consciously or subconsciously became the standard by which subsequent texts would be judged. This situation is gradually changing in both composition and in foreign languages. Teachers entering the field are more likely to be exposed to a knowledge base that extends beyond their textbook and, as a result, are less likely to surrender to the textbook as authority.

Nevertheless, the majority of classroom teachers, unlike researchers and material developers, have only a passing interest in and knowledge of research on the teaching and learning of foreign/second languages. These teachers, at least at the college level, have other, very legitimate and time-consuming interests. And they are, quite frankly, not well served by textbooks that change drastically from one year to the next. The real bottom line is that it takes time and energy to change the way a course is organized and taught, energy that is even less likely to be expended when such changes appear to be following the "swings of linguistic fashion" (Sheldon 1988, 239) rather than the realities of the classroom as teachers know it. In other words, the legitimacy of the text-teacher-student eco-system referred to above, based as it is on experience rather than the results of research, resists change that is not rooted in that very same experience.

Along this same line, it should be kept in mind that today's teachers have lived through varying portions of the past 30 to 40 years and have witnessed, as either students or teachers, the rapid progression from grammar translation to audio-lingual to functional and/or communicative language teaching. As Sutton (1988, 205) points out, "30 to 40 years is trivial when compared to the thousands of years of teaching foreign and second languages through reading the written word." In other words, 30 to 40 years of fairly chaotic change is trivial when compared to the much longer evolution of the eco-system of text-teacher-student.

In fact, it could be argued that the pedagogical, linguistic, and psychological conflicts of the past 30 to 40 years have been less than helpful to classroom teachers. This kind of rapid transition breeds uncertainty and a tendency to look outside of the classroom experience for expert answers. Classroom teachers, whose background in the relatively new fields of post-traditional linguistics and second language acquisition is slight, will have a tendency to become "grail seekers" (Maley 1984) at one extreme or to adopt a simplistic, reductionist strategy at the other (Clarke and Silberstein 1988). In either case, they will probably feel vaguely guilty.

Before leaving this section, let me emphasize that the discussion above is not an attack on the ignorance or poor preparation of teachers. Research into second language acquisition and learning, while important, has tended to ignore the equally important realities of teachers and students in classrooms. There are two points to be made here. First, the job second language teachers, and especially non-native teachers, are now expected to do, is vastly more complex than that expected even of audio-lingual teachers. The latter had to deal largely with matters of form in more or less easily controlled chunks; today's teachers are urged to reconcile the often conflicting tasks of dealing with form, meaning, and communicative act, while also attending to student affect and motivation (Medgyes 1986).

Second, there is a tendency for 'experts' to tell 'non-experts' (usually classroom teachers) what they should be paying attention to. The reason, of course, that experts can do this is because they are being paid to read, to research, to think, and to write. Effectively, this means that the 'experts' are those who teach the least and are, therefore, the least in contact with the eco-system of text-teacher-student discussed above (Brumfit 1985). This is probably inevitable, but I think it is extremely important to make it explicit.

As a result, teachers frequently find themselves caught in a double bind (Clarke and Silberstein 1988) where the very real, though often implicit knowledge they have developed in the classroom is viewed as unimportant or irrelevant, by themselves as well as the 'experts.' Thus, teachers may, on the one hand, expect materials to be the solution and set off on the search for the perfect textbook. On the other hand, they may opt out of the material wars altogether, disillusioned by the failure of the 'expert,' as represented by the textbook, to provide a definitive answer. Ultimately, they may do the sane thing and begin to depend on their own intuitions, informed but not driven by research findings and expert advice.

The situation of teachers has been discussed at some length because their role is central in the complex system linking text, teacher, and student. Teachers decide the texts that students use. Thus, teachers comprise the real market for publishers, and, as a result, their opinions are instrumental in decisons on the kinds of books that are developed, a subject to which we will return below.

Students

It will be noticed that students have figured only marginally in the discussion thus far. Ironically, students are probably the least understood and aruguably the least important of the individuals currently involved in textbook development. Students purchase the books and materials that their teachers tell them to; their opinions may influence a teacher's decision to continue using a book but only indirectly effect the initial decision. It would be interesting to know more about the role of students in textbook development and marketing. Do student comments about the adequacy or inadequacy of material carry any real weight when teachers make out book orders? Are materials ever revised because of student input during field testing, and if so, to what extent? At the moment, all we can do is speculate.

The textbook and its makers

Textbook authors and publishers often find themselves caught between the inherently contradictory forces of, in Ariew's (1982, 12) words, "innovation and salability." The publication of a textbook, especially an introductory text with its multiple colors, art work, and accompanying package of materials, requires the outlay of a large amount of money—between $100,000 and $250,000, and up to as high as $400,000 (Coser, Kadushin, and Powell 1982; Halpin and Addison 1985) long before the first copy is actually bought. Likewise, authors are required to produce their work—which may take from two to three, and up to five years—up front with no guarantee of compensation. Given these facts, publishers and authors, become understandably concerned about the reactions of the market—the teachers who will opt to accept or reject the book. Tibbetts and Tibbetts (1982, 855) point out that a textbook represents a product:

> By this, we mean that people design it, produce it, market it, sell it. All along the way there is a good deal of fretting and worrying about the product. Is it well designed? Can it be made at a reasonable cost? What is the best way to market it? Will anybody buy it? Will it be a Ford Mustang—or an Edsel?

On the other hand, a textbook is also more than a commodity. It is an attempt to reconcile the innovative with the traditional in the interests of improved learning and teaching. Although publisher and author keep both parts of the equation in mind, their perspectives make it inevitable that they view them differently.

Overall, most textbook writers are academics who make their living at something other than writing. According to Coser, Kadushin, and Powell (1982), they tend to have had the responsibility of running a large introductory course, to be middle-aged and middle-class. In general, they tend also to be academic second-class citizens. Textbook writers are, according to Bierstedt (1955), transmitters and not contributors of knowledge. Since prestige in academia accrues to those who advance (contribute) knowledge, authors of textbooks are in an academic no-man's land. Thus textbook writers who find themselves more closely allied with the marketplace than do most academics have a vested interest in maintaining an independent and scholarly profile.

Publishers, on the other hand, have their own priorities (Ariew 1982). Their activity will focus on avoiding the "distinguished failures" (Squire 1981, 28) that, while being innovative and of high quality, are ahead of what the market will accept. This is not to say that publishers see nothing but dollar signs; rather they cannot afford to ignore them. Publishers, although not unmindful of research, theory, and pedagogical fashion, will tend to focus on the market, the competition, and the bottom line. Of course, in the real world, such tendencies are matters of degree, and publishers and authors will both work to produce texts that are pedagogically sound and reasonably profitable.[5]

The textbook as negotiated compromise

What has been described thus far represents a system of checks and balances that seems to function relatively well. Teachers, the ultimate customer, serve as the pivot. They provide publishers, either directly through surveys and discussions with sales representatives or indirectly through their adoption decisions, with information upon which to base the decision to publish or not to publish a given text. Since teachers' biases tend to be conservative, they serve to constrain premature or over-enthusiastic publication of research results or 'expert' theory as textbooks.

Change does occur, but slowly. Alexander Pope's advice on publishing a successful text (cited in Schramm 1955, 129) is still apt:

Be not the first by whom the new is tried,
Nor yet the last to lay the old aside.

Issues in materials development

In this section, I examine at some length what I take to be the most pressing issues in current materials development: the relationship between academic values and textbook writing and the role of research in textbook development. I then briefly discuss selected issues involved in decisions concerning textbook content.

Textbooks and academic values

This is a particularly thorny issue. On the academic scale of things, theory ranks higher than practice and research is better rewarded than is teaching. Thus, generally speaking, a textbook, is seen as less valuable in terms of academic rewards than a scholarly book. My objective here is not to debate the merits of such a position; rather, more importantly, I want to look at its effect on textbook production.

Coser, Kadushin, and Powell (1982), in a survey of textbook authors, found that two thirds of new authors were actually recruited by publishing houses rather than having sought a publisher on their own initiative. Their comment is revealing: "Most *able* academics would rather write scholarly books or professional monographs; they need to be persuaded to write a textbook" [italics mine] (241). Boorstin (1981, ix) contends that "textbook writers, as distinct from monograph writers or the writers of articles in scholarly journals, are seldom the greatest thinkers of the subject." If, then, textbook writing is a second-class activity, why do professors do it? According to Tibbetts and Tibbetts (1982, 856), the obvious answer, money,[6] doesn't hold up either:

In the long run you [professors] will be much better off financially if you write scholarly books and work for academic promotion and the salary raises that go with it. In the so-called major universities, an untenured professor can even get fired for writing textbooks. In any case a writer of textbooks will progress more slowly up the academic ladder.

So, why then do people write textbooks? The cynical answer would be because they cannot or do not want to produce 'true' scholarly work. I would argue, however, that the talent and work behind an outstanding textbook, a piece of applied scholarship, while different in some ways from that necessary to produce an outstanding piece of pure scholarship, are nonetheless analogous. In both cases, large amounts of material must be internalized and reordered. In both cases, new information must be integrated with old in order to come to more or less original conclusions. The difference resides in the markets for which each is produced. Innovation in textbooks destined for large groups of teachers and students, is, of necessity, less obvious than is original insight in scholarly works destined for relatively small groups of specialists.

Further, it can be argued that, ultimately, the small advances made by textbooks are, due to their large audience, every bit as important as those made by scholarly works within their much more restrained sphere. The real crux of the matter comes in evaluating how good (or bad) a textbook is. Unlike scholarly work, which is largely evaluated by peer reviews, textbooks tend to be evaluated by how well they sell. Insofar as one considers sales an indication of teachers' informed judgments rather than a reflection of publishers' marketing techniques, this is not a bad metric. If, however, there is an inherent distrust of the marketplace as arbiter, the better a textbook sells, the more suspect its 'scholarship' becomes. Bierstedt's (1955, 124) interpretation of this phenomenon is worth, I think, quoting in full:

> Therefore, the prestige which an author gains through his production, gained indirectly through his financial emoluments, places his achievement close to the general societal norm but far from the academic norm. And the larger the financial return, the less is his academic prestige.

Perhaps this is as it should be. To the extent that textbook writing diverges from the academic norm, prestige should be withheld. A logical extension of this argument would have those texts that are produced for the small graduate market (e.g., specialist texts that resemble traditional scholarly work) accorded academic prestige. However, those texts produced for the large introductory markets (e.g., generalist texts that diverge significantly in form from traditional scholarly work) would be denied academic validity, on the assumption, perhaps, that what is lost in academic prestige will be made up in financial gain.

Here, however, we are back to our original question, only slightly modified. If the writing of introductory texts is not academically valid, that is, if they do not result in academic recognition (Kramsch 1988), who will write them? There are three possibilities, none of which appeals to me. The first sees the rise of a sub-class of material writers (much as we now have a sub-class of instructors). This, of course, would only serve to further separate the beginning levels from the more advanced ones. The second possibility acknowledges that textbook writing is indeed second-class work, suitable for those scholars who no longer wish to pursue original, intellectual thought but who are, instead, enthralled by the potential profit of a best-selling textbook. The final possibility is for publishers to abandon professors and to invest more heavily in what are called 'managed texts.' Managed texts are written by a team of writers at the direction of a publishing house, are carefully positioned vis-à-vis the market, and are produced according to certain specification. Although a complete discussion of such texts is beyond the scope of this chapter (see Coser, Kadushin, and Powell 1982, 269-282 for a fuller discussion), I think the implication is clear. The market wins and the delicate checks and balances currently in place collapse.

There is a last possibility, one that is appealing but whose future I feel less optimistic about. That is, the development of an evaluation metric for textbooks that parallels that for scholarly books. One way of setting about this would be to examine those textbooks that are considered outstanding or influential. Such textbooks would exhibit an awareness of current research and thinking while remaining firmly grounded in the reality of the classroom. They would not simply be derivative but would synthesize and innovate. A concern here would be that authors are seldom completely responsible for their textbooks. It would be necessary to separate out the constraints imposed by textbooks as basically conservative products that must remain responsive to market concerns from their authors' success in implementing considered innovation.[7] The development of such a metric is the only way to ensure that competent academics will continue to write textbooks. The alternative, as I see it, is to accept a gradual lowering of standards in the area of introductory textbooks. As Bierstedt (1955) pointed out over 30 years ago, textbook standards are directly related to the academic rewards received: "It is not inappropriate to wonder whether, if textbook standards are to be raised, it will not be necessary to raise the academic awards for writing them (125)."

There is an additional factor that must be taken into account here for the areas of English composition (Connors 1986)[8] and foreign language pedagogy. Until 30 to 40 years ago, both fields were largely defined by the material contained between the covers of textbooks. In other fields the continuum of knowledge that ranges from most accepted to most speculative was paralleled by publication outlets. Textbooks represented the most conservative knowledge, scholarly books held a sort of middle ground, journal articles contained more speculation, and working papers were the most daring. In foreign language pedagogy, however, textbooks represented if not the only, at least the most accessible outlet, and those advances that were made in the field were largely disseminated through textbooks. That tradition has continued today as evidenced by the fact that the publication of textbooks is probably seen as a more legitimate scholarly activity for applied linguists than for language teachers whose academic training has been literary.

At the moment, however, applied linguists have a respectable selection of journals in which to publish along with a respectable number of publishers willing to produce works other than textbooks. Thus, no longer restricted to textbooks as an outlet, and, indeed, encouraged by the academic reward system to avoid them, applied linguists may do so, leaving the field open to the possibilities of professional material developers, profit-seeking professors, and managed texts discussed above. It seems obvious that, if academic rewards go to research rather than to textbooks, and if opportunities for publication are no longer largely limited to textbooks, then many potential textbook writers are going to be lost. Again, let me emphasize that I do not want to pass judgment here on which is better—textbooks or scholarly books. I do want to point out, however, that the question of who will write tomorrow's books is far from settled.

The role of research in foreign language textbooks

Foreign language pedagogy has traditionally looked, in varying degrees, to other academic disciplines for its theory—to linguistics for language description, to psychology for learning, and to education for teaching. In addition, there has been an historical tendency to look for miracles, to search for ways that will make second language learning as painless as first language learning appears to be. One result has been the consistent call to apply the results of research to teaching and textbooks.

Research in second language acquisition

Much of the research that has taken place in second language acquisition seems to indicate that language learning takes place in relatively invariant stages that learners must pass through, and that, in many cases, these stages are the same for first as for second language learners.[9] A basic question, then, concerns the role of formal language instruction. Can languages be taught or are they only learned? Should teachers and textbooks attempt to respect this order of acquisition or should they ignore it?

An example from the literature on L1 and L2 French acquisition illustrates the problem. We have evidence that, for L1 learners of French, aspect is acquired before tense (Clark 1985). Bronckart and Sinclair (1973) asked children aged 3;0 to 8;0 years old to describe various actions and action sequences. Their findings indicate that actions clearly concerning a result are most often described in the *passé composé* (perfective aspect) while actions with no result or with no particular aim are described in the present (imperfective aspect). Similar results were obtained for a sample of adult, instructed L2 learners (Kaplan 1987). In other words, both L1 and L2 learners appeared to pass through a stage where the present contrasted with the *passé composé* before moving to the adult norm where the *imparfait* contrasted with the *passé composé*.

There are several problems with applying this research to materials development. First, before attempting to generalize specific research findings to a larger sample (students using a textbook), we would want to be sure that the observed sequence really exists. We would need to know if all learners go through this stage or if there are individual differences. We would also want to know more about this stage. Is it tied to other developmental phenomena? Is it general across all verbs or are there differences here as well? Second, if materials were to present French verb forms according to this observed, natural sequence, it would be necessary to teach an 'incorrect' contrast (present/*passé composé*). This seems intuitively unsatisfactory, but research could help us sort out whether or not the intuitively unsatisfactory could produce improved learning. In sum, although teachers and material developers should be aware of this type of research, they should hesitate before attempting to apply it directly to the sequence and grading of textbook materials.

Research in linguistics

Recent work in linguistics as applied to second language teaching/ learning[10] has focused on the relationship between form and function/ meaning. The underlying assumption is that the more explicit we can make this connection, the better we will be able to structure teaching materials. Kennedy (1987), for example, has studied the semantic category, quantification, in written English. Among other things, he found that the numbers *1*, *2*, and *3* and *first*, *second*, *third*, and *last*, were by far the most common cardinal and ordinal numbers. He also found that the subcategory of large quantities/degrees was more than four times as frequent as that of small, and that the quantifier *more* was seven times more frequent than *less*.

This poses a problem for materials developers. If large quantities are referred to more frequently than small ones, should the presentation of 'small' words be deferred relative to 'large' ones? Similarly, should the numbers 1-3 be referred to more often than the numbers 4-10 given their relative frequencies? Probably not, since factors other than frequency—need, learnability, usefulness, etc. (Carter 1987)—will have to be considered. Kennedy himself (1987, 275) has concluded that it is not clear how to determine which words should receive pedagogical focus.

Another example of this type of research is Ozete's (1988) study of meaning in relationship to the use of the preterit and the imperfect in Spanish. Basing his study on two contemporary short stories, Ozete attempted to define those attributes that favored High Focus (foreground information) from Low Focus (background information). He found that High Focus (preterite) verbs tended to have human and/or proper noun subjects and to be active. Low Focus (imperfect) verbs, on the other hand, tended to have non-human and/or common noun subjects and to be stative. He then goes on to apply these insights to the presentation and practicing of preterit and imperfect verbs. Here the application to teaching materials is made explicit. By making reference to how speakers structure their discourse rather than resorting to categorical and apparently arbitrary rules, learners may indeed be helped to understand how these verb forms function.

Research in instructional design

A third area of research with potential application to textbook development is concerned with the presentation rather than the content of the textbook. The central question here is how presentation effects learning. Within this field, an extensive literature exists on the role of illustrations in learning materials that could have implications for materials in foreign languages. Evans, Watson, and Willows (1987), for example, have looked at how illustrations are used in current textbooks. They surveyed textbooks (elementary and high school reading, math, environmental studies, spelling, and second language), interviewed people working in publishing, and observed teachers using illustrations in the classroom. Briefly, their findings indicate (1) that illustrations are more profuse and more colorful in lower-level books; (2) that the decision to illustrate by publishing houses is based less on consideration of the effects of illustration on learning than it is on what the competition is doing; and (3) that teachers do not use illustrations in the classroom. This latter finding is especially interesting in view of the fact that teachers say they want illustrations (thus influencing publishers to provide them).

Levin, Anglin, and Carney (1987) provide an overview of what is known about the effect of pictures on learning. They report that when pictures are relevant to the content (i.e., redundant or overlapping), recall is improved. When pictures are irrelevant (i.e., decorative), no such facilitation is observed. They also point out that, for less-skilled readers, relevant pictures may serve to organize the text (in Omaggio's [1979] terms, provide a schemata) or may even replace it.

Finally, Hammerly (1974; 1984) has shown that the use of pictures or film strips to present vocabulary directly without the intermediary of native language is inefficient at best and misleading at worst. He points out that the majority of learners 'play the game,' translating silently, but nonetheless translating rather than establishing any kind of direct link between picture and second language representation.

These studies, taken in conjunction with one another, have several implications for textbook development. First, the use of irrelevant illustrations may attract teachers and motivate students, but it does not seem to directly effect learning. Second, the use of relevant, representative or organizational illustrations (Levin, Anglin, and Carey 1987) may serve to help less-proficient readers (here foreign language students) make sense of material that is beyond their immediate level. Finally, pictures, although probably useful for practicing language, are only marginally useful for presenting it.

Research and textbooks

Overall, the answer to the question of whether research is useful in developing foreign language textbooks is a qualified but definite yes. In attempting to apply research findings, we are faced with a basic contradiction. Laboratory research where all the variables can be tightly controlled yields results of which one can be reasonably certain. Such research, however, is often difficult to apply directly to the classroom. Research done under conditions that more nearly resemble the classroom, however, yields results that are subject to the possible effect of uncontrolled variables. Such research can be generalized to other situations only with care (see Hatch and Farhady [1982, 7-10] for further discussion on the problem of reconciling what is also known as internal and external validity).

Thus, research results are useful, but only when used by knowledgeable decision makers who can weigh the cost of change within the educational context. To cite several specific examples, changing the traditional ordering of the structural syllabus to take into account stages found in L2 acquisition makes sense only if we are relatively certain of the validity of these stages (see Lightbown 1985 for further discussion). Basing vocabulary exclusively on frequency counts makes sense only if we are certain that frequency is the most important factor for the student population we are concerned with (see Carter 1987). However, varying a grammar explanation by adding additional information is probably cost effective, all else being equal. Likewise, attempting to make textbook illustrations more relevant to what students are learning is to be recommended but may be difficult to integrate into present texts.[11]

Two recommendations and a comment seem appropriate here. The first recommendation is that materials based on research findings should be field-tested before distribution (Brumfit 1985; Fleming 1987; Moody 1988). The application of research implies the generalization of a finding beyond the exact conditions that held during the original data collection. There is, therefore, no guarantee that similar results will be found in other settings. Adequate evaluation of materials in the field, of course, is easier said than done, with the result that often the first use of material by adopters also constitutes its first test in the field also.

The second recommendation concerns instructors manuals. Perhaps this is the place for research to lie fallow—to stand the test of time and use—before being translated into materials. For example, teachers could be made aware of the research concerning acquisition of aspect and tense in French and encouraged to observe their students to see if a similar pattern develops. Should this be confirmed, then teachers have the consolation of knowing there is an explanation (beyond pure stupidity and lack of effort) when students begin using present tense verbs for description in the past. Likewise, further information about language such as that described in Kennedy (1987) and Ozete (1988) can be offered. Finally, an explanation of the different roles that illustrations may play along with suggestions on how to make visual material more relevant could be included.[12] This would serve the dual purpose of educating teachers on the job, so to speak, while at the same time reducing the pressure to immediately apply more or less abstract research results to real-world classrooms. Ideally, this type of material in instructors manuals would be documented and would occupy a niche somewhere between a scholarly review of the literature and anecdotal wisdom, preferably closer to the former than the latter.

Issues in textbook content

There are several specific issues[13] that materials developers must deal with in producing the next generation of texts. For the most part, each of these has been discussed elsewhere; here, then, I simply identify them as issues, comment briefly, and refer interested readers to other sources.

Syllabus

The particular syllabus and/or methodology adopted in a particular situation will depend on the desired outcomes, the resources available, student needs, and teacher preferences (Krahnke 1988). Textbook authors and publishers, who want to reach the largest audience/market possible, do not have the luxury of tailoring material to individual situations. Instead, they must strive to project trends and tailor their production so that most people will be mostly happy with their texts. The advantage is that most teachers can use most texts if they will adapt them. The disadvantage is increasing length (as more options are added) and an eclecticism that, if not handled carefully, can degenerate into disparate materials with no common thread. In fact, most materials represent a more or less conscious compromise between various theoretical stances. Woods (1988, 227), summarizing his experience with text development, concludes:

> Whatever methodology we choose—communicative, functional, or any of the others I have mentioned—we are juggling and mixing all the building blocks of language. We are juggling the functions, the exponents, all of the grammar, the situations and the story line, and I have come to the conclusion that one is not more important than another. They must all fit. Superficially, a course may appear to be one approach or another, but in fact the developers must tug and pull all elements to make a course hang together.

Grammar

The problem here is how, when, and how much. Long (1988) has reviewed the literature on the efficacy of instruction, concluding that instruction does have positive effects on rate of acquisition as well as on ultimate level attained. Instruction does not, according to Long however, seem to be able to alter unfolding sequences of acquisition. Further, he cautions that the small amount of research in this area merits drawing only very tentative conclusions. The real issue, in research as in the classroom, is how instruction is defined. Instruction is not isomorphic with the overt teaching and testing of discrete grammatical forms, and the finding that instruction is helpful in some contexts does not imply that explict grammar teaching is to be encouraged (Long 1988).

Nevertheless, the grammatical syllabus is well established in classrooms and textbooks, particularly at the elementary and intermediate levels. I have argued elsewhere (Heilenman 1979) that grammar has remained at the core of foreign language instruction for reasons of expediency and academic suitability. I see no particular reason for this to change in the near future, although I think its modification may be a possibility (cf. Tibbetts and Tibbetts 1982 for a similar point of view in composition). We may also want to consider materials that explain less and do more; that is, material that helps teachers find things that students can do with the language (Prabhu 1987) while simultaneously paring the explicit teaching of grammar to a more manageable amount. We may also want to look at the traditional grammatical syllabus in terms of items that are likely to benefit from explicit instruction and items that are not (Pica 1985). Given that we have very little research in this area, the only principled way to do this would be to isolate those discrete items of grammar that students find difficult. In French, for example, we might target the article system, verbal aspect, and interrogatives as candidates for deemphasis in explicit teaching. We might also consider the wisdom of relegating systematic grammatical instruction to more advanced levels where learners could be made aware of the differences and similarities between their interlanguage forms and those of the language they are learning.

Pedagogical grammars

A pedagogical grammar, which I define here as the information about language that is made accessible to students, is not an applied, reduced, or otherwise diluted linguistic description. Its first concern is making sense to students. Unfortunately, since students seldom have much influence in deciding which books they will use, language explanations in textbooks are often written with authors uneasily aware of experienced teachers and academic linguists symbolically hovering over their shoulders. The pedagogical grammar found in many textbooks, then, represents an uneasy compromise between traditional explanations and current linguistic thinking.

Thus, Herschensohn's (1988) criticism of textbooks for their "complicated and exception ridden format" (411) assumes that a linguistically parsimonious and elegant explanation, (i.e., one that subsumes several individual rules under one more general rule) requires less effort to learn and apply. It could also be argued that traditional grammar explanations have persisted because they are, in some way, easier for human beings to learn/remember. A more pessimistic view of human nature, of course, would argue that traditional explanations persist because of human resistance to rethinking the accepted, that is, to simple inertia. I know of no directly relevant research on this issue, either one way or the other. In any case, Herschensohn and I are not the ones who matter; students are. Perhaps what we should do is test the adequacy of our textbook descriptions by having students read them and then write a variation on the immediate recall protocol (Meyer 1985) to test for their comprehensability. That would ultimately be more useful for textbook improvement than discussion among people who already know the rules.

Vocabulary

There are two issues here, one of initial selection and one of eventual learning. Selection is really only a problem at the beginning and early intermediate levels where material writers need to decide which words students should have and reconcile that with the words needed to write language that is as authentic as possible. Word frequency lists, although useful, are only starting points. Low frequency words are often central to understanding while high frequency words are less so. In addition, high frequency words such as 'take' are also polysemous and raise the question of which meanings should be taught and in which order (Carter 1987). The notion of "coreness" as proposed by Carter (1987, chapter 2) may be useful, but as he points out, the relative "coreness" of one word versus another is not always clear and will frequently need to be tempered by pedagogic intuition and experience.

Selecting words is only half the battle; textbooks must also provide activities that help learners develop their L2 lexicon. Such activities must move quickly from translation equivalents and lists to language in context. Activities dealing with collocations and semantic fields may be helpful. School activities used to help develop L1 learners' vocabulary may be adapted to the L2 context. Finally, research from the development of word associations in L2 (Meara 1984) should also be considered.

Register and level of language

Textbooks need to deal with variation in language in a principled way. The easiest path is to deal exclusively with sanitized language and to avoid registers above or below standard langauge use. A more realistic, although more time consuming, method is to introduce the idea of register from the beginning of study, emphasizing the need for discretion in use by L2 speakers, while exploiting the use of authentic documents to study register in context.

Authentic materials

The use of authentic materials is by no means a panacea. Woods (1988), for example, points out that immigrants are deluged with authentic materials, often to little avail. Besse (1988) contends that the use of authentic documents is a return to "morceaux choisis" (22) but that now, instead of literary texts, we have excerpts from newspapers and paraliteratures. Along with Nostrand (1989), Besse emphasizes the decontexualization of such excerpts, a decontextualization that can make them practically unreadable when separated from the events, conventions, institutions, and values that produced them. There are two separate issues here. First, the purposes that authentic materials can serve must be made very clear. Given that natural language seldom if ever falls into paradigms and conjugations, it is unrealistic to expect authentic documents to illustrate particular structural points. Assuming structural presentation to be the goal, we will probably have to resort to pedagogical subterfuge and create the texts ourselves, striving for as close a fit to authentic language as possible.

The second issue is the pedagogical apparatus that will accompany authentic materials. Rings (1986) notes that substantial pedagogical support will be needed if authentic documents are to be used from the beginning as more than decorative realia. Along the same lines, authentic non-print texts (video and audio tapes) need to be selected and processed in terms of appropriateness of text, task, and sequence (Rogers and Medley 1988).

Culture

As Robert (v) wrote in 1904, "It has been recognised [sic] as part of the modern language teacher's work that he should give his pupils some idea of the life and ways of the foreign nation whose language he is teaching." It is still so recognized today. The problem is not good will; the problem is how to serve/please all the constituencies involved. Let me list some of the problems: culture as cathedrals or croissants? compare and contrast or emphasize similarities? generalizations that border on stereotypes or specific details? whose culture? and so on. Questions such as these are beyond the scope of a brief comment. I would suggest, however, that the best way to resolve them is to focus on students rather than issues. Again, of course, the problem is that teachers and not students are the ones who select textbooks, and teachers tend to have strong ideas on issues.

Kramsch (1988) describes the different cultural realities of the foreign language textbook illustrating some of the difficulties that stand in the way of using text material produced and used in one culture to represent the reality of another. Her analysis and suggestions for change are cogent and should be taken seriously.

Technology

The real challenge for the next two or three or maybe four decades will be the integration of emerging technology into materials for teaching and learning languages. Sheldon (1988) suggests that the textbook as we know it could disappear to be replaced by core materials provided by publishers. Teachers, using desktop publishing technology, could modify and supplement this material and, in effect, 'publish' it themselves. The role of video and computers in mainstream materials is crucial. The complexities of the question, however, preclude anything here but the notation that this too is a major issue for materials development (see Smith 1987; 1989).

Conclusions

What kinds of conclusions can we take away from all of this? I see at least three. First, any real improvement in textbooks will come, not from discussions of details, but from an improved understanding of what teachers and students do with texts (Sticht 1981). Richards and Rogers (1986) have observed that, although we know a substantial amount about methods from the theoretical point of view, we know very little about how teachers actually implement them.[14] We know even less about materials. The complex public/private eco-system comprised of students, texts, teachers, authors, and publishers needs to be described, observed, and studied from as many angles as possible.[15]

A second area that needs attention is the problem of audience. As I have pointed out several times, students count for relatively little in the writing and selling of textbooks. Not only are textbooks sold to teachers rather than students, it is also relatively difficult for textbook writers and classroom teachers to put themselves in the shoes of learners. We need more information on how students react to contextualized exercises, for example, rather than on how material developers and teachers think they do.[16]

A third point concerns the role of textbook author as intermediary. Medgyes (1986, 112) has called for "language-teaching experts who would work halfway between the zealot and the weary." This is a good description of the ideal author—someone who knows both the research and the reality and who is willing to shuttle back and forth between them bringing news and happenings from one side to the other and back again.

Finally, as Tibbetts and Tibbets (1982, 855) have emphasized: "In this account, there are no villains." The textbook—the common repository of concerns of the different constituencies involved—will always be less than perfect. It will always represent a negotiated compromise. Insofar as this compromise is negotiated in good faith by competent professionals with a conscious awareness of the trade-offs involved, we can expect tomorrow's textbooks to improve upon today's.

Acknowledgement

I would like to thank Janet McDonald and Walter Tuman for their comments on an earlier version of this paper.

Notes

1. Kramsch's (1988) analysis of the textbook complements that presented here. Her emphasis is on the textbook as a cultural construct; mine is on the textbook as a social, economic, and political phenomenon.
2. I do not mean to imply that there have been no studies on the textbook. There have, but they have focused on features of the textbook—content and form—rather than on the questions of the textbook-in-use raised here. In a similar vein, Apple (1986, 85-86) has pointed to the lack of critical attention paid to "the ideological, political, and economic sources of its [the textbook's] production, distribution, and reception."
3. There is, of course in French the presentation of the *futur proche* (aller + infinitive) with the verb aller early in the sequence.
4. Teacher is used here in the generic sense. It can be read as 'instructor,' 'professor,' 'teaching assistant,' etc.
5. Kramsch (1988) contends that textbook authors in foreign languages engage in this activity for profit rather than in the interests of applying their theoretical knowledge. It should be noted that engaging in textbook writing in the interests of making money does not guarantee that one will become rich. Kramsch is describing motive; Tibbetts and Tibbetts, results.
6. I have just described utopia! It should not be left unsaid that the process of textbook writing and production is a series of compromises between these two. To the extent that all concerned act in good faith, the outcome is acceptable even if the process is often painful. See Coser, Kadushin, and Powell (1982) for a very readable sociological study of the publishing industry. Chapter 9, *Authors: A Worm's-Eye View*, is especially recommended for anyone considering writing a textbook.
7. As I will argue further on, instructors manuals may also play a part in evaluation. Here, authors could make the theoretical underpinnings and scholarly background of their work more explicit, a benefit for those using as well as those evaluating the text.
8. Connors deals only with the field of composition. Here, I extend his argument to foreign language pedagogy. Although I believe there are important parallels, there are also significant differences. Such pioneers as Henry Sweet, Harold Palmer, and others established an early concern for theory and research (largely linguistically based) in foreign language teaching beginning in the 19th century. Their influence, however, seldom extended as far as departments of foreign literatures in the United States, thus the parallel with composition.

9. Contributers to Hyltenstam and Pienemann (1985) summarize much of this research and consider its implications for the second or foreign language classroom.

10. Research on the role of Universal Grammar and parameter setting in second language acquisition is another candidate for inclusion here. See Felix (1985) or Schachter (1988) for further information.

11. Obviously, there are upper limits on the number of details to be added to grammar explanations as there are upper limits on how many representational versus decorative pictures should be included in a textbook. The question of quantity can only be answered by taking individual learners, language teaching situations, and textbook goals into account.

12. Fleming (1987, 150), for example, suggests that questions encourage learners to pay more attention to pictures. These could be provided in instructors manuals or in the text itself. Another possibility would be activities requiring learners to process visual information. Such activities could be useful in presenting cultural material for example.

13. Obviously many more topics (four skills, language—native or target—used in textbooks, literature, teacher-made material, pronunciation, intellectual level of material, etc.) could have been included.

14. I do not mean to imply that no such studies exist. They do but they do not focus on the text-in-use. Instead they attempt to identify how instruction might help second language learners (for example, Pienemann 1985) or they compare two kinds of instruction (for example, Scott 1989). Research of the kind I mean is exemplied by Guthrie (1984) who looks at the interaction between student, instruction, and teacher.

15. According to the Textbook Author's Association Newsletter (Briefs, July 1989, 12), a center charged with conducting, collecting, and disseminating research on textbooks has been established as a joint project of ERIC/RCS and Indiana University.

16. I strongly suspect that students are seldom aware that many exercises are contextualized; they are too focused on figuring out how to get the next item right before the teacher calls on them.

References

Allwright, R.L. 1981. What Do We Want Teaching Materials For? *ELT Journal* 36: 5-18.

Apple, Michael W. 1986. *Teachers and Texts: A Political Economy of Class and Gender Relations in Education.* New York: Routledge & Kegan Paul.

Ariew, Robert. 1982. The Textbook as Curriculum. In *Curriculum, Competence, and the Foreign Language Teacher.* The ACTFL Foreign Language Education Series, ed. T.V. Higgs, 11-33. Lincolnwood, IL: National Textbook.

Besse, H. 1988. Tendances actuelles des pratiques de l'enseignement du français aux Etats-Unis. In *L'Enseignement du français aux États-Unis: Perspectives Américaines et Etrangères*, ed. R.C. Lafayette, 13-29. Paris: Didier Erudition.

Bierstedt, Robert. 1955. The Writers of Textbooks. *See* Cronbach 1955, 96-128.

Boorstin, Daniel J. 1981. Introduction. *See* Sticht & Cole 1981, ix-x.

Bragger, Jeannette D. 1985. Materials Development for the Proficiency-Oriented Classroom. In *Foreign Language Proficiency in the Classroom and Beyond.* ACTFL Foreign Language Education Series, ed. C.J. James, 79-115. Lincolnwood, IL: National Textbook.

Bronckart, J.P. & H. Sinclair. 1973. Time, Tense, and Aspect. *Cognition* 2: 107-130.

Brumfit, Christopher. 1985. Seven Last Slogans. Chapter in *Language and Literature Teaching: From Practice to Principle.* Oxford: Pergamon Press.

Carter, Ronald. 1987. *Vocabulary: Applied Linguistic Perspectives.* London: Allen & Unwin.

Clark, Eve V. 1985. The Acquisition of Romance with Special Reference to French. In *The Crosslinguistic Study of Language Acquisition,* ed. D.I. Slobin, 687-782. Hillsdale, NJ: Lawrence Erlbaum.

Clarke, Mark A. & Sandra Silberstein. 1988. Problems, Prescriptions, and Paradoxes in Second Language Teaching. *TESOL Quarterly* 22: 685-700.

Cole, John Y. & Thomas G. Sticht, eds. 1981. *The Textbook in American Society: A Volume Based on a Conference at the Library of Congress on May 2-3, 1979.* Washington: Library of Congress.

Connors, Robert J. 1986. Textbooks and the Evolution of the Discipline. *College Composition and Communication* 37: 178-194.

Coser, Lewis A., Charles Kadushin, & Walter W. Powell. 1982. *Books: The Culture and Commerce of Publishing.* New York: Basic Books.

Cronbach, Lee J. 1955. *Text Materials in Modern Education.* Urbana, IL: University of Illinois Press.

_____. 1955. Text Production and Use, 188-216. *See* Cronbach 1955.

Evans, Mary Ann, Catherine Watson, & Dale M. Willows. 1987. A Naturalistic Inquiry into Illustrations in Instructional Textbooks. In *The Psychology of Illustration, Volume 2: Instructional Issues,* eds. H.A. Houghton & D.M. Willows, 86-115: New York: Springer-Verlag.

Felix, Sascha W. 1985. More Evidence on Competing Cognitive Systems. *Second Language Research* 1: 47-72.

Fleming, Malcolm L. 1987. Designing Pictorial/Verbal Instruction: Some Speculative Extensions from Research to Practice. In *The Psychology of Illustration, Volume 2: Instructional Issues,* eds H.A. Houghton & D.M. Willows, 136-157: New York: Springer-Verlag.

Guthrie, Elizabeth M. 1984. Intake, Communication, and Second-Language Teaching. In *Initiatives in Communicative Language Teaching: A Book of Readings,* eds S.J. Savignon & M.S. Berns, 35-54. Reading, MA: Addison-Wesley.

Halpin, William C. & Herbert J. Addison. 1985. College-Textbook Publishing. In *The Business of Book Publishing: Papers by Practitioners,* eds E.A. Geiser, A. Dolin, & G.S. Topkis, 290-295. Boulder, CO: Westview Press, 1985.

Hammerly, Hector. 1974. Primary and Secondary Associations with Visual Aids as Semantic Conveyers. IRAL 12: 119-125.

_____. 1984. Contextualized Visual Aids (Filmstrips) as Conveyors of Sentence Meaning. IRAL 22: 88-94. Hatch, Evelyn & Hossein Farhady. 1982. Research Design and Statistics for Applied Linguistics. Rowley, MA: Newbury House.

Heilenman, Laura K. 1979. A Realistic Look at the Function of Grammar in the Foreign Language Classroom. In *Teaching the Basics in the Foreign Language*

126 / Critical Issues in Foreign Language Instruction

Classroom: Options and Strategies, ed. D. Benseler, 90-100. Skokie, IL: National
Textbook.

Herschensohn, Julia. 1988. Linguistic Accuracy of Textbook Grammar. *Modern
Language Journal* 72: 409-414.

Hyltenstam, Kenneth & Manfred Pienemann, eds. 1985. *Modelling and Asssessing
Second Language Acquisition*. San Diego, CA: College-Hill Press.

Kaplan, Marsha A. 1987. Developmental Patterns of Past Tense Acquisition among
Foreign Language Learners of French. In *Foreign Language Learning: A Research
Perspective*, eds. B. Van Patten, T.R. Dvorak, & J.F. Lee, 52-60. New York:
Newbury House.

Kennedy, Graeme D. 1987. Quantification and the Use of English: A Case Study of
One Aspect of the Learner's Task. *Applied Linguistics* 8: 264-286.

Krahnke, Karl. 1987. *Approaches to Syllabus Design for Foreign Language Teaching*.
ERIC/CLL Language in Education Series. Englewood Cliffs, NJ: Prentice-
Hall/Regents.

Kramsch, Claire J. 1988. The Cultural Discourse of Foreign Language Textbooks.
In *Toward a New Integration of Language and Culture*, Northeast Conference on
the Teaching of   Foreign Languages, ed. A.J. Singerman, 63-88. Middlebury,
VT: Northeast Conference.

Levin, Joel R., Gary J. Anglin, & Russell N. Carney. 1987. On Empirically Validating
Functions of Pictures in Prose. In *The Psychology of Illustration, Volume 1: Basic
Research*, eds. D.M. Willows & H.A. Houghton, 51-85. New York: Springer-
Verlag.

Lightbown, Patsy M. 1985. Can Language Acquisition Be Altered by Instruction? *See*
Hyltenstam & Pienemann 1985, 101-112.

Long, Michael H. 1988. Instructed Interlanguage Development. In *Issues in Second
Language Acquisition: Multiple Perspectives*, ed. L.M. Beebe, 115-141. New York:
Newbury House.

Maley, Alan. 1984. "I Got Religion!"—Evangelism in Language Teaching. In
Initiatives in Communicative Language Teaching: A Book of Readings, eds. S.J.
Savignon & M.S. Berns, 79-86. Reading, MA: Addison-Wesley.

McMurry, Foster & Lee J. Cronbach. 1955. The Controversial Past and Present of
the Text. *See* Cronbach 1955, 9-27.

Meara, P. 1984. The Study of Lexis in Interlanguage. In *Interlanguage*, eds. A.
Davies, A. Howart, & C. Criper, 225-235. Edinburgh: Edinburgh University
Press.

Medgyes, Péter. 1986. Queries from a Communicative Teacher. *ELT Journal* 40:
107-112.

Meyer, Bonnie J. F. 1985. Prose Analysis: Purposes, Procedures, and Problems. In
Understanding Expository Text, ed. B.K. Britton & J.B. Black, 11-65. Hillsdale,
NJ: Erlbaum.

Moody, Raymond. 1988. Personality Preferences and Foreign Language Learning.
Modern Language Journal 72: 389-401.

Nostrand, Howard Lee. 1989. Authentic Texts and Cultural Authenticity: An
Editorial. *Modern Language Journal* 73: 49-52.

Olson, David R. 1980. On the Language and Authority of Textbooks. Journal of
Communication 80: 186-196.

Omaggio, Alice C. 1979. Pictures and Second Language Comprehension: Do They
Help? *Foreign Language Annals* 12: 107-116.

Ozete, Oscar. 1988. Focusing on the Preterite and Imperfect. *Hispania* 71: 687-691.

Pica, Teresa. 1985. Linguistic Simplicity and Learnability: Implications for Language Syllabus Design. *See* Hyltenstam & Pienemann 1985, 137-151.

Pienemann, Manfred. 1985. Learnability and Syllabus Construction. *See* Hyltenstam & Pienemann 1985, 23-75.

Prabhu, N.S. 1987. *Second Language Pedagogy*. Oxford: Oxford University Press.

Richards, Jack C. & Theodore S. Rodgers. 1986. *Approaches and Methods in Language Teaching: A Description and Analysis*. Cambridge: Cambridge University Press.

Rings, Lana. 1986. Authentic Language and Authentic Conversational Texts. *Foreign Language Annals* 19: 203-208.

Robert, Frank R. 1904. *Features of French Life*. First Part. London: J.M. Dent & Sons.

Rogers, Carmen Villegas & Frank W. Medley, Jr. Language with a Purpose: Using Authentic Materials in the Foreign Language Classroom. *Foreign Language Annals* 21: 467-478.

Schachter, Jacquelyn. 1988. Second Language Acquisition and Its Relationship to Universal Grammar. *Applied Linguistics* 9: 219-235.

Schramm, Wilbur. 1955. The Publishing Process. *See* Cronbach 1955, 129-165.

Scott, Virginia M. 1989. An Empirical Study of Explicit and Implicit Teaching Strategies in French. *Modern Language Journal* 73: 14-22.

Sheldon, Leslie E. 1988. Evaluating ELT Textbooks and Materials. *ELT Journal* 42: 237-246.

Smith, Wm. Flint, ed. 1987. *Modern Media in Foreign Language Education: Theory and Implementation*. ACTFL Series on Foreign Language Education. Lincolnwood, IL: National Textbook.

_____. 1989. *Modern Technology in Foreign Language Education: Applications and Projects*. ACTFL Series on Foreign Language Education. Lincolnwood, IL: National Textbook.

Squires, James R. 1981. Publishers, Social Pressures, and Textbooks. *See* Cole & Sticht 1981, 27-30.

Sticht, Thomas G. 1981. The Learning Process and the Text in Use. *See* Cole & Sticht 1981, 31-32.

Sutton, Michael. 1988. The Development of the Read Canada! Series. *TESL Talk: A Journal for Teachers of English* 18, Special Issue: 200-207.

Tibbetts, Arn & Charlene Tibbetts. 1982. Can Composition Textbooks Use Composition Research? *College English* 44: 855-858.

Walker, Decker F. 1981. Textbooks and the Curriculum. *See* Cole & Sticht 1981, 2-3.

Woods, Howard. 1988. Our Ottawa Experience in Development. *TESL Talk: A Journal for Teachers of English* 18, Special Issue: 221-233.

Annotated Bibliography

Allwright, R.L. 1981. What Do We Want Teaching Materials For? *ELT Journal* 36: 5-18. Focuses on types of publications language teachers need. Calls for material addressed to learners, for "idea books" containing collections of ideas for teacher adaptation, and "rationale books" that would help teachers understand and explain language learning theory.

Ariew, Robert. 1982. The Textbook as Curriculum. In *Curriculum, Competence, and the Foreign Language Teacher*. The ACTFL Foreign Language Education Series, ed. T.V. Higgs, 11-33. Lincolnwood, IL: National Textbook. Discusses the compromises that textbook authors must make along with the teachers' responsibility for adaptation of materials to their own situations. Recommends "healthy scepticism" in selecting a textbook along with boldness in making necessary modifications.

Besse, H. 1988. Tendances Actuelles des Pratiques de l'Enseignement du Français aux Etats-Unis. In *L'Enseignement du français aux États-Unis: Perspectives américaines et etrangères*, ed. R. C. Lafayette, 13-29. Paris: Didier Erudition. Discusses four issues that all methods and materials must consider: (1) how to give students access to meaning in the L2; (2) how to help them take advantage of grammatical and other regularities; (3) how to present language in the classroom; and (4) how a pedagogical progression encouraging acquisition can be structured.

Bragger, Jeannette D. 1985. Materials Development for the Proficiency-Oriented Classroom. In *Foreign Language Proficiency in the Classroom and Beyond*. ACTFL Foreign Language Education Series, ed. C.J. James, 79-115. Lincolnwood, IL: National Textbook. Describes how textbooks are produced. Analyzes text material from a proficiency point of view giving specific recommendations for lexical and structural coverage along with suggestions about exercises and activities.

Carter, Ronald. 1987. Vocabulary: Applied Linguistic perspectives. London: Allen & Unwin. Provides an overview of the English lexicon. Discusses "core vocabulary," the relationship of words in discourse, lexis and literary stylistics, lexicography, and the learning and teaching of vocabulary.

Cole, John Y. & Thomas G. Sticht, eds. 1981. *The Textbook in American Society: A Volume Based on a Conference at the Library of Congress on May 2-3, 1979*. Washington: Library of Congress. Participants drawn from the worlds of publishing and education attempt to define the issues involved in textbook development and use. Contains summaries of complete papers which were to be published by Academic Press but, to my knowledge, have never appeared.

Connors, Robert J. 1986. Textbooks and the Evolution of the Discipline. *College Composition and Communication* 37: 178-194. Gives a history of composition teaching illustrating the importance teacher qualifications or the lack thereof has had on textbooks.

Coser, Lewis A., Charles Kadushin, & Walter W. Powell. 1982. *Books: The Culture and Commerce of Publishing*. New York: Basic Books. Presents a sociological analysis of the world of books focusing on the interrelationships between academia, publishing houses, authors, editors, distributors, teachers, and students, among others.

Cronbach, Lee J. 1955. *Text Materials in Modern Education*. Urbana, IL: University of Illinois Press. The first, and one of the few, discussions of text materials in a broad perspective. Argues for a comprehensive theory of the textbook. Provides a broad view of the textbook as a philosophical construct, a factor in learning, and a product of authors and publishers.

Hauptman, Philip C., Marjorie B. Wesche, & Doreen Ready. 1988. Second-Language Acquisition through Subject-Matter Learning: A Follow-up Study at the University of Ottawa. *Language Learning* 38: 433-475. Reports on the learning of French as an L2 within the sheltered-context of a university Introductory Psychology class. Results indicate that students both mastered the subject matter material and made measurable progress in French.

Herschensohn, Julia. 1988. Linguistic Accuracy of Textbook Grammar. *Modern Language Journal* 72: 409-414. Discusses deficiencies in textbook presentations of French grammar from a linguist's standpoint. Calls for pedagogical grammars that are correct, that distinguish between spoken and written language giving primacy to the former, and for a consideration of the interactions between phonology, morphology, syntax, semiotics, and sociocultural concerns.

Houghton, Harvey & Dale M. Willows, eds. 1987. *The Psychology of Illustration, Volume 2: Instructional Issues.* New York: Springer-Verlag. Contributions dealing with the effect of illustration on learning. Articles include the history of textbook illustration, investigations of the effect of illustrations on learning, and computer graphics.

Howatt, A.P.R. 1984. *A History of English Language Teaching.* Oxford: Oxford University Press. Gives an account of the history of English language teaching from the Renaissance to the present including extensive references to materials used.

Hyltenstam, Kenneth & Manfred Pienemann, eds. 1985. *Modelling and Assessing Second Language Acquisition.* San Diego, CA: College-Hill Press. Contributors attempt to apply L2 acquisition research to classroom and materials. Although there is some optimism about the possibility, the general consensus is that this is premature.

Kramsch, Claire J. 1988. The Cultural Discourse of Foreign Language Textbooks. In *Toward a New Integration of Language and Culture*, Northeast Conference on the Teaching of Foreign Languages, ed. A.J. Singerman, 63-88. Middlebury, VT: Northeast Conference. Analyzes the culture of the textbook in the context of education and publishing. Discusses the kind of culture contained in textbooks and suggests directions for the future.

Olson, David R. 1980. On the Language and Authority of Textbooks. *Journal of Communication* 80: 186-196. Discusses the textbook as a register like babytalk or oral ritualized language. Posits that the separation of knowledge as represented in textbooks, from speakers (here the teacher) imparts authority and puts textbook content above criticism.

Prabhu, H.S. 1987. *Second Language Pedagogy.* Oxford: Oxford University Press. Describes the Bangalore project whose major aim was to develop a series of task-based activities where students' focus would be on message rather than on form. Includes a history of the project and a discussion of the issues involved in implementing curricular change.

Tibbetts, Arn & Charlene Tibbetts. 1982. Can Composition Textbooks Use Composition Research? *College English* 44: 855-858. Based on extensive experience authoring composition textbooks, the authors contend that there is little place for research in textbooks largely because teachers do not want it.

Willows, Dale M. & Harvey A. Houghton. 1987. *The Psychology of Illustration, Volume 1: Basic Research.* New York: Springer-Verlag. Gives an overview of current thinking and research concerning the role of illustrations in learning. Includes discussions of memory, affective response, the effect of pictures on prose learning, and the role of charts, graphs, and diagrams.

Woods, Howard. 1988. Our Ottawa Experience in Development. *TESL Talk: A Journal for Teachers of English* 18, Special Issue: 221-233. Gives a comprehensive guide to developing second language materials beginning with needs analysis, and including planning, development, and production concerns.

Basic Intercultural Education Needs Breadth and Depth: The Role of a Second Culture

Howard Lee Nostrand
University of Washington

Considering the great number of Americans who have been writing on the intercultural problems we face within the country and internationally, it is heartening indeed to find how wide a consensus exists on the description of the problems we face, particularly since this set of problems is quite without precedent. When we go beyond description to estimate the dimensions of an educational program we could count on to be adequate, the consensus still holds concerning its breadth: namely, a world perspective. On the question of sufficient depth, however, we come to a jumping-off place. But this need not deter any but the unadventurous. To build a consensus can be a more interesting adventure than just to discover one—provided you are convinced that the exercise is worth the work and patience it will take.

In this chapter, suppose we start from the existing consensus, and then, standing at the jumping-off point, look at a kind of in-depth experience that gives promise of supporting intercultural education with a sufficiently strong infrastructure.

The much-discussed intercultural problems of the United States fall into two categories: international and internal. As we review the two sets of problems, it will become apparent that they both generate a need for the same cultural infrastructure, namely, a capacity of individuals for cross-cultural relations which has come to be called "cultural competence." After we have surveyed the two sets of problems, therefore, and the progress of education toward a world perspective, we shall venture beyond the present consensus and examine what "cultural competence" ought to mean. There is only one, inescapable way to do this: a hands-on encounter with the building blocks, rough-hewn as yet and in need of polishing, from which the infrastructure can be made. But a stonecutter's quarry is no place to invite people dressed for a group discussion! The exhibit of building blocks, essential as it is for the argument, can best be presented as an Appendix to this chapter, which begins on page 153.

First, then, let us survey the agreed-on problems in our international and internal relations.

The international scene has evolved from one which the United States could dominate with impunity, at least for the short term, to one where even the several major powers can prevail only by persuasion—which involves knowing the other person's values and ways of establishing rapport. What happens for lack of such knowledge, in our embassies and in the competition for foreign markets, is illustrated by the Panama crisis of 1989. Before the U.S. invasion every multilateral resource had been tried, as was claimed, except that U.S. negotiators had never been able, in the years of trying to live down past interventions, to get their country accepted by its neighbors as a partner among equals and an *amigo* among *amigos*, the precondition for effective cooperation in the Hispanic culture.

Not only diplomacy and business have suffered from insufficient cultural competence, but scores of international fields, from the intergovernmental agencies' specialties to private banking, marketing, scientific research, labor organization, and unofficial cooperation on the environment or relief work. In all these activities, the many Americans who unexpectedly become our negotiators will continue to be at a disadvantage unless they are sensitive to cultural differences, at a depth that cannot be reached by ad-hoc briefing before a foreign assignment. Nor is there time for this in-depth education during the years of preparation for most of the professions. The education of a future ambassador or sales representative must begin long before, in childhood and the subsequent stages of human development.

Besides the leaders who are called unexpectedly to represent the country, there is of course the foreseeable need for specialists in the language and culture of each of the linguistic communities with which we have bilateral relations: specialists who combine culture-specific competence with expertise in a profession. The Japanese salesman who has spent four final years learning Hungarian naturally outsells one who came late to both parts of the double competence.

But international specialists and leaders cannot meet the need alone. The most enlightened public officials are still ineffectual unless they have the backing of a competent public opinion. What gets votes from some xenophobic constituency militates against carrying out the long-range policies where the self-interests of peoples converge. Our foreign policy has regularly sacrificed long-range advantage to please some voters or campaign contributors at home, and the practice has grown worse while the need to persuade has grown more demanding. Some degree of cultural competence is needed by the entire electorate and its successors now in school, as part of a common basic education.

Within the United States, we face the difficult task of managing an always precarious cultural pluralism of ethnic and religious traditions with conflicting beliefs and self-interests. The difficulty is compounded for us by the fact that we are in transition from the type of cultural pluralism we have known, where a main stream dominates the minorities, to a type unfamiliar to us, the type that is governed by an inherently unstable coalition. Diverse white, black, Hispanic and Asian components, each dominant in some constituencies, must somehow subordinate their conflicts to the shared purpose of maintaining a civilization. Political campaigns that exploit the ethnic rivalries will have to be resisted not only by the campaigners but by the public for which they design their appeal.

The home scene, therefore, calls for some minimum of cultural competence throughout the citizenry, not just expertise among the specialists in education and the relevant subject matter—notably conflict resolution, and cultural analysis to define the conflict points and latent common ground between antagonistic subcultures. Is the widespread *common* competence for intercultural relations at home basically the same as is needed for international relations? The two purposes are so similar that the same building blocks apparently could serve both. To the extent that this proves true we will be fortunate, not only because effective intercultural education can thus be more economical but because where local relations are too antagonistic for rational dialogue, conflict resolution can begin with a vicarious experience transferable from a remote setting.

Both the international and the internal needs we have surveyed are forces driving a current movement to reform American education by setting national standards. On the eve of the "Governors' Conference" of September, 1989, Ernest L. Boyer, president of the Carnegie Foundation for the Advancement of Teaching, who has won wide assent to his ideas for improving education, noted that "Concerns about economic competition abroad combined with our deepening fears about social pathologies at home have focused attention on the weaknesses of our schools." Observing the "growing conviction in the country that the nation's 83,000 schools, 16,000 districts and even the 50 states[1] acting on their own cannot adequately meet the challenge," he accepts the need for "a national strategy," with the caveat that "each school should be free to shape creatively its own program to achieve the overall objectives." (5)

It is significant evidence of a consensus that the national-standards movement has been espoused by successful politicians. President Bush and the governors of all fifty states, at the end of their unprecedented conference on education in September, 1989, issued a joint statement which concluded, "... We have entered into a compact... to enlighten our children and the children of generations to come."[2] The President elaborated upon the depth of the education implied in that objective of enlightenment: "We've discussed the need for educational reform in terms of our national competitiveness... But... there is more to learning than just our trade balance or the graying of our work force; it is broader than the important, but narrow, compass of economics and government." The objective will be attained, he proposed, only "when every young American can know the life of the mind."[3] Enlightenment does indeed require an inner life of experience, examined experience, of whatever building materials belong in a basic education.

Critics of the movement are disturbed, with reason, by the dominant emphasis, evident in the Governors' conference statement, on evaluating the end product of education:

> "... Teachers and school administrators are currently judged not on how much students learn but on the extent to which they comply with legislative and school board regulations. A movement is under way to base such evaluations on academic results...
>
> "When goals are set and strategies for achieving them are adopted, we must establish clear measures of performance and then issue annual Report Cards on the progress of students, schools, the states, and the Federal Government."[4]

William J. Gore, a political scientist distinguished for his research on Program Evaluation in the field of community development (a field which like education abounds in fall-out effects), cautions against the naïve reliance on "numbers" to tell what is happening in these complex fields. Teaching and learning are by nature processes, and so are vitiated by focusing not on process but on a product, discouraging teachers from devoting creative energy to human development in order to coach students for tests. There is a consensus, to be sure, that it is necessary to provide for accountability, but the consensus does not include basing accountability on the measuring of an end product as if it were independent of the processes which brought it about.

In contrast with the approach from product evaluation adopted by the Governors' Conference, the social studies are demonstrating in some pioneering elementary schools how the process of developing cross-cultural sensitivity can be begun. At Janesville, Wisconsin, Mike McKinnon, one of a succession of distinguished presidents of the National Council for the Social Studies, has third graders look through colored plastic "glasses" to see how different the same object can look. They grow interested in travel as they make a manila folder into a suitcase and draw inside it the possessions they would like to take with them. Flags of the world are permanently displayed in the hall, and, as one way of arousing interest, Mr. McKinnon has each child take home a color slide of some foreign scene, briefly identified, to "research" the place and tell the class about it. Clearly this is an excellent approach to the breadth of intercultural education. The depth, however, remains a problem for later stages of life.

In high school and college the departmentalized social sciences continue to broaden knowledge about other countries, interethnic problems and the worldwide humanitarian and environmental concerns for those students whose vocational programs permit electing such courses. But the rashes of racism in some of the best colleges would alone refute any claim that intercultural education is succeeding. The constructive consensus ends with the admission that our effort so far, except for the social studies in a minority of elementary schools, is simply too superficial to match the depth of the endemic human potential for racism and ethnocentrism. The conclusion is inescapable that we must devise an intercultural education that will go beyond knowledge to lifelong conviction. But how?

An Acceptable Extension of Consensus?

The thesis of the present chapter is that a second culture experienced in its own terms, namely its language, and placed in a multicultural framework, provides the best available infrastructure that would give intercultural education the strength to counteract the deeply rooted forces opposing its aims.

The proposed thesis does not deal with the contribution which the same experience can make toward skill in one's native language. Comparing cultures and their languages, like comparative anatomy, enables one to see how common needs and functions are served by different devices. But a second language and culture may not be the most cost-effective source of that kind of insight, while they are, according to this thesis, our one best hope of building an adequate intercultural component for a modern basic education.

The component in question is a combination of openness to other cultures, commitment to tolerance, and perspective on our own culture from outside it. The contrary force to be overcome is ethnocentrism with its flattering assumption that "we are number one" on a supposed single line of human progress. That assumption inevitably makes us see other peoples or minorities as if they were trying to imitate our highly individual-centered system of values which, as we sometimes admit, we wish were "kinder and gentler."

Knowledge about other cultures is essential to provide the framework for an adequate world view. A two-culture perspective would be narrow and inadequate. But *knowledge about*, by itself, produces only the intention to be tolerant of differences; and that good intention, as we see in every week's news of racism and bigotry, is prone to collapse at the very moment of crisis when it is most needed. *Knowledge about* is only an intellectual abstraction devoid of emotional commitment, unless it has been rooted in concrete *experience of*, in this case experience of another culture in its own terms. For one simply cannot experience that reality by first transposing it into one's own language. The old Swede was right—for him—when he lamented that "the only language which expresses feelings the way they really are, is Swedish."

The crux of the thesis is, first, that to counteract the deep affective force of racism and ethnocentrism requires an in-depth, examined, personal experience rooted outside one's home culture, and secondly, that among the possible types of experience, the likeliest to have a sufficient effect is the assimilation of another people's mentality to the point where one identifies oneself with the second culture—while still remaining one's own person with one's own values. The needed degree of this second self-identification requires a "critical mass" of experience, combined with organizing concepts to make it an examined experience. Why is the language of the culture essential to this experience? Because translation substitutes a different construct of meanings, a different cognitive grid through which reality is filtered before we interpret our perception. How often students find simply "weird" an isolated bit of a foreign way of life, seen through the grid which they assume reveals reality itself. Until that parochial assumption is broadened by concrete experience, intercultural relations will continue to lack dependable support.

The thesis is subject to testing. Can other kinds of examined experience achieve the needed result? Can the multicultural experience so brilliantly begun in elementary-school social studies be followed by sequels that dispense with the second self-identification? If so, how serious would be the loss of persons prepared from childhood for unexpected leadership in bilateral international relations? As another possibility, sensitivity training based just on our own culture has shocked American decision makers into realizing that their supposed freedom of decision is in fact shot through with unconscious cultural restrictions. (Cf. item 18 of the References.) Does the effect of the shock last? If it has to be repeated at intervals, does it hold interest and bring about the needed growth of personality? And does this approach achieve the whole intercultural objective of basic education?

The intercultural objective proposed here—openness to other cultures, commitment to tolerance, and perspective on oneself from outside the home culture—can be summed up as a certain attitude of cross-cultural relativism. Not the extreme, wide-open relativism that is rightly feared and condemned, but a golden mean between that and the opposite extreme, namely ethnocentrism, which precludes real respect for people who are different. This golden mean is characterized by the curiosity to learn about other ways of life, a relaxed acceptance of the fact that the way one was born into is not the only way known to humanity, and the ability to live by one's own values without feeling threatened by having to share the planet with people of other beliefs. The rarity of this generous attitude shows how difficult it will be to create a basic education that would make it a common achievement.

The Critical Consequences for the Language Teaching Profession

If an experience of a second culture as we have defined it is the likeliest adequate support for an essential part of the needed basic education, then language teaching in America moves from a sideshow of the curriculum to somewhere near center stage.

Since the whole movement reflected by the Governors' conference is at a formative stage, it is reasonable to assume that if we can reach a consensus soon enough within the field of languages and cultures, our recommendations will be built into the nationwide standards as they develop. One may not remember that this has happened before to the language teaching profession. When the Congress responded to the success of Sputnik—and the ensuing failure of the U.S. rocket—with the National Defense Education Act of 1958, the Modern Language Association was just completing a six-year operation called the Foreign Language Program. The FLP's recommendations became Title Six of the Act, with the resulting focus on "math, science *and* modern foreign languages."

Can we again rise to the occasion before it passes us by? We are prepared to define levels of oral "communicative competence." Since 1971 when that phrase was coined by the linguist Dell H. Hymes, remarkable progress has been made thanks to the initiative of ACTFL, The American Council on the Teaching of Foreign Languages. ACTFL is also leading an advance toward defining standards for reading and writing skills. (2) But in the area of cultural competence, and even in the sociolinguistic part of it which is essential to effective oral communication, we have only a basic consensus among members of the profession who have given the matter enough thought.

In the present open season, a nationwide consensus among language teachers on the definition of a minimal core of cultural competence becomes a central, critical issue of the 1990's for us and our organizations, particularly the Modern Language Association, ACTFL, Academic Alliances,[5] and the AAT's (the American associations of teachers of specific languages). Once we have a tenable definition to offer, a host of organizations devoted to global education and the spread of intercultural democracy will listen, for they share our concern to make cultural pluralism a success.

ACTFL included cultural competence in the *Provisional Proficiency Guidelines* of 1982, but suspended inclusion of that component in the revised edition of 1986, because it had not been defined satisfactorily for the purpose of testing. (2) ACTFL's position is nonetheless that knowledge of the sociocultural context is essential to language teaching. What ACTFL has since said about the teaching of reading applies as well to the ability to "read" a social situation: "In order to foster true reading, [...] students must have access to the cultural framework in which the work was produced and be guided by the teacher in such a way as to be able to derive this framework from the material itself" (3, p. 10). In other words, reading a text involves knowing or discovering the general patterns of a culture which affect its meaning and which can be derived from social behavior and institutions as well as from literature. The key patterns, in fact, are quite manageable: the major values, habits of thought, and widely shared assumptions about human nature and society.

If it seemed possible in the 1980's to postpone inclusion of the cultural component in the guidelines for proficiency and safe to treat the integration of that component into our language teaching just as a topic for discussion, we no longer can evade the issue in the 1990's. The movement toward nationwide standards, forced by a nationwide inadequacy, makes our handling of this unsolved problem a critical issue not of language learning alone, but also of the nation's ability to solve its epic-scale problems of national cohesion and persuasiveness in international relations.

"But You Can't Get There From Here."

Nonsense! Agreement on the essentials of cultural competence has in fact been developing over the past forty years among the educators who have been concerned about the logical need for it. The task of winning field-wide acceptance is not so much a matter of creating the substance of a consensus. In greater part, it is a problem of broadening participation in it.

The resistance to participation comes not from the reluctance to work hard. Language teachers are delighted at the chance to work their way into the mainstream of American education. Their chief concerns are the fear of the unknown and the fear of regimentation.

The often well-founded fear of not knowing "how to teach the culture" is yielding to the attractive resources that are becoming available. Not only are there workshops, study grants and helpful publications, but students are now communicating internationally by videotape and electronic mail; and in the more advanced countries, databases updated overnight, on line in the U.S., make it possible at a decreasing cost for students and teachers to obtain quickly the exact information they want about a culture area. (For the future successor to the textbook, already in use in teaching the Athenean culture, see page 151, item 19 of the References!)

Less common is a fear of losing the freedom to teach whatever one wants. But that freedom is already limited if one wants the advantages of a team enterprise. And furthermore, we owe it to our students to offer them a coordinated sequence from childhood to college, so that they can accomplish what they rightly expect of the time they spend with us. If the core of the sequence were nationwide, we could relieve the frustration of the many students who move about the country and find their experience of learning a language discouragingly incoherent.

Some nationwide centralization is not necessarily bad. In France, for example, determined individualists take a great deal of local freedom and initiative within a centralized program of education and examination whose effect on the quality of education we must admire. The danger in our case is that we may settle for a niggardly common core of education, by reason of our culture's pervasive focus on short-term, material results. The student who is unmotivated in the absence of a materialistic expectation is the victim of the same unduly limited goal in life as the scion of the privileged elite for whom "incentive" means only financial reward. We run the risk of defining basic education too narrowly, aiming at the productivity that will be profitable for an employer but neglecting the long-term character development including the competence and the commitment to support enlightened national and foreign policies.

The needed common core can—and it must—leave much classroom and homework time free for both local diversity and individual variation. A semester-long project adopted by a class produces enthusiastic motivation to learn to communicate in a second language, but it makes any uniform testing impossible except at long intervals. As for individual variation, the awareness among educators that learning must become learner-centered is as strong a force in the present reform movement as the awareness that American education needs more substance.

Diversity of approach is also imposed by the distinctive developmental tasks of the different age levels. The two components of understanding, "experience of" and "knowledge about," evolve quite independently. In childhood the experience and sociolinguistic performance advance ahead of "knowledge about." Later it is the contrary. Adolescent and adult learners, furthermore, have personal or vocational objectives on which their motivation depends. Many at high-school or college age are interested in one of the forty or more international careers. (25)

The basis for creating a common core starts with the demonstrable fact that a culture is a largely coherent whole, whose coherence results from the fact that its members share some major values and a cognitive grid which filters their perceptions, together with habits of thought and feeling, and habits of interacting with certain social institutions and customs. Equally demonstrable is the fact that all this patterned behavior is influenced by the culture's past, so that understanding of the present members' sense of identity requires knowledge of their history including the achievements they proudly allude to.

But precisely what skills and knowledge are needed for each level of competence in a specific culture—the levels of survival, social relations, vocational effectiveness? Does this sort of competence support the educational objective of openness, tolerance and perspective? And if it does, which level of competence is enough to provide reliable support? All these questions can be answered by research, just as in the case of a language it can be shown that errors of grammar impede communication more severely than do deficiencies of vocabulary.

Cultural competence turns out to comprise three interrelated areas: the sociolinguistic skills required for effective communication (8, 16); knowledge, based on experience, of the generalized features ("regularities") of one observed culture, together with similarly based knowledge of how to observe and analyze any culture; and finally, informed cross-cultural attitudes.

Cultural competence has the same meaning for a teacher as for anyone else. It is quite separate from pedagogical competence: the techniques for imparting one's skill, understanding and enlightenment to others. And while those techniques vary greatly from preschool to graduate-school teaching, the teacher still needs the same adult cultural competence. At each age level, even early childhood, one can impart some elements of an adult understanding, as the psychologist Jerome Bruner has shown. The quality of a teacher's or a parent's understanding inevitably reflects itself in the quality of a young learner's development.

Fortunately, an adult understanding of a culture requires only a manageable part of the vast amount there is to know about a whole culture area. Just as in language the world standard dialect suffices for all unspecialized communication, so it is with culture patterns and social institutions: a common core suffices for all learners except the specialist in some geographical region or socioprofessional milieu, who must add to the common competence in one direction or another. Within a culture area, such as those whose common language is English or Spanish, different nations have differing social institutions which lead of course to different sociocultural systems; yet they share a core of important central patterns, the building blocks of the culture.

Before we come to the building blocks there is a prior question: in this humanistic sector of education, is a testable standard really possible?

The Problem of Evaluation: Aiming at Attitudes Indirectly

This is a prior question first of all because many thoughtful humanists refuse to be a party to a program of nationwide standards if the process of education is to be vitiated, as so easily can happen, by reducing the objective, in practice, to a quiz kid's recall of unconnected facts.

It is a prior question secondly because the proposed objective of openness to other cultures, commitment to tolerance and perspective from outside, are attitudes, as is also, indeed, the all-encompassing enlightenment called for in the Governors' Conference statement. But education cannot aim directly at attitudes without indoctrinating, which is unacceptable.

Attitudes nevertheless can and must be examined, not as direct aims of education but as our means of knowing what the students bring to the interactive process of learning and how they are developing as whole persons. Attitudes can be defined operationally in terms of behavior, so that the real attitudes of a person can be discovered despite the human tendency to paint a virtuous self-portrait. Different instruments can be used in combination, among them Charles Osgood's semantic differential test (9, pp. 149, 390) where one reveals an attitude by choosing between paired adjectives; opinion questions on a 5- or 7-point scale; and the request to pick and describe an experience of a critical incident.[6] The attitudes of small children have been discovered by observing whom they choose to sit beside.

Teaching, testing and curriculum building, to avoid indoctrination, must be aimed at developing the skills or knowledge which enlighten the learner in the process.

The proof of how well the language and sociolinguistic skills have been assimilated is performance: interacting with a bearer of the foreign culture. The ACTFL interview test of the speaking skill inevitably includes cultural elements. The same type of interview, indeed the ACTFL test itself, can therefore yield a separate score for the sociolinguistic skills, based on a sampling of critical components such as the formal vs. informal ways of speaking and behaving, sensitivity to the social status of one's interlocutor, and the nonverbal factors that make for ease and rapport with an interlocutor.

There are indeed grave dangers to be overcome. Not only the general "washback" problem, the tendency to teach for the test and neglect everything but the illustrative details given in a syllabus, but a particular tendency of language teachers as they apply the ACTFL *Proficiency Guidelines*. A majority, as Claire Kramsch observes, have given proficiency "a distressingly functional, reductivist interpretation" which contributes little to the educational development of students. ACTFL and indeed all of us have neglected the connection between proficiency and the educational objective of understanding. The discussion of nationwide standards for *education* gives the opportunity to focus attention squarely on that relationship.

The danger of narrow interpretation appears in the way the supporting knowledge is taught and tested. Our teaching tends to neglect an essential process: simply to ask, as one comes upon a curious manifestation of a culture in social behavior or the arts, What pattern of the culture can explain this? What makes it significant? When knowledge of a culture is approached in this spirit of inquiry, even "objective" tests can then probe understanding, as indeed they can test critical thinking in any field where the examinee has sufficient background.

At least two kinds of test item can combat the danger of reductivism. The first is a type of multiple-choice question currently being developed at the Educational Testing Service by a perceptive humanist, Denise Asfar, with the help of consulting teachers: a type of question where the choice among proposed explanations of an act involves knowing a culture pattern, such as those collected in the Appendix. The second type of question asks for the ramifications of an act, a law, a position taken, so that answers can be graded 1, 2, or 3 according to a widening range of comprehension. Some experimenters are even inquiring whether this kind of question can be adapted to the multiple-choice format. If it turns out, however, that this purpose can be served only by an essay question which requires grading, it would still be well worth the expense. For the prospect of just one such question on a test motivates teachers and students alike to approach raw facts with an inquiring mind, indeed with increasing awareness that "facts are fuzzy around the edges."

There is a third reason why the feasibility of acceptable testing is a prior question. A nationwide standard cannot be applied unless it is first expressed in terms of operational definitions: not the elegant expression a humanist would like, in the form of generalized ideas, but in the form of particularized descriptions of what the person is able to do. It remains true, even so, that a part of the testing can deal with ideas. For the common core has to include those major values, habits of mind and assumptions which confer significance upon the concrete manifestations of a culture in behavior, institutions and works of art. Those abstract patterns are building blocks for understanding a culture, just as much as are the concrete facts.

The Building Blocks of Cultural Competence

For the purposes of a nationwide standard—namely teaching, curriculum building and testing—we need to define operationally the minimum "critical mass" of examined experience that will support the objective of basic education, tentatively proposed to be openness to other cultures, commitment to tolerance, and perspective on one's own culture. Research will have to find the minimum level.

While we await this extensive and expensive research, syllabi that have been revised over the years in several states lay a basis, provisory but empirical in a real sense, for choosing and sequencing cross-cultural learning experiences. Among these state "curriculum guides" that of Indiana, for example, is particularly explicit on the development of cultural competence. (11)

Most useful for a nationwide standard are the ACTFL levels of language proficiency. ACTFL benefitted by some 50 years of experience in the Interagency Language Roundtable (ILR) of the U.S. Government, which sets the qualifications for sensitive international positions and rates candidates on a scale of 0 to 5. In consultation with the ILR and a parallel British source, ACTFL adapted that scale for school use, subdividing the ILR 0 and 0⁺ into "Novice—Low, —Mid, —High"; ILR 1 becomes "Intermediate," and so on. (2) The top of the scale is the proficiency of the "educated native speaker," i.e., one with a secondary-school education. The top level of cultural competence is best named simply "Optimal," because the typical native often knows less about some parts of the culture area than the outsider needs to know, and also because the outsider cannot imitate native childhood experiences, the unconscious use of facial muscles, and the like.

The ACTFL proficiency standards will be truer to reality when the cultural dimension is again taken into account, for despite the effort to isolate language proficiency from culture, all four of the language skills involve cultural competence—the receptive skills (listening comprehension and reading) as well as the productive ones (speaking and writing). The meaning of a "message" cannot be separated from the intent of the sender, nor from the grid in the mind of the receiver. Neglect of this fact results in miscommunication and misinterpretation, and here research in Arabic and others of the less-taught languages has taken the lead.

The minimum standard of cultural competence will most likely fall within the level of survival competence, which ACTFL divides into three thresholds: "Intermediate—Low, —Mid, or —High." But wherever the minimum falls we should be ready with a definition of the next higher level, for no one is happy with the well-known tendency of a required minimum to become a maximum. Certainly a sequence stretching from preschool to high school, profiting from the child's ability to imitate speech effortlessly, can well reach a level which serves the purposes of basic education more than minimally. And since some students bring to school backgrounds of intolerance, more than the minimum may be good social insurance for the future.

The language teaching profession is concerned with the two subsequent levels as professional standards, one for beginning teachers and one for the fully qualified. The American Association of Teachers of French (AATF) has drawn upon ACTFL's "Advanced" level, "limited social competence," for the competence it calls "Basic"; and as a "Superior" standard for the fully qualified teacher, the AATF has adapted the "working social and vocational competence" which ACTFL also labels "Superior." (1) For the cultural component of each professional standard, the AATF has adapted to French culture the basic building blocks presented here in the Appendix, as the closest present approximation toward the future research-based norms for the ACTFL levels.

Sociolinguistic ability is the easiest of the cultural material to correlate with the language levels, since oral proficiency cannot do without it.

Knowledge of the culture is also a part of competence for the language tasks at each level, but the timing of its acquisition may not match the timing of language acquisition. With young learners the knowledge must be postponed, while for adults, learning becomes more efficient if the related cultural knowledge accompanies or even precedes practice in oral communication. "Related" means knowledge that the outsider is likely to need, such as social taboos, or that can be used to help in establishing rapport, such as major values or references to history.

Attitudes, too, contribute to successful rapport; so much so, in fact, that a person who radiates a general goodwill can create a warm social relationship with no more than the gestural equivalent of small talk. But specific attitudes do not correlate at all with the ACTFL levels, defined by tasks and the skills and knowledge they require. So unless research finds otherwise, one can only recommend that from the earliest level possible, priority be given to whatever experiences and knowledge will produce the ability to identify with a second culture and so will support the intercultural objective of basic education. In the Appendix, the most elementary intercultural attitudes have been placed tentatively at the Intermediate—Low level, the probable minimum.

The last major aspect of cultural competence, methods for observing and analyzing a culture, refuses entirely to attach to the succession of levels.

First, there is no counterpart in the language skills, since methods of language learning have not been included in the instruction. Secondly, this sort of enlightenment involves examining the experience of discovering and interpreting evidence, a process of reflection which is possible only for older learners, after the early age when the experience itself comes the most easily. A minimum of this sort of knowledge is tentatively assigned to Intermediate-Low, and all the rest is relegated to the "Advanced" level, "limited social competence," which certainly involves a critical approach to all the forms of unevenly reliable information one receives about a culture.

Now you might like just to look down into the quarry of building blocks. It begins on page 153.

The Critical Implications for Curriculum Design and Teaching

The intercultural essential for a modern basic education leads to several guiding principles for language education.

The first is to exploit the potential interplay between the culture and its language and literature. (21) But is it practicable to teach both language and culture in the limited time available? That limitation is not inexorable when it can be shown that a language is more than a "tool subject" or a spare set of equivalent symbols. Where a language course has been limited to less than five class hours a week, one university department has obtained an additional contact hour as "culture lab." But the great potential resource lies in student motivation.

The curiosity of today's students about different ways of life is a powerful means of arousing interest in a second language and literature. Their heightened motivation makes learning more spontaneous and therefore more effective. Their satisfying achievement then builds support for longer courses of study which overcome the constraint of time.

Language is tiresome to memorize by brute force, but when idiomatic expressions are found to illustrate culture patterns, they become interesting and memory is a by-product. Literature strikes a TV generation as an alien world of print, but it enters the world of the concerns that adolescents passionately discuss among themselves when one inquires into the values a people's literature conveys.

Language and literature, in turn, make ideas about cultures come alive. (8, 10, 20, 22) Any great novel illustrates the precept—so important for combating the tendency to overgeneralize about "national traits"—that there are three distinct levels of generalization, all useful in their place: about humanity, about a particular culture or subculture, and about unique individuals.

Anthropological linguistics, too, can illustrate this salutary precept. At the top level, humanity as a whole differs from other creatures in that we use symbols, i.e., signs that have multiple referents. (Other creatures are limited cognitively to signals: signs with a single referent). At the level where we generalize about one culture or subculture we are talking about separate sets of symbols, namely languages and dialects. At the bottom level are individual idiolects.

A linguistic insight can be used safely to illustrate the precept of cultural relativism when that idea confronts prejudiced attitudes. A British pronunciation of [o], the [ɛu] ridiculed by Americans as an affectation, can be shown to be a natural, further dissimilation of the already diphthonguized American [δu].[7]

No less important than exploiting the interplay between language and culture is the still controversial principle of teaching *in* the language from the start, including grammar—a near absolute, not only because using the language is the only way to develop communicative competence but for two further reasons. First, grammar has to be discussed in class if cultural insights are to make it interesting. (Students unprepared for language analysis will not waste time learning the terminology twice; and all the sciences require teaching a far more elaborate nomenclature.) Secondly, the student's self-identification with the second culture (12, Chapter 15), which is essential to the intercultural objective, requires a consistent mind-set of living and thinking in the language. The objective is completely frustrated by the common student assumption, "This language is for exercises. I think in my own language."

The imperative of self-identification leads to another controversial position: that the contrastive approach, inherent in the human mind, needs to be played down as far as possible until students are convinced that the foreign way of life, as well as theirs, makes sense in its own terms. Otherwise the "We do this, they do that" confirms their suspicion that the foreign way departs in all directions from *the* culture that makes sense. This is why elements of a foreign culture taken out of context strike students as "weird."

A fourth principle, study abroad, is fortunately not controversial, and it takes on much greater importance in the light of the self-identification problem. When a student has reached at least survival competence (preferably ACTFL Intermediate—High, ILR 1+), living in the culture area can rapidly build the critical mass of examined experience. The opportunity to observe and participate will be the most conducive to that result if the student has learned how to use organizing concepts such as the culture's major values.

A neglected pedagogical principle, the arrangement of learning experiences in progressive cycles, applies to understanding a culture and likewise to acquiring the conceptual tools for observing and analyzing cultures. The mass of experience involved will not really be assimilated until curricular planning produces long, coordinated sequences from preschool to college. This sort of coordination, revolutionary for American education, is now being pioneered by the Academic Alliances.[5]

To cope with the problem of influencing attitudes without indoctrinating we apparently have only two pedagogical principles: for the early age levels, to teach by example, and later, to discuss matters of verifiable fact such as the effects of tolerance and intolerance.

A final principle relates to the world context that becomes necessary if the examined experience of one culture is to contribute to a multicultural perspective. Even the study of a European culture can free us from our traditional fixation upon the Western sector of the globe, if the European country is placed in the context of the history of colonization, the cultures that have been colonized, the impact of world trade, immigration, the development of intergovernmental agencies, and the country's present relations with the Third World. Americans can learn a great deal from the greater sensitivity of a European country such as France to the ominous problems of the Third-World whose living standards, averaging the best with the worst, continue to decline by 1% a year despite three years of UN goals for its improvement.[8] Co-curricular experiences and resource materials, such as periodicals in the language, can reinforce the curriculum's cyclical insistence on this broad context, and horizontal coordination, particularly with the social studies, is as urgent as the vertical coordination of the language and culture sequence. Outreach to the surrounding curriculum can make languages much less foreign to it.

Critical Implications for Teacher Education and Self-Development

Undergraduate and graduate courses in language and literature should demonstrate the interplay of language and culture. In addition, the future teacher—indeed anyone who aims even at the Intermediate level—needs to study, at a minimum, the history and contemporary institutions of a major part of the culture area. (4, 21) In the case of French, the historian David Pinkney and this author found successful a team-taught undergraduate course on "The Making of Contemporary France," which each week traced the development of one theme from as far back as necessary to its present state: regional populations, centralization, the revolutionary tradition, two colonial empires and their outcome, industrialization, urbanization, education, the status of women... Lectures had to be in English for a mixed class of history and French students, but the reading and a discussion section were available in French.

The device of team teaching can similarly enable a present faculty to teach the history of a colonial power's interaction with the Third World. And if fully qualified teachers team with teaching assistants, a university can improve the meagre education in the humanities presently dispensed to many language students.

Research experience is valuable for any creative person, and a student at the "Advanced" level, through a team project or with some guidance, can have the satisfaction of participating in a significant venture. An example of a topic of manageable scope is a study of the values embedded in a literary work. Many such studies are needed.

At the Superior level, one can play a role as a specialist on one of the pioneering interdisciplinary teams, either in the field of describing a culture, in that of defining and evaluating cultural competence (6), or in one of the fields involving the humanities and the arts.

In-service courses, seminars, workshops and professional meetings are all useful as part of a plan of self-education. But one can also be more self-dependent, observing methodically and taking notes in the culture area, and reading such things as are marked • among the References below, beginning with any that strike one's interest. After all, no one in the first generation of cultural stonecutters ever took a course on the subject. There was none. Today, with much better resources available, one need not fear the effect of one's unskilled labor on such self-education.

Critical Questions For Research

Everyone wants educational policy to be based on accurate knowledge wherever questions of fact are involved. The most critical questions are these.

1. What are the tasks that characterize each level of competence defined in the Appendix?

For each of the commonly taught languages and cultures, the tasks need to be defined by questioning Americans about the problems they have encountered as tourists, students or interns, business representatives or diplomats in the language community, and by analyzing the reactions of persons in the host country to such visitors. Research-based composite or "generic" norms can then make research more efficient in countries where there are fewer researchers.

2. What sociolinguistic abilities, knowledge and attitudes correlate with success in the tasks at each level?

Good beginnings have been made, first by the Foreign Service Institute, the Defense Language Institute and the Educational Testing Service. The California Foreign Language Competency Project chaired by Professor Marjorie Tussing of California State University at Fullerton has included "Sociolinguistic Appropriateness" as one of seven components of "Accuracy" in its definition of proficiency levels. The Council of Europe, taking the functional/notional approach which targets situations that particular students may expect to encounter, has identified the vocabulary and knowledge required for the situations selected.

3. What parts of cultural competence call for special attention to teaching strategies?

Research by Kraemer (18, p. 13) indicates that particular difficulty arises from conflict with the learner's presuppositions, e.g., that an American "decision maker" is free of cultural conditioning. What conflicting presuppositions do students in a given school or college bring to the interactive process of education?

4. What points of consensus emerge from the relevant articles in the refereed journals, in ERIC, etc., as to the importance and the nature of the cultural component, including literature, for the study of foreign languages? Should a similar survey be undertaken of attitudes in the profession as a whole?

5. Assuming the objectives of understanding and critical thinking, what kinds of instructional unit and test item best develop the capacity to relate facts to one another, to organizing and explanatory concepts, and to new situations?

Kraemer comments (18, p. 8) that "The purpose of the exercise is to develop the participant's ability to recognize a great variety of manifestations of these cultural influences, not just the few which appear in the excerpts."

6. What structure best facilitates the application of knowledge about a culture and society to new situations? (Cf. the quote on p. 12 of item 3.)

Assuming the research-based principle that organized knowledge is the best retained, what structure will best help the learner to organize knowledge about cultures as it expands? Since the structure of the sociocultural system itself is more true to reality than any we arbitrarily impose, one logical approach is to relate the diverse surface manifestations, as they occur in teaching, to the "main themes" of the culture, following the anthropologist Morris Opler, namely the value system with its underlying habits of mind and assumptions. The surface manifestations of a sociocultural whole can be organized in an inventory under a cultural and a social subsystem, following the sociologist Talcott Parsons. (24) Research may discover a better structure, but meanwhile we are not at a loss for one that works.

Only a part of the questions of fact will have to be established by research. But even so, it is evident that we are confronted by a cost so great that we cannot afford multiple inventions of the wheel. Replications of some research will of course be needed, but any wasteful duplication must be avoided through national and also international coordination. Here we are fortunate indeed that an international network of databases makes it possible for the first time to find out what research has already been done anywhere in the world. The same databases will enable teachers and students themselves to find answers to questions about a country, even teaching materials made for native students, to meet needs that until now it has been quite impossible to satisfy.

Let the Case Rest

— But let not those of us rest who teach a language and culture! For on us depends a critical issue of American education: whether its intercultural breadth will have a deep enough infrastructure to withstand the endemic forces that thus far have been more than a match for it.

Notes

1. Evidence of the general concern shows also at the state level: by 1989, eight of the states had passed laws enabling them to take control of a solvent school district on grounds of educational inadequacy. *The New York Times*, 5 October, 1989, p. A 1.

2. *The New York Times*, 1 October, 1989, p. E 22, col. 5.

3. *Ibid.*, 8 October, 1989, quoted by Albert Shanker, p. E 7.

4. *Ibid.*, 1 October, 1989, p. E 22, cols. 1, 5.

5. Academic Alliances in Foreign Languages and Literatures, School/ College Faculty Collaboratives. Marymount College, P.O. Box 1368, Tarrytown, N.Y. 10591-3796. Publishes a bulletin, *Collaborare.*

6. A test combining these approaches is exemplified in the *Manuel du professeur* of item 25.

7. In the International Phonetic Alphabet, [ϵ] represents the open e in *pet* (except where it rhymes with *pay it*); [δ] represents the open o in *more* (except where it rhymes with *mower, mow*, or *mar*).

8. *The New York Times*, 5 November 1989, p. E 2.

References

The symbol • indicates particularly interesting reading.

1. AATF (American Association of Teachers of French). "The Teaching of French: A Syllabus of Competence. The Report of the Commission on Standards." *AATF National Bulletin* 14 (Special Issue, October), 1989.

2. ACTFL (American Council on the Teaching of Foreign Languages). *Provisional Proficiency Guidelines.* Hastings-on-Hudson [subsequently Yonkers], N.Y.: ACTFL, 1982. *Guidelines* [the cultural component omitted pending further research]. *Ibid.*, 1986.

3. _____. Faculty Workshop on the Use of Authentic Texts to Develop Cultural Understanding in Foreign Language Programs. *Ibid.*, 1987.

4. Allen, Wendy W. "Toward Cultural Proficiency." *Northeast Conference [on the Teaching of Foreign Languages] Reports,* (1985): 137-166. (Bibliography, 165-166.)

5. Boyer, Ernest L. "For Education: National Strategy, Local Control." *The New York Times*, 26 September, 1989: A19.

150 / Critical Issues in Foreign Language Instruction

6. Byrnes, Heidi. "Proficiency [test results] as a framework for research in second language acquisition." *Modern Language Journal* 71 (1987): 44-49.
7. • Carroll, Raymonde. *Evidences invisibles: Américains et Français au quotidien.* Paris: Seuil, 1987. Translated as *Cultural Misunderstandings: The French-American Experience.* Chicago: University of Chicago Press, 1988. Narrates and analyzes interesting situations at the points of conflict between two historically close and relatively similar cultures.
8. • Crawford-Lange, Linda M., & Dale Lange. "Doing the Unthinkable in the Second-Language Classroom: A Process for the Integration of Language and Culture." In Theodore V. Higgs, ed. *Teaching for Proficiency, the Organizing Principle.* Lincolnwood, IL.: National Textbook Co., 1984, pp. 139-177. ACTFL Foreign Language Education Series. Maintains that culture is a process in which language and culture interact; examines the relation to general and global education.
9. • Damen, Louise. *Culture Learning: The Fifth Dimension in the Classroom.* Reading, Mass.: Addison-Wesley, 1987. Second-Language Professional Library. An imaginative treatment of the basic topics enables one to browse in intriguing yet instructive byways: the *-Emic* vs. *-Etic* modes of cultural description; separating the social from the cultural; the Sapir-Whorf hypothesis; cultural identity; Lévi-Strauss and myth; cross-cultural research; culture shock; techniques of cultural training.
10. Gaudiani, Claire. *Strategies for the Development of Foreign Language and Literature Programs.* N.Y.: Modern Language Association of America, 1984. A well-rounded guide to department development and curriculum building. Clifford Adelman writes on "Language Study and the New Reform in General Education," Howard L. Nostrand on "The Fifth Language Skill: Understanding the Culture," and the editor's final chapter is "A Case for the Study of Literature in Foreign Languages".
11. *A Guide to Proficiency-Based Instruction in Modern Foreign Languages for Indiana Schools: Generic Competencies, Levels I-IV.* Lorraine A. Strasheim & Walter H. Bartz (eds.). Indianapolis, Indiana 46204: Indiana Public Schools, 1986. Proposes learning outcomes and instructional scenarios for nine areas of activity or discussion. Supplemental volumes elaborate the plan for individual languages, including Latin.
12. • Hall, Edward T. *Beyond Culture.* Garden City, N.Y.: Anchor Press/Doubleday, 1976. This perceptive anthropologist's contribution of tool concepts—here, chiefly "high and low context cultures," "monochronic and polychronic time"—would have won acceptance quite apart from his engaging style of presentation. Chapter 15 is devoted to the subject of self-identification.
13. • ____. *The Dance of Life: The Other Dimension of Time.* Garden City, N.Y.: Anchor Press/ Doubleday, 1983. "...time as culture, how time is consciously as well as unconsciously formulated, used, and patterned in different cultures." (p. 3) Among the cultural differences is the synchronizing of rhythm between interacting persons. A Glossary, pp. 209-213, defines many of Hall's tool concepts.
14. • ____. *The Hidden Dimension.* Garden City, N.Y.: Doubleday, 1966. The cultural differences in the conceptualizing of space, including proxemics (personal distancing) and the layout of houses and towns.

15. • _____. *The Silent Language*. Garden City, N.Y.: Doubleday, 1959. This first of his books explored the field of kinesics: gestures and body language.

16. Heny, Frank. "Theoretical Linguistics, Second Language Acquisition, and Language Pedagogy." *The Annals of the American Academy of Political and Social Science. Foreign Language Instruction: A National Agenda*. Richard D. Lambert, Special Editor. March, 1987: 194-210. Explores the interrelations among the three fields, including the sociolinguistic borderland, p. 202 and the footnote references there.

17. Hofstede, Geert. *Culture's Consequences: International Differences in Work-Related Values*. N.Y.: Sage Publications, 1980. This field of applied values shows differences among 40 countries in four basic variables: male dominance, individualism, power distance in interpersonal relations, and tolerance of ambiguity.

18. Kraemer, Alfred J. *Development of a Cultural Self-Awareness Approach to Instruction in Intercultural Communication*. Washington, D.C.: Human Resources Research Organization, 1973. HumRRO Technical Report 73-17. Rigorous experimentation with sensitivity training.

19. • Lambert, Craig. "Optical Disks in the Attic." *Harvard Magazine* (September-October, 1989): 4, 6. Videodisks and CD-ROM now enable a student to call up together the plan of the Acropolis, a view of the Parthenon, Attic vases, and texts of history, literature and mythology, foreshadowing the future of the language and culture textbook.

20. Lange, Dale L. "The Language Teaching Curriculum and a National Agenda," *The Annals...* (see Heny) 70-96. Eminent among the few discussions of the relation of language teaching to the nation's problem of general education.

21. Lehmann, Winifred P., and Randall L. Jones. "The Humanistic Basis of Second Language Learning." *The Annals...* (see Heny): 186-193. "The need to teach language in relation to social and cultural values affects educational choices with respect to curriculum, materials, and approaches and should be central to national planning and programs for professional development and the improvement of teaching." p. 186.

22. Lewald, H. Ernest. "Theory and Practice in Culture Teaching on the Second-Year Level in French and Spanish." *Foreign Language Annals* 7 (1984): 660-67. A last contribution from a reformer of this critical course.

23. Nostrand, Howard L. "Authentic Texts and Cultural Authenticity: An Editorial." *Modern Language Journal* 73 (1, Spring, 1989): 49-52. Argues that unless a student is enabled to see a text or situation against its authentic cultural background, the authenticity is lost.

24. _____. "The 'Emergent Model' (Structured Inventory of a Sociocultural System) Applied to Contemporary France." *Contemporary French Civilization* 2 (1977): 277-294. Based on a reconciliation, explained in an introduction, between the anthropologist Morris Opler's "main themes" description, specific to a given culture, and the sociologist Talcott Parsons' organization of data into subcultures, designed to apply to all sociocultural systems.

25. _____. Frances B. Nostrand & Claudette Imberton-Hunt. *Savoir vivre en français*. N.Y.: John Wiley & Sons, 1988. Presents the major values, habits of mind and prevalent assumptions of one culture area, and relates language to culture in a way suggestive for other languages and cultures. A sociocultural index at the end of the *Culture et communication* volume outlines the references to France, the

      francophone world, methods and concepts for cultural analysis, and international career interests. Would be • if it were in English.

26. Omaggio, Alice C. *Teaching Language in Context: Proficiency-Oriented Instruction.* Boston, Mass.: Heinle & Heinle, 1986. A thorough textbook. Chapter 9, "Teaching for Cultural Understanding," supplements Seelye with historical background and practical materials.

27. Robinson, Gail L. Nemetz. *Crosscultural Understanding.* N.Y.: Pergamon Press, 1985. One of the best discussions relating this concern to language education.

28. • Seelye, H. Ned. *Teaching Culture: Strategies for Intercultural Communication.* Lincolnwood, IL.: National Textbook Co., 1984. The most enjoyable reading on application in the classroom. Chapters 1, 2, and 11 are particularly recommended.

29. • Valdes, Joyce Merrill, ed. *Culture Bound: Bridging the cultural gap in language teaching.* New York, etc.: Cambridge University Press, 1986. Enlightening essays, including one on culture shock.

30. Valette, Rebecca. *Modern Language Testing.* N.Y.: Harcourt Brace Jovanovich. 2d. edition, 1977, pp. 262-281. The best book on testing; has a chapter on the cultural component.

Appendix
The Levels of Cultural Competence

Novice-High (0^+ on the ILR scale)

Sociolinguistic Ability
A person at this lowest level of useful ability
- can accompany a few memorized formulae with appropriate body language (nod, handshake, bow, accolade...), but understands responses only within memorized patterns.
- can be understood, but with difficulty, provided the context defines a single question at issue.
- can convey an attitude of goodwill via tone of voice and nonverbal means.

Knowledge
- understands the official instructions and warnings such as on trains and in parks or public buildings.
- interprets the behavior of interlocutors according to the code of the home culture, consequently misinterprets culture-specific non-verbal cues.
- lacks the knowledge requisite for the survival situations listed below under Intermediate.

Attitudes
- shows considerateness.
- should have one of the abilities listed under each of the three basic attitudes ascribed to Intermediate-Low.

Intermediate-Low "Survival competence" (ILR 1)
Note: Each level includes the abilities listed at all levels below.

Sociolinguistic Ability
A person at this level
- can meet minimal courtesy and travel requirements.
- can be understood by native interlocutors accustomed to such learners, but miscommunication is frequent.

Knowledge of the Culture Area
- can describe one major value, one common assumption about human nature or society, and one habit of mind, such as the way of establishing rapport for business.
- can manipulate the currency.
- can place on an outline map some main landmarks and sectors of one city in the culture area.

Knowledge of Cultural Analysis (24, 25)
- can describe and apply the following methods and concepts:
  observation of the culture, direct and remote through pen, tape and video pals, electronic mail, sister city relations; the complementary roles of inside and outside observers (25, pp. 29, 294-304).
  observation of differences among subcultures-regional, socioeconomic, and by age groups.

Attitudes (28 Chapter 11)
Openness to other cultures:
- shows curiosity about discovering similarities and differences between cultures, e.g., by the response to a question why some foreign custom may have arisen, or, to an inquiry concerning the ethnic heritage of an associate.
- can illustrate the proposition that the second culture makes sense in its own terms, by relating a behavior pattern, text or institution to a general value, assumption or habit of mind it exemplifies.
Commitment to tolerance:
- refuses to accept a stereotype as fair description of an ethnic group.
- resists overgeneralizing about "national traits"; e.g., can distinguish among three levels of generalization by classifying proposed statements as pertaining (1) to humanity as a whole, (2) to a culture or subculture, or (3) to individual differences.
Perspective on the home culture:
- shows self-identification with the second culture by being able either to describe a feature he or she would like to adopt, or to defend an apparently undesirable feature as part of a larger picture.
- can give an example of the problem of conforming to the norms of a foreign society while maintaining one's own values and identity.
- can show with examples that one's perceptions and judgments are patterned by one's home culture, and are subject to temporary influences such as the phases of culture shock (29 pp. 35-39).
- asked which of two customs or dialectal pronunciations is the correct one, takes the position that different does not necessarily mean wrong or inferior.
- asked to say whether a certain feature of a foreign culture is good or bad, shows awareness that the answer to such a question is relative to the culture from which one is passing judgment.
- can present objectively some judgments that foreigners make concerning the home country.

Intermediate-Mid (ILR 1⁺)

Sociolinguistic Ability
At this stage, the person
- can resolve three survival-level problems such as the seven listed under Intermediate-High.
- understands all conventional public signs such as P for parking area, and gestures such as thumb and index, or index and next finger, indicating "2."

- comprehends, though may not use, the common unconscious and symbolic gestures and facial expressions of the culture. (For the two kinds of gesture, cf. 25 vol. I, *Culture et communication*, pp. 138-141.)

Knowledge
- can describe three major values, a widespread assumption and a habit of mind, and can recognize these when evident in a text, a social convention or institution.
- can describe several main social conventions, such as those that govern dating, invitations to meals, common formulas for social letters.
- for one country of the language area, can place several main cities and regions on an outline map.
- can say which kinds of shops sell what kinds of merchandise, and knows where to go for information on such subjects.

Attitudes
Same as for Intermediate-Low

Intermediate-High (ILR 1⁺)

Sociolinguistic Ability
A person at this level
- can fulfill with civility all the requirements for survival as a traveler, such as to (1) obtain the information to reach an intended destination via public transportation; (2) secure lodging for the night; (3) order and pay for food and drink; (4) cash a check; (5) make a simple purchase; (6) conduct a simple phone conversation; and (7) take notes on information such as price, location, departure time.
- can explain the terms commonly used in culture-related texts such as menus, wedding or death announcements, and the abbreviations in classified ads.
- prompted by an example, shows awareness that compliments can arouse a reaction different from what would be expected in the home culture.

Knowledge
- can describe half a dozen major values (i.e., about half of the central value system), two habits of mind and two common assumptions, and can recognize manifestations of any of these.

- for one country in the culture area, can say how the country's institutions, regulations, and customs such as attitudes toward behavior and appearance in public, may affect him or her as a foreign traveler (or student, trainee, business person); and can name the official agencies which may hold the foreigner responsible for compliance with the regulations.

Attitudes
Same as for Intermediate-Low

Advanced "Limited social competence" (ILR 2)

Sociolingustic Ability
This person
- can (1) make requests politely; (2) offer and receive gifts and invitations; (3) apologize; (4) make introductions; (5) discuss, for example, a current events or policy, a field of personal interest, a leisure-time activity of one country in the culture area.
- can participate in a conversation if conducted in the standard (not colloquial) language, though may ask to have some expressions repeated or paraphrased.

Knowledge of the Culture Area
- can locate on a world map the main countries or areas where the language studied is the first or second language; can name their capitals, and add a sentence about their society or economy or international situation.
- concerning one country of the culture area, (1) can name the principal present political parties or factions, and (2) can describe two or three contemporary issues; (3) can discuss how the country's historic periods, prominent personalities and cultural achievements affect present attitudes and intergroup relations; (4) can produce a few proverbs or stock expressions which reflect a world view one encounters there.
- can describe the phases of "culture shock" and how they may affect perception. (29 pp. 35-39)
- can identify the truth or untruth implied in the common stereotypes concerning the home culture and one foreign culture.
- can write a simple social letter or a business letter that does not require legal or other technical language, with a beginning and ending appropriate to the given situation, though the style may be obviously foreign; on seeing such a letter, can interpret the evidences of formality or informality.

Knowledge of Cultural Analysis (24, 25)
- can describe and apply the following additional methods and concepts:
  the analysis of conceptions of space (14) and time: the monochronic and polychronic ways of "living" time (13 Index), and the distinction between high-context and low-context cultures (12).
  contrastive analysis-notably the identification of key cross-cultural variables (17), and the analysis of the contact points between cultures (7).

Attitudes
- asked to interpret statistics or an opinion poll, shows a critical approach by asking to know, e.g., the date, the size and composition of the sample, the capability and political orientation of the agency.

Advanced Plus (ILR 2⁺)

Sociolinguistic Ability
Here the person
- can handle any common social situation with an interlocutor accustomed to foreigners.
- can usually detect emotional overtones in speech, but may not detect subjective attitudes in a written text.
- can understand most announcements made over public address systems, gather the gist of a newscast if free to listen intently.
- after specific preparation, can grasp the main points of a lecture and take notes.

Knowledge
- almost always interprets reading correctly, reads between the lines, but may not appreciate stylistic nuances.
- for one country, can write on the main social institutions in terms of their underlying values and assumptions: for example, (1) the family in relation to the status of women and children; (2) friendship and the bearing of assumptions about outsiders; (3) religion and politics as affected by traditions of totalitarianism or pluralism; (4) the economy in its relation to government, and to the distinction between work and leisure; (5) business relations as affected by the conception of time and space; (6) education and the access to wealth and power; (7) the tastes reflected in the arts (and in the media, in the case of a developed country); (8) ecology and attitudes toward the environment.
- can identify, in a literary or a journalistic text, examples of elevated style and of familiar and popular expressions; and in reading, can point out some of the verbal indications of attitudes, hidden quotations or allusions.

Attitudes
Same as for Advanced.

Superior "Working social and vocational competence" (ILR 3)

Sociolinguistic Ability
The person at this level of competence
- uses cultural references and idioms, comprehends puns; uses the main unconscious and symbolic gestures of the culture (cf. 25 pp. 138-141); interacts with the rhythm of the interlocutor (13) and keeps the proper distance between persons — aspects of "proxemics" (15).
- consistently distinguishes between a formal and an informal way of speaking and behaving. (As an example of formal/informal behavior between speakers: if called upon to simulate meeting an old friend after a lapse of time, can judge whether an accolade, a handshake or a bow is appropriate, depending on the situation, social milieu and ages of the persons.)
- finds comic some culture-related humor: for example, a violation of a cultural value, or an incongruous cultural allusion. In a joking or teasing situation, can explain the danger of offending.

- can describe a type of compliment likely to be misinterpreted or embarrassing in the foreign culture.
- can participate in a formal meeting, an informal discussion where several persons talk at the same time, or as a test, can converse with an interviewer against a background of recorded speech.
- can infer the underlying intent of a speaker from what is said, or as a test, can draw this inference by reading between the lines of a written dialogue.
- can discuss abstractions, in fields of prior study such as a vocation, a hobby, an aspect of one country of the culture area: its main institutions, social stratification and mobility, the place of private organizations and unions, informal customs, sex- and age-group differences, *and* current cultural and social changes.
- can point out nuances of written style, but cannot vary writing style to fit accurately a variety of styles or audiences.

Knowledge
- can write three or four substantial paragraphs on an aspect of one additional country or region of the culture area. In the case of a developed country, knows the point of view of a few current political figures and periodicals; knows about the electoral procedure, and can describe briefly some recent cultural achievements—in film, song, art, architecture, or literature including TV and cartoon serials. In the case of a developing country, can write on topics such as the status of women, literacy, religious militancy, opposition between subcultures, terrorism, dictatorship, political and economic relations between the Third World and the developed countries. Can list main countries or regions of the culture area (half, in the case of French where there are over forty); can locate them on a map, name their capitals, and add a sentence about their society or economy or international situation.
- can discuss the metaphorical nature and cultural role of myth, a propos of a text in the language, such as an African legend.
- can explain features of the home culture that puzzle an inquirer from the other culture.

Attitudes
Same as for Advanced.

Near-Optimal (ILR 4)

Sociolinguistic Ability
At this level the person
- behaves in such a way as to win acceptance as an outsider equivalent to a bearer of the culture in all respects that matter for social or vocational relations, as evidenced in a simulated situation.
- can describe the institutions of one country, relating them to cultural values and assumptions, as outlined under Knowledge at the Advanced Plus level.
- can fashion writing to fit a variety of styles and audiences.

Knowledge
Same as for Superior.

<u>Attitudes</u>
Same as for Superior.

Optimal (ILR 5)

<u>Sociolinguistic Ability</u>
This person
- behaves in such a way as to permit acceptance into any group or clique in at least one country of the culture area, or as a test, can demonstrate the requisite sociolinguistic features.

<u>Knowledge</u>
- is informed on all the matters listed, plus those which a native typically retains from a secondary education.

<u>Attitudes</u>
Same as for Advanced.

Expanding the Vision
of Foreign Language Education:
Enter the Less Commonly Taught Languages

A. Ronald Walton
University of Maryland

Introduction

Amongst the many trends that have characterized foreign language instruction in the 1980's is the entry of the Less Commonly Taught Languages (LCTLs) into the educational mainstream. According to MLA statistics (Brod, 1988) the highest rates of enrollment growth in the U.S. at the college level are in Japanese (with a 45% enrollment growth between 1983 and 1986) and Chinese (with a 29% growth in the same time period). Walker (1989) has discussed at some length the causes for this new national interest in some of the LCTLs and has presented a rationale for the likelihood of future growth.

To say that the LCTLs, or at least several of them, have entered the mainstream does not mean that their presence is overwhelming. Enrollments in the LCTLs comprise less than 1% of all foreign language enrollments at the K-12 level (Dandonoli, 1987) and approximately 5-8% of total foreign language enrollments in colleges and universities (Brod, 1988). Nevertheless, even this very slight presence on the national scene has created new-found interest in the LCTLs.[1]

The growing presence of three of the LCTLs, Chinese, Japanese and Russian, can be seen as a test-case of what happens and what will happen in the future, as the less commonly taught languages enter an educational domain that has been dominated by the teaching of French, German, and Spanish. It is to the interface of the world of the LCTLs with that of the traditionally taught languages that this paper is addressed. In particular, its purpose is an attempt to foster a deeper understanding of the differences between the teaching and learning of the more and less commonly taught languages. The hope is that such a discussion will promote a smoother entry of the LCTLs into the mainstream and will engender an atmosphere of mutual cooperation between the "old timers" and the "new kids on the block."

Defining the LCTLs

From the perspective of foreign language education in the U.S., the LCTLs could be defined as all languages other than French, German, and Spanish. A crude division of the LCTLs recognizes three subgroups: (1) less commonly taught European languages such as Russian, Italian, Portuguese, and Swedish; (2) higher-enrollment non-Indo-European languages, such as Arabic, Chinese, and Japanese; and (3) lower-enrollment non-Indo-European languages such as Burmese, Indonesian, and Swahili. Obviously, using a single term such as "LCTLs" to define a group of languages so diverse and large is fairly meaningless other than in contrast to French, German, and Spanish. Equally evident is that no single person can characterize the teaching and learning of this enormous range of languages without the danger of overgeneralization.

Thus, this paper will focus mainly on the non-Indo-European languages as defined by subgroups (2) and (3) above. Languages falling within these two subgroups are sometimes termed "Truly Foreign Languages" (TFLs) to distinguish them from languages that are cognate to English, a distinction that is explained in detail below. While the discussion here applies in varying degrees to all TFLs taught in the United States, Chinese and Japanese will be singled out for special attention for several reasons: these languages are currently of high interest nationally; they are among the most difficult LCTLs taught in this country; and the author is familiar with them. Chinese and Japanese will thus serve as interesting representatives of other TFLs taught in the United States.

The Educational Tradition of the TFLs

While the TFLs have never occupied a highly visible position in American foreign language education, they have quietly developed in educational settings since World War II. Over the years the TFLs have evolved their own educational traditions and modes of organization. For the most part, TFL programs have been housed in larger universities (though not exclusively), have been tied to area studies programs, and have focused on the training of area scholars at the graduate level. However, some undergraduate institutions have long traditions in teaching one or another of the major TFLs. In addition, government language training organizations such as the Foreign Service Institute (FSI) and the Defense Language Institute (DLI) have an impressive history in providing instruction in a number of TFLs.

A crucial factor in the development and maintenance of the teaching of the TFLs in academe has been support under Title VI, first of the National Defense Education Act, currently of the Higher Education Act. The latter presently supports the teaching of approximately one hundred and fifty TFLs at the graduate level in over 90 universities and colleges. These funds are primarily used for fellowhips for budding area studies scholars, not for materials development, teacher training, curriculum design, and standardized test development. Other provisions within Title VI, however, do allow competition for modest grants to enhance some TFL development activities. Support from the U.S. Office of Education as well as from private foundations has played a critical role in developing and enhancing the infrastructure that supports on-going language instruction in these languages, though such support is, of course, never seen as adequate by those teaching the TFLs.

For some TFLs there are practically no instructional materials, for some there are materials from the home country of the native-speaking teachers, and for some there are a handful of texts produced by native English-speaking language specialists. In many cases, there are few modern linguistic analyses of the languages available, and for others there are only such analyses, often in the form of handbooks and reference grammars, but no instructional materials per se. For many of the low-enrollment TFLs dictionaries are either outdated or non-existent, and for the higher-enrollment TFLs there is a constant need for improved and updated dictionaries.

A number of the TFLs have teaching associations representing a single language, e.g. The Chinese Language Teachers Association. Others unite professionals who teach languages from a geographical area, e.g. African languages and Southeast Asian Languages. In the latter, a number of often quite different, linguistically unrelated languages are grouped together in a single organization. The National Association of Self-Instructional Language Programs (NASILP), headquartered at Temple University, has for nearly thirty years been instrumental in helping colleges and universities set up self-instructional programs in a wide range of LCTLs.[2]

For those TFLs that are frequently taught, pedagogical traditions have evolved and even become somewhat canonized. In the teaching of Chinese, for example, certain curricular structures, teaching methods, and testing and evaluation procedures are found in most programs, though there is considerable variability in how these are implemented. Likewise, experienced Chinese teachers have identified the pronunciation and grammatical features that present native English-speaking students with the most serious learning problems, and these are routinely discussed in the teaching literature on Chinese.

In sum, the LCTLs do have their own world within American foreign language education: their own history, infrastructure, pedagogical traditions, financial support structures (however weak), and of course, their own problems. However, it is a rather small world compared to that of French, German, and Spanish language instruction and one that operates largely on the fringes of foreign language education as a national endeavor.

Characteristics of the TFLs

The Foreign Service Institute and the Defense Language Institute have both divided the various languages that they teach into four categories based on learning difficulty for native English speakers. Difficulty is measured by the number of instructional contact hours required to reach prescribed levels of proficiency as determined by standardized proficiency tests. Proficiency is rated on a scale of 0 (no functional proficiency) to 5 (the proficiency of an educated native speaker). Category 1 languages, the easiest, include French, German, and Spanish and also languages such as Afrikaans, Norwegian, and Swahili.[3] Category 2 languages include Bulgarian, Farsi, Greek, Hindi, and Indonesian; Category 3 includes such languages as Burmese, Hebrew, Russian, Turkish, and Finnish. Category 4 languages include only Arabic, Chinese, Japanese and Korean.

For a student with average language learning aptitude the FSI experience indicates that to reach a proficiency level of 2 requires 480 contact hours for a Category 1 language such as French, German or Spanish, but 1,320 contact hours for a Category 4 language such as Chinese or Japanese. Assuming an academic Chinese program that alloted 10 contact hours per week at the elementary level, five hours per week at the intermediate level (many programs do not provide nearly so many contact hours at these two levels), and three hours per week at all subsequent levels, 1,320 contact hours would correspond roughly to eight years of academic study in order to reach the 2 proficiency rating. Based on the same contact-hour scheme it would require roughly one and a half years to reach this same level in French.[4]

Interestingly, the four languages most often targeted for mainstreaming these days include three Category 4 languages (Arabic, Chinese, and Japanese) and one Category 3 language, Russian (classified in this paper as an LCTL but not a TFL). What makes learning these languages so time-consuming for native English speakers? For the Category 4 languages there is no doubt that the non-alphabetic writing systems greatly slow the pace of learning, not just because of the complexity of their orthographies but because time spent on mastering the written medium cuts significantly into the time available to work on oral and aural skills.

However, there are learning problems for all the non-Indo-European languages that are rarely encountered in the teaching and learning of French, German, and Spanish. It was just because of such a poor fit between the nature of the traditionally taught languages and the LCTLs that the original ACTFL Generic Proficiency Testing Guidelines were of necessity revised.

The differences between the traditionally taught languages and the TFLs may be divided into at least two broad areas : (1) differences in the linguistic code, which includes the sound system, morphology, grammar, lexicon, discourse features, and   orthographies of a given language and (2) differences in the way that a language is used for interpersonal and interpretive intercultural communication.

Differences in the linguistic code are the most obvious, the most studied, and the most often discussed. The sound systems of various non-Indo-European languages, including such exotica as tones and clicks, can be much more challenging to learners than those of the traditionally taught languages. Morphological systems can contain tortuous morphophonemics; even the definition of the notion "word" may be problematic. Grammar may present not just complex sentence constructions but conceptual schemes for classifying human and material existence which are entirely alien to English speakers. Thus the learner must not only come to see the world or "Reality" in ways quite different from those described by the traditionally taught Indo-European languages, but must also learn to encode this new perception into language use. The honorific system of Japanese and its grammatical encoding in the language code is a typical example. The ways in which discourse is structured in the TFLS is likely to vary significantly from the Indo-European languages as well. The general avoidance of direct orders in Japanese and the tendency in both Chinese and Japanese to avoid direct negatives in response to requests are common examples.[5]

Perhaps the least obvious, least studied, and least discussed differences between Indo- and non-Indo-European languages are those dealing with the way that language is used within social contexts, an area now commonly termed "pragmatics." Leech (1983) recognizes two subsystems within general pragmatics that seem particularly pertinent in characterizing language use in the TFLs: "sociopragmatics," how language is used within the social contexts of a given culture, and "pragmalinguistics," how communicative language use is encoded into the language of the given culture. For the remainder of this discussion the term "pragmatics" will be used to label both of Leech's subsystems. Thus, the term "linguistic code," as noted above, refers to the linguistic systems of a language, such as the sound system and grammar, and pragmatics refers to how this code is used in social contexts.

The gap between the pragmatic systems of the Indo- and non-Indo-European languages can be enormous, so much so that the greatest hurdles facing learners of non-Indo-European languages may be in this realm rather than in that of the linguistic code. The problem is aggravated by the fact that our theoretical understanding of pragmatic systems is still quite rudimentary when compared to the rich and ever evolving theories and accumulated knowledge of the linguistic code. Yet, in teaching the non-Indo-European languages, every facet of instruction—dialogue study, drills, communicative use, the interpretation of texts, teaching style—is permeated with the reality of significant differences between the pragmatic systems of English and related languages and those of the various TFLs.

The Role of Culture in Teaching the TFLs

Hammerly (1982) divides the teaching of culture in the context of foreign language instruction into three categories: Achievement Culture, Informational Culture and Behavioral Culture. The first is associated with the features of "High Culture" (history, the arts, literature, for example), and the second with facts about a given culture or country (geography, political system). Hammerly's third category, Behaviorial Culture would seem to include the conventions for interpersonal communication or pragmatics.[6] With regard to the latter category, study of the TFLs involves much more than knowing, for example, that the Japanese bow upon introduction or that they exchange their shoes for slippers when entering the house. This third category fits somewhat with the notion of intercultural pragmatics discussed above and focuses on what should and should not be said in particular social interactions, which topics should and should not be discussed, and how topics and discourse should be tailored depending on the social status and the familiarity of the interlocutors, among other factors.

In the teaching and learning of the TFLs, it is quite clear that pragmatics ideally drives mastery of the linguistic code and that an enormous amount of attention must be devoted to the mastery of the particular TFL's pragmatic system from the first moment of instruction. In Japanese, for example, even to learn how to say "good morning," "thank you," and the usual classroom expressions (for example "please repeat") requires learners to understand that there are quite different grammatical forms for expressing these simple notions that depend on the social status of the speaker and the addressee and on their familiarity with one another: there is no single form for expressing such utterances, for there is no such thing as socially neutral speech in Japanese.

The pragmatic systems of various TFLs can be so different from that of English that it is even challenging to learn how to speak pragmatically appropriate English to members of these cultures who speak English as a second language. For example, a useful technique in preparing business-people who cannot devote the necessary time to study Chinese and Japanese would be to teach them how to speak English to a Chinese official or Japanese businessperson who speaks English. Well-trained and experienced teachers of Japanese understand that for an American high school student of Japanese, learning how to speak pragmatically appropriate English to an English-speaking Japanese will be a greater challenge than learning the Japanese sound system or the symbols of the Japanese syllabary.

Such a needed emphasis on pragmatics in the TFLs contrasts sharply with much of the literature on the teaching of culture in the European languages. For instance, the articles in the 1988 Northeast Conference volume, *Toward a New Integration of Language and Culture*, seem to place almost equal emphasis on the teaching of Achievement Culture, Informational Culture and Behavioral Culture. In teaching a Category 4 TFL such as Chinese or Japanese the complexity of the language itself—the linguistic code and the pragmatic system—is so great and the instructional time so valuable that there is simply no time to attempt a systematic introduction to thousands of years of Achievement and Informational Culture. A less systematic introduction to such elements of culture is likely to be a waste of time and may end up simply degenerating into the presentation of the very stereotypes regarding these cultures that one wishes to eradicate rather than reinforce.

Given the richness and complexity of these civilizations, in additition to the American student's total lack of familiarity with them, it becomes imperative that features of Chinese and Japanese civilization not directly related to Behavioral Culture be taught in separate courses, one obvious rationale for the traditional area studies model. Moreover, since mastery of the languages proceeds slowly, there is little likelihood that using the target language to teach about the civilization will be a viable process at the undergraduate level, certainly not nearly as effective as presenting such information in English.

The complexity and subtlety of the pragmatic systems of the TFLs likewise have serious implications for teaching methodologies and pedagogical practice generally. Many of the procedures common to instruction in the European languages are of questionable value in teaching the TFLs and may even be pedagogically harmful. For example, it is fairly standard practice in the teaching of European languages for students to practice speaking the target language to one another. Since the goal of language instruction is to prepare students to undertake intercultural communication, such practice may well encourage learners to continue using the English pragmatic system, though using it with the target language linguistic code. In fact, it is exactly the unlearning of the English (and broadly speaking, Indo-European language) pragmatic system that proves more challenging than mastering a new linguistic code. Since learners can assume that practically nothing in the English pragmatic system will transfer to communication with members of a TFL culture, and since the purpose of instruction is largely geared to acquiring this new pragmatic system, premature emphasis on students' speaking to one another in the target language must be seen for what it is, not intercultural communication, but "same culture" communication with a different linguistic code.

The same might be said of native English-speaking instructors teaching such languages as Chinese and Japanese in the classroom. This again is "same culture" communication, and while native English speakers may be competent in the target language code, they will never be authentic bearers of the pragmatic system, for they simply are not native Chinese or Japanese. This is revealed clearly in the differences between the classroom teaching styles of native and non-native teachers of Chinese and Japanese. Particularly noteworthy are the different reactions and attitudes of these two types of teachers regarding communication with English-speaking learners.

For the native-speaking teacher, classroom discussions of certain topics such as sex, death, and what might be seen as "negative features" of the culture (for example, the fact that Chinese rarely form lines but crash forward onto buses or toward service windows and counters) can be seen as inappropriate or even embarrassing. Such cultural phenomena are likely to be approached with a great degree of indirectness, even avoidance. Quite often, native speakers of Chinese and Japanese are not even aware of the very cultural and communicative features that foreigners regard as the most challenging and problematic.

However, a native English-speaking teacher of Japanese is quite unlikely to "feel" such embarrassment instinctively when communicating with American learners and may approach the discussion of such topics with the candor characteristic of an American mind-set: that is, there will not be the emotional, even chemical response of the genuine native speaker to such common teacher reactions as disappointment, disapproval, evasiveness, anger, frustration, approval, encouragement, surprise, patience, and urgency. Thus, since non-native teachers will not intuitively provide authentic pragmatic responses, the student will not be properly prepared for authentic intercultural communication with native speakers. The instructional process simply loses validity if it is not geared to genuine intercultural communication. A great fear in the teaching of the TFLs is that a learner will excel in the linguistic code, thus increasing native speaker expectations about the foreigner's control of the pragmatic system, but will fail in the pragmatic domain, thus creating more damage in intercultural situations than if the student were poor in both domains.

Issues related to authentic intercultural communication in the classroom also arise in oral proficiency testing. It is common practice in the traditional languages for both tester and student to be American. If the purpose of the test is to gauge the learner's ability to conduct intercultural communication, can there be any test validity when a member of one culture judges another member of the same culture? This is not a test of intercultural communicative ability but rather of "same culture" communicative ability. Surely a genuine test of intercultural communication must require the judgments of one who represents the target culture. Oral testing by native speakers of the target language is standard procedure in the long history of government-program language testing (e.g. at FSI and DLI).

The present emphasis in foreign language teaching on communicative competence is often described as a process of teaching students to negotiate meaning. What remains in the shadows is just what the negotiation process really represents when native English speaking students are negotiating meaning with one another or with a native English speaking teacher. They are indeed negotiating "meaning" if this refers to the process of using the linguistic code of the target foreign language, but it is difficult to understand how they are negotiating meaning across different cultures if they are members of the same culture. For the TFLs it is the negotiation of meaning across different cultures that should form the heart of the instructional process, for we are supposedly educating our students to interact successfully with members of another culture, not our own.

In sum, if in the traditional languages there is a constant attempt to try to figure out how to merge knowledge of culture with the teaching of the linguistic code, in the TFLs there is an equal amount of effort directed at how to constrain the teaching of culture, to off-load the teaching of Achievement and Informational Culture, and at the same time to insure that the teaching of Behavioral Culture will dominate the instructional process.

Pedagogical Practice in the TFLs

Two models of pedagogical practice seem to dominate foreign language instruction in the United States, that of the Indo-European languages and that of English as a Second Language (ESL). Some hints have already been presented that the former model may in many respects be inappropriate for the TFLs. ESL pedagogical practice, as developed and valuable as it is in the sphere of research and innovation, also meshes poorly with many facets of teaching and learning the TFLs. For example, ESL textbooks are invariably written in English, the target language of the learner. A student of Chinese or Japanese who could read textbook instructions and grammatical explanations in these languages would have to be, at a minimum, at the level 2 proficiency in reading, a goal that may well require the estimated 1,320 hours of instruction discussed earlier. English is alphabetic. ESL students have often been studying English since the seventh grade (or earlier) in their home countries. ESL students live in the target culture and can use the language daily for real communication. Many ESL students may wish to integrate into American culture (a real possibility in a pluralistic society), and quite a few ESL students are mastering academic English for study at an American university.

In contrast, Chinese and Japanese are not alphabetic languages and from the foreign learner's viewpoint the spoken and written media are like two unrelated languages. Unlike the case so often found in EFL/ESL where students can read English with some facility but arrive in the U.S. unable to speak it well, reading in Chinese and Japanese by foreigners is likely to come well after spoken ability and with great difficulty at that. Lengthy exposure to the non-phonetic or quasi-phonetic writing systems of Chinese and Japanese is less likely to contribute to development of oral and aural skills as is the case in studying languages with alphabetic writing systems. American students, unlike their ESL counterparts, are unlikely to have had any exposure to a TFL prior to college. Moreover, American students rarely study in Chinese and Japanese universities and thus do not seek such specialized and focused training, nor are they likely to desire to integrate into these cultures as their ESL colleagues might desire to fit into American society. In any case, such integration is highly unlikely in cultures where foreigners are forever seen as foreigners regardless of linguistic or pragmatic skills.

In addition, the ESL model generally does not follow the practice of systematically contrasting the learner's language and culture with the English language and with American culture. Indeed, ESL classes may well have members of a number of different cultures and such a procedure would place impossible burdens on ESL teachers. However, in teaching the TFLs, where the learners are essentially a homogenous cultural and linguistic group, contrast is inevitable and moreover highly efficient. This is particulary true of what Ellis (1985) terms "contrastive pragmatics." Assuming that one learns the new in terms of the known, the teaching of intercultural pragmatics requires that learners be made aware of their native pragmatic system as a way of modifying this system to fit in the new and quite different pragmatic system of a TFL.

The reason for mentioning the traditional-language and ESL models is that many foreign language educators seem to believe that teaching in the TFLs is somehow still dominated by audio-lingualism. For example, it is standard practice in much of the teaching of TFLs to have students work with dialogues for mastery and to devote considerable time to mechanical drills prior to communicative activities. The stress on dialogue mastery, where the dialogues have been properly designed (unfortunately not always the case) comes from the fact that they are ideal for presenting the highly contrastive pragmatic system of the TFL. Situated speech is everything. Moreover, the complexities of the sound, grammatical, and morphological systems are such that a great deal of work on just mechanics is a prerequisite for communicative practice.

The emphasis on inductive learning, often discussed in the teaching of the European languages, can prove problematic in learning the TFLs. Perhaps what makes successful induction possible in the learning of Indo-European languages is that most American learners already speak an Indo-European language and are already members of an Indo-European culture. The practice of guessing from context (either interpersonal or textual), for instance, presumes that the learner is able to "read" the foreign context. This is quite unlikely in teaching Chinese and Japanese to the beginner, for there is little in the learner's experience that would prepare him or her to understand the context at all. More probable is that guessing would lead to the wrong conclusion, particularly as regards pragmatics.

Examples such as these can be multiplied by the hundreds, because the teaching of each TFL has its own unique pedagogical practices that have evolved with time and experience. Yet many of these procedures would not be characteristic of pedagogical practice in either the traditional languages or ESL. Of course, to the degree that second language acquisition is based on universal psycholinguistic principles, the TFLs are subject to the same general canons of language mastery as are the European languages and ESL. Second language acquisition is not the same as second language teaching, however, and to the degree that TFLs have unique linguistic and pragmatic features it is only natural to expect different teaching practices.

Perceptions: The Cognate Languages and the TFLs

The picture of the TFLs presented so far suggests that their successful blending into a national system of language instruction based on French, German, and Spanish will require that those who practice within this long-standing and quite elaborated tradition see their world from a much broader perspective than is usually the case. Ruhlen (1987) divides the world's languages into seventeen phyla (plus four additional categories) including Khoisan, Nilo-Saharan, Afro-Asiatic, Altaic, Sino-Tibetan, Austric and Indo-Pacific as examples. Within any given phylum there may be hundreds of languages each with many millions of speakers. By our tradition and national history it turns out that what we mean by "foreign language teaching" in American culture is really the teaching of three Category 1 Indo-European languages to the speakers of another Indo-European language, English. A rough estimate based on figures cited above by Dandonoli (1987) and Brod (1988) is that at least 95% of all foreign language enrollments in the U.S. from kindergarten through college are in French, German, and Spanish. Walker (1989) estimates that over 90% of the enrollments in foreign language study in the U.S. are in languages that represent only 14% of the world's population.

It would seem more sensible, in broadening one's perspective about foreign language education in the United States, to classify French, German, and Spanish (among others) as "cognate" languages and cultures and reserve the term "foreign language" for non-cognate language and cultures.[7] Jorden and Walton (1987) term the latter group "Truly Foreign Languages," the term that has been adopted for the present discussion. The reason that this distinction is so crucial in approaching the gradual inclusion of the TFLs into the mainstream is that much of what is claimed or believed to be true about the teaching and learning of "foreign languages" may oftentimes be relevant to the teaching and learning of cognate languages only, as was discussed in the two sections above. Given Ruhlan's classification of the world's languages, it is fairly simple to make the case that cognate languages, when contrasted with languages from different phyla, are a very limited, special, even idiosyncratic subclass of languages; and cognate or related cultures are a very special subclass within the classification of the world's cultures.

In this light, then, our national system of language teaching with its emphasis on French, German, and Spanish can be viewed as a very atypical system from a global linguistic and cultural viewpoint, atypical in that what is termed "foreign" is actually not really very foreign. The use of terms such as "cognate" and "truly foreign" is thus not at all trivial. Indeed, much more than a mere academic tradition, the association of the notion "foreign" language" with French, German, and Spanish is a part of our national mind-set.

In order to reveal clearly the quite narrow and unique character of the cognate language tradition in foreign language education in the United States, it is useful to view this tradition as it is seen by those who teach in the world of the TFLs. First, it is worth noting that all three of the major cognate languages are classified in Category 1 with the implication that they are, relatively speaking, the easiest for native English speakers to master. Next, it should be pointed out that the American university is based on the Western European model and the cognate languages come with this model. As a consequence, one finds that the study of cognate languages is tied in intricate ways to the importance of a college education quite naturally steeped in the cultural values of European history and civilization. Since these cultural values are particularly pervasive in the definition of a liberal arts education, foreign language study within this model is closely linked to the humanities where it is often the "study" of a foreign language that has value rather than the ability to use the language for practical, functional communication (see Redfield, 1989, for a discussion of this latter point).

In making the case for the reinstatement of language requirements, it has been suggested, for example, that the "study" of foreign (read cognate) languages teaches the appreciation of another language, another culture, one's own language and culture, and in addition, enhances analytic and higher-order skill development. The latter rationale is often given for language study in grades K-12. Most noticeable about the cognate language tradition, however, is its close association with the study of literature, so that almost all cognate languages are taught at the tertiary level in literature departments (regardless of the department's name: "Department of Modern Foreign Languages," for example).

If it is acceptable to entertain the notion that foreign language education in the U.S. is most often cognate language education, then it must also be noted that this system is a consequence of American educational history. Our tradition has always placed foreign language study in the context of a liberal arts education, stressing literature and the other humanities disciplines. The picture would be radically changed if our foreign language requirement called for the study of at least two years of a truly foreign language and if the three major languages offered at post-secondary institutions were Shona, Japanese, and Tagalog. These languages would not fit with the European university model with its emphasis on the arts, history, philosophy and literature of the Western tradition. Given the difficulty of learning such languages one might expect to find linguists rather than literature specialists in charge of language programs. It is probable that the thousands of articles on foreign language teaching and learning that abound in journals on language pedagogy would be of a radically different nature than is now the case. In short, there might be a significantly different national and educational mind-set about what a foreign language is and how foreign languages are taught and learned.

This expanded perspective paves the way for a better understanding of the world of the TFLs. Instruction in these languages has usually developed within an area studies framework in contrast with the liberal arts model within which cognate language instruction evolved. Instruction in the TFLs has no necessary connection with the European educational system which teaches French, German, and Spanish, as well as Latin and Greek, in a context of the history and values of Western civilization. We have noted that Chinese and Japanese are Category 4 languages. Two years of college study, a typical requirement for Category 1 cognate languages, is merely an introduction to a language in Category 4. Better understanding of one's own language and culture or the development of analytic or critical skills is rarely, if ever, given by either students or teachers of the TFLs as a rationale for language study. There is no particular reason to associate the study of a TFL with the value of a liberal arts education nor with literature, though one would hope that the study of any second language would encourage such goals. Nor is there likely to be a constant concern with how to include culture in language courses, for culture properly subsumes study of the linguistic code from the outset in TFL teaching and learning because of the role that it plays in intercultural communication and pragmatics.

The teaching of Achievement and Informational Culture in Chinese, for example, is typically the responsibility of area studies experts who offer highly specialized courses in Chinese History, Chinese Political Science, Chinese Anthropology, Chinese Economics, and Chinese Philosophy. On the other hand, one often finds the notion in the teaching of the cognate languages that students should learn about the "civilization" of a given European culture, the features of Achievement and Informational Culture, in the language classroom; one is less likely to find individual specialists in French History, French Political Science, French Economics, French Anthropology, and French Philosophy. Most accessible to students of French will be specialists in French literature.

Finally, the linguistic nature of the TFLs and the unique pedagogical approaches necessary to teach and learn them would seem to require of the cognate language teaching community, not merely a wider perspective of foreign language education, but one that is radically different. It is clear that TFL language study should have its own model, distinct from that of the cognate languages and ESL. There will, of course, be similarities among all three models. This does not, however, logically lead to the conclusion that the TFLs should adopt either of the other two models. In fact, logic suggests that the teaching and learning of cognate languages be a special subset of the teaching of TFLs and not the other way around. The same logic would suggest that the teaching and learning of Category 4 languages, and related research, be the highest order models for the teaching and pedagogical research agendas of Category 1, 2, and 3 languages since all pedagogical issues in these three categories are presumably subsumed under those facing Category 4 languages.

At present, this is not the case. Truly foreign languages and Category 4 languages do not lead the way in foreign language education, though the potential for such leadership surely exists. TFL teaching, learning, and second language acquisition research has suffered from national neglect and an appalling lack of resources. Thus, we should not be surprised at the low quality of text materials in many (though not all) of the LCTLs, the lack of teacher training, and the lack of more sophisticated curricular designs. What is needed by the TFLs is not pedagogical guidance from the cognate languages and ESL, for this may prove inapplicable, but rather assistance informed by the knowledge of the special features of the TFLs. Above all, what is needed is the allocation of sufficient resources for those in the LCTLs themselves to improve their pedagogical practice and implement their own agenda of second language acquisition research.

Administrative and Program Features of the TFLs

The mainstreaming of the TFLs seems nowadays focused on the creation of new programs in colleges which have historically taught only the cognate languages and in the high schools that likewise have a strictly cognate language tradition. In college settings it is likely that TFLs such as Japanese and Chinese will be added to cognate language departments or will be administered in special programs. A typical scenario is to try out one or two TFLs in an experimental mode and move to a more permanent structure only if there is enough enrollment growth to support a full-time and/or tenure-line appointment. When such language programs are successful there is likely to be some thought given to introducing several area studies courses as well.

Those who teach in cognate language departments are familiar with the fact that there are differences between native and non-native teachers. They are also aware that the educational systems and intellectual traditions of French, German, and Spanish differ not only among themselves but also contrast with educational practice and intellectual values of the American tradition (see Kramsch [1989] for an interesting discussion of this point). However, all four traditions share common roots and an enormous similarity when compared with the educational and intellectual traditions of truly foreign languages and cultures.

When a TFL is added to a cognate language department, administrators should not expect that just another language is entering the curriculum. Both the languages and the teachers will be distinctly different. Native speaking teachers of Chinese and Japanese, for instance, bring with them educational backgrounds and styles of interaction, both professional and personal, that may contrast sharply with administrative and educational practices heavily steeped in the European tradition.

For example, it is not uncommon for native speaking Japanese teachers to feel uncomfortable in giving D's and F's. Moreover, the concept of a Japanese "sensei" or a Chinese "laoshi" is really not the same as that of an American "teacher." The educational tradition in these cultures places the "teacher" on a higher plane than his or her American counterpart. It has traditionally been the practice in Chinese classrooms in China for students to refrain from asking questions in case the teacher might lose face if he or she does not know the answer. There is little student-teacher interaction in such classrooms. Thus, the notion that language teachers should be "facilitators" or "managers" or that classrooms should be "student centered" are quite alien to many native Chinese and Japanese teachers. They are much more comfortable as the presenters of information in a lecture format, the mode in which they themselves were educated. An even more alien and threatening idea is that students might actually evaluate teachers.[8]

When dealing with administrative matters, a chairperson may misjudge the Japanese tendency to refrain from frankness on sensitive issues or the tendency to avoid saying "no" as a signal of agreement. In fact, the teacher may disagree quite strongly but would rather that his or her views be leaked to the Chairperson through a third party.

Another common problem for those not familiar with Asian cultures is to assume that Chinese, Japanese, and Korean languages and cultures are similar and thus to assume that one mode of administrative conduct will work for teachers of all three languages. A visit to an established East Asian language and area studies program will quickly reveal that differences among these cultures are in all likelihood much greater than those between French, German, and Spanish. This is to be expected, for though these Asian languages and cultures are geographically proximate, the cultures do not share the degree of similarity among each other that is so often assumed. Even with respect to the languages themselves one must remember that Chinese and Japanese, for example, are genetically unrelated and are at almost opposite ends of the language-typology spectrum: Chinese is a Sino-Tibetan morphosyllabic tone language with essentially no inflectional system, whereas Japanese is an Altaic polysyllabic pitch-accent language with an extremely rich and complex inflectional system.

There are native English-speaking teachers of such TFLs as Chinese and Japanese, but it is often the case that they work in coordination with native teachers. The tradition of native target-language teachers runs deep in the TFLs. This is partly because the cultures are so different from that of the American learner that native English-speaking teachers are sometimes seen as weak substitutes. In addition, among the small number of Americans who reach higher levels of competence in a Category 4 language, few elect to become language teachers. The cultural gap and the linguistic complexity of the languages are not, however, features that necessarily argue for the exclusive presence of native Chinese and Japanese teachers in a language program for foreign learners. The view that these native teachers have of their languages, their own experience in learning them and their educational traditions may sometimes interfere with presenting the language for acquisition by foreign learners. Jorden and Walton (1987) have suggested that native-speaking teachers of the TFLs do not know what it is like to learn their language as a second language, nor what it is like to function as a foreigner in their home cultures. They also may lack the experience of having participated themselves as students within the American educational system. They are thus limited in what they can offer the foreign learner in formal educational settings in America. On the other hand, the native English-speaking teacher who has studied either Chinese or Japanese, has functioned as a foreigner in these cultures, is a product of the American educational system and has had pedagogical training may be better positioned to assist fellow Americans in the language learning process. Yet, such native English-speaking teachers are neither native speakers of the target language nor authentic cultural models for students, whose primary challenge is to become effective intercultural communicators. Jorden and Walton thus propose a team-teaching model—a teacher from the learner's own culture working hand-in-hand with a teacher from the target culture—as an approach that insures the best possible education in both language and culture for the American student.

The team-teaching approach may strike many teachers of French, German, and Spanish and educational adminstrators who make budgetary and staffing decisions for language programs as an extravagent use of precious resources. We can probably ascribe this to the mind-set of Category 1 cognate language teaching and the concomitant lack of experience in dealing with Category 4 TFLs.

At the same time, those who work in the cognate language tradition will need to be aware that American students who take the TFLs may differ significantly in motivation and purpose from the typical cognate language student. It is unlikely that a student will take a Category 4 language just to satisfy a language requirement. Rather, the typical TFL student comes with curiosity and a plan, however vague, to use the language in some way as part of his or her post-graduate career. Thus, there is less concern with creating motivation than in maintaining and strengthening the learner's initial motivation as the complexity of the TFL becomes apparent.

Ethnic students can present certain problems in program administration. For example, many Chinese-Americans enroll in Chinese, often as a way of strengthening their cultural heritage and frequently under pressure from their parents. This can create the problem of how to place and evaluate "semi-native" speakers and would seem to resemble the same sort of problem so often encountered in Spanish language programs in the United States. However, the Chinese case is much more complex since some students may speak Mandarin at home (with familiar register) but may be unable to read and write Chinese characters, a learning process that is certainly worthy of academic credit. Many Chinese Americans speak Cantonese, another Chinese language thought to differ from Mandarin about as much as French differs from Spanish, or even German. Thus learning Mandarin is obviously worthy of credit. It may be that a Cantonese American can read and write Chinese characters so that learning them in a Mandarin class is less difficult and worthy of credit, since the Cantonese character set, with some exceptions, is identical to the Mandarin character set, though the characters are pronounced quite differently. In short, questions of placement and credit can become fairly complicated when TFLs are part of a language program.

Those who have functioned only in the academic world of the cognate languages should be aware that this tradition harbors a number of expectations that may well not apply to the TFLs. For example, the emphasis on literature by the second or third year of cognate language instruction differs significantly from a Category 4 language where literature, generally not the primary interest of undergraduate TFL students, is more appropriately treated as "language for special purposes" and is probably best reserved for the graduate level in all but very strong undergraduate programs.

Likewise, the difficulty of Category 4 languages argues against the probability of high enrollments that many administrators look for during the trial period when they decide whether or not to make a TFL a permanent feature of the curriculum. The failure to allot sufficient and appropriate resources, for example, by hesitating to utilize a native/non-native teaching team for a Category 4 TFL, can place a fledgling TFL program in an unfair position when comparisons are made with enrollments and attrition rates in a cognate language. Expectations of collegiate behavior, when it comes to working with TFL native speakers, especially those with little familiarity with American academic culture, will require a meaning of "collegiate" that goes beyond the European and American definition. In brief, teachers and administrators will need to be aware that the entry of a TFL into a school may well bring with it new and unfamiliar exercises in intercultural communication. Expectations about business as usual may require a fundamental reassessment in all matters, pedagogical and administrative.

Mainstreaming the TFLs: The Future

The mainstreaming of the TFLs is not for the most part a movement that began with mutual cooperation and building within the language teaching community, for this might have occurred many decades ago. It is rather a movement that has been recently imposed on this community by outside forces. It has in fact been generated by national concerns, especially that of economic competitiveness. These have trickled down from policy makers at the state and federal levels, the military and intelligence communities, business, parents, and students, to state foreign language adminstrators, college presidents and deans, school districts, language departments, and finally to the classroom. Just how the more and less commonly taught language traditions react to this new state of affairs will have much to do with the future of the TFLs in educational institutions. While this paper has emphasized the desirability of cognate language teachers and administrators coming to appreciate the distinctive features of TFL language education, it is quite clear that understanding is a two-way street and that it will behoove the TFL teaching community to become more familiar with the educational and pedagogical work of their colleagues in the cognate languages.

Mutual cooperation and understanding between these two worlds is necessarily predicated on a desire to work together. Some in the cognate language teaching community apparently see the entry of the TFLs as an unwelcome intrusion. This is understandable, for some administrators insist that the inclusion of a TFL portends the exclusion of a currently-taught cognate language. The reduction or elimination of German and Latin programs, in particular, is seen by some high-school administrators as a price that must be paid for bringing aboard a TFL, or even a cognate LCTL such as Russian.

At the same time TFL teachers, few in number, often lacking in formal training and besieged with serious problems in the realm of text materials, curriculum design, professional standards, and especially a long-standing lack of adequate resources, have not been clamoring for expansion into additional instructional settings and instead are often more concerned with maintaining and strengthening enrollments in existing programs.

In this somewhat charged atmosphere one can imagine at least two different scenarios for the future mainstreaming of the TFLs: the coexistence model and the integration model. In the coexistence model, cognate language teachers may accept the fact that national demands and student interest argue for making a place for the TFLs, but may well be unenthusiastic about such a troublesome addition, sensing increased competition for students and the possible shrinkage of cognate language enrollments and programs. At the same time, practitioners within the TFL teaching community who have long since learned to survive outside the language education mainstream may prefer to be left alone to pursue their own agendas.

The coexistence model will work and in fact, may already be the dominant model that has arisen in the 1980s. It is, however, a model that diminishes the potential of foreign language education (and education more generally) in a nation whose global role in the twenty-first century will certainly depend on a citizenry capable of functioning in a great variety of international and intercultural contexts. For those TFL teachers who do wish to see the national expansion of their languages, the coexistence model, while perhaps preferable and comfortable in the short term, is no doubt the more precarious route in the long run. As long as the TFL paradigm remains on the margin of the national educational infrastructure, however well it evolves internally, it will be in constant jeopardy of retrenchment and reduction: last added, first eliminated.

The integration model, by contrast, does more than just allow for coexistence. Rather than competing for space in a room of fixed dimensions, the integration agenda looks deeply into the nation's educational goals and long-range needs and creates a larger and more richly furnished room. This room is, of course, simply a metaphor for an enriched vision of foreign language education. What makes such enrichment appealing is that both the cognate language and TFL traditions have much to offer one another.

The cognate language tradition has accumulated decades of experience in the broader contexts of foreign language education in the United States, from K-12 to the graduate level, whereas the TFLs have limited experience in much more restricted contexts. High school language teaching, in particular, is a world largely unknown to TFL teachers. The cognate languages, dealing as they must with larger and more complex programs have evolved administrative and organizational skills and procedures that may be of considerable value to TFL programs as they move into the mainstream.

The cognate language tradition has a more extensive, more varied exposure to the American language learner's mind-set, knowledge of considerable value to the TFL teaching community which historically has often had the luxury of working with small numbers of highly motivated and perhaps even linguistically gifted students, although this luxury has been gradually vanishing in the teaching of some of the higher-enrollment TFLs. Even experience in how to popularize foreign language study is untraveled territory for many TFL teachers. Whereas language study in the TFLs has been predicated largely on the notion that the only legitimate goal is the development of functional skills for career and professional purposes, expansion into more varied educational contexts may argue for the value of the study experience itself, again an area of accumulated experience and thinking in the cognate language domain.

Issues of professionalization and standards, as well as the significant role that can be played by carefully structured, multiple-agenda national membership organizations are commonplace for the cognate language community and no doubt deserve serious study by the TFL community as it emerges from its historical confines.

For the teachers of cognate languages, the contribution of the TFLs centers on years of accumulated experience in grappling with linguistic, pragmatic, and pedagogical issues that may well provide fresh and intriguing insights into the teaching of European languages. Some of the issues involving the teaching of culture in the TFLs have already been mentioned earlier, but there are many others. It has been suggested (Walton, 1987), for example, that in dealing with members of non-cognate cultures where foreigners are forever marked as obvious foreigners, and where there exists a code of interpersonal behavior expected of foreigners as contrasted to natives, the proficiency scale might better have as its ultimate target the "ideal foreigner" rather than the educated native speaker. Would this make sense for cognate languages as well? Is there a definition of intercultural communication as it is viewed in teaching the TFLs that contrasts with the definition in teaching the cognate languages? If so, how would these differences carry over into pedagogical practice in the two traditions and what can both learn from this comparison?

Because the TFLs obviously take longer to master, hour-by-contact-hour, there has evolved, in some languages at least, the practice of requiring considerable self-management of learning by the student. Would knowledge of the design of self-managed language learning environments acquired through this experience in the TFLs be of value to teachers of cognate languages? Research and pedagogical practices in teaching the reading of non-alphabetic writing systems result in a view of the reading process that differs rather dramatically from the view of this process in the cognate languages. Moreover, the relationship between oral/aural skill acquisition and development of the reading and writing skills has been and continues to be an area of concern and research in the TFLs. Cognate language teachers may discover in this research and instructional practice a fresh way of thinking about the skill of reading as well as its relationship to the acquisition of conversational skills. Likewise, years of experience in using the team teaching model followed in some TFL language programs has revealed the complementary strengths and weaknesses of native and non-native teachers. Perhaps the insights garnered from this experience would be revealing for teachers of the cognate languages.

Chinese was the first language to develop a nationwide standardized proficiency test for listening and reading and the first to devise a national standardized indirect oral proficiency exam (using audio tape). Teachers of the LCTLs played a central role in developing the new revised ACTFL generic proficiency guidelines. Again, teachers of the cognate languages may wish to tap into the experience that TFL educators have accumulated in these efforts.

While the coexistence model is unlikely to result in what could be a fruitful exchange of teaching experience, curriculum design, pedagogical practice, and research on cognitive and second language acquisition factors that differ between the cognate and truly foreign languages, the integration model is predicated on precisely such exchanges. Beyond searching for commonalities and sharing differences in the pedagogical realm, however, true integration can be achieved only when the administrative infrastructure includes the teaching and teachers of the TFLs on an equal basis with cognate language teaching and teachers. Thus the role of administrators and decision makers both within foreign language education and the larger educational environment will be crucial in the movement to mainstream the TFLs.

From the administrator's point of view the coexistence model is a necessary, expedient, experimental first step. At the same time, this model brings with it all the ingredients for potential failure. The TFLs must demonstrate that they are viable. This requires resources and effective inclusion in the language teaching infrastructure. Yet they are often excluded from such resources and the infrastructure until they can demonstrate their viability.

Administrators, working to get things going, may not require that standards for accountability and teaching credentials for TFL teachers be identical to those of cognate language teachers. Some college, community college and high school programs are so desperate for teachers of Chinese and Japanese that normally required teaching standards are being by-passed through special certification procedures. As a result, one finds the incredible situation that strict certification procedures are required for a Category 1 cognate language, but are slighted for teachers of a Category 4 TFL. Thus, complex languages that require a high degree of pedagogical sophistication and teacher training have less stringent certification procedures than the instructionaly less demanding Category 1 cognate languages. While some states might require that a native-speaking Chinese or Japanese teacher have an academic degree in some subject from the home country and thus be an "educated native speaker," there seems little awareness that what might count most for members of other cultures teaching American high school students is familiarity with the American high school environment, or at least preparation to teach in this environment through study in an American school of education, complete with supervised practice teaching.

The same syndrome may surface at the college level. Here programs and administrative decision makers are placing emphasis on finding "experienced" teachers rather than pedagogically trained teachers. There is a difference, since experience alone is no guarantee of quality or pedagogical sophistication. As a result of such administrative decisions, cognate language faculty may drift toward lowered rather than revised expectations for the TFLs. Just because these languages are difficult does not mean that they are somehow immune to the usual canons of quality in teacher certification and curricular design and especially in objective accountability to the learner.

One would hope that foreign language education policy and decision makers would thus adopt a dual track agenda in their efforts to mainstream the TFLs. One track would place emphasis on short-term, clearly transitional strategies to set up and staff TFL programs. The other would place equal emphasis on formulating longer-term plans to create an educational and administrative infrastructure that actually integrates the TFLs into the mainstream.

What one finds nowadays is much more emphasis on short-term planning than on a long-range vision. For instance, relaxing certification standards and relying on untrained TFL teachers (untrained in language teaching and/or education generally) to teach in the high schools is an emergency response to instructional demands. What seems to be missing are the much-needed discussions for building the long-term infrastructure to train and supply well-qualified teachers: are schools of education currently studying ways to include teacher training in the TFLs? Are efforts being made to identify the qualifications of those who will train future TFL teachers? Are schools of education going to transfer the cognate language and ESL teacher training models over to the TFLs, or are they approaching teacher training in these languages by first attempting to ascertain whether these two models are appropriate for TFL language education?

The TFLs are in desperate need of massive resources if they are to move from the fringes of language instruction into the mainstream. Where is the planning and strategy formulation that will make these resources available? Efforts to integrate the TFLs into the mainstream, rather than just allowing them to coexist with the cognate languages, must surely begin to address such issues.

In summary, the future of a new and expanded role for the TFLs within the context of American education rests on whether compelling arguments can be made to language teachers, both cognate and TFL, and to educational administrators and policymakers that the coexistence model should evolve into the integration model through conscious effort and thoughtful planning. For such a transition to succeed, educators and decision makers are much in need of data and analysis of current TFL resources, of the successes and failures of the various components of the initial coexistence model as well as attempts to move toward the integration model. Such data is now being collected in national surveys of the teaching of Chinese, Japanese and Russian conducted by the National Foreign Language Center.

Conclusion

The LCTLs and the TFL subgroup have long since established a presence, however limited, in American foreign language education and will continue to hold a place regardless of whether or not they enter the national mainstream. Thus, it is not so much the fate of the LCTLs that is at stake but rather that of foreign language education for future generations of American citizens. Language educators must face not only what to do about current demands for the teaching of Arabic, Chinese, Japanese, and Russian but more importantly the issue of the integration of the LCTLs into the definition of foreign language education on a national scale. The LCTLs of concern today may not be the same ones of import in a decade. What we have before us now is simply a test-case. The coexistence model of LCTL/TFL language instruction prevalent today is clearly a reactive model, a first response to unanticipated demand. Those outside foreign language education, from policymakers to parents may come to judge the field of foreign language education, and perhaps in indirect ways the allocation of resources to it, according to how well it satisfies the educational needs of the American populace. This would not seem to be an unreasonable demand on the field of foreign language education, since it is one constantly applied to education in the humanities, in literacy, in science, in math, in medicine, and in technology, to name just a few current foci of the public's interest in national needs.

Foreign language educators have long advocated the importance of their subject matter, have presented their case to the public with vigor and have created an impressive rationale for the centrality of foreign language study in the American educational system. Yet, to be a foreign language educator must surely mean to be concerned with the teaching and learning of foreign languages beyond French, German, Spanish and other cognate languages. Otherwise we have the unfortunate division of "cognate language educators" versus "truly foreign language educators." There is a challenge here and one that involves the integrity of the field itself: that challenge is to become proactive rather than reactive in expanding the vision of foreign language education in the United States.

Notes

1. The National Foreign Language Center, with assistance from the U.S. Department of Education has sponsored three annual meetings of representatives from LCTL language teaching organizations. These representatives now plan to form a new Council of The Less Commonly Taught Languages to begin planning a national agenda for the enhancement of instruction in a number of LCTLs.

2. NASILP now has over a one hundred and twenty member institutions. These programs are designed to provide instruction in institutions which would not normally be able to offer an LCTL. Students are expected to take a major role in instructing themselves using text and tapes, but normally meet with a native speaker, generally untrained, for several hours per week to receive feed-back on outside preparation and to practice material already studied prior to these tutorial sessions. Most courses stress the development of conversational skills. Grades are determined by a single final exam, ideally conducted by an outside examiner who normally teaches the language. Many NASILP programs are eventually supplanted by regular course offerings.

3. DLI classifies German as a Category 2 language but the FSI categorizes it as a Category 1 language.

4. The comparison of classroom contact hours to years of academic study is, of course, quite hypothetical. Students in academic programs may spend considerable language study time outside of classes. Well-designed

and well-taught programs may move students to higher levels of proficiency faster than pedagogically poor programs. Intensive programs may promote the attainment of higher proficiency levels, not merely because of increased classroom contact hours, but because of immersion in the language. Undergraduate students in the TFLs often attend intensive summer and study-abroad programs and may thus attain reasonable levels of proficiency prior to graduation.

5. See Jorden and Walton (1989) for a more detailed discussion of the contrasts between the linguistic, discourse and pragmatic features of the TFLs and those of the Indo-European languages.

6. Hammerly's definition of Behavioral Culture as "the sum of everyday life" (Hammerly 1982:514) no doubt encompasses the notion of intercultural pramatics, but only in a broad, indirect manner. Thus, while I use the term "Behavioral Cuture," I mean it to refer exclusively to intercultural pragmatics.

7. The term "cognate" is used here as a convenient short-hand for the meaning "cognate to the Indo-European languages of Europe." The author is aware that other languages, such as Hindi, are in fact members of the Indo-European language family, though they are distinct enough, both lingusitically and culturally, from the languages of Europe to be classified as TFLs.

8. In the summer of 1989 the author was asked to help prepare, as a part of a Hokkaido Foundation sponsored teacher workshop, approximately 50 graduate students from Japan to function in American university language programs and departments. More than any other topic discussed during the author's week in residence at the workshop was that of student evaluation of teachers. The Japanese graduate students were not only nervous about, and distrustful of, such a procedure, but were somewhat shocked that such evaluations might be taken seriously by administrators and other faculty.

Annotated Bibliography

Brod, Richard. 1988. "Foreign Language Enrollments in US institutions of Higher Education Fall 1986." Association of Departments of Foreign Language Bulletin, January, 19:39-44. Presents figures for foreign language enrollments in the United States at institutions of higher learning for the years 1983 through 1986.

Dandonoli, Patricia. 1987. "Report on Foreign Language Enrollment in Public Secondary Schools, Fall 1985." Foreign Language Annals, 20:457-70. Presents enrollment figures for the years 1985 through 1987 in U.S. public schools.

Ellis, Rod. 1985. *Understanding Second Language Acquisition*. Oxford; New York: Oxford University Press. Introduces the emerging field of second language acquisition by presenting current issues, problems, and approaches and summarizes the state of current research in many domains. Points out areas of needed research and theory development.

Hammerly, Hector. 1982. *Synthesis in Second Language Teaching. An Introduction to Languistics*. Preliminary ed. Blaine, Washington: Second Language Publica-

184 / Critical Issues in Foreign Language Instruction

tions. Presents a comprehensive introduction to issues and practice in second language teaching. Author attempts to evaluate the effectiveness of teaching approaches and perspectives rather than presenting a menu of the current approaches.

Jorden, Eleanor H. and Walton, A. Ronald. 1987. "Truly Foreign Languages: Instructional Challenges." Annals of the American Academy of Social and Political Science 490: 110-124. Contrasts the teaching and learning of Indo-European languages with the study of non-Indo-European languages, using Chinese and Japanese as the main examples. The authors emphasize the role of culture in teaching, learning, teacher qualifications, and program administration.

Kramsch, Claire J. 1989. *New Directions in the Teaching of Language and Culture*. Washington, D.C.: National Foreign Language Center. Emphasizes the role of discourse in merging language and culture into "linguaculture," a bonding of language and culture. Takes a societal and educational, rather than anthropological, view of culture, contrasting and comparing American notions of culture with those of several European cultures.

Leech, Geoffry. 1983. *Principles of Pragmatics*. London; New York: Longman. Addresses the complex and under-researched topic of pragmatics, how language is used in communication. Attempts to distinguish pragmatics from semantics and lays out a framework for defining and theoretically constraining the emerging field of pragmatics.

Redfield, James. 1989. "The Politics of Language Instruction," Association of Departments of Foreign Language Bulletin, April:5-12. Offers a Dean's view of the problems of governance with regard to foreign language instruction in the American university setting. Maintains that foreign language teaching in the university is at a political disadvantage because language teachers are powerless, a fate that derives from their lack of prestige within the academy. Concludes with little hope of changing the present situation.

Singerman, Alan J. and Williamson, Richard C. 1988. *Toward a New Integration of Language and Culture*. Middlebury, Vermont: Northeast Conference on the Teaching of Foreign Languages, Inc. Contains a collection of papers by various authors addressing a number of domains from teaching to textbooks to study abroad as avenues for better integrating the teaching of culture and language.

Ruhlen, Merritt. 1987. *A Guide to the World's Languages. Volume 1: Classification*. Stanford, California: Stanford Press. Attempts to classify the world's languages genetically while at the same time presenting a historical view of previous efforts at classification for most language groups. Author tries to present a rationale for the proposed classifications. Contains useful charts and tables in summarizing the proposed taxonomy of the world's languages.

Walker, Galal. 1989. "The Less Commonly Taught Languages in the Context of American Pedagogy," in Helen Lepke (ed.) *Shaping the Future: Challenges and Opportunities*. Middlebury, Vermont: The Northeast Conference on the Teaching of Foreign Languages, Inc. 111-137. Discusses the growing political and economic importance of the Less Commonly taught languages with particular emphasis on East Asia and Eastern Europe. Examines the uniqueness of the LCTLs in the American tradition of emphasis on French, German, and Spanish with respect to teacher qualifications, teaching approaches, textbooks, curricular design, and program management and offers advice on how the LCTLs can be successfully brought into the larger context of American pedagogy.

Walton, A. Ronald. 1988. "The Case of Chinese," in Charles Stansfield and Chip Harman, eds. *ACTFL Proficiency Guidelines of the Less Commonly Taught Languages*, The Center for Applied Linguistics, Washington, DC and The American Council on the Teaching of Foreign Languages, Hastings on Hudson, New York: 24-25. A report based on the author's efforts in helping to develop the ACTFL Revised Generic and Chinese Proficiency Guidelines. Pays special attention to the problems of reading and writing and the perceived shortcomings of the Guidelines to address complex issues in intercultural communication.

The Upper-Division Curriculum in Foreign Languages and Literatures: Obstacles to the Realization of Promise

David P. Benseler
The Ohio State University

Despite appearances, the foreign language profession in America seems not to have any commonly accepted *definition* of the content of its upper-division curriculum. Upper-division courses are expected to enhance student language abilities, their level of literacy, their knowledge of the target culture(s) and its/their people, and enhance their general education as well. Such courses are often accessible to major and non-major alike, depending mostly on language ability. Intellectual rigor, stimulation, challenge are not necessarily characteristics of upper-division offerings and depend mostly on the individual instructor. In some institutions upper division is where courses are numbered 300 or higher; in others, it's where literary study—the interpretation of literature as opposed to the reading of literary works for the specific purpose of enhancing the language learning process—begins; where students begin to read *authentic* texts of whatever variety; in other places it's where many faculty members get paid to teach—finally!—what they are most interested in; in still others it's where the content of our courses is regarded as actually living up to our billing as a humanistic or liberal arts endeavor; in many or most, it's where numerous colleagues will tell us that we "go" from learning the language to a point where we're "using" it. And, unfortunately, in nearly all locations it's where the solid base of registrations on the crucial lower-division level develops sharply tapered sides as the enrollment pyramid continues its steep climb to the point in the senior year where the two sides meet.

Renate Schulz (1981, 43) has characterized the plight of students at the start of their upper-division studies, clearly a transition phase of their learning process: "American college students," she wrote, "are expected to experience a rather sudden and magic improvement in reading ability as they enter the third year of foreign language study. To this point they have been carefully nursed with small amounts of structurally graded texts containing high frequency vocabulary. Now, after three to four semesters of spoon feeding, they are usually started without mercy on the chronological study of the literary masterpieces of the target language in a survey course....we do not just expect to wean the students from the bottle to the cup. We hand them knife, fork, and the uncooked ingredients for a gourmet meal and expect them to enjoy a Lucullan repast."

By any standard, the published course list of a department is a reflection of what its faculty regards as essential knowledge in the subject area to be introduced to students and to be mastered by them (to varying degrees, of course). Definitions of curriculum that do exist are remarkably similar, although some are more wide-ranging than others. What most definitions share is a seeming determination to be specific—in terms of content and objectives—only about language study. To cite but a few examples: Rivers says that we must acknowledge six classes of goals for foreign language study: "1) to develop the intellectual powers of the individual by involving him in the study of foreign languages; 2) to enrich his personal culture through a study of literature and philosophy; 3) to increase the learner's understanding of how language works and thus also to increase his awareness of his own native language; 4) to teach the reading of the foreign language with literary and research aims in mind; 5) to increase cross-cultural understanding and appreciation; 6) to teach the skills of communication" (cited in Banathy, 107).

Bela Banathy defines curriculum as "an organized attempt to respond to such inquiries as what to teach, to whom, and why; how to teach, with what, when, and where; and how to organize, evaluate, and improve instruction. According to this, the design, development, and management of curriculum are decision-making operations requiring a structure and a strategy." Banathy goes on to advocate a "systems concept," according to which "curriculum is a deliberately designed entity, assembled of components, forming a coherent and integrated whole for the attainment of an educated goal. Curriculum components are based on their potential to provide for educational functions that will best facilitate the proposed learning" (105).

Kathy Heilenman echoes Banathy: "The word *curriculum*, as commonly used, refers to a course of study and is primarily concerned with issues of course content, sequence, and articulation. In this sense, a foreign language curriculum can be identified with a foreign language program or course of study. Decisions made about the curriculum or program are based on assumptions regarding what should be learned (subject matter), how it should be taught (method), and the way in which successful learning should be defined (objectives, course prerequisites, exams, grades, degrees). These assumptions are also part of the curriculum but have more in common with what is usually termed approach or philosophy than with the program per se" (57).

Vicky Galloway sees curriculum as a coordinated series of develop-mental steps in *language* use: "It would seem that if proficiency is a goal of language instruction, complementary considerations would apply to selecting the learner's grammar for functional use. Thus, three concerns might be prominent: 1) on the linguistic plane, that learner performance be authentic and accurate; 2) on the evaluative plane, that each level of instruction provide for maximum proficiency attainment and prepare for future growth; and 3) on the psychological plane, that instructional planning provide learners with a sense of reward and the feeling that they are communicating" (56-57).

Louis Kelly offers the most terse statement of interest to us here, although he gives no indication of how to distinguish between the goals he mentions: "The purposes for which foreign languages are taught," he writes, "fall into three groups: literary, scholarly, and social or practical" (183).

Although Kelly's pronouncement has strong implications regarding content, as does Rivers', none of the scholars I have cited attempts to define what should be taught on the upper-division level in colleges and universities. Whether they feel that particular chore is best left to local institutions and their faculties or whether they, not unlike the remainder of the profession, *take this level for granted* is unclear. The fact remains that we have indeed no common or accepted definition of what an advanced college level foreign language curriculum is or what its content should comprise save by the courses we decide to list in college and university catalogues and bulletins. Moreover, the definitions I have cited seem concerned primarily or only with the development of language competence or proficiency. Little or no attempt is made to conceptualize, define, support the philosophical foundations of *what* should be taught.

This situation poses—or ought to pose—a professional dilemma. Teaching and scholarship are based on rationales of what and why we present what we do, yet we seem to lack common definitions in this instance. Heidi Byrnes phrases the faculty's dilemma here quite eloquently in terms of teaching: "we generally feel comfortable teaching an introductory language course; we are already less sure about the articulation between introductory and intermediate courses and lack considerably in evidence about what it means to learn a language at this level. Finally, at what should be the advanced level we are so bereft of substantive knowledge that we typically abandon the progression altogether and teach conversation or literature courses or simply go to any of a wide variety of topics that are deemed necessary for a foreign language major. Not only do our course offerings reflect this increasing uncertainty, our materials parallel it as well" (37).

Unfortunately, the MLA Commission on Foreign Languages, Literatures, and Linguistics did little to alleviate the problem: its recommendations, published in 1986, do not even refer to the upper-division; indirectly, however, the Commission acknowledges its existence by recommending that "Departments...offer literature courses organized along thematic, formal, or interdisciplinary lines as well as courses on the works of minorities and women" (48). Prior to that report, the Task Force on the Commonly Taught Languages had merely recommended that the ADFL "should sponsor one or more conferences on the development of new options in major and minor language-and-culture programs in the commonly taught languages." The President's Commission on Foreign Language and International Studies, formed by Jimmy Carter in 1978, was evidently not asked (by the President or the profession) to address definitions of curriculum, since the background papers requested by the commission skirt the issue altogether. Some of our own publications simply assume a common knowledge of "curriculum" as well: among others, ACTFL's own 1982 publication, *Curriculum, Competence, and the Foreign Language Teacher*, does not define the term.

My point here is not to belittle the efforts of those who serve us so well on commissions and task forces, not to mention in the preparation of their thoughts for publication. It is quite simply to reinforce what we probably all know anyway: the upper-division curriculum in foreign languages and literatures qualifies for designation as the most neglected area of our entire enterprise. We have invested countless gallons of ink in the planning, description, and analysis of lower division courses, and in learning outcomes for them, and in the conception and realization of the knowledge and skills we want new PhDs to be armed with as they join the profession. The middle area of our curriculum, though, has not received similar attention. It and its content are taken for granted; we assume—and can doubtless justify to our own *local* satisfaction at least—what that level ought to consist of, and we proceed accordingly. It might even be termed the "default curriculum," so little have we examined, discussed, questioned it in the professional literature. We should try to understand possible reasons for our benign neglect of what is, when all is said and done, the content and organization of what we seek to teach, of the knowledge and skills we want undergraduate majors to possess at the conclusion of their studies.

Factors Influencing the Present Upper-division Curriculum

Scanning upper-division course offerings in foreign language departments in the United States yields an impression of remarkable consensus from institution to institution. This level of the curriculum has three basic components: 1) literary studies, whether historical, thematic, theoretical, or by genre; 2) continuing language studies, primarily in the form of composition and conversation courses (normally "intermediate" and "advanced"—one is hard-pressed to find even local definitions that distinguish between those although, according to Hoffman and James, Hunter College seems to have integrated them well with the *ACTFL Guidelines*); 3) some culture and civilization courses as well as listings for film in particular target cultures, and related courses in current events. Rather than a curriculum that contains courses on a wide variety of reading materials (not just a change in literary genre or century) and discourse styles, students are offered essentially the same program as majors from one institution to the next: a requisite number of courses in each of the three categories just mentioned.

Why is this so? What factors have influenced what we do to such an extent that duplication, in *type* of course at least, is virtually assured from one institution to the next? Let us consider a number of possible reasons.

First, our curricular traditions are based on a desire to have upper-division courses enhance language capability and to build on the knowledge and skills gained in elementary and intermediate courses. Simultaneously, we expect them to add strong elements of intellectual rigor and challenge by enhancing literacy and the appreciation of literature, adding to student knowledge of the target culture (a comprehensive term) and its people, and contributing to the general education of the students who populate them, whether major or non-major.

Second, upper-division course offerings in foreign languages and literatures are the result of an evolution dating from the time when some of them, at least, were *lower* division courses. In those days, language itself was taught by the "reading" and translation of selected literary masterpieces, a process that began in the first term and continued to the point where the undergraduate student was either graduated or simply went on to studies in other disciplines. As notions about the nature and content of "language" study began to change, so too did the point at which literary works were read and eventually discussed.

Our upper-division course offerings are susceptible to numerous vicissitudes which I choose to designate as "pressure points." Academic humanists have a traditional and, I assert, *healthy* resistance to change. Modern professors of literature, no matter what the language involved and not unlike their counterparts in history, art, philosophy or music, tend to regard themselves as co-guardians of the intellectual treasures of particular eras and cultures, as trustees of a subject matter, the merits of which have withstood various tests of time—if not necessarily analysis—of their role in the curriculum. While our predecessors in the academy used foreign literatures as a means to achieve language learning via translation, today's professors of literature see their calling much differently. Moreover, they are often heard to lament their perceptions of a decline in appreciation for the intrinsic merits of reading, in general, and literary study in particular. Some can still recall reading and appreciating—though possibly with Herculean effort—in the third semester of "language" study literary works which do not appear in today's curriculum until the fifth or even sixth semester. Teachers of languages (in English departments it's Creative Writing) are at times seen as being among the principal villains in this context since they "don't teach enough reading and culture."

Next is an equivalent notion shared by many foreign language educators (foreign language education degree holders) that they should not try to interfere with the content of those course offerings not clearly labeled as "language" courses. Since their education has been in methodology and related areas, they reason that most of the upper-division is not their "turf." And, like their counterparts who specialize in the analysis and teaching of literature, they have their own list of grievances, not the least of which is that literature courses do not stress enough—if at all—the continuation of *language* learning; that indeed many of these courses are taught in English. Classes of this nature are taught on too high a level, they claim; student language capabilities simply are not sufficient to get the job done. Gaudiani responds to them by warning (74): "The only serious(ly) dangerous trend that I see in FLL curriculum changes involves the move away from the skills and content of the humanities. As the emphasis on teaching oral-aural competency meets the demands of career-oriented FL programs, faculty may find themselves distracted from teaching reading and writing, which are the fundamental skills of humanities education." She sees these not as teaching literary history, but as means of enhancing cultural literacy. Ariew (64) and many others see the *ACTFL Proficiency Guidelines* as possessing the potential to provide a unifying statement and concept for the curriculum, while Ernst Hoffmann and Dorothy James assure us that the *Proficiency Guidelines* can become a standard for all levels of traditional departments without displacing the centrality of literary studies: "We no longer expect our students," James writes, "to become literary critics in four years, but we do not consider that we have therefore lowered our standards. We have tried to raise them by building into our program a workable and demonstrable form of ... in-depth study..." She goes on to describe testing that now takes place between levels in German at Hunter College, noting that the changes they have implemented based on their use and interpretation of the ACTFL Proficiency Guidelines have led to a 33% increase in the number of students completing the foreign language requirement, and to a 50% increase in successful upper-division literature course enrollments. She goes on to advocate the "transformation of the entire college curriculum in foreign languages... into an *integrated* [my stress] sequence of courses, grounded firmly in humanistic, literary content, but teaching linguistic skills actively throughout... [S]imply diversifying the subject matter of courses will not improve language instruction unless these courses are part of a program which is linguistically sequenced."

The root of what James describes, namely a divided professoriate, is devastating in its effects on the entire curriculum and indeed on both our self-concept and the ways in which we are seen by outsiders. We have a senior professoriate basically disinterested in language teaching, coupled with a junior one engaged in it primarily because it provides the stepping stone to what members of that junior faculty really want to teach.

Also not to be overlooked in our discussion of pressure points affecting the upper-division curriculum, and in recent years, at least, a major one, is college and university administrations and their insistence on cost effectiveness—that is, on a curriculum that will *populate courses in quantities sufficient to justify their existence.* Our professional literature overflows with descriptions of courses conceived and born as a result of this pressure, courses which nevertheless attempt to address the concerns of the first two groups I have mentioned. Indeed, successful endeavors in this particular arena comprised a major portion of Renate Schulz's 1977 survey of successful undergraduate programs: her book and the NEH-funded survey on which it is based list nearly two hundred courses which owe their addition to the curriculum primarily to a desire to build enrollments. Numerous descriptions of such courses, and indeed even entire programs, have appeared in our professional journals as well.

Janet Swaffar has begun the process of addressing the concerns of the first two pressure points, and by implication the third, by recommending a conceptual shift in the upper-division (304):

Upper Division Shift: Radical Changes

Pre-existing Paradigm	*New Paradigm*
canon of literature as genres, periods	lit. as part of cultural values: popular culture, multi-media; inter-textuality rather than genre, thematic rather than period emphases
language for surface accuracy (major=elitist scholar)	pragmatic use of language in: double majors culture tracks language in careers study abroad

Fourth, still part of our *Leitmotiv* of pressure from within and still within our framework of tradition, the nature of what is "fit" to be taught has its origins in the universities of Europe rather than in definitions (other than by implication) of what is necessarily best for the education of American undergraduates. For centuries, what has been taught in France in departments of French is literature (with reference to other disciplines depending on the interests of the professor). The same applies to German departments in German universities, Spanish departments in Spanish universities, etc. Early American academics left the United States to study in these universities and when they returned, they tended to teach by and large—though with embellishments—as and what they themselves had been taught. Foreign academics who immigrated to the United States to teach added impetus to these transfers of courses. Department faculties have the same pressure points today. Witness the present struggle between older colleagues who profess a close reading of literary texts and those younger scholars who teach in theoretical terms and in those of how a given text was received in its time; indeed, witness the same between older ALM proponents and those who come from a notional/functional, personalized, or proficiency orientation to language learning.

But the structure we created by default, as it were, has been absolutely devastating in its resistance to change. In his excellent books on the history of the profession, Gerald Graff (1987, 1989), although talking specifically about English departments, places responsibility for the state of affairs that I address directly on what he calls the "field coverage principle" which dominates so much of the upper-division curriculum. In turn it seems to have dominated even the way faculty are assigned to teach courses. To allow Graff to speak for himself here (my point being that one could doubtless make a case for the applicability of the same principle to the foreign literature curriculum as well):

> The field coverage principle seems so innocuous as to be hardly worth looking at, and we have lived with it so long that we hardly even see it, but its consequences have been far reaching. Its great advantage was to make the department and the curriculum virtually self-regulating. By assigning each instructor a commonly-understood role—to cover a predefined period or field—the principle created a system in which the job of instruction could proceed as if on automatic pilot, without the need for instructors to debate aims and methods... The second advantage of the field-coverage principle was to give the institution enormous flexibility in assimilating new ideas, subjects, and methods... Fierce resistance to innovation arose frequently... but since all instructors were on their own, the absorption of innovation did not oblige pre-established habits to change, so that in the long run—and increasingly it was not a very long run—resistance tended to give way. It is only the field-coverage principle that explains how the literature department has managed to avoid incurring paralyzing clashes of ideology during a period when it has preserved much of its earlier traditional orientation while incorporating disrupting novelties such as contemporary literature, black studies, feminism, Marxism, and deconstruction... By making the teaching staff and the curriculum self-regulating, the principle let instructors get on with the job of teaching and research in an efficient and untroubled way, but it also relieved them of the need to discuss the reasons they were doing what they were doing.

The penultimate pressure point of importance here is the power exercised by local curriculum committees, both departmental and other, by peer pressure from other departments about the "level" of X's curriculum (not to dwell on opinions about turf or what department should be teaching a course on French or Russian literature if the materials to be read are in English), and by regional and national visitation and accreditation teams. All tend to value the traditional, or the new cloaked in the rich garb of tradition. Curricular concerns of the type now surfacing in departments across the country come but slowly.

Sixth and last, but certainly not to be overlooked, is what might be termed an unofficial alliance of textbook authors and publishers; it provides still another barrier to the comprehension and correction of curricular problems, and the enactment of remedial measures. Appropriate textbooks for upper-division courses have been among the most urgent of desiderata for years now. They are unavailable primarily because new ones have not been written and/or published, or they are out-of-print and mostly unobtainable due to generally small enrollments in upper-division courses

(=markets). The situation is similar to that of the protagonist in *Der Hauptmann von Köpenick*, a drama by Carl Zuckmayer. Wilhelm Voigt, an ex-convict, is frustrated by a bureaucracy that will not let him be employed without its various permits and papers—yet will not issue them to him unless/until he is employed. Publishers maintain that a market substantial enough to justify the expense of new materials on the upper-division level in foreign languages does not yet exist again, while the professoriate asserts that it cannot get that market without well-conceived and reasonably priced texts and materials.

Conclusions and Recommendations

It is more than merely disturbing that upper-division course work in modern languages and literatures in the United States is based so heavily on tradition and assumption rather than on explicit definitions, rationales, and objectives. We owe it to ourselves and to the students who populate our courses to correct the situation, taking into account the pressure points I have described. While articulation at all levels has always been both an objective and a major pedagogical problem for us, it cannot be accomplished until we have a clear concept of *what* we are trying to articulate.

A joint commission (MLA/AAT/ADFL) of the profession is urgently needed. It should be comprised of (in no particular order) methodologists, literary scholars, and colleagues specializing in broader issues of culture and civilization. Its purpose should be to define the principles, parameters, and objectives of a model upper-division curriculum. Its work, which might well begin with ADFL summer seminars devoted to a thorough historical analysis of the curriculum, should encompass conceptually the relationship of the upper-division to the content and structure of the whole. The membership of such a body should incorporate both traditional and non-traditional thinkers well acquainted with the pressures of the profession.

In 1985, Jacques Laroche noted the changing face of language studies in this country: "From effete and gainless, the image of language studies has become pragmatic. However, and for equally pragmatic reasons, the upper-division levels of undergraduate programs are suffering from another problem: traditional literary curricula are no longer revered as the ultimate consecration for the language major, and many departments are desperately seeking realistic course topics likely to attract respectable enrollments." To Laroche's commentary I would add only that the absence of a definition of our upper-division curriculum, especially when coupled with the lack of a clearly defined set of goals for students to achieve, ultimately makes tenuous at best preparations for a probable and nearly wholesale retooling/rethinking of our discipline that could be necessary by the late nineties—as we again take up the task of preparing a vast new body of needed young professionals.

References

Ariew, Robert. "Integrating Video and CALL in the Curriculum: The Role of the ACTFL Guidelines." *Modern Media*. Ed. W. Flint Smith: 41-66. Media in the language curriculum.

Banathy Bela H. "Current Trends in College Curriculum: A Systems Approach." *Foreign Language Education: An Overview*. Ed. Emma M. Birkmaier. Skokie, IL: NTC, 1972: 105-40. Theoretical implications of then current language curriculum trends.

_____ & Dale L. Lange. *A Design for Foreign Language Curriculum*. Lexington, MA: Heath, 1972.

Benseler, David P. "Culture, Civilization and the College Foreign Language Curriculum of the Future." *Essays on the Teaching of Culture*. Ed. Howard B. Altman & Victor Hanzeli. Detroit: Advancement Press, 1974: 165-90. Intensive language study and in-depth study of foreign cultures.

_____. "Factors Affecting German after the Requirement." *Monatshefte* 73 (1982): 265-70. Five factors, including the lack of a diverse curriculum, impact negatively on upper-division enrollments.

_____. "Increasing Upper-Division Language Enrollment through Intensive Language Learning." *Foreign Language Annals* 11 (1978): 415-19. 320-hour intensive courses lead directly to upper-division literary studies.

Brod, Richard. "Back to the Center: Activism and the Humanities." *ADFL Bulletin* 12,iii (1981):9-15. Plea for activism and argumentation for expanding the activities of (especially the senior) professoriate.

_____. "Options and Opportunities: New Directions in Foreign Language Curricula." *ADFL Bulletin* 10,iv (1979): 16-17. Trends in the foreign language curriculum during the seventies.

Buck, Kathryn. "Report on the 1974-75 Survey of Non-Traditional Curricula." *ADFL Bulletin* 7,i (1975): 12-16. Report of USOE-funded survey of non-traditional courses and degree programs.

Bundy, Jean D. et al. "The Colby College Conference on the Undergraduate Major in French." *French Review* 42 (1968): 66-73. A thorough analysis of the undergraduate major in French.

Byrnes, Heidi. "How Do You Get There from Here? Articulating the Foreign Language Major Program." *ADFL Bulletin* 20,i (1988):35-38. Focus on faculty accountability, program definition, and pragmatisim in designing major curriculum.

Carroll, John B. "Foreign Language Proficiency Levels Attained by Language Majors near Graduation from College." *Foreign Language Annals* 1 (1967): 131-51. Data-based report of a seminal project.

Clark, John L. *Curriculum Renewal in School Foreign Language Learning*. Oxford: Oxford Univ. Press, 1987. Language curriculum in the schools.

Connor, Maurice W. "New Curricular Connections." *The Language Connection*. Ed. June K. Phillips: 95-121. Describes a wide variety of courses and concepts that apply to upper-division: intensive courses, interdisciplinary courses, language camps, and festivals that enhance K-l2 learning.

Crouse, Gail, Krin Gabbard, Leanne Wierenga & D.L. Schrader. "Foreign Languages and the Total Curriculum: Exploring Alternative Basics." *Teaching the Basics in the Foreign Language Classroom: Options and Strategies*. Ed. David P. Benseler.

Skokie, IL: National Textbook, 1979: 63-77. Business, music, film, interdisciplinary studies and foreign languages.

Curriculum, Competence and the Foreign Language Teacher. Ed. Theodore V. Higgs. Skokie, IL: National Textbook, 1982.

Devens, Monica. "Graduate Education in Foreign Languages and Literatures: A View from Five Universities." *ADFL Bulletin* 17,iii (1986): 14-18. Report of campus visits to five large doctoral-degree departments.

Elling, Barbara. "Special Curricula for Special Needs." *The New Imperative.* Ed. June K. Phillips: 83-115. Concerned essentially with K-12 programs.

Foreign Language Proficiency in the Classroom and Beyond. Ed. Charles J. James. Lincolnwood, IL: National Textbook, 1985. Annual review.

Fryer, T. Bruce. "Free to Explore: Curricular Developments." *Perspective: A New Freedom.* Ed. Gilbert A. Jarvis. Skokie, IL: National Textbook, 1975: 9-46. Annual review summary. 21) Galloway, Vicki. "From Defining to Developing Proficiency: A Look at the Decisions." *Defining and Developing Proficiency.* Ed. Heidi Byrnes & Michael Canale: 25-73. Focus on the "ACTFL Proficiency Guidelines."

Gaudiani, Claire et al. *Strategies for the Development of Foreign Language and Literature Programs.* New York: MLA, 1984. Focus constantly on building enrollments; contains numerous ideas about curriculum and its strengthening: structural changes (18-22), content changes (26-28), changes in major programs (28-34). Part II (97-244), sixteen essays by as many scholars, is devoted entirely to curriculum design. Emphasis almost exclusively language curriculum; theoretical issues of design not treated.

German Studies Association. *Guidelines for Curricular Organization at American Educational Institutions.* Tempe, AZ: GSA, 1987. Reports results of extended committee project.

German Studies in the United States: Assessment and Outlook. Ed. Walter F. W. Lohnes & Valters Nollendorfs. Madison: Univ. of Wisconsin Press, 1976. Essays on the diverse history of teaching German as a profession.

Graff, Gerald. *Professing Literature: An Institutional History.* Chicago: Univ. of Chicago Press, 1987. A seminal work describing part of the evolution of present upper-division [English] curriculum.

_____ & Michael Warner. "Introduction." *The Origins of Literary Studies in America.* Ed. Graff & Warner. New York: Routledge, 1989: 1-14. Important collection of essays "on the early history of the profession of academic literary studies."

Graman, Tomas L. "The Gap between Lower- and Upper-Division Spanish Courses: A Barrier to Coming up through the Ranks." *Hispania* 70 (1987): 929-35. Results of internal survey at the University of Utah revealed that very few students took upper-division courses without significant non-academic experience in Spanish.

Harper, Jane. "A Flexible Foreign Language Curriculum." *ADFL Bulletin* 16,iii (1985): 18-21. Community College Foreign Language Curriculum.

Heilenman, Laura K. & Isabelle M. Kaplan. "Proficiency in Practice: The Foreign Language Curriculum." *Foreign Language Proficiency.* Ed. Charles James: 55-78. Focus on the language curriculum.

Hoffmann, Ernst Fedor & Dorothy James. "Toward the Integration of Foreign Language and Literature Teaching at All Levels of the Curriculum." *ADFL Bulletin* 18,i (1986): 29-33. Impact of integration of the *ACTFL Proficiency*

Guidelines into curriculum; literature retains its position as the focal point of the curriculum.

Huberman, Gisele & Vadim Medish. "Content Courses in Foreign Languages." *ADFL Bulletin* 4 (September 1972): 62-64. Teaching varied upper-division series of courses developed with an NEH grant.

James, Dorothy. "Reshaping the 'College Level' Curriculum: Problems and Possibilities." *Northeast Conference Reports* (1989): Literature and proficiency, with literary study retaining its centrality in the curriculum.

Jurasek, Richard. "Integrating Foreign Languages into the College Curriculum." *Modern Language Journal* 72 (1988) 52-58. Follow-up report on effects of NEH grant reported in next entry.

_____. "Practical Applications of Foreign Languages in the College Curriculum." *Modern Language Journal* 66 (1982): 368-72. Effects of a $179,000 NEH grant to internationalize the curriculum across departments at Earlham College.

Kelly, L.G. *25 Centuries of Language Teaching.* Rowley, MA: Newbury House, 1969. To date the definitive history.

Kelly, Thomas E. "Interdisciplinary Studies." *Responding to New Realities.* Ed. Gilbert A. Jarvis. Skokie, IL: NTC, 1974: 129-60. Annual review chapter.

Lafayette, Robert C. "Toward an Articulated Curriculum." *Our Profession: Present Status and Future Directions.* Ed. Thomas Geno. Middlebury, VT: Northeast Conference, 1980: 61-76. Proposes a "united thrust toward articulated curricula."

The Language Connection: From the Classroom to the World. Ed. June K. Phillips. Skokie, IL: National Textbook, 1977. ACTFL Annual Review.

Laroche, Jacques M. "Undergraduate Internship in Conversation." *Foreign Language Annals* 18 (1985): 209-12. Using undergraduates to help peers.

Lipton, Gladys K. "Curricula for New Goals." *Foreign Language Education: A Reappraisal.* Ed. Dale L. Lange. Skokie, IL: National Textbook, 1972: 187-218. Annual review chapter.

Modern Media in Foreign Language Education: Theory and Implementation. Ed. Wm. Flint Smith. Lincolnwood, IL: National Textbook, 1987. Concludes: "Modern Media, including video and CALL, will make an impact on the foreign language curriculum... The use of the Media brings about complications in the structure of the curriculum—new and complex machines introduced in the classroom and laboratories..." (p. 62).

Modern Technology in Foreign Language Education: Applications and Projects. Ed. Wm Flint Smith. Lincolnwood, IL: National Textbook, 1989. Has serious implications for all levels of foreign language learning via the use of technology: interactive TV, interactive videodisk, computers, satellite reception of authentic spoken texts, interactive audio—learning centers.

The New Imperative: Expanding the Horizons of Foreign Language Education. Ed. June K. Phillips. Skokie, IL: National Textbook, 1980. ACTFL Annual Review.

The Origins of Literary Studies in America: A Documentary Anthology. Ed. Gerald Graff & Michael Warner. New York: Routledge, 1989.

Ort, Barbara A. & Dwight R. Smith. "The Language Teacher Tours the Curriculum: New Horizons for Foreign Language Education." *Foreign Language Annals* 3 (1969): 28-74. Focus on the high school language curriculum, but with interesting course titles and descriptions revealed by a survey.

198 / Critical Issues in Foreign Language Instruction

Papalia, Anthony & Joseph Zampogna. "The Changing Curriculum." *The Challenge of Communication.* Ed. Gilbert A. Jarvis. Skokie, IL: NTC, 1974: 299-328. See esp. pp.316-23. Isolated course titles and descriptions in annual review.

Parsons, R.A. "Language, Literature, and Curriculum Revision in the 1980s." *Foreign Language Annals* 18 (1985): 213-18. Proposes the addition to the curriculum of three courses intended to ease the transition from language to literature studies.

Perspective: A New Freedom. Ed. Gilbert A. Jarvis. Skokie, IL: NTC, 1975. ACTFL Annual Review.

Practical Applications of Research in Foreign Language Teaching. Ed. Charles J. James. Lincolnwood, IL: National Textbook, 1983. Application of research in language teaching does not give direct consideration to the upper-division.

President's Commission on Foreign Language and International Studies: Background Papers and Studies. Washington: GPO, 1979; rpt. *Modern Language Journal* 64 (1980): 9-57. The important report to which the renewed interest in foreign language study of the 1980s is often attributed.

"Recommendations of the Commission on Foreign Languages, Literatures, and Linguistics." *Profession 86.* Ed. Phyllis Franklin. New York: MLA, 1986. Text of the Commission report.

Refield, James. "The Politics of Language Instruction." *ADFL Bulletin* 20,iii (1989): 5-12. 53) *Responding to New Realities.* Ed. Gilbert A. Jarvis. Skokie, IL: NTC, 1974. Nearly the entire issue is devoted to curriculum.

Sachs, Murray. "The Foreign Language Curriculum and the Orality-Literacy Question." *ADFL Bulletin* 20,ii (1989): 70-75.

Schulz, Renate A. "Literature and Readability: Bridging the Gap in Foreign Language Reading." *Modern Language Journal* 65 (1981): 43-53. Measuring readability of texts prior to their utilization.

_____. *Options for Undergraduate Foreign Language Programs: Four-Year and Two-Year Colleges.* New York: MLA, 1979. See esp. pp. xi & xii; pp. 3-7 give a comprehensive listing of innovative courses reported by her NEH-funded survey.

Shepard, Joe W. "Beyond the Language Requirement: The Role of Foreign Languages in the Upper-Level Curriculum." *ADFL Bulletin* 14,ii (1982): 14-16.

Stern, H.H. *Fundamental Concepts of Language Teaching.* Oxford: Oxford Univ. Press, 1983. Notes (435-36) that recent years of reform have even led to a theory of curriculum; it is "concerned with 1) the underlying ideological and philosophical assumptions of curriculum (curriculum philosophy); 2) the conceptualization of three main components of curriculum: a) purposes and content, b) instruction, and c) evaluation; and 3) curriculum processes: a) systematic curriculum development, b) the implementation of curriculum in educational institutions, and c) curriculum evaluation."

Stevick, Earl W. "Curriculum Development at the Foreign Service Institute." *Teaching for Proficiency: The Organizing Principle.* Ed. Theodore V. Higgs. Lincolnwood, IL: National Textbook, 1984: 85-112. Describes five component skill-oriented curriculum development at the United States Foreign Service Institute: relevance, function, communication, comprehension, imagery (p. 87).

Swaffar, Janet K. "Competing Paradigms in Adult Language Acquisition." *Modern Language Journal* 73 (1989): 301-14. Emergence of an interactive model of second-language acquisition.

Teaching German in America: Prolegomena to a History. Ed. David P. Benseler, Walter F.W. Lohnes & Valters Nollendorfs. Madison: Univ. of Wisconsin Press,

1988. Eighteen essays and one interview on various aspects of the history of German studies in the United States.

Resetting the Margins: The Outsider in French Literature and Culture[1]

Elissa Gelfand
Mt. Holyoke College

"Nowhere is one more an outsider than in France... And yet, nowhere is it *better* to be an outsider than in France."[2]

"Marginality": a term that presupposes a dynamic between the center and the margins, between what is integrated and what is "other." As a category for research or pedagogy, "marginality" is now being used to reevaluate the traditional study of most national literatures and cultures. Critical of the narrowness of standard courses and approaches, some scholars are pressing for greater inclusiveness in area-studies curricula. They are in part imbued with the concept of "otherness" central to contemporary continental theory; they also point to the historical reality of marginality, an undeniable cultural fact of concern to our increasingly diverse student body. Further, the analytic viability of "marginality" itself is currently the subject of hot debate. In the arena I know best, French studies, some scholars (like myself) see marginality as a useful tool not only for dismantling the persistent myth of a coherent French cultural heritage, but also for making explicit the politics of reading and teaching literature. Others, however, reject the concept as a false reification of human experience which, more dangerously, only reinforces the "otherness" of social and literary outsiders. The debate might be viewed as between those who subscribe, albeit with reservations, to a traditional binary or "'interest model,' which construes canons 'as the expression of the interests of one social group or class against those of another'"[3] and those for whom adopting that model is "to deny process" and "inevitably to become involved with the law"—that is, with the destructive oppositional concepts (e.g., masculine/feminine, active/passive) on which western thought and culture have been based (Jardine and Menke, 231). This paper will attempt to navigate somewhere between these two positions in its presentation of the theoretical and practical questions surrounding marginality.

Marginality has also emerged as an ancillary issue of the current quarrel over the "new historicism," or the interdisciplinary methodology that studies history as "a *construct* made up of textualized traces assembled in various configurations by the historian/interpreter" (Howard, 23-24, her emphasis)[4] and all cultural "texts" as the products of dynamic processes. An outgrowth of Michel Foucault's structural approach, especially in his *Histoire de la sexualité*,[5] in which the human subject is viewed as fragmented and incoherent and relationships of power as constantly producing social inequalities, the new historicism renounces "the illusory quest of an older historical criticism to recover objective, authentic, or stable meanings" (Montrose, 305). But, the new historicism is being challenged by feminist and minority scholars who claim its generalizing frameworks deny the concrete political, economic, and social differences brought by race, sex, class, and ethnicity. It focuses, they argue, on "the public and political over the private and domestic" (Boose, 738) and on the discourse of the dominant culture alone, thus displacing the material elements that constitute the identities of "otherness."

My position on marginality is both a political and a strategic one. As a feminist, I believe in the agency of authors and historical subjects and in the interpenetration between cultural and literary texts. And, as teacher and scholar, I believe that acknowledging otherness means attending to alternative forms of historical action and subjectivity. I also speak as a teacher for whom the demands of undergraduate course syllabi preclude in-depth excursions into theoretical terrain. What is more, I believe that reading works by marginal groups can have important ethical consequences: having students enter life experiences different from their own encourages a kind of imaginative empathy. That is, to really make sense of textual otherness, students must dislocate themselves and read beyond what they know; they must, in relation to *l'etranger*, "*be in his or her place*, which is tantamount to thinking and making oneself other to oneself" (Kristeva, *Étrangers*, 25, her emphasis).

Because choosing texts for courses or research is an exclusionary act, making the criteria of choice visible helps students and readers themselves participate in demystifying the selection process. That is, studying French culture self-consciously makes palpable the fact that all aesthetic judgments are socially grounded—it was people who chose what was and wasn't read in France—and that the literary canon is a fact of history as well as of art.[6] What is written and read depends on access to the tools of cultural production. It also reflects a series of judgments, first on the level of the individual who asserts or censors her or himself, then on the level of the collectivity that accepts, rejects, or tolerates. Reading marginal works exposes those judgments and reveals a society's desires, hypotheses, and possibilities (Turner, *Dramas*).[7] By unveiling the host culture's values and obsessions, the literature of outsiders engages us in a process, not a reification: the changing dynamic between groups "within" and "without." Alain Finkielkraut's evocation of the "febrile and unending process" that has constituted social exclusion in France gets to the heart of the implications of using marginality as intellectual and pedagogical category:

> It is not possible to infer a single, all-inclusive binary opposition that would be the ultimate cause of the conflict between the 'inside' and the 'outside.' On the contrary, the more fragmented our world becomes, the more numerous the criteria for exclusion. Racism based on aesthetica and dress; local xenophobias; compartmentalizations by speech; segregation by age, race, social class, and life-style: all these intersecting mistrusts are moving toward replacing the notion that only one factor differentiates the Frenchman from his or her Other (Finnkielkraut, 112).

Reading works by outsiders gives access to a point of view different from that of "worldliness," a fresh optic "from which the world (and its discursive domains) is perceived, entered, and experienced" (Miller, "Men's Reading," 45). Rather than merely including marginal works in existing structures, in a static effort to "balance" the curriculum, I think they can be more richly used to dislodge traditional aesthetic criteria, and thus destabilize and problematize the boundaries of inclusion and exclusion themselves.

A powerful example of the elasticity of cultural exclusion Finkielkraut describes—and one whose vividnes strongly affects studenta at the outset of a course—is the historical status of the *fou* or mad person in Europe. The visual impact of Fellini's *Juliette of the Spirits*, of the several film versions of Nosferatu, and of various Renaissance paintings puts in place the haunting image of the *nef des fous* (poorly translated as "ship of fools").[8] Long barges sailing past us in total silence, with their cargo of pale, crazed faces being sent from town to some unknown destination, remind us that the *nef des fous* is not just a literary or filmic symbol, it is a social fact. Medieval and Renaissance European cities often exiled mad people on such boats, thereby relegating them to a life of permanent wandering on the margins of society. But the "ship of fools," a phenomenon of real physical and social exclusion, served society's mythic needs as well. In a culture that viewed body and soul as indissoluble, any abnormality was considered evidence of divine judgment and had to be exiled for the community to regain spiritual unity.[9] Thus, the heroic literary trope of the *nef* or *navire* ("ship") was applied to the *fous'* epic voyage that was to cleanse society as a whole. It was also hoped that the pilgrimage of these "unanchored" individuals, spiritually "lost at sea," would bring them to the safe harbor of reason.

Further, the tragic figure of the lunatic has been viewed differently by each century and culture. From the magical sacred, but also fear-inspiring and leper-like creatures that medieval society set apart, the *fous* became relatively integrated into sixteenth-century European cultural imagery. They were symbols of comic derision or veiled truth (visible in the grinning skulls and *danse macabre* motifs of the time) for an increasingly secularized and reason-centered culture. By the next century, the complete separation of madness from reason brought by Descartes, association of madness with error lead to the harsh exclusion of *fous*: their detachment from rational thought made them socially unassimilable and, worse, potentially criminal elements that had to be interned in state hospitals. This view of madness in relation to the faculty of judgment continued in the eighteenth century but was accompanied by the first medical definitions of brain illnesses. For example, the entries under *folie* in Voltaire's *Dictionnaire philosophique* (1764) and in the *Encyclopédie* (1751-72) distinguish by degree of "fever," "dementia," "derangement," "feeblemindedness," and "frenzy." They also point to a disease of the organs of the brain (Voltaire, *Dictionnaire*). With the subsequent development of animist and mechanistic "sciences," nineteenth-century positivism gave its full weight to the emerging empirical field, psychiatry. The emphasis on treatment, still in its early stage, is echoed, for example, in Nerval's *Aurélia*, in which the author analyzes his descent into schizophrenia and his "cure" at the hands of the famous Dr. Blanche. Finally, modern French thinkers, particularly the absurdists, appropriated the *fou* as the essence of rational revolt in an insane world. For a society that hypothesized the fragmentation and the incomprehensibility of the human condition, internal dissidence was deemed the most plausible response. The historically changing status of the mad person tells us something about his or her life, yet it tells us far more about the values and obsessions of the host culture. That explains why, at any given time, the condition of the *fou* was highly ambiguous: the liminal image of the fools' ship, sailing at the margins of the tragic and the sacred, suggests this dual status.

And, if we go one step further, we could say that mad people seem to be the group most alienated from voicing their own experience, at least in terms we recognize. We have few direct accounts of their stories. Among the texts that give access to the experience of madness in French society are *Moi, Pierre Rivière*, the stunning confession of a nineteenth-century murderer; Nerval's apocalyptic quest for psychic unity in *Aurélia* (1853), as well as his hallucinatory poetry of the 1840s and 1850s; Marc Blanc-Lapierre's modern account of the nightmare of hospitalization, *Suis-je donc fou?*; and Michel Thévoz's collection of writing fragments by psychiatric patients, *Le langage de la rupture*.[10] Thévoz's analytic framework, which embraces all forms of representation, raises the issue of the relationship between originality and language: "These authors take up writing in an unself-conscious frame of mind, one of gratuitous and disrespectful invention, of jubilant subversion... [but] this attitude is in reality an initial discomfort with all the rules of self-expression, a feeling of not belonging that resolves itself by means of inventive aggression against language." (11-12). The difficulty of self-expression for these "intruders in their own language, these thieves" (13), has generally succeeded in silencing them.[11] In a similar vein, the psychoanalyst Luce Irigaray has argued that the language of schizophrenia is not commensurable with standard socialized discourse. Rather, in its irreducible otherness, this language constitutes, says

204 / Critical Issues in Foreign Language Instruction

Irigaray, a form of cultural contestation ("Expression" and *Le langage*). And, the essays Kristeva collected in *Folle vérité* posit that the words of the mentally ill expose the basic "malaise" of all language, that of an oscillation between shared communication and distance or *altérité*. The paucity of direct accounts by *fous* in part explains their being made the object of the most varied and contradictory societal projections. Mad people have been virtually silent or silenced, and those more able than they to speak and write have told us about madness, not from within, but from without. Through their projections, literary witnesses reveal a good deal more about themselves and their milieu than about what is outside them.

As conceptual category, marginality elicits strong visceral responses. For that reason, the problematics of "otherness" need to some degree to be elaborated at the outset of any course or project and a common vocabulary needs to be developed. One thorny question is that of the origins of social and literary otherness. For purposes of teaching, I have found two works particularly useful, not only because the difference in historical contexts from which they arose is itself an example of the elasticity of cultural definitions, but also because the two texts establish important conceptual tensions. Evoking these tensions throughout the course keeps students self-conscious as readers and works against unitary, authoritative "explanations" of why particular groups were excluded. Rousseau's *Discours sur l'origine et les fondements de l'inégalité* of 1754 puts forth a classically descriptive enlightenment view of the origins of human inequality. Taking as his premise that, by natural law, equity exists *a priori* in the universe and that inequality is perforce a human creation, Rousseau studies this transformation from natural justice to social injustice. In his nature/civilization typology, the positive physical, mental and moral qualities that define the originary individual are destroyed by progress and the human interdependency it engenders. Rousseau's focus on the dangerous consequences of sociality—on the inevitable sense of superiority produced by comparison of self with other—puts in place a both relational and hierarchical framework within which to consider political and economic inequities. Yet, despite his insistence on the human interactions self-interest motivates, Rousseau's model is, finally, a static one; its essentialist view of human nature renders the weak, the poor, and the enslaved permanent victims of social institutions.

In a very different treatise, Sartre's *L'être et le néant*, the post-modern, anti-positivistic, and a-historical tendencies that mark twentieth-century French philosophy—in sharp contrast to the eighteenth-century sense of the term—become apparent. In place of Rousseau's monolithic question, "Who is man?" Sartre explores the dynamic relationship between self and other. In his framework, human action derives from the desire for the absent "other" or the "néant." This fundamental gesture toward the "other" informs, of course, the major currents of modern continental linguistics, psychoanalysis, and feminist thought, and establishing it at the outset facilitates subsequent reading of such important works as Beauvoir's *Le deuxième sexe*, Fanon's *Peau noire, masques blancs*, and Sartre's own *Réflexions sur la question juive*. *L'être et le néant* also posits the full agency of the "other," or her/his simultaneous status as other and as active subject. Thus, the notion of the complete objectification of marginal groups is contested; rather, Sartre points the way toward the crucial realization that "others" have continually formed traditions parallel to the dominant one. Or, as John Guillory puts it, in his reformulation of the traditional/marginal or canonical/non-canonical dichotomy, "The most conspicuous aspect of the current legitimation crisis is surely the fact that the non-canonical is not that which does not appear within the field of criticism, but that which, in a given context of reading, signifies exclusion. The non-canonical is a newly constituted category of text production and reception."[12] Marginality is thus conceived as a site of cultural production. *L'être et le néant* does, however, have important limitations arising from its highly mechanistic view of the inevitable conflict between self and other. They also stem from existentialism's illusory ideal of transcendence, one that culturally oppressed "others" have faulted for ignoring the fact of historical constraints. Nonetheless, Sartre's analysis—and it is analysis rather than description—has the advantage of not postulating pre-existent social groups and of therefore allowing for the elasticity brought by ideological change.

Another theoretical issue is that of the very different positions, at a given time, of different marginals in relation to the hegemonic culture, and also of the same group at different historical periods. In *La civilisation de l'Occident médiéval* (and its revised version, "Les marginaux dans l'Occident médiéval"), the historian Jacques Le Goff elaborates, first, the epistemological difficulties for historians in determining these cultural positions. At the least, says Le Goff, there is the problem of sources: often social outsiders were silent or illiterate, or their works were published anonymously. Further, the circumatances under which they wrote, and thus the degree of sincerity in their writings, must be considered. The medievalist Guy Allard puts it this way: "When one is being hunted down by the authorities, reduced to speaking in private and to writing texts that circulate *secretly*, dissemination of works depends on the attentive care of a disciple or the obligingness of a publisher... When a witch is subjected to judicial torture or when an alchemist reveals the secrets of his or her art to a disciple, we need to understand that the site of their discourse is usually that of 'dissembling' or 'pretending.' Morcover, how can we blindly give credence to *official* texts when they tell us about mad people, beggars, witches?" (Allard, 16-17, his emphasis). Linked to that, the fact that self-expression could in some cases have worsened their situation no doubt led marginal authors either to soften their contestation or to adopt the values of the dominant society in their writing.

Another problem for research is the tension suggested earlier by Rousseau's and Sartre's texts: how to reconcile the need for descriptive categories of marginality with the awareness of the processes that continually undo and transform those categories. Victor Turner's three categories or "aspects of culture," are useful in that they refer to "rites" or transitional states of social separation: "liminality," or an ambiguous movement among fixed points of classification; "outsiderhood," or a more distinct condition of being "outside the structural arrangements of a given social system"; and "structural inferiority," or a "caste" position of outcast "without status qualifications or characteristics" (233-234). Le Goff, too, tries to incorporate process into his study of marginality by drawing fluctuating social attitudes, rather than fixed labels. These attitudes are further complicated, says Le Goff, by their own internal ambivalences, by the oscillation between fear and attraction within the host culture ("Les marginaux"). The consequence of external conditions auch as plagues, famine, or wars, this ambivalence also arises from internal psychological mechanisms at the individual and collective level. The "other" is the locus of varied myths that exhibit the host culture's irreconcilable contradictions.[13] With all these nuances in mind, Le Goff goes on to distinguish four categories of "otherness": first, the "excluded," who are the most threatening in the eyes of the host culture and are therefore banished to the limits of the social order. For medieval Europe, the "excluded" were criminals, prostitutes, heretics, and Jews. Le Goff also attributes to these groups a certain will to self-isolation, as was the case, for example, with those Jews who wished to develop their culture separately from Christiandom. Second, the "devalued" were those who did not exercise self-exclusion; rather, they were contained within the dominant society and controlled by it. Women, the poor, and the illegitimate, among others, filled certain of the culture's needs and were thus kept in check by it. Third, the "marginals," medieval madpeople and beggars, were deemed barely tolerable and were driven, though not banished, from the social nexus to the threshhold between within and without. Finally, the "imaginary marginals," or the monsters and human "savages" conceived by the medieval European imagination, were relegated unalterably beyond the pale. Mohammed, for example, was seen as the monstrous "anti-Christ." While Le Goff's categories refer to the European medieval context, they are applicable to other cultures and eras as well.

The third set of framing issues regarding marginality has to do with the specific posture adopted by outsiders themselves. We can ask, first of all, whether a writer's marginality is self-selected, imposed, or both. For instance, in her provocative essay, "A Double Margin: Reflections on Women Writers and the Avant-garde in France," Susan Suleiman compares the relationships of both these authorial categories—women and avant-garde—to mainstream French literature: "If... culture is 'like' a space to be mapped or a printed page, then the place of women, and of avant-garde movements, has traditionally been situated away from the center, 'on the fringe,' in the margins. One difference is that avant-garde movements have willfully chosen their marginal position—the better to launch attacks at the center—whereas women have more often than not been relegated to that position: far from the altar as from the market place, those centers where cultural subjects invent and enact their symbolic and material rites" (151). Suleiman goes on to discuss the dual marginality of women writers who are also part of the avant-garde. She evokes this modernist phenomenon, in which "woman" and "the feminine," metaphors for previously repressed cultural forces, are twice put into discourse. Further, using Marguerite Duras's comments in *Les parleuses* and, especially, Hélène Cixous's feminist manifesto, "Le rire de la Méduse," Suleiman argues that such double marginality can, paradoxically, provide "the female subject with a kind of centrality in *her own eyes*" (153, her emphasis). That is, the woman avant-garde writer can adopt an empowered stance if she, like Duras and Cixous, seeks to combine "a revolutionary practice of writing" with "the disruption of existing cultural and social institutions and ideologies" (154).

A second question regarding the outsider's position is, to the extent that an author may self-conscioualy choose to write from the margins, does she or he refuse to participate in the existent order or instead master the rules of the game in order to effect personal or social change? In *Les voleuses de langue*, Claudine Herrmann describes the options available to women writers historically as "conformity" or "eccentricity," that is, "[the] acceptance of masculine values," versus "[the] refusal of all values" (38). The only way out of this impasse was to write "coded" books: women writers used and subverted the master's discourse for their own ends. Thus, for example, Madame de Lafayette mastered seventeenth-century salon French, but in order to attack the very values of the milieu that produced it—specifically, the codes of gender comportment that rendered female happiness impossible: "If women scorn social rules, they themselves are scorned, but if they enforce them unquestioningly, they bring on irreparable misfortune. The game offered to them is therefore completely rigged: it's a game they can never win" (24). Lafayette's Princesse de Clèves (in her novel of the same name) does not explicitly contest her no-win situation as woman. But she undermines it indirectly by rejecting the court language that circumscribes her status. She refuses the impersonal discourse of social rules and instead makes language her own instrument of sincerity—her remarkable confession of infidelity to her husband is but one example. Thus, the princess "steals" social discourse and makes it a tool of subversion, just as her creator does.

In a similar vein, Hélène Cixous studied the "exceptional" criminal Pierre Goldman, accused of murder and armed robbery in the 1960s (*Un K...*). For Cixous, Goldman was "singular" and "excessive," "exclusion's chosen one" who attacked the society that had marginalized him. A Jew born in France but denied French citizenship, he was haunted by his Polish parents' persecution and lived through them a life of pre-ordained "fatality." He was the antithesis of the ineffectual outsider: unlike "those anxious and talkative experimenters, the 'marginals of History,'" Goldman was "in truth a formidable person because, like K. [Kafka], he is one of those individuals who are in league with the History of this society, those who call it to account, those who tear away the mask, who break the silence" (57). Goldman's refusal of the judicial process that condemned him was also symbolic for Cixous of his struggle against the Law and his nostalgia for the "maternal": for his mother's native Poland, her suffering during World War II, her separation as woman from the normal categories of cultural identity. In a word, Goldman was a "conscious pariah," Hannah Arendt's term for the only posture in which a Jew could maintain her or his integrity in a hostile society: marginal in relation to both European society and the assimilated Jewish community, conscious pariahs take responsibility for their situation and refuse to escape. They stand "outside the real world" and yet are "attached to it from without" (Arendt, 73). They use their hearts and minds as weapons of self-preservation, as Jews and as Europeans.

The postures marginal writers assume force us to attend both to lived experience and to imaginative transformations of that experience. To give marginality grounding, we need to take into account the material facts from which texts arose, but also respect the distance between biography and art. One useful method of reading marginal texts is to explore the parallels between social and textual structures: rather than a one-to-one relationship of reflection between text and individual biography, we can search for evidence of the interplay between a given society's views of outsiders and a particular author's responses to those views. For example, the corpus of writings by women imprisoned in France during different eras reveals a rich and varied interaction between paradigms of female normality and the authors' representations of themselves (Gelfand, *Imagination*). Marie Cappelle-Lafarge, convicted of poisoning her husband in 1840, wrote from a culture rife with contradictions about female criminality: Romantic sentimental views vied with positivistic "scientific" ones; moral ideologies centering on women's spiritual "nature" clashed with empirical "truths" concerning their physical capacities. Cappelle-Lafarge takes the notion that she is representative of the female criminal "type" and transforms it into the reclaiming of her natural wholeness that prison has sundered. Further, she takes the paradigms of empirical discourse and reinfuses them with her own "observable facts" about her identity (ch. 5). Similarly, the infamous belle époque *femme fatale*, Marguerite Steinheil, imprisoned for strangling her mother and husband in 1908, used the theatrical and "psychologizing" lexicon of her accusers (who had deemed her a "great hysteric" and an "immoral actress") in order to defend herself. Her memoirs read like a bourgeois melodrama in which Steinheil "re-creates" herself as virtuous victim. And she responds to the harsh aesthetic judgments that couched views of her deviance by asserting her own superior artistic sensibility (ch. 6). Finally, the contemporary prison novelist, Albertine Sarrazin, turned the 1950s psycho-sexual "explanations" of her deviance on their head: if prison officials saw her illegitimacy and her troubled childhood as pushing her toward prostitution and theft, Sarrazin herself exalts her burgeoning sexuality in thoroughly positive terms. She also inverts the criminological discourse of her day, whose stress on external causes such as social conditioning lessened the role of individual free will, by insisting on the power of her self-determination as criminal (ch. 8).

In another example of the exploitation and subversion of normative paradigms, the overture to *Sodome et Gomorrhe*, Proust takes the idea of homosexuality as the "inversion" of "normal" genital sexual expression and transforms it in his famous formulation: "something strange, or natural, if you will" (12). While observing an encounter between two men, the narrator, Marcel, mimics a biologist and expounds a taxonomy of homosexual "types"; by the end, he reverses the parallels between the "natural" and "artificial" worlds and defines homosexuals as the most vital of the human sub-species. Their "hermaphrodism," says Marcel, is the only vestige there is of the primordial union and harmony of the species, of the true "fecundation" from which humanity has since fallen. Thus, the homosexual is a natural force of order, the contrary of the threatening "foreigner" society judges him to be. Further, Proust combines his metaphor of the narrator as organizing zoologist with stylistic devices that suggest textual order: first, the use of an "overture" to establish the theme of harmony; second, the technique of observation followed by explanation, in order to parrot the scientific method; and finally, the play with the notion of "visibility" in which the characters' self-revelation as "men-women" parallels the narrator's revelation of the true nature of social organization.

A last, very powerful case of the textual subversion of marginality is Violette Leduc's stunning autobiography, *La bâtarde*. Not only does Leduc respond to a multiplicity of "othernesses"—she is illegitimate, lesbian, mad, often poor, and a woman—she ultimately makes negativity and rejection the very basis of her self-affirmation. Leduc refuses to please her reader; she transmits without mediation her mutilated vision of reality. But what makes her transcription of her otherness so potent is that it is filtered through her body, the very source of her self-loathing and alienation. As a result, Leduc's constant evocation of her ugliness becomes the symbol of her detachment from herself and from others. What is more, this fundamental rejection of herself is compounded by the self-destructive relationships in which she becomes involved. Paradoxically, Leduc renders the most debasing of situations with the most dazzling and hallucinatory prose. She makes her anguish and solitude the very instrument of her defiant appeal to her interlocutor, whose attention she both deflects and implores.

Perhaps the most exciting theoretical work on marginality can be found in two recently published books, Julia Kristeva's *Étrangers à nous-mêmes* and Tzvetan Todorov's *Nous et les autres*. Though it does not present a single sustained argument, *Étrangers à nous-mêmes* offers some extremely suggestive germs for ways to conceive of *l'étranger*.[14] First, as in her previous work on the psychic dissidence that marks all human subjects,

Kristeva locates *l'étranger within* us. That is, each individual is, by definition, fragmented and incoherent. As a consequence, "otherness" can never be assimilated, and collective homogeneity is an impossible goal. Rather, says Kristeva, we need to seek new modes of living with alterity, and she argues for "cohabitation," or the coexistence of cultural "particularisms." Second, Kristeva refuses to fix or "chosifier" *l'étrangeté*, adopting the image of "toccata and fugue" to suggest its constant movement. The movement or "errance" of *étrangers* puts them in a position utterly divergent from that of members of the host culture: the former are adaptable, they can "relativize" themselves, and are thus a force of life; the latter are "monovalent"— that is, unable to have any perspective on human relations—and are thus in a position of "death." Third, Kristeva categorizes *étrangers* as either "ironists" or "believers," or those who remain divided within the configuration of inside/outside and whose stance is never consonant with the host culture, versus those who transcend the in/out dichotomy and get to the "beyond," the creative space of the "believer." Though she does not elaborate further on these marginal positions, Kristeva implicitly carries forward her earler ideas on the revolutionary potential of cultural "negativity," a productive place outside of known coordinates (see *La révolution*; "Sujet"; and "Pratique"). Finally, Kristeva's comments on *l'étranger*'s relationship to language illuminates why he or she can effect little change on the literary canon. On the one hand, the outsider may never truly acquire the dominant language. She or he will thus choose silence which, for Kristeva, means exile from one's own "maternal" language, as well as absence from "paternal" canonical discourse.[15] On the other hand, *l'étranger* may master the host language. In the eyes of the host culture, however, this perfectly adopted discourse will carry no weight, it will remain "pure rhetoric," ineffectual formalism that leaves no trace on the canon.

The rest of *Étrangers à nous-mêmes* examines these facets of cultural estrangement in specific historical contexts, from ancient Greek cosmopolitanism through modern European nationalism. The overall value of this study is its intertwining of philosophical with socio-cultural perspectives in a way that asserts an ethical stand. In response to a 1988 French government commission finding that France now has the largest population of foreigners in its history (*Étrangers*, 287), Kristeva challenges the commission's call for "integration" as the national goal. The foreigners' affirmation of their particularity, says Kristeva, renders homogeneity impossible. Rather, responsibility for living with "those who are different" lies with the individual, in the personal moral codes we all must follow (290).

Todorov's approach is far more applied and historical and, paradoxically, personal than Kristeva's. His is an eloquent call for a complete reconceptualization of the relationship between "us" and "others," and it arises from his own experience as exile both in Bulgaria and in France. Todorov makes clear at the outset that *Nous et les autres* is a "moral essay" on human diversity that examines how "otherness" has been thought in the past, but also how it must be re-thought in the future (11). In this cogent study, Todorov engages in a dialogue with the principal French thinkers of the seventeenth through twentieth centuries whose works influenced not just cultural ideologies of difference but, more importantly, human behavior. The book's framework is the fundamental dualism of universalism versus relativism that underlies the ongoing tension in French thought between a generalizing insistence on human unity and a particularizing focus on diversity. Beginning with seventeenth-century classicism's internal contradictions—its point of departure is a profound ethnocentrism, yet it pretends to "humanistic" transcendence—Todorov unmasks the evolving intellectual contexts in which the discourse of the universal/relative dualism changes, but the contradiction at heart remains. Thus, post-Enlightenment "scientism," nineteenth-century "racialism," modern "nationalism," and various modes of "exoticism" elaborate the problem of a single human species in conflict with multiple cultural sub-groups, variously delineated. Worse, all the sytems of thought superimpose a hierarchical and judgmental interpretation on the universal/specific opposition.[16]   In this light, Todorov rereads such formative thinkers as Montaigne, la Bruyère, Rousseau, Diderot, Condorcet, Helvétius, Renan, Barrès, and Lévi-Strauss, among others, and locates the flaws in each one's intellectual project. Further, Todorov carries forward the negative political consequences of each writer's interpretation of diversity and commonality. Aside from the benefits of nuanced analysis, *Nous et les autres* also provides crisp linguistic distinctions useful for developing a shared critical vocabulary among students. For example, the differences between "racism" and "racialism" and between "assimilationist" versus "associationist" colonialism deepen any discussion of western humanism and its implications.

Todorov's final chapter is as thought provoking as any I've read on solutions to the individual and communal damage wrought by earlier ideologies of otherness. Speaking for and as himself, Todorov exhorts us to break with the illusion of fixed differentiations between "us" and "them." Instead, our analytic starting point should be ethical principles, principles that embrace the unresolvable ambiguities of our at once individual and collective statuses. Further, while acknowledging that the political entities of "nations" exist, we should be aware of the limitations and historical modifications of distinct "citizenships," as well as of the idea of a universal "humanity." Todorov's overall plea is for a "new humanism," which he calls a "critical humanism" (427): even while we all partake of specific cultural determinations, we also have in common the capacity to refuse these determinations; our recognition of social heterogeneity must also attend to our universal freedom to affirm moral values: "Wisdom is neither hereditary nor contagious: we achieve it to one degree or another, but we always do so by ourselves and not because we belong to a group or a nation. The best form of government in the world is merely the least bad, and even if we live under it, we still have everything left to do. Learning to live with others is part of that wisdom we have yet to achieve." (437).

I mentioned at the outset that marginal literature serves the vital function of debunking the myth of a monolithic French culture and literary tradition. Works that present a broad range of human experience, rather than a narrow view of concerns from which false generalizations are drawn, affirm that factors such as gender, race, class, age, religion, and sexuality shape people's lives and have shaped French culture. Further, if we ignore works of marginal authors, we reinforce the invisiblity and the silence these groups have, historically, endured. Feminist and cultural theory of the past twenty years has exposed the ways social and symbolic systems, the laws of life and literature, have excluded certain dimensions of experience. The "feminine," these critics claim, by which they mean elements inconsistent with the rationality, authority, and unity western culture has always prized, has been devalued. In this feminist light, the idea of a homogeneous French national identity and literature is seen as a myth founded on the exclusion of otherness and the repression of difference.[17]

The received idea of French universalism and fraternity in fact masks an impulse in that culture to assimilate difference and betrays a profound uneasiness with cultural pluralism.[18] This less than glorious aspect of France's past can be studied and taught as straightforward social history. The expulsion of Jews in the fourteenth century, the ghettoization of the poor in the nineteenth century, the de-naturalization of immigrants in the twentieth century, and the ongoing economic and political exclusion of women—these are all events we need to use to reshape the study of French civilization and to undo the traditional centrality of male political and military history.

French intolerance for cultural diversity can also be examined from the literary-theoretical perspective of canon formation. This important new field of French criticism looks at how "the authorial and reading practices as well as the social 'preferences' of a given cultural moment are erased, forgotten, and rewritten as a transcendent literary history" (Miller, "Authorized Versions," 406). It traces the origins of the canon to the mid-eighteenth century, specifically, to the development of pedagogical manuals for use in the Church-run secondary schools (see Joan Dejean, "Teaching Frenchness" and "Classical Reeducation"). Previously, "literature" had referred loosely to virtually anything written or read "by an adult public active in the world rather than a public isolated in an educational establishment" (Dejean, "Classical Reeducation," 28); best-selling authors such as Mademoiselle de Scudéry and Madame de Sévigné were therefore included in literary collections. But, by the 1740s, figures such as l'Abbé Batteux began selecting works as teaching materials "for a program of study of the French tradition that aim[ed] to eliminate all literature deemed dangerous to civic virtue" ("Classical Reeducation," 32).[19] What is useful in the context of marginality is the relationship between the aesthetic judgments made by educators and the concept of "Frenchness." According to Dejean, decisions about what texts were appropriate for molding white Christian males into model French citizens reflected the biases of the era's entrenched conservative powers, Church and State. And so, women's texts, deemed morally corrupting and thereby threatening to the social order, were excluded.[20] Likewise, male educators made judgments based on a hierarchy of literary genres. Since classical criteria deemed "noble" forms such as epic and tragedy more conducive to developing the positive qualities of "human nature," less lofty forms such as Christine de Pisan's epistles or Sévigné's letters were relegated to the margins. What is most regrettable for modern readers is that these eighteenth-century judgments of gender and genre by which non-Christian, non-white, and non-male authors were excluded were perpetuated uncritically by each generation of literary historians and anthologizers. As a consequence, our students continue to study what is an impoverished residue of the once-heterogeneous mix of writing that existed in France; that rich and varied corpus became the "narrow and fixed literary tradition we study, write about, teach, and pass on" (Miller, "Authorized Versions," 410).

The evolution (or lack of evolution) of the French literary canon over time can also be examined through the lens of the history of ideas and ideological movements. For example, Elaine Showalter's observation suggests fruitful interconnections between politics and writing: "It is a curious fact of literary history that canon formation has been particularly aggressive following wars, when nationalist feeling runs high and there is a strong wish to define a tradition" ("Introduction," 11). In a course I taught on "Literature and Politics in Modern France, we studied the historical correlation between such efforts to define a French national identity and prescriptive ideas about a French literary style.[21] For example, Maurice Barrès's *Scènes et doctrines du nationalisme* (1902) and George Sorel's *Réflexions sur la violence* (1915) draw the political landscape that followed the 1870 French defeat. Whether in the form of Barrès's right-wing patrimonial cult of "the Land and the Dead" or Sorel's bellicose left-wing anti-parliamentarianism and syndicalism, the ideological climate was one of discontent with the government in place and a restless desire for a renewed national vigor. Concomitantly, André Gide's *Journal* of the early twentieth century expressed his wish for cultural invigoration through a purified "French" writing. He believed France should once again assert its literary distinctiveness. Thus, describing the Jews' inability ever to possess the French language, he echoed the exclusionary anti-Semitism characteristic of the French cultural xenophobia of the time: "It is enough for me that the qualities of the Jewish race are not French qualities... the contribution of Jewish qualities to literature, in which nothing is of value that is not personal, brings fewer newer elements, that is, an enrichment, than it cuts short the speech, the slow explication of a race, and falsifies gravely, intolerably, its signification."[22] Similarly, for the defeated France of the 1930s and 1940s, one can read the political journals of Robert Brasillach together with Jean Giraudoux's aesthetic considerations put forth in his tract, *Pleins pouvoirs* (1939). Brasillach's German-inspired vision of a purified France based on "the qualities of our nation, our race, our history" (*Notre avant-guerre*, 244) reaffirms the same fear of an undermining of national integrity by "foreign" elements expressed by Giraudoux: "They bring wherever they pass a sense of imprecision, secrecy, misappropriation, corruption, and are constant threats to the spirit of exactitude, good faith and perfection that was characteristic of French artisanry."[23]   And, Brasillach and Giradoux share the desire for a spiritual renaissance in a France rendered base and materialistic by (Jewish) bankers and speculators.

One can push further the relationship between "the notion of 'French literature'" and the "theological and nationalist discourses" in which it is embedded by pursuing not just the question of canon formation, but the more radical one, as Elaine Marks puts it, of "how texts are read and for what purpose" (Marks, 175).   Marks's article sets aside the reading of marginal texts "as forgotten or neglected pieces" and instead uses them as "case histories of the ways in which prescription and proscription operate in discourses that inform literature and culture" (175).   While Marks goes on to expose the inclusionary and exclusionary principles common to proponents of three different traditions—French national, women's, and lesbian—one could adopt her approach to study similarities among other traditions or among other marginal experiences viewed as discrete.   One could, for instance, compare the discursive strategies Simone de Beauvoir uses in *Le deuxième sexe* to delineate the ontological condition of "woman"— her position as sexual identity in relation to that of man and of (ideal) humans in general—with those Frantz Fanon uses in *Peau noir, masques blancs* to situate colonized blacks in relation to whites and to other blacks. The two works elaborate models of absolute alterity: both blacks and women are not just "other" in regard to the male and white norm, they are "other" within and in relation to themselves.   Both women and blacks are over-determined, that is, their sex and race—their bodies—establish their identities in advance.   Yet, the existential precepts Beauvoir and Fanon use posit a universal human subject, and thus in some sense contradict the specificity of black colonial and female experience.   Or, one could compare Simone Weil's criteria for the physical and mental alienation experienced by assembly line workera (in *La condition ouvrière*) with those Catherine Erhel and Catherine Leguay utilize to describe women prisoners (*Prisonnières*). The particular forms of dehumanization both female inmates and the poor confront inform Weil's letters and Erhel and Leguay's testimony, and this dehumanization can be traced, for example, in such textual elements as representation of the body and narrative chronology.   Marks's method is effective because it illuminates the politics of reading, that is, the ways in which similar languages of marginality can be used and interpreted for utterly different ends.

It is crucial that we not only tell students that French democratic principles are contradicted by that nation's history (this seems particularly imperative in this bicentennial year), but also have them read the words of marginalized groups themselves. This makes audible voices that contradict the illusion of a single, coherent French cultural legacy. Only primary sources such as Fanon's testimony on racism, d'Eaubonne's essay on "féminitude," Villon's prison poetry, or Elie Wiesel's rendering of the Holocaust, offer readers the content of being black, or a woman, or an outlaw, or a Jew in that society.

One can also develop, along with contentual familiarity with marginal experiences, students' critical abilities, by considering the question of point of view in texts.[24] The narrative technique most powerfully inflected by difference (sexual, racial, class, ethnic, religious), point of view and its shifts make cultural relationships tangible. Not only the author's and narrator's, but also the reader's point of view can be articulated so their prism of interpretation can be defined. And, the different kinds of connections between and among reader, narrator, and author can be analyzed as configurations of social interaction—between men and women, masters and subordinates, colonizer and colonized. If, for example, students read in pairs texts that treat similar experiences, but from different vantage points, they can seize the limitations of any account. When they compare Voltaire's (*Traité sur la tolérance*) or Sartre's (*Réflexions*) ideas about Jews with Wiesel's, or Rousseau's views of women (*Émilé*) with Beauvoir's, or Louis Chevalier's discussion of working-class poverty with Victorine B...'s, they get a sense of what is fashionably called cultural "positionality," or the subject's posture in regard to the dominant discourse. A comparative study of incommensurable literary viewpoints alao makes it clear that outcast groups have been active cultural agents rather than mere victims of cultural hegemony.

Further, awareness of point of view is necessary for students and readers to recognize their own subjectivity, that is, the biases and values they themselves bring to their encounter with a text. When, for instance, a young woman or man of the 1990s reads Madame de Lafayette's "La Comtesse de Tende" or Rousseau's *La Nouvelle Héloïse*, in which the heroine "falls" morally, becomes pregnant, and eventually dies, they reject the heroine's limited choice between virtue or death. From their post-Freudian and post-contraception viewpoint, sexuality implies some element of volition. Or, students' resistance to the young protagonist's tragic recreation of her parents' impoverished life in Christiane Rochefort's *Les petits enfants du siècle* betrays their American middle-class field of vision. They see the wish to break from the cycle of poverty as sufficient and disregard the economic conditions necessary for that wish to take hold. Finally, readers who are frustrated by the prison escapee Anne's apparently self-destructive return to "the joint" in Albertine Sarrazin's *L'astragale* need to confront the very real constraints "freedom" can pose. Nurtured and sustained by prison's limitations, Anne is paralyzed by the structurelessneas of her liberty. When we deliberately work from a point of view that is not our own, our analysis of necessity changes; we experience the hegemonic parts of our own identity—for example, whiteness, heterosexuality, maleness—"as relative states" and not as "authoritative positions" (Rich, "Toward...," 96).

An appreciation of individual "positionality" in regard to text and context can also illuminate certain issues of language and cultural identity. At a sophisticated level, we can read along with Julia Kristeva texts that manifest ruptures in the linguistic and social fabric: late nineteenth-century avant-garde poets like Mallarmé or Lautréamont, or fascist/"psychotic" authors like Céline (*La révolution* and *Pouvoirs*). Though Kristeva focuses on modern and post-modern writers and skirts the question of authorial intentionality, her work allows us to read backward through the grid of marginality: we can look for evidence in earlier writers of a self-structuring exclusion, of marginality consciously used as a way to gain access to writing. For example, Tilde Sankovitch argues in *French Women Writers and the Book* that Marie de Gournay's self-portraits in *Peincture de moeurs* (1626) exploit the metaphor of her "alterity" or her mythic otherness to counter dominant definitions of Frenchness. Her epic language translates her embattled status as a woman, and it also works against the forces of Malesherbian linguistic purification at work in the seventeenth century. Similarly, Stephen Nichols has argued that medieval women "explored [the] alterity of language" to create texts that allowed them to confront "the hidden dimensions of desire." From their position of illiteracy they "cross[ed] over from the discourse of the every day world to that other language, the discourse of writing" (78). If we posit that canonical texts reflect the stylistic and linguistic preferences of insiders—for example, that Louis XIV's centralization of power is mirrored in the standardization of seventeenth-century French—then we can ask if marginal works diverge from those established tastes and priorities. Do they adopt, manipulate, or reject the linguistic biases of their time? How do those marginal works communicate a life experience that is problematic?

In the French classroom, we can make marginality the subject of linguistic exercises. We can, for example, consider the profound difference between the use of the term "nègre" by French colonialists and the use of the word "négritude" by French-speaking Africans: the same term conveys racial prejudice in one context, racial pride in the other. Or, we can compare the phrase "la femme" with "les femmes," a lexical distinction that often signals sexual stereotyping on the one hand, attention to concrete realities on the other. We can also point out that in current French feminist discourse, "la femme" and "le féminin" designate philosophical concepts of otherness that contrast with the cultural priorities of materialist feminists. And, we can talk about "le Juif" versus "l'Israélite," two terms anchored in the troubled history of French Jewry. A label used by anti-Semites and rejected by French Jews themselves during the Third Republic, "Juif" was deemed too particularistic and "Israélite" appropriately assimilationist. Significantly, many contemporary French Jews now self-identify as "Juifs," an affirmation of cultural pride. Studying the use of language can open to discussion of widely divergent ideological views.

There is another way we can use marginality in reshaping our courses and our research, one that could change them radically. While it is essential to correct distorted and inaccurate perceptions about being a woman, poor, gay, or black, it is equally important not to reinforce the marginality of those lives and works. By simply adding texts to existing curricula or standard areas of research, we are in a way keeping those texts apart. What is more, by "adding marginals and stirring," to use the feminist formulation, we do not re-think our courses or our projects as a whole, we do not reevaluate previous criteria of intellectual coherence. If, however, we move these marginal works to the center, if we displace previous social and textual norms, we are forced to reconstruct the entire logic of the literary or cultural corpus we are studying. We are forced to break from the dualistic structure of insider-outsider, center-margin, a dualism of unequal terms, and we are made to reconceptualize the human relationships involved. We have no choice but to find new grounds for reading these and formerly canonical works together, grounds that are incompatible with traditional criteria such as "greatness," "beauty," or "importance."

For example, Jean Genet's *Miracle de la Rose* illuminates to some extent the content of the prison world that formed him. It reflects the passage in penal ideology from the need for banishment—the young Genet experienced the *bagne* or deportation to forced labor—to the belief in the prisoner's capacity for rehabilitation. It also conveys the evolution of the nineteenth-century cult of the great criminal in France.[25] Genet goes beyond legitimizing his imprisoned heroes to glorifying their criminal acts; and Genet's own sanctification as author and criminal shows the link in modern French culture between the literary and criminal imagination. *Miracle de la Rose* also transmits the pain and anger Genet, as pariah, felt, as well as the beauty of his life through his eyes. But, if we use the text as a lens through which to look back on interwar France as a whole, we can see the complex response of the prevailing non-criminal and heterosexual society to Genet's world, that is, the fear he inspired in those who imprisoned him and censored his writing, and the admiration he aroused in those who glorified his life and work. And, more broadly, we can raise new and larger questions about human subjectivity. We can, for instance, ask with Genet if there are ways to think about human identity that transcend the conventional opposition between self and other. Genet's post-modern destabilizing of the concept of a fixed identity occurs on a multitude of levels: chronological (past and present interpenetrate); metaphysical (good and evil are interchangeable); linguistic (the vulgar and the poetic coexist); and sexual (masculine and feminine continually blend). Genet's movement between and among triangular relationships that both verify and undo individual identity, and his insistence on absolute subjectivity, or his evocation of the void within the self, transform dualisms into alchemical myth.

Another, in some ways easier work through which we can reconceptualize human relationships is Marguerite Duras's *Moderato Cantabile*. To approach this book, we have to actively displace our expectations and ourselves as readers: the characters are shadows possessing no conventional psychological depth; the narrative is built not on traditional linearity, but on the repetition of scenes; the atmosphere is stifling, the action non-existent, the conclusion open-ended; and language and dialogue, far from facilitating communication, instead continually undo the acquiring of knowledge and meaning, for the characters and for us. Students, and all readers, are confronted here with a text that resists being read with comfort or familiarity. As a result, we must dislocate ourselves and reach beyond what we know; we must read in a new way. Like the novel's heroine, Anne, a tentative figure who seeks to understand an irrational act of murder and who attempts to assume the identity of the dead woman, we, too, will try to make sense of something our knowledge cannot fully grasp—the novel itself—and we, too, must make ties to other lives—in this case, to Anne's world of intense feminine alienation. Thus, by reading Duras, together with our students, we make connections both with the text and with one another, we actually experience the process of textual interpretation as a community activity.

Finally, in another, dramatic instance of the consequences of displacing our view, this time in a research context, the critic Jeffrey Mehlman has studied works by well-known French authors which reveal affinities with the discourse of France's "sustaining anti-Semitism" (Mehlman, 4), works deemed secondary or peripheral by critics. In *Legacies of Anti-Semitism*, Mehlman examines texts by Gide, Blanchot, Giraudoux, and Lacan that until now have been labelled merely "polemical." By moving these "minor" pieces to the center, pieces marked by the racism of their culture, Mehlman shows how the landscape of each author's entire opus looks very different: in this new light, canonical landmarks reveal structures and strategies of exclusion that were previously invisible. For example, Giraudoux's tragedy *Judith*, in the context of World War II French collaboration, now appears to be "a play lamenting a failed genocide" (39). Or, Lacan's apologetic misreading of Léon Bloy's anti-Jewish tirade, *Le salut par les Juifs*, suggests Lacan saw both psychoanalysis and Judaism as "divergent traditions": as Bloy had deemed New Testament theology superior to that of the old Testament and criticized Jews for refusing to integrate it, so Lacan sought an improved reading of Freud that "pretended to restore [psychoanalysis] to its originary energy" (27). Finally, Mehlman reads Gide's *Les caves du Vatican* for intertextual parallels with Céline's *Bagatelles pour un massacre*. Gide's insistence on style as more important than substance, along with his making style the sole criterion for the designation "French literature," constitute an apology for Céline's venomous anti-Semitism (65). By placing the taboo subject of anti-

Semitism at the center of his analysis, Mehlman makes us see subtle forms of aesthetic and political collaboration in texts. The possibilities for choice of marginal texts are vast, but I would like to mention three others that work well for displacing ourselves as readers. First, Claire Etcherelli's novel, *Élise ou la vraie vie*, is a richly-textured story that makes cultural alienation palpable on many levels. The heroine, Elise, is a poor, orphaned, provincial-born woman, and the hero, Arezki, is an Algerian-born factory worker living in Paris. Thematically, all the characters are separated from what they see as "la vraie vie" ("true life"), or the happiness that is ever-deferred because of the untraversable gap between their desires and reality. Character depiction also reinforces this sense of alienation: there is a constant ironic disjuncture between the protagonists' sense of themselves and external perceptions of them. For example, his white racist co-workers see Arezki as a stereotypically animalistic, over-sexed Arab, when in truth he is tender, shy, compassionate, and thoroughly self-controlled. The novel's central metaphor of "the look" underscores the key role of visibility in the marginalizing of North Africans and women, since both groups are over-determined and assimilated to their physical appearance. Because the novel presents no direct psychological information about characters, the reader is made to confront images and behavior and to sort out preconception from observation. Finally, *Élise ou la vraie vie* illustrates the problem of communication that underlies social exclusion. There is, literally, no dialogue between the Algerians and the French. Even the lovers, Elise and Arezki, cannot transcend the forces that separate them. Among the North Africans themselves, writing as medium of contact is superceded by other forms such as songs, gestures, looks, and signs. This symbolic refusal of French language on the part of the foreigners reflects their adherence to their native culture; and it forces the reader to interpret scenes without benefit of verbal exposition. Ultimately, language as site of otherness inheres to the novel itself, since the book mimes internally its own production. That is, the writing of the novel is reflected in Elise's coming to writing as story's end. The initially silent, alienated heroine promises to recount the race, class, and sex oppression she has experienced—she will tell the story we have just read. And, when we, the readers, speak or write of the novel, we, too, inevitably make alienation an issue of language.

Albertine Sarrazin's sprawling fresco of prison life, *La cavale*, brings us into the alien world of the criminal *milieu*. The novel recounts the five months Sarrazin spent in Versailles, Compiègne, and Amiens prisons during 1961. The apparent substance of the narrative is the daily monotony of prison routine that Anne, Sarrazin's autobiographical heroine, endures: eating, cleaning, sewing, sleeping. Sarrazin makes tangible the immobility of time and space in this self-contained world. And yet, in subtle ways, we are drawn in beyond the description of prison's external features to the novel's true life center, Anne's imagination. For the real story here is Anne's writing of the novel that will become *La cavale*. The true textual chronology is not wake-ups or mail calls, but the evolution of Anne's creative vitality; her intellectual movement toward the book's completion, along with her barren intervals of silence, constitute the novel's true structure and its dramatic tension. What gives the book immediacy is Barrazin's use of a double perspective, that of Anne the narrator and Anne the prisoner/character she observes. The result is a freshness of voice and a sharp irony, as Anne watches herself function physically in this world from which she feels intellectually removed. By putting her ironical narrator in the position of the observing reader, Sarrazin establishes a critical prism for us. Through it, we see prison as from her eyes, and less through our own prejudices. As we focus on Anne's mental pulse, we are made to feel the debilitating effects of imprisonment on an active human spirit.

A last, extremely powerful outsider's text is Françoise d'Eaubonne's "La féminitude ou la subjectivité radicale," the introduction to her ecological/feminist tract, *Le féminisme ou la mort*. This highly personal essay defines woman's state in masculine culture: one of "radical subjectivity," or the ever-present awareness of a self in contradiction. D'Eaubonne's paradigm for woman's condition is the double-bind: "No matter what I do, I'm wrong" (42). Woman lives eternal paradox: she is at once part of and separated from the hegemonic male culture; she is most unnatural to herself precisely when she conforms to the "feminine nature" masculine culture ascribes to her. And, the more she internalizes her condition and tries to turn it to her advantage, the more justification she gives to her oppressor's view of her. What makes d'Eaubonne's evocation of *la féminitude* so compelling is that she walks the reader through its stages. She begins with the moment of self-discovery every woman encounters, the recognition of an irremediable break that constitutes her relationship with the male world, and also with herself. D'Eaubonne's lexicon for this sense of rupture is rich: "separation," "curse," "anguish," "alienation," "strangeness," "condemnation," "punishment." The text also sustains juridical metaphors that suggest woman's potential at any moment for breaking patriarchal Law. In fact, the entire piece creates the effect of a legal defense, of a dialogue with an imagined accuser whose objections d'Eaubonne foresees. Through the chronology of self-discovery and the use of dialogue with an interlocutor, the reader, like the woman d'Eaubonne describes, is brought to consciousness of female alterity. She or he is made to abandon the univocal posture of judge and enter into the conflictual condition of womanhood.

Focusing on medieval witches, or 1950s Algerian rebels, or belle-époque saphists illuminates all of French history and literature in a fresh way. These marginals can be seen as prophets of cultural transformation, as signs of larger strains and crises in western humanity. Jules Michelet made this point when he argued in *La sorcière* that, not coincidentally, the fear of witches intensified just at the time the Church was losing power. Likewise, some of the most virulently misogynistic texts—for example, Jean de Meun's part of *Le roman de la Rose* (c. 1277), Rousseau's *Émile* (1762), or

Montherlant's *Les jeunes filles* (1936-1939)—appeared at moments of feminine or feminist activity in France. Familiarity with the thoughts and acts of outcasts can deepen our sense of cultural movement and change in general. In addition, focusing on outsiders can, paradoxically, be a way to reconstitute human community. Outsiders have told us repeatedly, through the centuries, that there is what Genet calls "a void" at the heart of things (*Miracle*), that is, a chasm between different groups vying for equal claim to selfhood. But, by displacing our view, by multiplying the texts we read and reconceiving the ways we read them, and by entering into life experiences different from our own, we can encourage empathy, in ourselves and in students. The empathic restoration of social and literary community is also a moral and political geature that can go far to fill the void outsiders have experienced. As Adrienne Rich exhorts us, "My hope is that the movement we are building can further the conscious work of turning Otherness into a keen lens of empathy, that we can bring into being a politics based on concrete, heartfelt understanding of what it means to be Other" ("If Not...," 203).

Notes

1. The ideas for this article originated in a seminar I taught at Mount Holyoke College in 1980 on "'L'autre' in French Culture and Literature." They were given further shape in a paper presented at the American Association of Teachers of French Regional Conference in November 1985. All translations are mine.
2. Julia Kristeva. *Étrangers à nous-mêmes*. Paris: Fayard, 1988, 57-59, her emphasis.
3. Lucienne Frappier-Mazur. "Marginal Canons: Rewriting the Erotic." *Yale French Studies* 75 (Fall 1988), 112. She quotes Robert von Hallberg, "Editor's Introduction." *Critical Inquiry* 10 (September 1983), iii.
4. I am grateful to the participants in the Harvard University Feminist Theory Seminar for bringing references to the new historicism to my attention and for supplying copies of articles. It is in the area of English Renaissance studies that the material on the new historicism has been particularly rich.
5. Besides Foucault, other "founding fathers" of new historicism are Walter Benjamin, Hayden White, and Louis Althusser.
6. Two recent journal issues address the issue of canon formation in France and contain particularly provocative essays: *Yale French Studies*, no. 75, "The Politics of Tradition: Placing Women in French Literature" (Fall 1988); and *The French Review* 61:3 (February 1988).

7. See especially ch. 1 for his elaboration of the concept of "liminality, " a "movement between fixed points [that] is essentially ambiguous, unsettled, and unsettling" (274), a "threshold cultural position" that is "betwixt and between" the "status occupying" structure and the "inferior" margins (232).
8. Michel Foucault's informative discussion of the *nef des fous*, which he calls a "figure" or representation that exists in the general social consciousness, appears in the first chapter of his *Histoire de la folie à l'âge classique*. Paris: Gallimard, 1972.
9. See Jacques Le Goff. *La civilisation de l'Occident médiéval*. Paris: Arthaud, 1967; and his "Les marginaux dans l'Occident médiéval," in *Les Marginaux et les exclus dans l'histoire, Cahiers Jussieu* no. 5. Paris: UGE-10/18, 1979, 19-28.
10. There is also the remarkable film *Aloíse* (dir. Chantal Akerman), the story of a gifted painter whose aphasia is treated as mental illness. The film not only raises the issue of women's alienation from masculine language, it addresses normative codes of visual representation as well.
11. The same term, "voleuses" ("thieves"), is used to describe women's historical relationship to language by Claudine Herrmann in *Les voleuses de langue*. Paris: des femmes, 1976. The pun in "voleuses"—women both "steal" and "fly" when they write—echoes Thévoz's view that psychiatric patients' words are both "magical substances" and dangerous instruments that threaten "[the] fundamental principle of sociality" (19).
12. John Guillory. "Canonical, and Non-Canonical: A Critique of the Current Debate," *ELH* 54 (1987), 484, his emphasis. Cited in Stephen C. Nichols, "Medieval Women Writers: *Aisthesis* and the Powers of Marginality." *Yale French Studies* 75 (Fall 1988), 78.
13. Beauvoir's section on "Mythes" in *Le deuxième sexe* is a brilliant compendium of the coexistent images of woman (virgin/whore, nature/ artifice, etc.) in Western culture. An example of the contradictory mythologies surrounding the working class poor in nineteenth-century France is Zola's *Germinal*. In the novel, bourgeois mine owners view the coal miners as both docile and dangerous, as animals at once savage and resigned.
14. The term *étranger* presents difficulties for translation, since it is at once adjective and noun, and also simultaneously means "strange," "alien," "outside," and "estranged."
15. For Kristeva's views on language and the maternal, see "La femme ce n'est jamais ça." *Tel Quel* 59 (Autumn 1974), 19-25; and "Héréthique de l'amour." *Tel Quel* 74 (Winter 1977), 30-49.
16. Hélène Cixous's formative feminist essay, "Sorties," in Catherine Clément and Hélène Cixous. La jeune née. Paris: UGE-10/18, 1975, 114-246, argues eloquently that all symbolic systems are rooted in hierarchized oppositions and that the perception of difference in terms of superior/inferior is masculine. For Cixous, *homme/femme* is the fundamental opposition upon which culture is built.

17. For an overview of the French feminist reevaluation of *altérité*, or the problematics of difference in which "woman" and "the feminine" have been oppressed and repressed, see Virginia Thorndike Hules, "A Topography of Difference," in Elissa Gelfand and Virginia Thorndike Hules. *French Feminist Criticism: Women, Language, and Literature.* New York: Garland Publishing, 1985, xv-lii. Se also Alice Jardine. *Gynesis: Configurations of Women and Modernity.* Ithaca and London: Cornell University Press, 1985.

18. The fact that this assimilationist impulse can, under certain conditions, turn to intolerance is the thesis underlying Michael Marrus and Robert O. Paxton's definitive study, *Vichy France and the Jews.* New York: Basic Books, 1981.

19. L'Abbé Batteux's best-known collection is his *Cours de belles-lettres* (1747).

20. This rejection of women's works on moral grounds intersects with another socio-literary event of eighteenth-century France, the debate on the novel. Conservative defenders of classical aesthetics and of the social status quo were also generally the strongest opponents of the novel, whose focus on love and on women they deemed morally and socially dangerous. See Georges May. *Le dilemme du roman au XVIIIe siècle: étude sur les rapports du roman et de la critique (1715-1761).* Paris and New Haven: PUF and Yale University Press, 1963; also, Elissa Gelfand and Margaret Switten. "Gender and the Rise of the Novel." *The French Review* 61:3 (February 1988), 443-453.

21. For opposing views on the issue of style versus content in relation to political engagement, see André Gide. *Littérature engagée* (1935). Paris: Gallimard, 1950; and Jean-Paul Sartre. *Qu'est-ce que la litterature?* Paris: Gallimard, 1948.

22. Gide, Journal, 1889-1939, entry of 24 January 1914, cited and translated by Jeffrey Mehlman in his *Legacies of Anti-Semitism in France.* Minneapolis: University of Minnesota Press, 1984, 64-65.

23. Giradoux, *Pleine pouvoirs*, cited and translated by Mehlman in *Legacies*, 47.

24. For useful introductions and distinctions concerning point of view, see Wayne Booth, "Distance et point de vue." *Poétique* 4 (1970), 511-524; Roland Bourneuf and Réal Ouellet. *L'univers du roman.* Paris: PUF, 1972; and Gérard Genette. *Figures III.* Paris: Seuil, 1972.

25. Balzac's Vautrin is the classic example, as is Lacenaire, the criminal-poet of the same era.

References

Allard, Guy, ed. *Aspects de la marginalité au Moyen Age.* Montréal: L'Aurore, 1975.

Arendt, Hannah. *The Jew as Pariah: Jewish Identity and Politics in the Modern Age*, ed. Ron H. Feldman. New York: Grove Press, 1978.

Barrès, Maurice. *Scènes et doctrines du nationalisme.* Paris: Plon, 1902.

Beauvoir, Simone de. *Le deuxième sexe.* Paris: Gallimard, 1949.

Blanc-Lapierre, Marc. *Suis-je donc fou?* Paris: Laffont, 1978.

224 / Critical Issues in Foreign Language Instruction

Boose, Linda. "The Family in Shakespeare Studies." *Renaissance Quarterly* 40 (Winter 1987), 707-742.

Brasillach, Robert. *Notre avant-guerre*. Paris: Plon, 1941.

Brocher, Victorine. *Souvenirs d'une morte vivante*. Paris: Maspero, 1977.

Chevalier, Louis. *Classes laborieuses et classes dangereuses à Paris pendant la première moitié du XIXe siècle*. Paris: Plon, 1958.

Cixous, Hélène. "Le Rire de la Méduse." *L'Arc* 61 (1975), 39-54.

_____. "Sorties." In Catherine Clément and Hélène Cixous. *La jeune née*. Paris: UGE-10/18, 1975, 114-246.

_____. *Un K incompréhensible: Pierre Goldman*. Paris: Ch. Bourgeois, 1975.

Dejean, Joan. "Classical Reeducation: Decanonizing the Feminine." *Yale French Studies* 75 (Fall 1988), 26-39.

_____. "Teaching Frenchness." *The French Review* 61:3 (February 1988), 398-404.

Diderot, Denis (& d'Alembert). *Encyclopédie* (1751-1772). In Diderot. *Oeuvres complètes*, vols. 13-17. Paris: Garnier, 1875-1877.

Duras, Marguerite. *Moderato Cantabile*. Paris: Minuit, 1958.

Eaubonne, Françoise d'. *Le féminisme ou la mort*. Paris: Pierre Horay, 1974.

Erhel, Catherine and Catherine Leguay. *Prisonnières*. Paris: Stock, 1977.

Etcherelli, Claire. *Élise ou la vraie vie*. Paris: Denoël, 1967.

Fanon, Frantz. *Peau noire, masques blancs*. Paris: Seuil, 1965.

Finkielkraut, Alain. *Le Juif imaginaire*. Paris: Seuil, 1980.

Foucault, Michel. *Histoire de la folie à l'âge classique*. Paris: Gallimard, 1972.

_____. *Histoire de la sexualité*. vol. I. Paris: Gallimard, 1976.

_____, ed. *Moi, Pierre Rivière, ayant égorgé ma mère, ma soeur et mon frère. Un cas de parricide au XIXe siècle*. Paris: Gallimard, 1973.

Frappier-Mazur, Lucienne. "Marginal Canons: Rewriting the Erotic." *Yale French Studies* 75 (Fall 1988), 112-128.

Gauthier, Xavière and Marguerite Duras. *Les parleuses*. Paris: Minuit, 1974.

Gelfand, Elissa. *Imagination in Confinement: Women's Writings from French Prisons*. Ithaca: Cornell University press, 1983.

Gelfand, Elissa and Virginia Thorndike Hules. *French Feminist Criticism: Women, Language, and Literature*. New York: Garland, 1985.

Genet, Jean. *Miracle de la Rose* (1943). Paris: Gallimard, 1977.

Gide, André. *Journal, 1889-1939*, vol. 1 of 2. Paris: Gallimard, 1948-1954.

_____. *Littérature engagée* (1935). Paris: Gallimard, 1950.

Giraudoux, Jean. *Pleins pouvoirs*. Paris: Gallimard, 1939.

Goldman, Pierre. *Souvenirs obscurs d'un Juif polinais né en France*. Paris: Seuil, 1975.

Guillory, John. "Canonical, and Non-Canonical: A Critique of the Current Debate." *ELH* 54 (1987), 483-527.

Herrmann, Claudine. *Les voleuses de langue*. Paris: des femmes, 1976.

Howard, Jean. "The New Historicism in Renaissance Studies." *English Literary Renaissance* 16 (Winter 1986), 13-43.

Irigaray, Luce. "Expression et signe." *Études psychopathologiques* (February 1971), 17-28.

_____. *Le langage des déments*. The Hague/Paris: Mouton, 1973.

Jardine, Alice. *Gynesis: Configurations of Woman and Modernity*. Ithaca: Cornell University Press, 1985.

Jardine, Alice A. and Anne M. Menke. "Exploding the Issue: 'French' 'Women' 'Writers' and 'The Canon'?" *Yale French Studies* 75 (Fall 1988), 229-258.

Kristeva, Julia. *Étrangers à nous-mêmes*. Paris: Fayard, 1988.

_____. *Folle vérité: Vérité et vraisemblance du texte psychotique*. Paris: Seuil, 1979.

_____. *Pouvoirs de l'horreur: Essai sur l'abjection*. Paris: Seuil, 1980.

_____. "Pratique signifiante et mode de production." *Tel Quel* 60 (Winter 1974), 21-33.

_____. *La révolution du langage poétique: L'avant-garde à la fin du XIXe siècle: Lautréamont et Mallarmé*. Paris: Seuil, 1974.

_____. "Sujet dans le langage et pratique politique." *Tel Quel* 58 (Summer 1974), 22-27.

Lafayette, Madame de. "La Comtesse de Tende." In *Histoire de Mme. Henriette d'Angleterre; La Princesse de Montpensier; La Comtesse de Tende*. Ed. Claudine Herrman. Paris: des femmes, 1975.

Leduc, Violette. *La bâtarde*. Paris: Gallimard, 1964.

Le Goff, Jacques. *La civilisation de l'Occident médiéval*. Paris: Arthaud, 1967.

_____. "Les marginaux dans l'Occident médiéval." In *Les margineaux et les exclus dans l'histoire. Cahiers Jussieu* 5. Paris: UGE-10/18, 1979, 19-28.

Marks, Elaine. "'Sapho 1900': Imaginary Renee Viviens and the Rear of the *belle époque*." *Yale French Studies* 75 (Fall 1988), 175-189.

Marrus, Michael and Robert O. Paxton. *Vichy France and the Jews*. New York: Basic Books, 1981.

Mehlman, Jeffrey. *Legacies of Anti-Semitism in France*. Minneapolis: University of Minnesota Press, 1984.

Michelet, Jules. *La sorcière (XIXe)*. Paris: M. Didier, 1952-1956.

Miller, Nancy K. "Authorized Versions." *The French Review* 61:3 (February 1988), 405-413.

_____. "Men's Reading, Women's Writing: Gender and the Rise of the Novel." *Yale French Studies* 75 (Fall 1988), 40-55.

Montrose, Louis. "The Elizabethan Subject and the Spenserian Text." *Literary Theory/Renaissance Texts* (1986).

Nerval, Gerard de. *Aurélia* (1853). In *Les Filles du feu, suivi de Aurélia*. Paris: Gallimard, 1972.

Nichols, Stephen C. "Medieval Women Writers: Aisthesis and the Powers of Marginality." *Yale French Studies* 75 (Fall 1988), 77-94.

Proust, Marcel. *Sodome et Gomorrhe* (1921-1922). Paris: Gallimard, 1954.

Rich, Adrienne. "Toward a More Feminist Criticism" (1981) and "If Not with Others, How?" (1985). In *Blood, Bread, and Poetry: Selected Prose, 1979-1985*. New York and London: Norton, 1986, 85-99 and 202-209.

Rochefort, Christiane. *Les petits enfants du siècle*. Paris: Grasset, 1961.

Rousseau, Jean-Jacques. *Discours sur l'origine et les fondements de l'inégalité parmi les hommes (1754)*. Paris: Gallimard, 1965.

_____. *Émile* (1762). Paris: Garnier, 1964.

_____. *Julie ou la Nouvelle Héloïse* (1761). Paris: Flammarion, 1967.

Sankovitch, Tilde. *French Women Writers and the Book*. Syracuse: Syracuse University press, 1988.

Sarrazin, Albertine. *L'astragale*. Paris: Jean-Jacques Pauvert, 1965.

_____. *La cavale*. Paris: Jean-Jacques Pauvert, 1965.

Sartre, Jean-Paul. *L'être et le néant: Essai d'ontologie phénoménologique*. Paris: Gallimard, 1943.

_____. *Qu'est-ce que la littérature?* Paris: Gallimard, 1948.

226 / Critical Issues in Foreign Language Instruction

_____. *Réflexions sur la question juive*. Paris: Gallimard, 1954.

Showalter, Elaine, ed. *The New Feminist Criticism: Essays on Women, Literature, Theory*. New York: Pantheon, 1985.

Sorel, Georges. *Réflexions sur la violence* (1915). Geneva: Slatkine, 1981.

Suleiman, Susan Rubin. "A Double Margin: Reflections on Women Writers and the Avant-Garde in France." *Yale French Studies* 75 (Fall 1988), 148-174.

Thévoz, Michel. *Le langage de la rupture*. Paris: PUF, 1978.

Todorov, Tzvetan. *Nous et les autres: La réflexion française sur la diversité humaine*. Paris: Seuil, 1989.

Turner, Victor. *Dramas, Fields, and Metaphors: Symbolic Action in Human Society*. Ithaca: Cornell Univeraity Press, 1974.

Voltaire. *Dictionnaire philosophique* (1764). Paris: Garnier, 1935-1936.

_____. *Traité sur la Tolérance* (1763). Geneva: Cheval Ailé, 1948.

Weil, Simone. *La condition ouvrière*. Paris: Gallimard, 1951.

Wiesel, Elie. *La nuit*. Paris: Minuit, 1958.

Annotated Bibliography

Ajar, Émile. *La vie devant soi*. Paris: Mercure de France, 1975. Older Jewish woman looks after North African children in Paris; basis for the film, *Madame Rosa*.

Arcadie: Être homosexuel en France en 1970. Jan. & Oct. 1970.

Arendt, Hannah. *Antisemitism*. San Diego/New York/London: Harcourt Brace Jovanovich, 1951. Major, if controversial study of the situation of European Jews in relation to social and political contexts; important section on Third Republic French Jews.

Aymard, Christine. *On ne voit pas du tout la mer*. Paris: Seuil, 1979. Novel about poverty and juvenile delinquency.

Bâ, Mariama. *Une si longue lettre*. Dakar: Nouvelles Editions Africaines, 1983. A moving memoir-novel that presents a synthetic view of women's status in Senegal; traces the different steps and the generational changes in women's lives.

Beauvoir, Simone de. *Djamila Boupacha*. Paris: Gallimard, 1962. The case of a young Algerian woman accused of terrorism and brutalized by her captors during the Algerian war; her attorney was Gisèle Halimi.

_____. *La femme rompue*. Paris: Gallimard, 1967. A collection of stories about older women and the pain of aging.

Benoit, Jean. *Dossier E... comme esclaves*. Paris: Alain Moreau, 1980. Racism in France.

Bernay, Jérôme. *Grand'peur et misère des homosexuels français*. Paris: Arcadie, 1977. Testimonies of discrimination.

Besnard, Marie. *Mes mémoires*. Production de Paris, 1962. The memoirs of a provincial woman wrongly accused of poisoning her family in 1947.

Bonnet, Gabriel and Jean Bonnet. *La France et l'intolérance*. Paris: Roblot, 1975. A history of the intolerance of difference in France, from the earliest sources to the end of the Fourth Republic.

Bonnet, Marie-Jo. *Un choix sans èquivoque: Recherches historiques sur les relations amoureuses entre les femmes, XVIe-XXe*. Paris: Denoël, 1981. A thorough historical study of lesbianism in France.

Cahiers de doléances des femmes et autres textes. Paris: des femmes, 1981. Collection of documents by women of the 1789 revolution demanding political rights.

Césaire, Aimé. *Discours sur le colonialisme.* Paris: Présence Africaine, 1955 & 1962. Analysis of the sources and devastating effects of colonialism, from a marxist perspective.

Chénier, André. *Oeuvres poétiques d'André Chénier.* Paris: Garnier, 1889. Contains prison poems by the great 18th-century poet killed during the Terror.

Cohen, Albert. *Solal.* Paris: Gallimard, 1930 & 1958. Sprawling novel about a Jewish family living in Greece.

Colette. *Ces plaisirs (Le pur et l'impur).* Paris: Ferenczi, 1932. Colette's subtle, often brilliant analysis of homosexual experience.

Condé, Maryse. *La parole des femmes: Essai sur des romancières des Antilles de langue française.* Paris: l'Harmattan, 1979. Testimonies about the lives and writing of Caribbean women.

Condé, Maryse. *Moi, Tituba, sorcière: Noire de Salem.* Paris: Mercure de France, 1986. Forceful novel that uses parallels between Caribbean women and colonial witches.

Curtis, Michael. *Three Against the Republic: Sorel, Barrès, and Maurras.* Princeton: Princeton University Press, 1959. Still-pertinent study of three figures representative of early 20th-century French proto-fascism.

Dadié, Bernard. *Un nègre à Paris.* Paris: Présence Africaine, 1976. An African's encounter with French racism.

Diallo, Nafissatou. *De Tilène au Plateau: Une enfance dakaroise.* Dakar: Nouvelles Éd. Africaines, 1975. Straight autobiographical account of her childhood and the influence of both her father and Islam.

Dreyfus, Alfred. *Souvenirs et correspondance.* Paris: Grasset, 1936. Reveals, in spite of his adherence to assimilation, some facets of Dreyfus's life as France's best-known Jew.

Dufrancatel, Christiane, et. al. *L'histoire sans qualités.* Paris: Galilée, 1979. Essays on women's status during different periods of French history.

Duras, Marguerite. *Aurélia Steiner.* In Duras, *Le navire night,* etc. Paris: Mercure de France, 1980. Haunting rendition of female madness, alienation and pain.

Eaubonne, Françoise d'. *Éros minoritaire.* Paris: A. Balland, 1970. A general history of lesbianism in western culture.

Ega, Françoise. *Lettres à une Noire: Récit antillais.* Paris: l'Harmattan, 1978. A Caribbean woman writes home about her experiences of racism.

Exclus et systèmes d'exclusion dans la littérature et la civilisation médiévales. Actes du Colloque du CUERMA (1977). Paris: Champion, 1978. Collection of essays.

Farge, Arlette. *Vivre dans la rue à Paris au XVIIIe siècle.* Paris: Gallimard/Julliard, 1979. Collection of documents (police reports, travel logs, court testimonies) that recreates the colorful but dangerous lives of Paris' 18th-century impoverished street people.

Femmes en France dans une société d'inégalités (les): Rapport au ministre des droits de la femme. Paris: Documentation française, 1982. Useful compendium of what remains to be done.

Fénélon, Fania. *Sursis pour l'orchestre.* Paris: Stock, 1976. First-person account of her experience in an all-woman orchestra at Auschwitz.

Forster, Robert and Orest Ranum, eds. and trans. *Deviants and the Abandoned in French Society.* Selections from the *Annales,* "Economies, Societes, Civilisations," vol. 4, 1978. Excellent collection of essays on marginality: 15th-century prostitutes; 18th-century prisoners and abandoned children; 19th-century prisons and insane asylums.

Foucault, Michel. *Surveiller et punir*. Paris: Gallimard, 1975. Formative work that sets imprisonment in the historical context of other forms of social control in France.

Friedländer, Saul. *Quand vient le souvenir*. Paris: Seuil, 1978. Very moving recollection of his surviving the Holocaust by passing as a Catholic child.

Funck-Brentano, Frantz. *Légendes et archives de la Bastille*. Paris: Hachette, 1901. Testimonies and letters of 17th and 18th century Bastille prisoners.

Gaspard, Françoise. *La fin des immigrés*. Paris: Seuil, 1984. North Africans in French cities.

Geertz, Clifford. *The Interpretation of Cultures*. New York: Basic Books, 1973. Important collection of anthropological essays that connect the symbolic structures of creativity to social structures in the world.

Genet, Jean. *Journal du voleur* (1949). Paris: Gallimard, 1976. Angry and poetic account of Genet's becoming the criminal society judged him to be; portraits of the important lovers/criminals in his life.

Gérard, Nicole. *Sept ans de pénitence*. Paris: R. Laffont, 1976. Journal in which the author recounts why she murdered her husband to save her child; good description of the affective bonds women form in prison.

Geremek, Bronislaw. *Truands et misérables dans l'Europe moderne (1350-1600)*. Paris: Gallimard/Julliard, 1980.

Gide, André. *Corydon*. Paris: Gallimard, 1924. Gide's fullest treatment of homosexuality.

Gobineau, Joseph Arthur (comte de). *Essai sur l'inégalité des races humaines*. Paris: Firmin-Didot, 1853-55. Influential work for 19th and 20th century European racialist doctrines of white superiority.

Gouges, Olympe de. *Déclaration des droits de la femme et de la citoyenne* (1791). In Elyane Dezon-Jones, *Les écritures féminines*. Paris: Magnard, 1983. De Gouges' response (for which she was beheaded) to the *Déclaration des droits de l'homme*.

Gripari, Pierre. *Pierrot la lune*. Paris: Table Ronde, 1963. Early collection of testimonies by French homosexuals.

H. comme Histoiré, no.3: *Les Juifs en France*. Paris: Hachette, 1979. Articles about Jews in French history, the socio-demographic profile of the current French Jewish community, and images of Jews in French literature.

Hahn, Pierre, éd. *Nos ancêtres les pauvres: La vie des homosexuels sous le 2nd Empire*. Paris: O. Orban, 1979. Testimonies of 19th-century homosexuals.

Harris, André and Alain de Sédouy. *Juifs et Français*. Paris: Grasset, 1979. Interviews with French Jews from a variety of cultural and generational backgrounds.

Hyman, Paula. *From Dreyfus to Vichy: The Remaking of French Jewry, 1906-1939*. New York: Columbia University Press, 1979. First-rate social history of Jews in post-Dreyfus France.

Irigaray, Luce. *Ce sexe qui n'en est pas un*. Paris: Minuit, 1977. Essays that provide an invaluable overview of this feminist psychoanalyst's contributions to rethinking female sexuality and her critique of traditional conceptions of woman.

Jameson, Frederic. *The Political Unconscious: Narrative as a Socially Symbolic Act.* Ithaca: Cornell University Press, 1981. This marxist critic's important elaboration of the connections between literature and politics.

Katz, Jacob. *Exclusiveness and Tolerance: Jewish-Gentile Relations in Medieval and Modern Times.* 3rd ed. New York: Schocken, 1973.

Kriegel, Annie. *Réflexion sur les questions juives.* Paris: Hachette, 1984. In response to Sartre's metaphysical *Réflexions sur la question juive,* this historian/journalist treats a variety of concrete and problematic issues: the Holocaust; the status of the contemporary Jewish community in France; Zionism; and Israel's foreign policy.

Kristeva, Julia. "La femme ce n'est jamais ça." *Tel Quel* 59 (Autumn 1974), 19-25. One of the most complete articulations of Kristeva's ideas on "woman-as-absence" and on the revolutionary potential of woman's "negativity" in relation to the dominant culture.

Langfus, Anna. *Le sel et le soufre.* Paris: Gallimard, 1960. Novel about a young Jewish woman in Poland during World War II.

Lazare, Barnard. *L'antisémitisme, son histoire et ses causes (XIXe).* Paris: PTO, 1969. Classic and controversial analysis by a prominent Third Republic Jewish thinker.

Lévy, Bernard-Henri. *L'idéologie française.* Paris: Grasset, 1981. Highly intelligent and much-criticized study of the French brand of fascism; this "new Philosopher" traces the historical origins of native-French intolerance.

Lévy-Stringer, Jacques. *Les marginaux: une nouvelle force politique en France.* Paris: Fayolle, 1977.

Livrozet, Serge. *Aujourd'hui, la prison.* Paris: Hachette, 1976. Essay on the steps in the French penal process and the "truth" about life "inside" by a former inmate and prisoner-activist.

Malraux, Clara. *Et pourtant j'étais libre.* Paris: Grasset, 1979. The volume of Malraux's memoirs that deals with her life during World War II; touching account of her struggle to survive as a Jew and a single mother, as well as her work with the French resistance.

Malraux, Clara. *Rahel, ma grande soeur...* Paris: Ramsay, 1980. Malraux's biography of the important 19th-century German Jewish *salonnière,* Rahel Varnhagen, in which the author's identification with her subject reveals a good deal about Jewish women of both eras.

Marks, Elaine and Isabelle de Courtivron. *New French Feminisms: An Anthology.* Amherst: University of Massachusetts Press, 1980. The now-standard collection of important writings about women, woman, and the feminine that emerged during the different stages of post-1968 French feminism.

Memmi, Albert. *L'homme dominé.* Paris: Gallimard, 1968. Study of the commonalities in the experiences of blacks, colonized peoples, Jews, the working class, women, and servants; combines individual stories with theoretical efforts to systematize the processes of oppression.

Memmi, Albert. *Portrait d'un Juif.* Paris: Gallimard, 1962. A presentation of the contemporary Jewish condition, whose point of departure is Memmi's own experience as Jew and as colonized Tunisian; a search for definitions of "the misfortune of being a Jew."

Pastre, Geneviève. *L'espace du souffle.* Paris: C. Bourgois, 1977. A *récit* of her experience by one of France's most accomplished self-identified lesbian writers; evokes her joy in her sexuality.

230 / Critical Issues in Foreign Language Instruction

Pavesi, Julie. *La nuit des buchers*. Trevise, 1979. Study of medieval witches and the condition of women in the Middle Ages.

Paxton, Robert O. *Vichy France: Old Guard and New Order, 1900-1944*. New York: Knopf, 1972. Now-classic study of the moral discourse underlying the Vichy regime.

Perceval le fou, ed. G. Bateson. Paris: Payot, 1975. The text of an 1830's autobiography by a schizophrenic.

Perrin, Elula. *Les femmes préfèrent les femmes*. Paris: Ramsay, 1977.

Philippe, Béatrice. *Etre juif dans la société française*. Paris: Montalba, 1979. Excellent historical overview of how Jews have lived in France—"tolerated, excluded, persecuted, integrated"—from the 2nd century to the present.

Poètes sous les verrous (les). *Poésie*, no. 20 (Nov.-Dec. 1971). Small but useful collection of poems by well-known French writers who have spent time in prison (from Villon to Sarrazin).

Quetel, Claude and Pierre Morel. *Les fous et leurs médecins, de la Renaissance au XXe siècle*. Paris: Hachette, 1979. Combines literary samples with clinical analysis.

Regard d'en France. Des Africains parlent, qui les écoute? Paris: L'Harmattan, 1979. Collection of testimonies.

Roland de la Platière, Jeanne. *Mémoires particuliers de Madame Roland* (1793). Paris: Firmin-Didot, 1929. Political and personal thoughts of the Girondins' "Egeria," written in prison during her final months.

Russier, Gabrielle. *Lettres de prison*. Paris: Seuil, 1970. Letters from prison of a school teacher whose love affair with her student led to her condemnation, punishment, and eventual suicide; disturbing portrait of the destruction of a human spirit.

Sayre, Robert. *Solitude in Society: A Sociological Study in French Literature*. Cambridge: Harvard University Press, 1978. A marxist interpretation of the relationship, since the Middle Ages, between the "modern phenomenon" of solitude in society and the "socio-economic system of capitalism."

Schwarz-Bart, André. *Le dernier des Justes*. Paris: Seuil, 1959. A "family saga" novel that traces the legend of the "Justs" through the lineage of the Lévy's; Middle Ages through Ernie Lévy's experience at Auschwitz.

Senghor, Léopold. "Qu'est-ce que la négritude?" In *Négritude et civilisation de l'universel. Liberté* 3, 1966 & 1977. An essential presentation of the cultural and political underpinnings of the concept of *négritude*.

Senghor, Léopold. *Négritude et humanisme. Liberté* 1, 1964. Earlier version of Senghor's ideas on négritude as cultural affirmation.

Staal-Delaunay, Mme de. *Mémoires de Madame Staal-Delauney* (1718). Paris: Mercure de France, 1970. Implicated in the political machinations of her employer, the Duchesse du Maine, Staal-Delaunay recounts her 18 months of unusual happiness in the Bastille.

Stambolian, George and Elaine Marks. *Homosexualities and French Literature*. Ithaca: Cornell University Press, 1979. A collection of essays and interviews that use lesbianism and homosexuality as criteria for reevaluating the French cultural tradition and for articulating new literary traditions.

Sternhell, Zeev. *La droite révolutionnaire, 1885-1914: Les origines françaises du fascisme*. Paris: Seuil, 1978.

Trigano, Shmuel. *La République et les Juifs apres Copernic*. Paris: Presses d'aujourd'hui, 1982. Polemical but persuasive analysis of the Copernic synagogue bombing and other recent anti-Jewish events in France; blames the precepts of French republicanism itself for encouraging intolerance.

Waller, Marguerite. "Academic Tootsie: The Denial of Difference and the Difference it Makes." *Diacritics* 17 (Spring 1987), 2-20. Cogent refutation of the assumptions of the new historicism on the grounds it erases the effects of concrete cultural differences.

Weber, Eugen. *The Nationalist Revival in France, 1905-1914*. Berkeley and LA: University of California Press, 1959. Still-pertinent and important study of the early 20th-century right-wing factions in France.

Zehraoui, Ahsène. *Les travailleurs algériens en France*. Paris: Maspero, 1971.

Zola, Émile. *L'assomoir* (1877) and *Germinal* (1885). Two of Zola's many novels that treat 19th-century poor and working-class life in France.

Training and Supervision in Foreign Languages: A Diachronic Perspective

Gerard L. Ervin
The Ohio State University

Introduction

Teacher training, including the training and supervision of the graduate teaching assistants (TAs) who do so much of the elementary language instruction at the nation's research universities, could serve as a point of unification for many of the other themes of this volume. It is arguably in the training of new teachers, for example, where research in the areas of psycholinguistics and second language acquisition, materials development, implementation of educational technology, proficiency, and articulation find their most direct application. Perhaps, then, it is not surprising that the issues of training and supervising college foreign language teachers, making their training and supervision an integral part of the mission of institutions that have graduate programs, and ensuring that the execution of these duties becomes part of the reward structure at those same institutions, have received increasing attention in recent years.

Review of literature

In the bibliography of his landmark study of TA trainers and supervisors in foreign languages, Hagiwara (1970), cites sources from as early as the 1940s urging that more attention be paid to the preparation of college teachers of foreign languages. Indeed, if one examines the literature on the topic from the 1940s to the present, some common threads emerge.

One obvious grouping within this body of literature consists, quite simply, of exhortations. Numerous writers over the past forty-five years (e.g. Pargment, 1944; Sacks, 1961; Ervin, 1975; Dvorak, 1986; Van Cleve, 1987) have asserted that undergraduate language teaching is a noble and important calling; that graduate programs surely serve as the preparation ground for future generations of college teachers as well as of scholars; that undergraduate students are entitled to instruction by qualified, experienced and/or supervised personnel; and that most foreign language faculty, whatever other assignments they may have (especially early in their careers), will spend much time teaching basic language courses. These admonitions betoken not only enlightened self-interest on the part of these members of the foreign language teaching profession, but also their adherence to an almost moral imperative, i.e., that both undergraduate and graduate students deserve the best that faculty can provide.

A second division in the literature comprises program descriptions. These "how-we-do-it" (or "how-it-should-be-done") articles are widely represented (cf. Stein et al., 1961; Dalbor, 1967; Meiden, 1970; Hagiwara, 1970; Gibaldi and Mirollo, 1981; Di Donato, 1983; Chism, 1987; Lee, 1987; Lide, 1988). No newly appointed foreign language TA supervisor or coordinator need reinvent the wheel: descriptions, examples, and checklists for successful training programs, methods courses, supervision models, and evaluation practices are readily available. The scope of such writing is, not surprisingly, quite broad: TA training and supervision programs reflect the institutions and language programs that they have been developed to support, and these institutions and language programs (even programs within one institution) differ markedly from one another.[1]

A third, and extremely interesting, element within the literature is composed of empirical, principally descriptive, research. Though not many in number, articles in this category have treated, for example, a) the *characteristics* of TA training and supervision programs (e.g., Hagiwara, 1970; Schulz, 1980; Gibaldi & Mirollo, 1981); b) the *content* of TA training programs (e.g., Nerenz, Herron and Knop, 1979; Ervin and Muyskens, 1982); and c) *personnel issues* associated with TA training and supervision programs (e.g., Hagiwara, 1970; Schulz, 1980; Teschner, 1985).[2]

As increasing numbers of institutions of higher education have come to recognize the importance of quality and consistency in TA training and supervision, the need for a new kind of specialist has emerged. In foreign language departments these specialists typically exhibit a desire to work with TAs, possess excellent knowledge of the contemporary foreign language and culture, and have formal training in areas such as program supervision, curriculum and materials development, language teaching methodology, and language testing. Some may have a background in applied linguistics and second language acquisition research. As the number of these specialists, whom Teschner (1987) calls "educational linguists," has grown, so has their professional visibility: a new association, the American Association of University Supervisors and Coordinators of Foreign Language Programs (AAUSC), was established in the early 1980s.

The founding of AAUSC was clearly a response to the interests of the growing numbers of TA supervisors and their need for a standing professional channel through which to share information. The existence of AAUSC also offers a new research opportunity, namely, the chance to collect, compare, and analyze the experiences and opinions of a broad cross-section of professionals working in the field of TA supervision in foreign languages. In so doing we can begin to define and establish the parameters of this new academic specialty.

Population and instrument

A questionnaire was developed to send to TA supervisors. Comments on a pilot version of the questionnaire were solicited from a sampling of active TA supervisors, and appropriate revisions were made. The final form of the questionnaire concentrated on the following issues:

a.   In what kinds of institutions and departments are TA supervisors commonly employed?
b.   What are the working conditions and responsibilities of TA supervisors?
c.   What do they perceive to be important to their on-the-job success?
d.   How do they discharge their duties?
e.   How do they perceive the future of their specialty?

The final version of the questionnaire, a copy of which is included in Appendix A, was sent directly to the 122 members of AAUSC.[3] The original recipients were also encouraged in a cover letter to duplicate the questionnaire and pass it along to non-AAUSC colleagues active in the field of TA training and supervision who might not have received a copy.

Response rate. Over seventy (70) responses were returned. Many were accompanied by examples of TA handbooks, class visitation forms, and teaching guides that shed valuable light on the the extent of the variety in patterns of organization and execution of the TA supervisors' duties. Some respondents indicated that they were not currently active as program coordinators/supervisors; their responses, as well as responses that were largely incomplete or were received too late to be tabulated, have been excluded from the results and discussion presented here. A total of sixty-three (63) responses was tabulated.

Findings

Institutions (Table 1). The institutions that the responses represent are in the main large and state-supported. Though respondents were not asked to identify themselves nor their institutional affiliation, most did so voluntarily. They represented thirty-seven (37) different campuses (see list at Appendix B).

Departments (Table 2). A plurality (41.3%) of the responses represent "language family or area" departments (e.g., "Slavic," "East Asian," "Romance Languages"); somewhat fewer (36.5%) represent single-language departments (e.g., "German," "Spanish"); and the smallest group (23.8%) came from multi-focus departments (e.g., "Foreign Languages," "Languages and

Linguistics.") This pattern of the division of academic units seems consistent with the size characteristics of the responding institutions, i.e., the larger the institution, the more likely it will be to have its languages divided into specific units.

Table 1. Institutions from which responses were received.

	*CT.	%	LOW	HIGH	MEAN	ST. DEV.
Enrlmt	56		6,000	60,000	27,902.1	14,953.8
State	48	76.2				
Private	15	23.8				

*CT. = number of responses to this item (count). Not all respondents provided all information requested, hence the sum of subtotals may not equal totals.

Table 2. Departments from which responses were received.

	CT.	%	LOW	HIGH	MEAN	ST. DEV.
Type						
Single-lang.	23	36.5				
Fam/area	26	41.3				
Multi-focus	15	23.8				
Number FT fac	59		2	53	19.9	11.7
Undergrad. majors	56		4	200	82.9	47.3
Grad. majors	58		6	100	35.2	21.2
TAs in dept.	59		3	100	29.8	21.5
Students in supv courses	52		70	2,500	649.9	462.0

The departments themselves are typically large (mean number of full-time faculty = 19.9), have large undergraduate and graduate programs (mean numbers of majors = 82.9 and 35.2, respectively), and have substantial numbers of TAs (mean = 29.8).

Responsibilities (Table 3). Most of the TA supervisors (60.3%) work alone (i.e., without other faculty assistance), supervising an average of 18 TAs. Typically they are responsible for the instruction of some 650 students in 27 sections spread over four separate course levels (this would make the mean section size 650/27, or approximately 24). The supervisors make anywhere from one to five visits per term to a TA, with the mean being 1.8. Just over a third of the supervisors (39.7%) also report being responsible for assigned extracurricular activities: those most commonly mentioned are language clubs, a foreign language day, and organizing workshops for high school teachers.

Table 3. Responsibilities reported by respondents.

	CT.	%	LOW	HIGH	MEAN	ST. DEV.
1. Work alone (Yes)	38	60.3				
2. Assigned extracurr (Y)	25	39.7				
3. No. TAs respon for	59		3	50	18.0	12.4
4. Pre-term trng prg (Y)	59	93.7	6	100	35.2	
Grade/credit (Y)	15	23.8				
Required (Y)	57	90.5				
5. During-term sem/crs (Y)	57	90.5	3	100		
Grade/credit (Y)	49	77.8				
Required (Y)	51	81.0				
6. Number sep course levels	63		1	12	4.0	2.5
Number total sections	62		5	95	27.4	19.3
7. Evaluation method			70	2,500	649.9	
Class visits (number)	63	100.0				
Individual confs.	61	96.8				
Checklist	22	34.9				
Letter of evaluation	25	39.7				
Student evaluations	58	92.1				

Over 90% of the supervisors report using one or more of the following means of evaluating and providing feedback to their supervisees: class visits, individual conferences with the TAs, and student evaluations. Less frequently mentioned are letters of evaluation (39.7%) and checklists (34.9%). A substantial number of respondents (21%) also specifically mentioned the use of videotapes. Over 90% of the supervisors also report that their TAs are required to attend a *pre-term* training course, although only 23.8% of these courses bear a grade or credit. Finally, over 90% of the respondents also state that they offer formal *during-term* methods instruction. This course is required of students in 81% of the cases, and in most instances (77.8%) it also bears a grade and/or credit.

Rank and tenure (Table 4). The present data confirm that TA supervision remains a job most typically done by junior, untenured personnel. Only 44.5% of the respondents to this questionnaire are tenured (cf. 65% of faculty in all fields nationwide, according to 1988-89 AAUP figures), and only 36.5% hold the rank of associate or full professor (cf. 65% of faculty in all fields nationwide, again according to 1988-89 AAUP figures).

There was no clear consensus regarding the question of whether supervisory duties would help (or had helped) the respondents towards promotion and tenure. Comments ranged from "It has been stipulated that a supervisor never gets promoted," and "No recognition whatsoever!" to "It depends who is sitting on the tenure committee," and "I was hired for this very purpose; of course it counts." Almost all respondents reported that research and publishing are important (indeed, expected), but were divided on whether *textbook* publication would count.

Table 4. Rank and tenure status of respondents.

	Non-Ten.-Trk.		Tenure-Trk Unten.		Tenured	
	No.	%	No.	%	No.	%
Lecturer	10	15.9	2	3.2	3	4.8
Instructor	2	3.2	0		0	
Assist. Prof.	2	3.2	17	27.0	1	1.6
Assoc. Prof.	1	1.6	1	1.6	14	22.2
Professor	0		0		7	11.1
Other	0		0		3	4.8
TOTALS	15	23.9	20	3.18	28	44.5

Working conditions (Table 5). Nearly 70% of the respondents report that they receive some form of special compensation for their duties, most often in the form of a course reduction.

Table 5. Working conditions of TA supervisors.

	CT.	%	LOW	HIGH	MEAN	ST. DEV.
1. Special comp (Y)	44	69.8				
2. Special budget (Y)	7	11.1				
3. Special assistance (Y)	40	63.5				
4. Visits/term to 1st-yr TA	60		1	10	2.3	1.4
Specified by dept. (Y)	8	12.7				
Semester system (Y)	39	61.9				
Quarter system (Y)	22	34.9				
5. Specificity of duties						
Highly specific	10	15.9				
General	20	31.7				
At liberty	30	47.6				

A majority (63.5%) report that they have special assistance, usually in the form of a TA or (less often) a work study student, a lecturer, or a secretary. Nearly 80% of the respondents reported that they are at liberty to do the job as they see fit, or that their duties are only generally prescribed.

Time (Table 6). The respondents overall estimate that they spend over 56 hours per week on the job. Some fifteen hours per week are devoted to their own lesson planning and teaching, ten are devoted to their own research, and of the remaining 30 hours per week, over 22 are devoted to their supervisory and coordinating duties.

Table 6. Time-on-job reported by TA supervisors.

	CT.	LOW	HIGH	MEAN	ST. DEV.
Total Hrs/Wk	*59*	*25*	*96*	*56.4*	*13.2*
Teaching	59	2	12	6.6	2.3
Lesson planning — own	59	1	32	9.2	5.9
Planning, etc. — supervis.	56	0	20	6.0	3.8
Admin.	58	1	30	6.6	5.3
Vis/obs classes	56	0	12	3.3	2.6
Indiv. TA meetings	55	0.25	16	3.3	2.7
Student meetings	59	1	10	3.7	2.0
Own research	51	0	25	10.0	6.1
Other	30	1	25	7.7	6.5

(Many other activities were also mentioned, prominent among them being institutional duties such as committees and preparing grant proposals.)

Characteristics Supervisors Consider Important (Table 7). The two characteristics of a TA supervisor that this population rated most necessary for job success are one's ability to establish rapport, and one's sense of ethics and discretion. The importance accorded these qualities is followed closely by mention of the supervisor's knowledge of teaching methods and his or her own teaching ability, and knowledge of the target language and culture. Many other qualities were proposed by the respondents, as well, including the following:

- boundless energy.
- professional visibility (conferences, organizations, contacts).
- support (from colleagues, family, chair).
- imagination and creativity.
- organization.
- leadership.
- mediation skills.

The Future of the profession. Several types of responses could be identified from the answers to the open-ended question posed in Section H about the future of the specialty:

Table 7. Qualities and qualifications cited as necessary for success as a TA supervisor.

	CT.	LOW	HIGH	MEAN	ST. DEV.
Personal					
Rapport*	**62**	**3.5**	**5**	**4.9**	**0.3**
Appearance	62	1	5	2.9	1.2
Humor	62	1	5	4.0	1.0
Ethics/discretion*	**62**	**1**	**5**	**4.8**	**0.6**
Professional					
Methods*	**62**	**1**	**5**	**4.6**	**0.8**
English	58	2	5	4.2	0.8
Terminal degree	54	1	5	4.1	1.0
FL Educ. lit.	62	1	5	4.3	0.9
Admin. skill	60	1	5	4.4	1.0
Teaching ability*	**62**	**2**	**5**	**4.6**	**0.6**
2nd Lang. Acquis.	62	1	5	4.2	1.0
Target Language					
List/speak*	**62**	**1**	**5**	**4.7**	**0.7**
Read/write*	**62**	**1**	**5**	**4.5**	**0.8**
Grammar*	**62**	**1**	**5**	**4.6**	**0.8**
Culture*	**61**	**1**	**5**	**4.5**	**0.8**
Country	62	1	5	3.9	1.0
Other (Y)	17				

* Item in boldface if **mean** > 4.4 *and* **SD** < 1.0.

1. *Professionalization and recognition.* Almost all respondents mentioned in some way the need for increased professionalization of their field. They clearly see their role no longer as a transitional phase through which junior members of language and literature departments must pass on their way to developing a serious academic specialty, but rather as a career path to which they can, and want to, make a commitment. They appear to recognize, however, that it is one thing for them as individuals to make a commitment to a given field, and that it is quite another for senior colleagues, departments, deans, and institutions to give that field full recognition within the academy.

While aware of this difficulty, some of them feel isolated and boxed in. As Teschner (1987) puts it, "A vicious cycle reigns: because professionally trained educational linguists are a small minority and their field is relatively nascent and scattered around campus, educational linguists who direct [lower division foreign language] programs are usually expected to publish in a 'traditional' field, i.e., literature or theoretical linguistics; and because they are expected to publish in literature or linguistics they do not always succeed in contributing what they could to turn educational linguistics into the respectable field it needs to be if future scholars wish to claim it unapologetically as their main academic activity" (p. 33).

This issue, while being far from resolved, is nevertheless being confronted: the TA supervisors who responded to this survey seem to recognize that it is in large measure their own responsibility to define their field and to establish a research agenda and an investigative methodology (or methodologies) that will serve the needs of their department, add to the frontiers of knowledge, and stand up to the academic scrutiny that must precede their being recognized. There seems to be an implicit recognition, alluded to by Kramsch (1987), that only in this way can those committed to TA supervision hope to have their work recognized within the academic reward structure.

2. *Language Proficiency.* Although the precise definition of this term (not to mention its manifestation in language teaching and testing practice) is currently being debated, the need to ensure that language students, TAs, and, by implication, TA trainers and supervisors are familiar with the basic concepts of language proficiency runs throughout the responses.

3. *Educational Technology.* The respondents agree that TAs and TA supervisors need to be (or become) familiar with computer-assisted instruction, videodiscs and interactive video, the use of foreign television broadcasts, and other technology of the late '80s. It is probably safe to say that the pace of technological innovation and implementation in the classroom will accelerate into the '90s and beyond. Keeping abreast of these innovations represents a major, time-consuming, challenging, and ongoing responsibility for TA supervisors. (Indeed, just as AAUSC was formed in response to changing conditions in the language teaching profession, the mid-'80's saw the birth of a professional association of technology-minded language educators: the Computer-Assisted Language Learning and Instruction Consortium [CALICO].[4] This organization, though still comparatively small, has been growing rapidly.)

Another area of future change and concern (not mentioned by the respondents, but which this writer considers worth attention) will be the increasing need for specialists in the teaching of the less-commonly taught languages, i.e., languages other than French, German, and Spanish. Although enrollments in languages such as Arabic, Chinese, Japanese, and Russian are very low in comparison to those in the "Big Three," the world influence of the nations where other languages are spoken is vast and growing. Many of the insights, methods, and techniques developed for the teaching of French, German, and Spanish have applicability to the teaching of other languages, but if these advances are to find their way into the canon of the teaching of the less-commonly taught languages, language teaching specialists who know those languages must be found.

Summary and conclusion

In many respects the present study confirms much of the anecdotal, essay, and research work that has preceded it. Moreover, it provides additional information that allows us to fit the earlier writing into a comprehensive picture of the emerging status, role, and working conditions of TA supervisors. With regard to the specific questions that this study set out to examine, the following points can be made:

a. *In what kinds of institutions and departments are TA supervisors employed?* Large, state-supported institutions with large language departments are the most likely employers of TA supervisors in foreign languages.

b. *What are their working conditions and responsibilities?* Few TA Supervisors hold the rank of Professor, but a substantial number of them (just under half) have tenure or equivalent job permanence within their departments. While job particulars vary widely from one situation to the next, special support for TA supervisors and considerable latitude for them to determine how to carry out their duties are not unusual.

c. *What do they perceive to be important to their on-the-job success?* TA supervisors are a pragmatic group, reporting that familiarity with the target language and contemporary culture, teaching ability, and the ability to establish rapport are paramount to their job success.

d. *How do they discharge their duties?* The supervisors surveyed for this study put in long work weeks. Many are assigned extracurricular duties, most work alone (i.e., as the sole faculty TA supervisor in their department), and virtually all carry out their supervisory functions using a variety of pre-service, in-service, and one-on-one strategies to work with TAs.

e. *How do they perceive the future of their specialty?* The respondents are divided on this issue. There is an undeniable hint of pessimism in the responses of some, but at the same time there seems to be a growing sense of purpose and professionalism that many of the respondents now share.

Mooney (1989) reports that in the next fifteen years, academia will face a serious shortage of professors. While the predicted personnel needs will likely be most acute in the sciences and technology, the humanities will not be unaffected. At the same time, more and more voices, not traditionally identified with foreign language study, are calling for a renewed emphasis on foreign language and international studies at both the secondary and the post-secondary levels.[5] If the foreign language profession does not take steps now to ensure that the availability of *qualified* foreign language educators keeps pace with the demand, we could face a return to the 1960s, when, as Anderson (1963) reported, the need for foreign language teachers was so great that many marginally qualified individuals were hired.

Colleges and universities of the type whose faculty provided information for the present study can play a key role in ensuring a supply of qualified language teachers that will carry us into the next millennium. But such a supply cannot be taken for granted. Recently Saporta (1989, p. 20) described the situation prevailing in large language departments this way: "...the structure of the modern foreign language department, particularly at the large state universities, is quite clear. Graduate students begin their 'career' as teaching assistants in elementary language courses. Simultaneously, they provide the enrollment in advanced courses and seminars, taught by tenured and tenure-track faculty. The interests of the latter are essentially in some form of literary criticism or linguistic analysis; their attitude toward elementary language instruction ranges from indifference to outright contempt."

Given the direct link between the undergraduate and graduate teaching missions common in the kinds of institutions in which educational linguists work, the situation Saporta describes should be intolerable. But even if his characterization is reasonably accurate, the results of this survey, taken together with results presented in other studies that we have cited, seem to indicate that there is a growing recognition of the importance of TA training and supervision and of the role played in large language departments by language teaching specialists. Thus, there may be room for cautious optimism over the future of this emerging specialty and for the careers of those who have chosen to make it their own.

Notes

1. In some institutions, for example, TAs serve mostly as adjuncts (drillmasters, test graders) to faculty; in others, there is a gradual phase—of increasing amounts of responsibility; and in stall others, TAs function virtually autonomously (planning lessons, making up and grading tests, and assigning final grades) from the first day they walk into their classrooms. Cf. Schulz, 1980.

2. If one scans articles of this last type, it becomes apparent that many TA trainers and supervisors have had the feeling of constantly swimming upstream. Study of these assignments reveals, for example, that they are disproportionately filled by junior, untenured (or even non-tenure track) faculty, many of whom express doubt that their work in this area will significantly contribute to their chances for tenure and promotion.

3. The author wishes to recognize the College of Humanities and the Foreign Language Center at The Ohio State University for their support of this research; Prof. Carol Klee of the University of Minnesota, AAUSC Secretary/Treasurer, for providing the AAUSC address list and labels; and Mr. David Chamberlain for his many hours of careful data entry.

4. The founding of CALICO, encouraging though it certainly is, is only a beginning. Implementation of technological innovations in the classroom is proceeding slowly, at best, and colleges must bear part of the blame. See, for example, "Teacher-Training Colleges' Slow Move to Computers Blamed

for Schools' Lag in Integrating Technology," *Chronicle of Higher Education*, July 19, 1989, pp. A9-A10.

5. Such calls are not new, but they are becoming ever more frequent and include statements from bodies well outside the foreign language teaching profession. For example, in February, 1989, the National Governors' Association called for increased emphasis in secondary schools on world history, world culture, and foreign languages, and for foreign language study beginning as early as the first grade. The Association further urged that all college graduates should be conversant in a second language. In a strikingly similar statement in July, 1989, the American Council on Education called on the nation's colleges and universities to require competence in a foreign language for recipients of bachelor's degrees.

Annotated Bibliography

American Association of University Professors (AAUP), "The Annual Report on the Economic Status of the Profession, 1988-89" *Academe*, March-April, 1989. Gives statistics on salary, rank, tenure status, and many other aspects of the professoriate. An annual publication.

Andersson, Theodore, "Do We Want Certified Teachers or Qualified Ones?", *Modern Language Journal* XLVII (1963), 6:231-35. Cites the fallacy of hiring unqualified foreign language teachers, and proposes that certification not be the only criterion used for hiring.

Chism, Nancy, *Institutional Responsibilities and Responses in the Employment and Education of Teaching Assistants: Readings from a National Conference*. Columbus: The Ohio State University Center for Teaching Excellence, 1987. Dozens of papers from conference strands, including conditions of TA employment, TA development consideratins, matters relating to international TAs, and task force reports suggesting continuing directions for investigation and policy formulation.

Dalbor, John B., "A Realistic Look at the Training of College Foreign Language Teachers," *Modern Language Journal* 51 (1967), 4: 209-214. Presents a rationale and defense of the need to train college foreign language teachers, then describes the program at Pennsylvania State University.

Di Donato, Robert, "TA Training and Supervision: A Checklist for an Effective Program." *ADFL Bulletin* 15 (1983), 1: 34-37. Provides a list of suggested inclusions in a complete TA orientation, in-service training, and evaluation program.

Dvorak, Trisha, "The Ivory Ghetto: The Place of the Language Program Coordinator in a Research Institution," *Hispania* 69 (1986): 217-22. Suggests that TA supervisors/language program coordinators are in positions at large research institutions, where their managerial duties and the academic expectations placed upon them for promotion are not congruent.

Ervin, Gerard, "The Role of the Language Teaching Specialist in the College Foreign Language Department." *ADFL Bulletin* 7, 2 (1975): 15-16. Description of the role, duties, and qualifications of a college language department's language teaching specialist.

_____, and Judith Muyskens, "On Training TAs: Do We Know What They Want and Need?" *Foreign Language Annals* 15 (1982), 5: 335-344. Report of a survey in which foreign language TAs were asked to select the knowledge and skills they considered most necessary as a part of their preparation to teach.

Gibaldi, Joseph and James V. Mirollo, *The Teaching Apprentice Program in Language and Literature.* New York: Modern Language Association of America, 1981. Compilation of results of a major survey of TA-using departments of English and foreign languages, and descriptions of selected programs.

Hagiwara, Michio P., *Leadership in Foreign-Language Education: Trends in Training and Supervision of Graduate Teaching Assistants.* New York: Modern Language Association of America, 1970. (Also available as EDRS microfiche ED 041 523.) One of the earliest and most extensive surveys of foreign language departments with TA programs and supervisors. Large annotated bibliography.

Kramsch, Claire J., "The Missing Link in Vision and Governance: Foreign Language Acquisition Research." *ADFL Bulletin* 18, 3 (1987): 31-34. Proposes that the new field of second-language acquisition can establish itself as intellectually valid as its practitioners carry out badly needed data-based theoretical and empirical research.

Lee, James F., "Toward a Professional Model of Language Program Direction." *ADFL Bulletin* 19, 1 (1987): 22-25. Describes past practice and current efforts to make TA supervisory duties part of the promotion and tenure mainstream at large research institutions.

Lide, Francis, "On Constituting and Institutionalizing a Foreign Language Discipline: The Example of Rhetoric and Composition in Departments of English." *Modern Language Journal* 72, i (1988), 42-51. Draws upon the experience of the acceptance by departments of English of rhetoric and composition as a legitimate field of academic specialization to suggest that foreign language acquisition and teaching are no less deserving of recognition.

Meiden, Walter, "Training the Inexperienced Graduate Assistant for Language Teaching," *Modern Language Journal* 54 (1970), 3: 168-74. Describes the TA training program in the Department of Romance Languages at The Ohio State University.

Mooney, Carolyn J., "In 2003, Colleges May Need to Recruit a Third More Professors Than in '89," *Chronicle of Higher Education*, July 19, 1989, pp. A1 ff. Describes a study by two administrators at Franklin and Marshall College that confirms predictions of other, similar studies in recent years that large numbers of faculty retirements in the near future will lead to shortages of professors.

Nerenz, Anne G., Carol A. Herron, and Constance K. Knop, "The training of Graduate Teaching Assistants in Foreign Languages: A Review of Literature and Descriptions of Contemporary Programs," *French Review* 52 (1979): 877-81. Survey of TA trainers to ascertain what was included in training programs, and of TAs to determine what they consider beneficial in their training.

Pargment, M.S., "Preparation of College Teachers in Modern FL's," *Educational Record*, 25 (1944): 75-86. As described by Hagiwara (1970), "Advocates that teacher training should precede training in scholarly research and that each department should accept the responsibility for both types of training and develop a program adapted to the needs of individual prospective instructors."

Sacks, Norman P., "Training the New College Instructor," *Reports of Surveys and Studies in the Teaching of Modern FLs.* Modern Language Association of

America, 1961: 176-78. As described by Hagiwara (1970), "Training of graduate students as teachers must receive equal emphasis as training in research."

Saporta, Sol, "Foreign Language Departments and Ethics: An Editorial," *Modern Language Journal* 73, ii (1989): 119-20. Describes the incompatibility between what academicians in the humanities say about the intrinsic value of their field and the reality that prevails, both within the academy and outside.

Schulz, Renate A., "TA Training, Supervision, and Evaluation: Report of a Survey," *ADFL Bulletin* 12, 1 (1980): 1-8. Results of an extensive questionnaire survey of TA-employing foreign language departments. Describes changes since the 1970 Hagiwara report. Makes recommendations for an effective TA training, supervision, and evaluation program.

Stein, Jack M. et al., "The Preparation of College and University Teachers," *Northeast Conference on the Teaching of Foreign Languages: Report of the Working Committees, 1961*, ed. S.L. Flaxman, Princeton University Press, 1961: 32-41. As described by Hagiwara (1970), "Points out the reluctance of many tradition-bound departments to pay attention to pedagogical matters. Gives an outline of a minimal program [of TA training and supervision]."

Teschner, Richard V., "A Profile of the Specialization and Expertise of Lower Division Foreign Language Program Directors in American Universities," *Modern Language Journal* 71, i (1987): 28-35. Report of a survey of the academic background, areas of publication, and academic rank of lower division foreign language program directors.

Van Cleve, John, "Graduate Study and Professional Responsibilities: Bridging the Gap," *ADFL Bulletin* 18, 2 (1987): 18-19. Suggests that fresh Ph.D.'s in foreign language have usually not been given the tools nor pragmatic knowledge of the profession that will enable them to succeed at an operational level in obtaining and retaining their first job.

Appendix A
Foreign Language TA Supervisor Questionnaire
February, 1989

A. Your institution
1. _____ Approx. total enrollment.
2. _____ State-assisted or _____ private?

B. Your department
1. Type (check one):
   ___ single-language (e.g., French, Russian)
   ___ single-language family/area (e.g., Romance, Classics, Slavic, Asian)
   ___ multi-focus (e.g., Foreign Languages, Languages & Linguistics, German & Russian)
2. _____ Approx number of full-time faculty
3. _____ Approx number of undergraduate majors
4. _____ Approx number of graduate student majors
5. _____ Approx number of TAs in the department
6. _____ Approx number of students in courses under your supervision in Fall Term, 1988 (do not include any workshops or seminars you taught for your TAs).

C. Your responsibilities
1. Do you work alone, or do you share TA training/supervision responsibility with faculty colleagues in your department?
2. Do you have specifically-assigned extracurricular responsibilities (language club, outreach activities such as organizing a language day or contest for high school students, etc.)? If so, briefly, what are they?
3. How many TAs do you have primary supervisory responsibility for? _____
4. Do you have a pre-term training program for your TAs? _____ If so, do students get grades and/or credit for taking it? _____ Is it required of them? _____
5. Do you have a during-term seminar or methods course for your TAs? _____ If so, do students get grades and/or credit for taking it? _____ Is it required of them? _____
6. How many separate course levels (101, 102, etc.) do you supervise in a typical term? _____ Approximately how many sections, total? _____
7. How do you evaluate or provide feedback to your TAs? Check as many as apply:
   _____ Class visits (approx. number per TA per term: _____)
   _____ Individual conferences or interviews with TA
   _____ Checklist (could you include a sample?)
   _____ Letter of evaluation
   _____ Student evaluations of the TA's teaching
   ___ Other:

D. Your rank & tenure status

Rank	Non Tenure-Track	Tenure-Track, Untenured	Tenured
Lecturer			
Instructor			
Assistant Prof.			
Associate Prof.			
Professor			
Other			

How do you feel your TA supervisor duties affect you with regard to promotion and tenure? (E.g., will such work be recognized when the time comes? Will your publishing/research record in this area count? Will published textbook or teaching materials authorship help?)

E. Your working conditions:
1. Do you receive any special compensation (e.g., salary, release time) for your work was a TA supervisor? _____ If so, could you describe the arrangement in a few words?
2. Do you have a special budget allocation (e.g., for supplies and/or equipment) for the program you supervise? _____ If so, could you describe it?
3. Do you have any special assistance (secretarial, work-study students, senior TAs) assigned to you to assist in your supervisory duties? _____ If so, could you describe that assistance?
4. Approximately how many visits per term do you typically make to a first-year TA? _____ Is this number specified by your department? _____ Are you on a _____ quarter or _____ semester system?
5. How specifically are your TA-supervisor duties described by your department? (i.e., are there clear expectations of you, written down somewhere, or are you generally at liberty to do what you think is needed?)

F. Your views: How important do you think the following are to the functioning of a TA supervisor? (Rate them: 5 = extremely important, 3 = moderately important, 1 = not important) Please add unlisted qualifications/traits that *you* think are important.

	Less Important « » More Important				
	1	2	3	4	5
Personal traits Ability to establish rapport					
Appearance					
Sense of humor					
Academic ethics, discretion					
Professional qualifications Formal knowledge of teaching methods					
English language competence					
Terminal degree					
Knowledge of FL Education literature					
Administrative skill (planning, budgeting)					
Exemplary teaching ability					
Formal knowledge of 2nd lang. acquisition					
Target language competence Listening/speaking fluency					
Reading/writing fluency					
Formal knowledge of TL grammar					
Formal knowledge of target culture					
Frequent trips to target country					
Other					

G. Your time: How do you spend your time on the job? Rough estimates of a "typical" week would be very helpful.

Hrs/Wk	Activity
	Teaching
	Lesson planning for your own teaching
	Planning lessons, syllabus, tests, etc. for courses you supervise
	Administrative work: scheduling courses, ordering texts, dept. meetings, etc.
	Visiting/observing TA's classes
	Meeting TAs individually
	Meeting students (your own, or those in courses you supervise
	Your own research
	Other:

H. The future: Briefly, how do you think TA training and supervision will change in the next ten years? Be as specific as possible. What changes would you *like* to see?

I. What else? What did you want or need to be asked that this questionnaire did *not* address? (Feel free to answer this or any other question at length on an extra sheet of paper.)

THANK YOU for your assistance. This questionnaire is anonymous, and we appreciate your confidentiality and your limited time. But if you would be available for a 15-minute follow-up telephone interview, please indicate your name, phone number, and the best time to call:

NAME: _____ Institution: _____

PHONE: (____)_____ Time to call: _____ am/pm

If you would like to be sent a copy of the tabulation of this questionnaire, please give your name and address here:

Finally, if you have any documentation relating to your position or duties (e.g., a departmental or institutional letter of instruction or set of guidelines to the TA supervisor, or a departmental or institutional TA manual) that you would be willing to share, it would be most appreciated.
RETURN TO: Gerard Ervin, OSU Foreign Language Center, 155 Cunz Hall, Columbus, OH 43210

Appendix B
Institutions from which responses were received

Boston College
Brown University
Columbia University
Duke University
Harvard University
Indiana University
Louisiana State University
Michigan State University
Northwestern University
Ohio State University
Pennsylvania State University
Purdue University
Stanford University
UNC at Chapel Hill
University of Arizona
University of California - Davis
University of California - Irvine
University of Chicago
University of Cincinnati
University of Delaware
University of Georgia
University of Illinois - Urbana
University of Illinois at Chicago
University of Iowa
University of Kentucky
University of Massachusetts
University of Michigan
University of Minnesota
University of Montana
University of Nebraska at Lincoln
University of Pennsylvania
University of Texas - Arlington
University of Texas - El Paso
University of Texas - San Antonio
University of Utah
University of Virginia
University of Wisconsin - Madison

Beyond Language Proficiency:
The Construct of Knowledge

JoAnn Hammadou
University of Rhode Island

Béralde:	...Faites-vous médecin vous-même...
Argan:	Mais il faut savoir bien parler latin, connoître les maladies, et les remèdes qu'il y faut faire.
Béralde:	...L'on n'a qu'à parler avec une robe et un bonnet, tout galimatias devient savant, et toute sottise devient raison (pp. 844-845).[1]

Le Malade Imaginaire, Molière

Importance of teacher training

Education in general, and teacher training in particular, are back on the government policy agenda with a vengeance.[2] Many reformers currently seem to see teacher training as the key focus for solving a myriad of problems facing education today. This importance foisted on teacher education may or may not be justified, and some of the problems being addressed within the context of teacher training may be more effectively dealt with in other areas. Good teacher education is not the panacea for all of education's ills, because good teachers working under bad conditions, for example, may still fail to achieve society's desired results. Nevertheless, the key role that preservice teacher training plays in expressing a society's and a profession's intents put it unavoidably at the center of current attention. Society's mandate to foreign language teacher training seems to be part of broader demands that range from the mundane (end teacher shortages) to the lofty (provide humane teachers who can reach disenfranchised youth turned off to learning). The bottom line, of course, is a strong cry for improved teacher quality. While lawmakers and policy writers grapple with ways to legislate improvements in education, it is incumbent on teacher educators to continue in their own efforts at educational improvements.

Current reform movements in states like Connecticut, Massachusetts, and New Jersey have begun offering alternate routes into teaching. These states offer programs in which individuals with undergraduate degrees participate in brief training programs on generic pedagogical skills in order to obtain teacher certification. A primary assumption of these programs is that subject matter knowledge is the principal ingredient in teacher preparation. In other policy reform movements subject matter knowledge is also gaining attention. The Carnegie[3] and Holmes Group[4] reports advocate the abolition of an undergraduate degree in education in favor of an undergraduate degree in a subject-matter specific discipline for elementary school teachers. One sees, therefore, a revival of interest in the preservice teacher's knowledge of subject matter possibly being mandated by policymakers. This follows a period of time in which teaching, as well as learning, were both viewed as generic phenomena in educational research. Currently, research is affirming the policymakers' concerns, however, about subject matter knowledge as central to teaching. This paper will not attempt to look at the vast area of preservice teacher education in its entirety, but rather will focus on the issue of teachers' knowledge of subject matter and its role in foreign language teacher education.

Importance of subject matter knowledge

Buchmann has regularly asked her teacher candidates to rank the categories of teacher, learner, content, and environment in order of importance to education. She reports that these preservice teachers have regularly voted "learner" at the top and often give no votes at all to content.[5] Buchmann also notes that subject matter knowledge or content was never mentioned in Improving Educational Standards and Productivity: The Research Basis for Policy, a book sponsored by the National Society For the Study of Education in 1983.[6] Such neglect is no longer evident today. The widely cited Carnegie and Holmes Group reports, for example, both emphasize the critical importance to teaching of content knowledge. So who is right? Are we once again witnessing the swing of the seemingly inevitable educational pendulum? Is it automatic that what did not get mentioned last year, must get top billing this year? More likely what we are witnessing is the natural ebb and flow of new information about an age-old debate.

Recently this author overheard one preservice teacher announce: "I decided that I wanted to teach in a high school not in an elementary school because I wanted to teach the subject, not the kids." Others looked aghast—"But you don't do that; you're always ultimately teaching the student not the subject." The preceding conversation is only a small subset of a larger dialogue. This dialogue is part of the debate over the role of content knowledge in good teaching and the priority that it or other aspects of teaching should be given in the formal education of prospective teachers.

Teachers and teacher educators from all disciplines have been struggling with this debate. It is surprisingly unclear what rank or significance subject matter knowledge plays in the making of a good teacher. But foreign language teaching is one arena in which past practice provides ample evidence of the complexity of the question. A non-scientific survey of personal acquaintances may produce samples of two extremes in failure: the non-native foreign language teacher who knew no foreign language to teach or the native speaker, clearly fluent in all uses of the language, who was equally ineffective at imparting new knowledge to students. The myth of the expertise of the native speaker as teacher of a language exposes a natural desire on the part of some to seek simplicity of solution where no such simplicity exists. Clearly there is more to subject matter knowledge than first meets the eye.

At the very heart of the question lies a simple truth. A teacher who knows no French cannot teach French to others. In this, its most basic form, all can agree that content knowledge is, indeed, a precondition of teaching. Classrooms in which the French teacher never asks nor answers a question in French, never explains nor demonstrates anything in French may be sites of some worthwhile activity, but that activity will not be the learning of French. All of the myriad of teaching behaviors—disciplining, motivating, planning, evaluating, sequencing—presuppose content knowledge on the part of the teacher. Buchmann again reminds us, "When student achievement is disappointing, it is useful to recall that teaching is conditional upon the presence of educational content knowledge of teachers."[7]

In fact, subject matter knowledge distinguishes teaching from social work, counseling or other human service professions. All must know about children, their needs and their environment and its influences. Teachers must also have a body of knowledge that they can impart to students. Without content knowledge, the teacher becomes "like an actor who was exquisitely sensitive to the reactions of an audience, a master of gesture and of subtle inflections of voice, but who omitted to do one thing—to learn his words."[8] It seems most likely that the policymakers, mentioned at the beginning of this paper, are referring to this basic truth when they legislate increased content coursework for prospective teachers or seek alternative entry mechanisms into teaching for subject matter experts.

It is precisely within the classroom of some subject matter experts, however, that the added complexities of content knowledge become most apparent. Picture the native speaker of Spanish, with a Ph.D. in linguistics, master of the language in all of its subtleties. Imagine this content expert in the American high school class of Spanish. Naturally we question this expert's knowledge of American culture, children, school environment. But there is another question as well, very closely associated with subject matter knowledge. The question under inspection now is whether there are fundamental differences between subject matter knowledge in general and subject matter knowledge necessary for teaching. If there are fundamental differences, the reforms mentioned earlier recommended by policymakers are overly simplistic and doomed to failure.

The probability of such a difference between types of knowledge was noted earlier by Dewey. "Every study of subject thus has two aspects: one for the scientist as a scientist; the other for the teacher as teacher. These two aspects are in no sense opposed or conflicting. But neither are they immediately identical."[9] Currently, research in history education,[10] English education,[11] math education,[12] and science education[13] supports Dewey's claims. There is certainly reason to believe that analogous results might also be found in foreign language educational research. Among a list of seven categories of the knowledge base of teachers, Shulman includes "content knowledge; general pedagogical knowledge, with special reference to those broad principles and strategies of classroom management and organization that appear to transcend subject matter;... [and] pedagogical content knowledge, that special amalgam of content and pedagogy that is uniquely the province of teachers, their own special form of professional understanding...."[14]

Complexity of subject matter knowledge

It is of critical importance for educators to examine both the depth and breadth of the knowledge construct if the development of teachers is to be better understood and influenced. The depth of subject matter knowledge refers to components and complexities within content knowledge. It refers, for example, to the richness of examples of each element of the subject that the scholar possesses as well as the quality and quantity of links the scholar can make among elements of the discipline. The breadth of knowledge implies the ability, possibly unique to good teachers, to understand the subject on other people's terms and the ability to influence other people's understanding of and proficiency in the subject. Later, we will examine the characteristics of those other types of knowledge that are relevant to the teacher, but first we must look at the complexities of content knowledge itself.

Content Knowledge

As educators, we use the terms "content knowledge" or "subject matter knowledge" easily and interchangeably and roughly equate them with what we know about a subject. Grossman, Wilson, and Shulman suggest that there are, in fact, four broad features within subject matter knowledge—content knowledge, substantive knowledge, syntactic knowledge, and beliefs about the subject matter. They label "factual information, organizing principles, central concepts" as content knowledge.[15]

For the foreign language teacher, the ability to use the imperfect and the preterite correctly, accurate spelling, the naming of foreign political institutions or works of art, the contrasting of two different dialects, the themes of the great works of literature are all examples of the factual information that is content knowledge. Within foreign language education, concern over teachers' content knowledge has usually surfaced as a concern about teachers' target language proficiency. A survey of the research base of foreign language teacher education revealed that target language proficiency (under various labels of language skills, fluency, linguistic ability, or proficiency) was the only subject-matter-specific topic included in the literature on foreign language teacher development.[16]

Language proficiency already has been proposed as an "organizing principle" for foreign language education.[17] The construct of proficiency, although suggested to be an organizing principle for foreign language instruction, is not yet fully articulated. Nevertheless, models of language proficiency are influencing teachers' thinking and having an impact on what transpires in classrooms. Other related "central concepts" such as language functions and communicative competence are also influencing the structuring of language instruction. These concepts provide the language teacher with a vehicle for looking at the messages and intents of language rather than just its forms.

It is a difficult task to articulate what are the organizing principles and central concepts of any field. In foreign language education we can see different outcomes or teaching behaviors that result from different teachers' priorities. If language analysis or communicative competence or literary theory are seen as the organizing principle of the discipline, different classroom activities (and presumably different learning) result. Certain sets of factual information and a given organizing principle probably tend to develop together. A given organizing principle and given key concepts are most likely interwoven along with given factual information into the complex mosaic that constitutes the teacher's content knowledge.

If teacher educators wish to influence the prospective teacher's teaching, they must learn about his or her current content knowledge. Case studies in other areas of education have provided examples of how teachers' content knowledge influences the way in which they use textbooks, select material, and plan and sequence instruction.[18] Preservice teachers must see similar examples in their own teaching and must see the benefits of continually expanding their content knowledge.

Content knowledge alone does not adequately describe subject matter knowledge. Rather, content knowledge is seen emerging from two other elements of knowledge—substantive structures and syntactic structures.[19] Substantive structures are the paradigms or frameworks that guide research in a discipline. Syntactic structures are the procedures of research and the methods of accepting or denying proof of new knowledge in the discipline.

Substantive Knowledge

Prospective teachers will vary in their awareness of the substantive structures of their discipline. Substantive structures guide the kinds of questions researchers ask when studying the discipline. Prospective teachers from undergraduate programs may have a much better sense of the answers than of what were the original research questions. In history, for example, students may have discussed different perspectives on a historical event without explicitly identifying the types of research questions that guided the formation of those perspectives.

In foreign language, preservice teachers will have studied literature, but may or may not have explicitly studied different critical perspectives. They may or may not be able to identify the critical tradition of the *explication de texte* or the consequences of Reader Response Theory. The prospective teacher will have some notion or notions of the substantive structures of foreign culture. Questions that have framed the study of foreign culture have come broadly from attempts to identify culture's impact on language and, vice versa, to identify mutually beneficial elements across cultures, and to foster self understanding. Beyond the arena of literature and culture into the realm of language itself, the substantive structures may come from traditional inquiry in phonetics, phonology, lexicology, sociolinguistics, comparative linguistics, psycholinguistics, or second language acquisition, among others. The prospective teacher's understanding of the source of knowledge within the discipline may be more tacit than explicit. This does not mean that it will not influence the focus and structuring of his or her teaching.

Syntactic Knowledge

The methodology of research within the foreign language field is diverse and varies among branches within the discipline. How new foreign language teachers perceive the growth of new knowledge in their field taking place may well influence how they organize their classroom instruction. How they see this process working is most likely linked with what they define the discipline to be (based on personal content knowledge) and what intellectual questions they perceive the discipline to be answering (based on personal substantive knowledge).

The first danger that faces prospective teachers and their teacher educators is a lack of knowledge of syntactic structures. Case studies in other domains have provided evidence of missing syntactic structures. For example, a prospective social studies teacher who was an undergraduate political science major demonstrated a lack of awareness of the syntactic structures of history.[20] In foreign language education the syntactic structures of the discipline need to be articulated more fully. In "A Syllabus of Competence: The Report of the Commission on Professional Standards, AATF," several syntactic structures for knowledge of foreign cultures are summarized. The "methods and conceptual tools for observing and analyzing a culture" are (1) field study, direct and remote; (2) the differentiation of subcultures—regional, socioeconomic, age groups; (3) the analysis of space and time concepts; and (4) contrastive analysis, especially cross-cultural variables and the analysis of the contact points between cultures.[21] Other syntactic structures come primarily from a range of studies within linguistics, literary criticism, and history. Prospective teachers frequently come to the profession with only a rudimentary knowledge of the syntactic structures of any branch of their discipline and often with a subset of possible syntactic structures. Grossman details the instructional outcomes in English education of two new teachers who differ in their outlook on syntactic structures of literature: one teacher who saw the text as central to the process of literary interpretation and another teacher who considered the reader's response to literature to be the key of literary understanding.[22] These different orientations are shown to generate differences in motivations to teach, selection of content to teach, structuring of classroom activities, and responses to teacher education.

Limitations of the syntactic knowledge of the teacher have direct consequences on the learning of the students. Lack of syntactic knowledge leads to the failure to incorporate syntactic knowledge in the new teacher's own lessons. The net result may be a misrepresentation to students of what the discipline is. If the prospective teacher sees the syntactic structure of cultural studies to be the collection of facts, his or her students will be presented with staid sets of facts. If cultural studies are seen to come from field study and contrastive analysis, the classroom may include collecting data from penpal letters regarding similarities and differences in native/target culture school systems.

A second consequence of limited syntactical knowledge is the inability to learn new information on the part of the new teacher. The teacher who views foreign culture as a static set of facts will be increasingly left behind as the target culture continues to change and to evolve. Without an awareness of syntactic structures, the new teacher will be unable to evaluate the legitimacy of various claims about the culture with consequences in such areas as textbook evaluation and the evaluation of students' own hypotheses and conclusions about the facts they have learned. These difficulties will arise in all domains of the discipline, of course, not just in culture. As the language itself changes, the teacher as student of the language needs to stay informed. As new linguistic ammunition is added to the "natural order" debate of language acquisition, the teacher needs some understanding to evaluate the strength of the evidence. An awareness of how new knowledge is brought into the field will influence new teachers and how they in turn influence their students.

Belief about Subject Matter

The final dimension, belief about subject matter, may be difficult to differentiate from the other components of subject matter knowledge; however, Grossman, Wilson and Shulman define belief as relying heavily on "evidence that is largely affective or subjective rather than objective" and "more disputable than knowledge."[23] Foreign language teachers may attribute characteristics to the language they teach—it is "logical", "beautiful", "rhetorically superior/inferior" to other languages, and these attributes may influence what and how they teach in the language. Teachers may decide that the substantive and syntactic structures of one branch of the discipline are the "right" ones. Foreign language educators have yet to study these beliefs about subject-matter proper and their impact on learning.

More attention has been given to attitudes and belief about language learning. Horwitz cautions that beliefs about language learning can interfere with new learning in the foreign language methods class.[24] She recommends confronting belief systems with prospective teachers and examining differences in beliefs between students and teacher. Two instruments, the Foreign Language Survey and the Beliefs About Language Learning Inventory, have been devised to measure beliefs about learning and teaching languages.[25] Less attention has been given in foreign language education to what aspects of the study of languages prospective teachers value and why.

The components of subject matter knowledge—content knowledge, substantive and syntactical knowledge and beliefs all serve as the foundation for teachers in the act of teaching. But teachers must go beyond their knowledge of their subject. They need not only a solid grounding in the subject matter themselves but also a view of the subject as others may see it. They must know ways in which to influence how others understand it. For this, they need knowledge of models, analogies, demonstrations, processes and activities that enlighten others. In short, they must find ways to transform their own subject matter knowledge to make it accessible, visible, usable by others.

Pedagogical content knowledge

Much has been written about what comprises the expertise of teachers. There is a growing trend to move away from attempts to describe qualities of teaching that apply to all teachers toward an attempt to describe the expertise needed to teach a particular subject matter.

Probably the most familiar attempts in the past to define teacher expertise were organized by the accountability movements of the 1970s. These efforts produced competency-based education for teachers with an emphasis on demonstratable teacher behaviors common to all teachers along with explicitly stated means of evaluation. This work is based, for the most part, on empirical research studies of teaching effectiveness, which has been summarized recently by Brophy and Good[26] and by Rosenshine and Stevens.[27] Proponents of this line of inquiry have attempted maximum generalizability across subject areas. This attempt at widescale generalizability is now being labeled by some as the greatest weakness of this body of work because of the difficulty of documenting relationships between teachers' behaviors and learners' outcomes in a given class. Concepts such as "wait time" and "time on task" are part of general pedagogical knowledge common to all teachers. Although important, they will not be dealt with here. Rather, our focus will be toward an emphasis on foreign language and away from an emphasis on the generic.

Research efforts that are currently getting a great deal of attention are attempts to highlight the unique features of teaching and learning a particular subject. The crux of the individual teacher's knowledge is at, what Shulman calls, "the intersection of content and pedagogy"[28] or pedagogical content knowledge. This body of knowledge is what teachers must have beyond the scholar's knowledge of content. Shulman outlines the creation/use of pedagogical content knowledge: "The idea is grasped, probed, and comprehended by a teacher, who then must turn it about in his or her mind, seeing many sides of it. Then the idea is shaped or tailored until it can in turn be grasped by students. This grasping, however, is not a passive act. Just as the teacher's comprehension requires a vigorous interaction with the ideas, so students will be expected to encounter ideas actively as well. Indeed, our exemplary teachers present ideas in order to provoke the constructive processes of their students...."[29]

The key feature of teachers' understanding that differs from that of other subject matter experts is the ability to transform understanding for students. Transformation of content knowledge takes many forms. Preparation includes the ability to segment and structure content and to interpret areas of content critically. Preparing may also include tailoring content in anticipation of learners' preconceptions, aptitude, interests, age, social class, culture, attention span, past difficulties, etc.

Shulman emphasizes the concept of representation in pedagogical content knowledge. Multiple forms of representation, such as analogies, metaphors, examples, demonstrations, and simulations of new knowledge for students, are important. The repertoire of representations that a teacher has constitutes, to a large degree, that teacher's pedagogical content knowledge. Multiple instructional routines that are linked to multiple knowledge representation go beyond lecture or question and answer formats to include many different instructional modes. The key word in multiple representations is "multiple." It is flexibility in understanding of content that is so necessary for teachers. Little, if any, systematic work seems to have been done in foreign language education to document the development in new teachers of such representations.

It is insufficient for the teacher to believe that aspects of the foreign culture should be related to the native culture of the students because unanswered questions still remain. What pieces of daily life in the foreign culture does the teacher choose for students to look at? What media are used? What elements of the culture will fairly represent the culture's complexity? What stereotypes or prejudices do given students of a given age tend to possess, and how do they interact with the elements of culture selected? What activities can students participate in that will have the greatest impact on them? Clearly, learning to represent aspects of content knowledge is a formidable task for new teachers.

Pedagogical content knowledge involves all aspects of subject matter knowledge. Content knowledge proper is clearly involved in what is taught and how it is taught, but substantive knowledge and syntactical knowledge are also factors. For example, the beginning teacher's culture lessons may represent the substantive knowledge of anthropological research via the types of questions that are voiced and may represent the syntactic process by the means by which students' answers in class are evaluated.

Current content knowledge curricula

Unfortunately, we do not seem to have a very clear picture outside of our own regions or local institutions of what are the curricula currently taught to foreign language teacher candidates. Despite some attempts to extrapolate from other areas such as ESL,[30] most of the literature consists of various calls or proposals for new additions or changes without much evidence of what is currently in place.[31]

In a survey of 500 foreign language education programs at small private universities, Schrier discovered that 45% of small colleges emphasize literature for their teacher candidates, 36% emphasize basic language mastery, but that the selectivity of the school's admission policy was related to an increased emphasis on linguistics that was nonexistent in non-competitive small colleges. She also found that differentiation between subject matter studied for teacher candidates versus that studied by foreign language majors existed primarily in highly selective schools and less often in other settings. In the "competitive" institutions where curricula for teacher candidates differed from curricula for foreign language majors, the emphasis on literature decreased by 76% and the emphasis on basic language skills increased by 14%. Culture and civilization increased by 213% and linguistics by 139%.[32]

Obviously, the content and emphasis of coursework plays a major role in defining the subject matter knowledge of beginning teachers. These data are an important first step in assessing the knowledge base of beginning teachers. Schrier noted an extremely high response rate of 70% and an eagerness to provide baseline information of this sort that was reflected in spontaneous comments and unsolicited documents that were provided along with survey responses.[33] Due to such interest in providing this sort of information, local programs can compare their own emphasis with that of other institutions and professionals now can ask: "Is this the subject matter emphasis that is desirable?"

Implications for preservice teacher development

Curricula

First, we must look at large global pictures, such as that provided by Schrier, of what the curricula are for preservice teachers today in the United States. Secondly, we must examine the content and syllabi of our local programs in order to identify the content knowledge, substantive and syntactic structures, and pedagogical content knowledge that are natural outgrowths of such programs. Thirdly, through national organizations / networking we must share the outcomes of our study of local programs with colleagues around the nation. Through systematic identification of the content of local programs we can begin to identify the current knowledge base of foreign language teachers. This background information will give greater meaning to the continuing debate over what the knowledge base should be.

One useful place to start working is from the springboard of the ACTFL Provisional Program Guidelines for Foreign Language Teacher Education. Under "Area II: Acquisition and Use of Knowledge," these Guidelines imply the importance of substantive and syntactical structures when they caution: "What is learned through the liberal arts study may ultimately be less important than how it is learned."[34] Under the broad category of "Specialist Development" there is plenty of room for individual programs to identify more specifically the nature of the content knowledge and pedagogical content knowledge that their own teacher candidates are using.

Research is giving credence to the policymakers' concerns that subject matter knowledge is central to teaching. Before policymakers make arbitrary decisions about access to teaching for subject matter experts, educators must clearly spell out what the intricacies of subject matter knowledge and pedagogical content knowledge are. There is a need to do so immediately.

This is not to say that descriptive studies should be made automatically prescriptive. The identification of outstanding teaching will still remain elusive. General educational researchers have noted for a number of years the difficulty in confirming the existence of superior teaching.[35] Foreign language has not been immune to the pitfalls that await those who seek to uncover the elusive "outstanding teacher." As a result we must view with caution, for example, study results that label teachers as exemplary based on number of votes from former students, because this method does not allow for the possibility for more votes as a simple result of longevity and therefore more students.[36] We would hope to recognize more than longevity as a key factor in outstanding teaching, but are often stymied by such questions as outstanding teaching of which students, of which types of knowledge, under which conditions?

Influence of Subject Matter Knowledge on Other Domains

In connection with local study of the content knowledge (in all of its dimensions) stressed in local curricula, a variety of interesting research questions emerge. Foreign language teacher educators must be interested in seeking evidence, such as that found by Grossman in English education, of ways that substantive and syntactical knowledge influence students' responses to teacher education.[37] It seems likely that teacher candidates' views on the nature of their discipline affect how and what they learn during teacher education, but these reactions should be documented so that all may be aware of them. Some nebulous "conflicts" within the infamous triad of cooperating teacher, student teacher, and university supervisor may be more clearly explained, using subject matter knowledge structures as a comparison.

The topic of subject matter knowledge and especially pedagogical content knowledge is receiving a lot of professional press right now. Despite occasional critiques,[38] most reactions are enthusiastic. The concept of pedagogical content knowledge, which is by definition discipline specific, seems to be an idea whose time has come. A number of profitable lines of inquiry in foreign language education open up as a result. First of all, case studies of foreign language teachers that focus primarily on knowledge structures should confirm whether foreign language teachers' knowledge fits into the paradigms previously outlined.

One idea that should not be implied from the current interest in this line of study is that case study research methodology is to replace empirical quantitative research. The potentially fruitful results from one in no way negate the importance of the other. Surveys, case studies, and quantitative studies are all necessary components in the search for further understanding of the teaching/learning process. At all costs, further skirmishes in the research "paradigm war"[39] must be avoided.

Knowledge Components

One intriguing question is: How far can expertise in one area compensate for weaknesses in another? Hints of just such a possibility exist in foreign language. Earlier in this paper the myth of the automatic superiority of the native speaker was examined. One possible explanation for superior teaching on the part of the non-native speaker is greater ability to simplify speech, maximize use of cognates, and restrict language use to accessible structures for the benefit of complete comprehension on the part of the novice listener. Research has provided evidence of these adaptive features in foreign language classes and documented their varied use—more adaptive features for less proficient listeners and fewer linguistic adaptations for more proficient listeners.[40] It is unknown whether competency in such classroom communication can compensate for weaknesses in other subject matter knowledge and if so to what degree? Such a question could also be posed about any subject matter expertise (e.g., in film, literature, politics, speaking vs. writing, representations for learning grammar but not for learning culture) offsetting weaknesses in another area.

The research area of teachers' beliefs about their discipline and its substantive and syntactic structures is, at present, uncharted territory in foreign language study. No literature exists that documents the nature of foreign language teachers' conceptualization of their subject matter and the subsequent effects on what they teach or how they influence students.

If nothing else, foreign language educators are pushed by the above information to view subject matter knowledge as a vast and complex topic. Too often it has been simplified to mean linguistic accuracy alone. It seems necessary to go beyond the albeit legitimate concerns over preservice teachers' language proficiency and look at the full range of competencies that make a foreign language teacher. Also, language teachers' knowledge has been traditionally grouped around the areas of language skills, culture, literature, linguistics, and methodology as they are in the Syllabus of Competence.[41] The inclusion of syntactic structures, substantive structures, beliefs, and pedagogical content knowledge in the analysis of subject matter knowledge provides useful perspectives for teacher educators to talk about the ways beginning teachers use their knowledge and about ways to influence that knowledge and its application.

It is beyond the scope of this paper to respond to all the needs raised here. There are a number of different avenues that are currently being pursued in order to bring new insights to preservice teachers. What follows is simply one sample of one avenue that is currently under investigation.

A sample intervention in teacher development

What do we want foreign language teachers to know? And at the same time how can we best teach the preservice teacher this knowledge? One suggestion that has a growing number of supporters is still rarely seen in foreign language education: the case method. The Carnegie Report *A Nation Prepared: Teachers for the 21st Century* specifically mentions the case method among its recommendations. "Teaching cases illustrating a great variety of teaching problems should be developed as a major focus of instruction."[42] Similarly, The Presidents' Forum on Teaching, a group of 37 college presidents, has listed among its goals: "Promote ... case study methods of clinical education for prospective teachers."[43]

A case is a narrative, story or vignette that is a "case of something" or, in other words, an instance of a larger category.[44] Cases may be exemplars of a general principle or representative of some larger class of experiences—e.g., the pitfalls of a peer relationship with students or criteria for foreign language error correction. Inherent in casewriting is an attempt to make sense out of an experience and more likely an attempt to share the insights of an experience with a larger educational community.

For some advocates, cases are part of an important effort to capture the accumulated wisdom of experienced teachers. These advocates reason that much important understanding of teaching is being needlessly lost as experienced teachers leave the profession for whatever reason. They argue that in the push of recent years to expand useful research-based knowledge, practical knowledge has been unnecessarily neglected.[45]

Foreign language educators may be doubly hindered when asked to define their profession's knowledge base. A case literature of teaching experiences unique to foreign language does not yet exist, and empirical research studies are undeniably fewer in number than in such areas as math education or first language reading. A case literature may be financially more immediately within reach than a body of data-based research, and both are essential in order to improve the knowledge base of foreign language teachers.[46]

Cases are seen not only as a part of a case literature of practical knowledge from the field storehoused in written form. They are also presented as part of a process of interaction between students (usually preservice teachers), the case and the instructor. From this perspective, cases are seen as a method of fostering teacher decision making. In describing the case method of the Harvard Business School's teacher education program, McCarthy explains, "Pre-service case based classes give participants a chance to think on their feet, to take risks, to take trial and error stabs at problem solving—all in a safe(r) environment."[47] The cases used to instruct future teachers at the Harvard Business School are always true rather than invented but are written from the onset by an experienced educator/case writer as a teaching tool.

Other cases are written by the teacher, often a novice, as a sort of cathartic experience of reflection. For these cases the process of writing the case is the focus of attention as a means of promoting self-analysis. The insights of a given teaching experience can therefore be created out of the process of describing the experience in written form. Novice teachers writing for The Intern Teacher Casebook and novice supervisors (experienced teachers) writing The Mentor Teacher Casebook[48] attest to the illuminating capacity of the process of writing a case. One case author gives an example: "My vignette about the unsuccessful lesson was particularly helpful. When I wrote that I told my class that we were going to read [a play] 'because the curriculum guide said so,' I was startled. I said it, but my postrealization was especially shocking. It made me aware that sometimes the classroom context is a place completely isolated from other customs and norms. Outside of the classroom, I could not envision myself saying something like that, and expecting my students not to question me."[49]

Cases appear to be a promising tool to help prospective foreign language teachers gain from the wisdom of experienced teachers, grapple with the difficult decision making that is a daily part of teaching (and for which, frustratingly, there is rarely "one right answer"), and reflect on their own early forays into the classroom. Experienced and novice foreign language teachers alike should look at classroom events that were memorable to them and consider the usefulness both to themselves and to others of recording as vivid a picture of the event as possible.

The use of cases as simulations of on-the-spot decision making seems particularly promising. Thoughtful discussions about criteria for error correction during the foreign language methods course bring up such issues as comprehensibility, focus on meaning versus form and frequency of error. Instructor and students can discuss criteria for choosing which student errors to correct and ways to correct student error. A case could be written by an experienced teacher that is representative of the teacher's options in reacting to learners' language in the classroom. Prospective teachers could vicariously choose their course of action and defend it.

Novice teachers often comment on the overwhelming onslaught to the senses of the early days of teaching. Experienced teachers and novice teachers alike soon have their own tales to tell about, for example, learners' anxieties about foreign languages. Research studies exist on sources and manifestations of foreign language learner anxiety. A case literature of teachers' responses to it could also be readily compiled.

The tools of the foreign language teacher educator need to be varied, diverse. Between discussion of educational concepts and immersion in the act of teaching, there need to be multiple techniques available to gain knowledge about foreign language learning/teaching. Practice teaching a lesson to one's peers, the other preservice teachers, primarily gives practice in the performance of the teaching act but lacks the reality of novice language learner response and input. Practice teaching in the secondary classroom is, of course, the "real thing" but does not lend itself, in all its complexity, to the focus on a single topic, nor is it always a benign and forgiving environment for blunders. Naturally both forms of practice teaching are useful learning tools. They can be complemented by case analysis whose niche seems to be its ability to make theory and principles of learning more vivid and the opportunity it provides for exploring the decision-making process that is now so commonly identified with teaching.

The following is an excerpt from a case written by a cooperating teacher:

> Marilyn Johnson felt a bit nervous; today she had to present a difficult grammar point to the ninth grade Spanish II class. She didn't know quite what to do about this group; the only time they really seemed to be paying attention was when Mrs. Graves, her cooperating teacher, was in the classroom to observe. She often felt frustrated to the point of tears. Things were especially difficult on days when she would introduce a new grammar point....
>
> Just then Mrs. Graves entered the room and quietly took a seat in the back. Marilyn began the next part of her lesson....

The students chattered as they opened their books. Oh, dear, how was she ever going to get them to settle down? Well, she'd just begin; they'd probably stop talking once they realized that she'd begun giving notes.

"The subjunctive is used after verbs and expressions of prohibition, suggestion, command, request, demand, desire and permission. A subjunctive que clause is used only if there is a change in person. Otherwise, a dependent infinitive is used. Look at these examples: 'Deseo que usted escriba la carta en español.—I want you to write the letter in Spanish.' 'No quiere que yo entre.—He does not consent to my coming in.' and finally—look at this one closely, class—'Prefiero salir solo—I prefer to go out alone.'" Marilyn was very proud of the definition and those examples. Just yesterday, when she and Mrs. Graves had talked about the best way to approach the lesson, Mrs. Graves had cautioned her against merely repeating what was in the students' textbook. Marilyn had found these in one of her college texts.

"Miss Johnson, could you give us more examples?"

Marilyn froze. More examples? She wasn't prepared for that question; she thought that the three she'd found in her college text would be sufficient. She hesitated; what should she do next...?[50]

A case, such as the one excerpted above, does not teach itself. But note that it raises the question of the role of subject matter knowledge for prospective teachers in a much more compelling manner than the question, "What is the influence of one's own knowledge of Spanish on how one teaches Spanish?"

Foreign language educators have gathered further evidence that foreign languages can be learned more effectively or efficiently when the language is studied within some context. Through numerous negative examples, we have seen that isolated words and sentences strung together only to illustrate a grammatical concept are learned with less facility than those that occur within a meaningful context. Foreign language teacher educators can benefit from the same lesson. Rather than bemoan student teachers' inabilities to apply the principles that they seem so willingly to espouse in the methods class, teacher educators should strive to provide the knowledge of those principles within a context that can make them more meaningful and therefore easier to assimilate.

Kennedy warns, however, against treating teacher education solely as case analysis of problems in theory or general principles.[51] She questions, for example, one's ability to recognize a particular case in real life as an example of a general principle or to adjust to unique features of each new case, unless the decision-making process is tied to one's own "deliberate action." She suggests that expert practitioners conduct "mental experiments," envision the consequences of their plan, and judge the consequences against their definition of the problem and against their impact on other goals. These mental experiments involve first making sense of a new problem by imposing a structure on it, often derived from previous experience, before imagining various actions to take on the problem as defined. Only after such deliberation are decisions acted upon.[52] Finally, the results from actions are used to assess both the original definition of the problem and the expert's actions based on the actual outcome.

This course of action seems still to be applicable to the use of the case method, if (1) the cases are approached as such "mental experiments," (2) the cases are firmly grounded in subject-specific pedagogical content knowledge, and (3) links are explicitly drawn to the teacher candidates' own practice.[53]

Conclusions

The brother of Molière's *malade imaginaire* in our opening quotation suggests that he should be his own doctor. In response, Argan questions his own ability to master all the knowledge needed for the job. The brother, Béralde, believes that by simply acquiring the trappings of the discipline, the knowledge would come of itself. Teaching, like medicine, has also been the recipient of skepticism over the rigor or the very existence of its knowledge base.

Subject matter knowledge is back in the limelight as its components and its role in the development of prospective teachers are under close scrutiny. Recruitment pressures and pressures from policymakers will demand entry mechanisms into teaching for subject matter experts. Researchers in other fields of education are focusing considerable attention on the composition and influence of subject matter expertise.

Foreign language educators can and should join the process of delineating subject matter knowledge and exposing its influence on how teachers teach in a uniquely foreign language context. Sandstedt identifies research in the area of pedagogical content knowledge to be "of special importance" although "the implication that this research has for foreign language teaching is yet to be seen."[54] This area of research has the potential to help respond to several calls for reform in foreign language education. For example, Phillips states: "No one argues against greater mastery of subject matter... [but] the profession must define more accurately the competencies which relate to effective classroom teaching of foreign languages."[55] Making implicit knowledge about the structure of subject matter explicit will be an important vehicle toward such a long range goal. One step at a time, we can begin responding to these challenges and responding to the unanswered questions about what actually constitutes the knowledge base of foreign language teaching. Armed with this information about the knowledge base and how it influences teaching decisions, we will be better equipped to aid new teachers entering the foreign language teaching field.

Notes

1. Robert Jouanny (ed.), *Oeuvres complètes de Molière Tome Premier.* (Paris: Garnier Frères, 1962).

2. Bernard Shapiro, Teachers and Teacher Education Today: Lessons for the United States from Research in the Western Developed Countries of the OECD (Paper presented at the American Educational Research Association Annual Meeting, San Francisco, March 27, 1989); James H. Case, Schools of tomorrow (Paper presented at the Seminar on a Doctoral Program in Education for the Future, University of Rhode Island, Kingston, September 22, 1989).

3. Carnegie Corporation, *Teachers for the 21st Century* (New York: Carnegie Forum on Education and the Economy, 1986).

4. Holmes Group, *Tomorrow's Teachers: A Report of the Holmes Group* (East Lansing, MI: Holmes Groups, Inc., 1986).

5. Margret Buchmann, "The Priority of Knowledge and Understanding in Teaching," in Lilian G. Katz and James D. Raths, eds., *Advances in Teacher Education* (Norwood, NJ: Ablex Publishing, 1984), pp. 29-30.

6. Buchmann, p. 30.

7. Buchmann, p. 33.

8. Richard Stanley Peters, *Education and the Education of Teachers* (London: Routledge & Kegan Paul, 1977), p.151.

9. John Dewey, The Child and the Curriculum, in Jo Ann Boydston, ed., *John Dewey: The Middle Works, 1899-1924, Volume 2: 1902-1903* (Carbondale, IL: Southern Illinois University Press, 1983), pp. 285-286.

10. Suzanne M. Wilson, *Understanding Historical Understanding: An Analysis of the Subject Matter Knowledge of Teachers* (Paper presented at the American Educational Research Association Annual Meeting, San Francisco, March, 1989).

11. Pamela L. Grossman, *A Tale of Two Teachers: The Role of Subject Matter Orientation in Teaching* (Knowledge Growth in a Profession Publication Series), (Stanford, CA: Stanford University, School of Education, 1987).

12. **Matthew Lambert, "Choosing and Using Mathematical Tools in Classroom Discourse," in James Hiebert, ed., *Conceptual and Procedural Knowledge: The Case of Mathematics* (Hillsdale, NJ: Erlbaum, 1986).

13. **Maher Z. Hashweh, "Effects of Subject Matter Knowledge in Teaching Biology and Physics," *Teaching and Teacher Education: An International Journal of Research and Studies* 3 (1987).

14. Lee S. Shulman, "Knowledge and Teaching: Foundations of the New Reform," *Harvard Educational Review* 57 (1987), p. 8.

15. Pamela Grossman, Suzanne Wilson, and Lee Shulman, "Teachers of Substance: Subject Matter Knowledge for Teaching," in Maynard C. Reynolds, ed., *Knowledge Base for the Beginning Teacher* (Oxford: Pergamon Press, 1989), pp. 23-36.

16. Elizabeth Bernhardt and JoAnn Hammadou, "A Decade of Research in Foreign Language Teacher Education," *Modern Language Journal* 71 (1987):289-298.

17. Theodore V. Higgs, *Teaching for Proficiency, the Organizing Principle* (Lincolnwood, IL: National Textbook, 1984).

18. Grossman, Wilson, and Shulman, p. 26.

19. Joseph Jackson Schwab, cited by Grossman, Wilson, and Shulman, p. 29.

20. Wilson, pp. 1-76.

21. American Association of Teachers of French, "The Teaching of French, A Syllabus of Competence: The Report of the Commission on Professional Standards, AATF," *AATF National Bulletin* 15 (1989), p. 14.

22. See Grossman.

23. Grossman, Wilson, and Shulman, p. 31.

24. Elaine K. Horwitz, "Using Student Beliefs about Language Learning and Teaching in the Foreign Language Methods Course," *Foreign Language Annals* 18 (1985):333-340.

25. Horwitz, p. 333.

26. Jere J. Brophy and Thomas L. Good, "Teacher Behavior and Student Achievement," in Merlin C. Wittrock, ed., *Handbook of Research on Teaching*, third edition (New York: Macmillan, 1986):328-375.

27. Barak Rosenshine and Robert S. Stevens, "Teaching Functions," in Merlin C. Wittrock, ed., *Handbook of Research on Teaching*, third edition (New York: Macmillan, 1986):379-391.

28. Shulman, p. 15.

29. Shulman, pp. 12-13.

30. JoAnn Hammadou and Elizabeth Bernhardt, "On Being and Becoming a Foreign Language Teacher," *Theory Into Practice* 26 (1987): 301-306.

31. Leslie L. Schrier, *A Survey of Foreign Language Teacher Preparation Patterns and Procedures in Small, Private Colleges and Universities in the United States*. Unpublished doctoral dissertation, The Ohio State University, Columbus, 1989, p. 33.

32. Schrier, pp. 109-112.

33. Schrier, p. 65.

34. "ACTFL Provisional Program Guidelines for Foreign Language Teacher Education," *Foreign Language Annals* 21 (1988), p. 73.

35. David Berliner, "In Pursuit of the Expert Pedagogue," *Educational Researcher* 15 (1986):5-13.

36. Gertrude Moskowitz, "The Classroom Interaction of Outstanding Foreign Language Teachers," *Foreign Language Annals* 9 (1976):135-157.

37. See Grossman.

38. E.g., Hugh T. Sockett, "Has Shulman Got the Strategy Right?" *Harvard Educational Review* 57 (1987):208-219.

39. N. L. Gage, "The Paradigm Wars and Their Aftermath: A 'Historical' Sketch of Research on Teaching Since 1989," *Educational Researcher* 18 (1989):4-11.

40. For further discussion of the construct "teacher talk" see Barbara H. Wing, "For Teachers: A Challenge for Competence," in Gilbert A. Jarvis, ed., *The Challenge for Excellence in Foreign Language Education* (Middlebury, VT: Northeast Conference on the Teaching of Foreign Languages, 1984):11-41. See also Richard R. Day, ed., *Talking to Learn: Conversation in Second Language Acquisition* (Rowley, MA: Newbury House, 1986).

41. American Association of Teachers of French, p. 2.

42. Cited by Marina McCarthy, "Teaching Cases at the Harvard Business School: A Model for Teacher Training and Faculty Development," (Paper presented at the American Educational Research Association Annual Meeting, San Francisco, March, 1989), p. 76.

43. Presidents' Forum, American Association for Higher Education, What's the Agenda? cited by Holmes Group Forum, 4 (1989), p. 26.

44. Lee S. Shulman cited by Judith H. Shulman and Joel A. Colbert, eds., *The Intern Teacher Casebook* (Eugene, OR: ERIC Clearinghouse on Educational Management, 1988), p. ix.

45. E.g., Shulman and Colbert, pp. 5-6; Lee S. Shulman, "Those Who Understand: Knowledge Growth in Teaching," *Educational Researcher* 15 (1986):4-14.

46. Although cases can be and are developed inexpensively, not all are less expensive than empirical research studies. Elaborate teaching cases such as those of the Harvard Business School can cost $10,000 each, including salary and production costs. McCarthy, p. 29.

47. McCarthy, p. 7.

48. Judith H. Shulman and Joel A. Colbert, eds., *The Mentor Teacher Casebook* (Eugene, OR: ERIC Clearinghouse on Educational Management, 1987).

49. Shulman and Colbert, *Intern Casebook*, p. 72.

50. Coleen Griffith, unpublished case study, 1989. The case first gives the environmental context in which the incident takes place and concludes with the actual responses that the student teacher selected.

51. Mary M. Kennedy, "Inexact Sciences: Professional Education and the Development of Expertise," *Review of Research in Education* 14 (1987), pp. 143-147.

52. Kennedy, p. 148.

53. Suzanne M. Wilson, A Case Concerning Content: Using Case Studies to Teach Subject Matter (Paper presented at the American Educational Research Association Annual Meeting, March, 1989), p. 28-30.

54. Lynn A. Sandstedt, "Foreign Language Teacher Education Reaction Paper," 1989.

55. Responses are possible (in part) not only to the widely known reforms suggested by the Holmes Group and Carnegie reports but also to the call for validation of program content by Strasheim and the call for self-study by Knop: Lorraine A. Strasheim, "Preservice and Inservice Teacher Education in the Nineties: The Issue is Instructional Validity," (1989); Constance K, Knop, "Reaction to Preservice and Inservice Teacher Education in the Nineties: The Issue is Instructional Validity," (1989); June K. Phillips, "Teacher Education: Target of Reform," in Helen S. Lepke, ed., *Shaping the Future Challenges and Opportunities* (Middlebury, VT: Northeast Conference on the Teaching of Foreign Languages, 1989), p. 14.

Annotated Bibliography

"ACTFL Provisional Program Guidelines for Foreign Language Teacher Education." *Foreign Language Annals* 21 (1988), 71-82. These guidelines were intended to help in the creation or improvement of teacher education programs for foreign language teacher candidates. The guidelines focus on the areas of personal development, professional development, and specialist development. The latter area is divided among language proficiency, culture and civilization, and language analysis. Program indicators are listed for each guideline.

American Association of Teachers of French. "The Teaching of French, A Syllabus of Competence: The Report of the Commission on Professional Standards, AATF." *AATF National Bulletin* 15 (1989), 2-35. The commission proposes two sets of standards: Superior level of competence and Basic level of competence for teachers of French. Each set is accompanied by a range of recommended knowledge and skills. One of the unique features of this document is the host of concrete examples of most categories mentioned.

Bernhardt, Elizabeth and JoAnn Hammadou. "A Decade of Research in Foreign Language Teacher Education." *Modern Language Journal* 71 (1987), 289-298. The authors summarize the research base on foreign language teacher education from 1977-1987 which is categorized according to seven descriptors: (1) global position statements; (2) teacher behaviors; (3) training of teaching assistants; (4) training of university professors; (5) inservice opportunities; (6) supervision; and (7) methods course curricula. The major problems for education that were identified by the Holmes Group are outlined and their implications for foreign languages analyzed.

Buchmann, Margret. "The Priority of Knowledge and Understanding in Teaching." In *Advances in Teacher Education*. Volume 1. Eds. Lilian G. Katz and James D. Raths. Norwood, NJ: Ablex, 1984, pp. 29-50. Buchmann argues for the return of "content" to a position of equal rank among topics of teacher education and cautions against expansion of other studies at the expense of teacher candidates' content knowledge. Evidence is provided that overconcerns with process to the detriment of product may come by default when teachers lack the minimal knowledge to evaluate students' product. Buchmann also claims that a firm grasp of subject matter is not sufficient and that teachers need to be flexible enough to incorporate new ideas and tolerate alternative points of view.

Grossman, Pamela, Suzanne Wilson, and Lee Shulman. "Teachers of Substance: Subject Matter Knowledge for Teaching." In *Knowledge Base for the Beginning Teacher*. Ed. Maynard C. Reynolds. Oxford: Pergamon Press, 1989, pp. 23-36. This thorough article explains the dimensions of subject matter knowledge. In a review of research the writers provide evidence of features of subject matter knowledge that influence teaching: e.g., depth of knowledge, organization of knowledge, and transformation of knowledge as it relates to students, curriculum and teaching situation. The dimensions of subject matter knowledge for teaching are also analyzed. Research examples are given of the impact on teaching of deficits in content knowledge, syntactic knowledge, and substantive knowledge. Examples are also given of beliefs about subject matter and their import.

Grossman, Pamela. *A Tale of Two Teachers: The Role of Subject Matter Orientation in Teaching*. Knowledge Growth in a Profession Publication Series. Stanford CA: Stanford University, School of Education, 1987. Grossman compares two teachers of English who participated in the same teacher preparation program. Although the two teachers had basically the same content knowledge of literature, the author found marked differences in their "orientations" toward the teaching of literature. The case study highlights these differences and the resulting consequences during the teachers' induction into teaching.

Hammadou, JoAnn and Elizabeth Bernhardt. "On Being and Becoming a Foreign Language Teacher." *Theory into Practice* 26 (1987), 301-306. This article discusses what is unique about the situation of foreign language teachers and about the professional programs that prepare these teachers. The principal thesis is that generic teacher preparation programs inadequately speak to the needs of future foreign language teachers. The authors suggest that the greatest needs are in the areas of (1) perspectives on the nature of language and language learning, (2) overcoming professional isolation, and (3) maintaining subject matter knowledge.

Hollingsworth, Sandra. "Prior Beliefs and Cognitive Change in Learning to Teach." *American Educational Research Journal* 26 (1989), 160-189. This is a report of the first year of a longitudinal study of changes in preservice teachers' knowledge and beliefs about reading instruction. Fourteen teacher candidates from six different disciplines were interviewed and observed. The ultimate goal of "task awareness" (understanding learning from text-related tasks from the students' perspectives), was achieved by two of the participants. A critical factor influencing change seemed to be the placement of preservice teachers with cooperating teachers with somewhat contrasting views of teaching and learning that were still willing to allow their student teacher to teach differently from themselves. Matched pairing seemed to promote rote copying without true belief changes. Two additional years are planned for the study.

Horwitz, Elaine. "Using Student Beliefs about Language Learning and Teaching in the Foreign Language Methods Course." *Foreign Language Annals* 18 (1985), 333-340. This paper describes two instruments for measuring beliefs about language learning and teaching. Horwitz illustrates the kinds of beliefs that teacher candidates may hold and how these beliefs can directly interfere with learning during a foreign language methods course.

Kennedy, Mary M. "Inexact Sciences: Professional Education and the Development of Expertise." *Review of Research in Education* 14 (1987), 143-147. Kennedy examines four broad perspectives on general pedagogical expertise. The definitions of expertise that result are critiqued and each one's weaknesses are identified. The author also hypothesizes about factors that may influence a profession's definition of expertise: unique demands of the profession, quality of students, response to critics of the profession.

Knop, Constance C. "Reaction to Preservice and Inservice Teacher Education in the Nineties: The Issue is Instructional Validity." Unpublished manuscript, 1989. Knop calls for surveys of teachers' needs that should be provided to universities and to professional organizations. She also suggests that greater use should be made of cross-disciplinary teaching of teacher candidates. Furthermore, she emphasizes the importance of self-evaluation and teaching of self-evaluation strategies to preservice teachers.

McCarthy, Marina. "Teaching Cases at the Harvard Business School: A Model for Teacher Training and Faculty Development." Paper presented at the American Educational Research Association Annual Meeting. San Francisco, March, 1989. McCarthy describes the Harvard Business School type case teaching and proposes that this case method could be used effectively in a large number of teacher education programs. This style case usually consists of a "flashpoint" or attention-getter, the contextual background information, a description of the teacher/protagonist and the events of the case. The case sets up a teaching problem without telling how the teacher resolves the problem. In addition, most cases have a (B) or (C) case that provide another participant's perspective or explain how the problem was handled.

McDiarmid, G. Williamson, Deborah Loewenberg Ball, and Charles W. Anderson. "Why Staying One Chapter Ahead Doesn't Really Work: Subject-Specific Pedagogy." In *Knowledge Base for the Beginning Teacher*. Ed. Maynard C. Reynolds. Oxford: Pergamon Press, 1989, pp. 193-206. The authors outline a response to the call for greater emphases on pedagogical content knowledge for beginning teachers. Their goal is flexible subject matter understanding on the part of teacher candidates. Toward that end they describe preservice teacher-generated "representations" of subject matter that they wish to foster during the methods course.

National Board for Professional Teaching Standards. *Toward High and Rigorous Standards for the Teaching Profession*. Detroit: 1989. The purpose of this board is to establish high standards for what teacher should know and do and eventually to certify experienced teachers who meet these high standards. This initial policy statement outlines in broad terms what teachers should know. Position statements cover such categories as: commitment to students and their learning, subject matter knowledge and how to convey the subject to students, managing and monitoring student learning, commitment to lifelong professional development, and collaboration with the community.

Phillips, June K. "Teacher Education: Target of Reform." In *Shaping the Future Challenges and Opportunities*. Ed. Helen S. Lepke. Middlebury, VT: Northeast Conference on the Teaching of Foreign Languages, 1989, pp. 11-40. The reform movements in foreign language teacher preparation programs are outlined and their outcomes identified. Phillips gives samples of work done in the areas of Academic Preparation, Professional Education, Teacher Testing, and Induction to Teaching. A principal challenge that she identifies is the ability to move as a profession away from a defensive, reactive posture to a proactive, offensive posture in politics and in state and national credentialing and assessment movements.

"Project 30 Newsletter" Vols. I-III. Texas A & M University. These publications include up-to-date information on new projects in teacher education. supported by the Carnegie Corporation. The three primary goals of the projects are to increase teachers' competence and authority, to provide for the development of the intellect of students, and to strengthen the profession of teaching. Eventually a book will be published that will describe each of the thirty new curricula.

Sandstedt, Lynn A. "Foreign Language Teacher Education Reaction Paper." Unpublished manuscript, 1989. In reaction to the paper by Strasheim, Sandstedt concurs that graduate level in-service is of critical importance and he outlines suggestions for summer institutes for teachers. He also proposes the strengthening of field service through the use of "Effective Teacher/Adjunct Professors" from area schools. Sandstedt places greatest importance on fostering more flexible pedagogical content knowledge, which he believes requires intense cooperation between Education and Arts and Science faculties. While calling for further research, Sandstedt also calls for the use of the existing pedagogical reports of the 1980s.

Schrier, Leslie L. A Survey of Foreign Language Teacher Preparation Patterns and Procedures in Small, Private Colleges and Universities in the United States. Unpublished doctoral dissertation, The Ohio State University, Columbus, 1989. This study provides important baseline data on the characteristics of the teacher educator, the students, and the curriculum in foreign language teacher preparation programs at small colleges. These institutions were found to train a growing percentage of the nation's future teachers.

Shulman, Judith H. and Joel A. Colbert. *The Intern Teacher Casebook*. Eugene, OR: ERIC Clearinghouse on Educational Management, 1988. This volume is a collection of cases written by novice teachers from the Los Angeles Unified School District for use during teacher preparation and staff development. Each account illustrates a teaching dilemma (e.g., "teaching with minimal content knowledge") and is followed by a reaction from other teachers or educational scholars.

Shulman, Judith H. and Joel A. Colbert. *The Mentor Teacher Casebook*. Eugene, OR: ERIC Clearinghouse on Educational Management, 1987. This text is a collection of cases or vignettes written by experienced mentor teachers in the Los Angeles Unified School District that highlights the process of helping beginning teachers. Each case describes a real-life situation between mentor teacher and novice teacher.

Shulman, Lee. "Knowledge and Teaching: Foundations of the New Reform." *Harvard Educational Review* 57 (1987), 1-22. Shulman discusses four issues: (1) the sources of teacher knowledge, (2) the conceptualization of these sources, (3) the nature of the process of pedagogical reasoning, and (4) the implication that this image of teaching and teachers has for teaching policy and educational reform. He argues for the development of a knowledge base for teachers and for a conceptualization of teaching as a cognitive process.

Strasheim, Lorraine A. "Preservice and Inservice Teacher Education in the Nineties: The Issue is Instructional Validity." Unpublished manuscript, 1989. After a review of the progress of teacher education in this century, Strasheim evaluates the "instructional validity" of current practices in foreign language teacher education. Strasheim emphasizes the need to strengthen the language proficiency component, the eclectic-style of the methods component, and the testing of teacher competency. Before changes are made, however, they should be subjected to widescale professional review in regional meetings.

Wilson, Suzanne M. A Case Concerning Content: Using Case Studies to Teach Subject Matter. Paper presented at the American Educational Research Association Annual Meeting, March, 1989. Wilson offers a sample case dealing with a student teacher of English trying to teach the concept of "theme" to high school students. The case provides background information about the student teacher's educational experiences and reasons for teaching. The paper explains how the case was used during teacher training and how teacher candidates analyzed and reacted to the case.

Wilson, Suzanne M. Understanding Historical Understanding: An Analysis of the Subject Matter Knowledge of Teachers. (Paper presented at the American Educational Research Association Annual Meeting, San Francisco, March, 1989). This study explores the knowledge of American history of 10 participants categorized according to both pedagogical and subject matter expertise: novice, developing, and expert. Differences in understanding of history were classified among four qualitative dimensions of understanding: differentiation, elaboration, qualification, and integration.

Foreign Language Faculty Renewal: A Case Study

Eileen Burchell
Ellen S. Silber
Marymount College, Tarrytown

> "Il n'est désir plus naturel que le désir de connoissance.
> Nous essayons tous les moyens qui nous y peuvent mener.
> Quand la raison nous fault, nous y employons
> l'expérience..." (Montaigne, "De l'expérience," *Essais*)[1]

Introduction

In this final chapter of *Critical Issues in Foreign Language Instruction*, we have chosen to explore professional development from a particular perspective, that of two teachers of French at a small Northeastern liberal arts college for women. As teaching faculty we feel compelled to rethink established paradigms of foreign language education research that have until recently excluded most classroom practitioners. By presenting a case study model rather than using the traditionally accepted forms for research, we hope to empower foreign language teachers across the profession to voice the questions most important to them about their own professional growth. Bernhardt's and Hammadou's study implies how little we know about what foreign language teachers actually value in their continuing education (1987). We want to tell a story of faculty development by recording and reflecting on the concrete experiences which have furthered our own renewal in the field of foreign language, literature, and culture.

Beginnings

How do college faculty in foreign languages decide what it is they don't know and want to learn about? We believe that, in most cases, there are forces both within and beyond the individual campus that have a direct impact on what we choose to study. For example, national trends for the reinstitution of foreign language requirements, state mandates for proficiency-oriented curricula, and growing student interest on our campus in foreign cultures all played a part in shaping our initial efforts at faculty renewal.

Organized professional development in foreign languages at our institution began in 1982 when one of us, as Chair of the Department of Modern Languages, attended a workshop for the improvement of foreign language and literature programs, conceived by Claire Gaudiani and funded by the Exxon Foundation and the University of Pennsylvania. As a result of this experience, we learned that graduate specialization in literature did not prepare most college teachers of the commonly taught foreign languages to keep up with current theory and research in language acquisition and pedagogy. Our exposure to innovation at this workshop became the catalyst for foreign language curriculum change and expanded faculty development efforts at our institution.

The First Grant

The Exxon workshop stressed two things above all: 1) curriculum change costs money; and 2) raising funds requires effort, not genius. Before writing a grant proposal, however, we were advised to interview the entire student body through a questionnaire. We wanted to know more about their views, expectations, and preferences in the foreign language classroom. The consensus was striking. Our students expressed overwhelming interest in speaking a foreign language confidently, and in learning about contemporary cultures. Majors in International Business were also receptive to including commercial French and Spanish courses as part of the language component of their programs. As a department, we decided to continue studying some of the new content areas and methodologies we had recently learned about.

At this juncture we had a stroke of luck. A new government grants officer approached us with information about the Department of Education's Undergraduate Foreign Language and International Studies Program. She was eager to support our efforts in creating a plan for faculty development activities within the Modern Language Department. In this effort, her help was indispensable since grant writing was a skill which neither we nor any of our colleagues possessed. We were, however, fully aware that if we didn't submit something, we wouldn't get anything. We learned that there is no such thing as the perfect proposal. If we hadn't been funded the first time, we would have asked for the reviewers' comments and tried again.

We conceived a program that would radically alter the format of all elementary and intermediate language instruction at the College, transform the study of foreign cultures, add courses in commerical language, and train faculty in oral proficiency testing. In February 1984, we received a grant. Implementation of the grant required department-wide faculty renewal which took a variety of forms, both individual and collective. For example, five of the six members of the language faculty attended a training workshop in the Dartmouth Intensive Language Model which we had decided to adopt. We also went as a group to the Defense Language Institute in Monterey, California for ACTFL-sponsored training as oral proficiency interviewers. Since the focus of our grant was on strengthening the foreign language component of our international studies program, funds from the grant provided an opportunity for several of us, including one adjunct faculty member, to visit exemplary programs on other campuses and talk to colleagues about their experiences in internationalizing curricula.

Participation in grant activities has a way of focusing one's sense of professional direction. This is what happened for one of us, with the support of this first DOE funding. Drawing upon fresh knowledge and momentum, she undertook new endeavors, such as developing commercial language courses at the College, training faculty in oral proficiency testing and submitting interesting proposals to workshops and conferences around the country. In her energetic pursuit of these professional interests within the foreign language field, this faculty member has recognized her participation in the original grant activities as having had a spiralling effect in her personal story of professional development.

Our experience most clearly demonstrates that when the experts in a discipline—teachers themselves—are empowered to chart the course of their own intellectual and professional growth, their commitment to program implementation and personal renewal is strong. Interestingly, we discovered that each of us was motivated to participate in renewal efforts for different reasons. For some, the prospect of innovation was challenging in itself; for others, sustained enthusiasm for learning was the motivation; still others proceded very practically to expand the content knowledge necessary for specialty courses. For our then-adjunct faculty member, the successful grant was a major turning point: the grant allotted funds for a new full-time appointment in French, a striking example of what grant monies can do. Faculty development then took on new meaning with the possibility of tenure in her chosen field. And yes, we had our sceptics in the department who made us all aware of the need to reexamine regularly our assumptions and our progress.

We believe that it is largely because our individual and collective commitment to each other and to the renewal process was so strong, that the changed curriculum was unusually vital. These changes remain in place today, for us, a testament to the power of faculty-generated professional development.

Another critical dimension of our project involved an outside evaluator who reported on our efforts. Richard Jurasek, a colleague in German from Earlham College, served as a consultant on our project. We would like to share with you his observations which confim our own analysis and intuition about the benefits of renewal at any educational institution:

> This group enterprise had another critical benefit: the professionalization of the department and teachers. This is not to suggest that the faculty were lax

professionals before the [Dartmouth] workshop, but rather that they were collectively energized by the enterprise to rethink their instructional methods and collectively experiment with some promising ideas. An additional benefit is their new intellectual solidarity. This is not to suggest that each of the six persons now speaks with one voice. Indeed, there seems to be ongoing discussion about curriculum methods and future directions. But they are now more focused on their task and share more critical paradigms, terminology, and experiences. This solidarity and increased professionalism count among key changes in intellect and affect for this faculty. (Jurasek, 1)

Although we did not have "professionalism" and "solidarity" in mind when we wrote the grant, we know now that such by-products are as important in renewing faculty efforts as are plans for curriculum change.

The Tarrytown-Lakeland Foreign Language Teachers Association

While one way to effect college faculty development is through the acquisition of outside funding, there is another cost-free model. An Academic Alliance school-college collaborative has as its purposes to improve foreign language education programs in the local area and to better members' intellectual and professional lives. At Marymount College we founded the Tarrytown-Lakeland Foreign Language Teachers Association in 1983. This group is also part of the network of Academic Alliances in Foreign Languages and Literatures.

In the Tarrytown-Lakeland collaborative, we have organized many professional development activities that take into account the needs of our members from four participating institutions: two public high schools, a private school, and a liberal arts college. We have held workshops on oral proficiency testing, use of computer-assisted instruction for the foreign language learner, integration of telecommunications advances in the foreign language classroom, teaching contemporary culture through reading and composition, the role of literature in Eastern Europe, writing individual grants, and experiencing unfamiliar teaching methodologies. Our own faculty would not have studied together in this way had it not been for the Academic Alliance model. (For more background on this national collaborative movement, see Gaudiani's and Silber's publications in the annotated bibliography.)

There is yet another benefit for foreign language faculty who participate in Alliances: for those of us who genuinely enjoy teaching beginning language courses, the Tarrytown-Lakeland collaborative (and others like it) provides a natural setting in which we come together with colleagues of like mind, the majority of them from the schools. As college teachers, we have found renewal through these regular discussions about elementary language teaching, because it is a subject often devalued by our professional college/ university culture.

The Westchester Consortium for International Studies

When we joined the profession, we imagined the life of a college faculty member to include long hours alone spent on research. If there were any collaborative activity, it was to be with other faculty from our department. Once we had challenged this stereotype by extending our professional community to include foreign language teachers in the local schools, our mind-set changed. It was therefore a natural next step to come together with faculty from other colleges.

The occasion was the formation of the Westchester Consortium for International Studies funded by Hitachi to provide interdisciplinary faculty development opportunities for teachers at member institutions. Central among the program activities is a series of faculty seminars. Topics for the semester-long seminars have brought together colleagues from the humanities and social sciences to consider art and culture in East Asia, the political economy of developing nations, and a comparison of educational systems in Japan and the U.S. Such collaboration affords faculty in our discipline the opportunity to show other teachers that knowing foreign languages heightens one's ability to more nearly identify with people from other cultures.

As an outgrowth of participation in the international studies consortium, one of us proposed a project on gender perspectives in literary texts from French, Spanish, and Japanese cultures. This particular program is an example of our discovery that professional development opportunities can be occasions not only to expand one's horizons as a learner and classroom teacher, but in addition to become a leader and facilitator of knowledge for one's peers. Starting with an original idea and building it into a full-fledged program of faculty reading, study, discussion and writing, lends an added dimension to the concept of renewal: we become catalysts for the learning of our colleagues.

Back on our Own Campus: College-wide Faculty Renewal

Renewal programs for foreign language faculty need not always be limited to the fields that have traditionally informed our teaching. One of the most significant faculty development experiences for us, and indeed for the thirty-eight faculty and staff who attended in 1987, was a two-day workshop entitled "Gender and its Implications for Teaching and Learning." Based on research done for *Women's Ways of Knowing* by Belenky, Clinchy, Goldberger and Tarule (1986), this faculty development seminar helped participants to examine epistemological processes of women students and the effects of pedagogical styles in facilitating or discouraging student knowing. This kind of experience supplements others on foreign language pedagogy by highlighting gender issues in the classroom and by shifting the focus of instruction to the learner.

Reflections

Never in the history of foreign language education in this country has re-visioning professional development been more urgent. In the words of Adrienne Rich, this transformation is, literally, "an act of survival" (35). Why? Impacting us as foreign language teachers in the 1990s we find an overwhelming number of changes: non-traditional and "differently-abled" learners (Brown 1; Spinelli 139); dramatic advances in telecommunications technology; growing interest in less commonly taught languages; calls for a global curriculum and multi-cultural literacy; the highly increased demand for communicative and cultural competence. In order to respond to these challenges, individual classroom teachers of foreign language, from all educational sectors must be at the center of the decision-making process. It is these teachers who know about students; it is they then who know what tomorrow's foreign language faculty will need to know.

Our own narrative of renewal has evolved considerably through the very process of conceptualizing, writing, and reflecting on this paper. When we began thinking about faculty development for foreign language educators, it was in an abstract, generalized frame of reference. Trained to value the theoretical rather than the experiential frame of reference, we did not immediately think of our own experiences as sufficiently representative or "scholarly" for inclusion in a volume on critical issues in foreign language education. Yet as we read, we discovered that it is only from personal experience and reflection that genuine faculty renewal flows.

What Have We Learned?

We have learned that faculty development can take many forms but that the most successful experiences are based on teachers' own perceptions of their needs.

We have learned that personal relationships and interaction are the basis for successful renewal.

We have learned that teachers most often learn better from other teachers.

We have learned that risk-taking is an integral part of any ambitious faculty development program.

We have learned that the worst case scenario in submitting a grant proposal is not rejection but missing the deadline, due to the drive for perfection.

More than anything else, we have learned that you have to start somewhere. We are tempted to say that it doesn't matter where you start; for when you begin to notice possibilities for innovation, you then go on to see many others. This habit of mind stays with you; like a new pair of glasses, it can give you vision where before you had none. Reflecting on how we felt at the beginning of our own faculty renewal efforts, we are reminded of James Russell's observation in A Fable for Critics (1848): "In creating, the only hard thing's to begin."

Notes

1. "There is no desire more natural than the desire for knowledge. We try all ways that can lead to it. When reason fails us, we use experience—" (Montaigne, "Of Experience." *The Complete Essays of Montaigne*, vol. III., trans. Donald M. Frame. Garden city, NY: Doubleday, 1960, 309.)

References

Babcock, Charles L. "What Do We Really Mean by Faculty Development?" *ADFL Bulletin* 20, 3 (1989):31-34. Expands the concept of post-secondary faculty development as self-renewing activities by stressing the importance of personal relationships within the context of collegial interaction.

Belenky, Mary Field, Blythe McVicker Clinchy, Nancy Rule Goldberger, Jill Mattuck Tarule. *Women's Ways of Knowing*. New York: Basic Books, 1986. Describes five perspectives for understanding women's cognitive development, based on interviews with 135 women of various ages and educational backgrounds. Quotations for the interviews and the epistemological schema can provide insight useful to any faculty member.

Bernhardt, Elizabeth and Joann Hammadou. "A Decade of Research in Foreign Language Teacher Education." *Modern Language Journal* 71,3 (1987):289-99. Responds to Homes Group Report by calling for "subject matter specific research in teacher education" (296). Only nine of seventy-eight articles cited (1977-87) treat inservice opportunities for professional development.

Brown, Christine. Interview in "The Race to the Future." *Collaborare* 5 (1990):1,4.

Combs, Arthur W. "New Assumptions for Teacher Education." *Foreign Language Annals* 22,3 (1989): 129-34. Re-evaluates traditional assumptions underlying teacher education programs. Argues for an experiential frame of reference that acknowledges the importance of personal belief systems in professional growth and development.

Durant, Stephen W. "The Myth of Mentoring." *ADFL Bulletin* 19,3 (1988):42-47. Examines implications of two recent developments in foreign language education on mentoring: increased standards of professionalism for faculty and rapid transformations in literary theory.

Gaudiani, Claire L. and David G. Burnett. "Academic Alliances: A New Approach to School/College Collaboration." *Current Issues in Higher Education*. Washington, American Association for Higher Education. Washington, American Association for Higher Education, 1985-86. Gives an excellent overview of the Academic Alliance concept. Discusses how to establish a faculty collaborative and incentives for participation. List of fiscal resources and bibliography.

Holly, Mary Louise and Caven S. McLoughlin, eds. *Perspectives on Teacher Professional Development*. London: Falmer Press, 1989. Explores professional development, viewed as a career-long process for educators, from multiple perspectives: historical, sociological, psychological, pedagogical, cross-cultural. Chapters 4, 6, 7, 8, 12 deal with practitioner's viewpoint.

Jarvis, Donald K. "Junior Faculty Development and Language Department Quality." *ADFL Bulletin* 19,3 (1988):32-37. Addresses need for programs to assist junior faculty in developing as teachers and scholars. Contains good overview of faculty development literature in general and cites examples of specific programs.

Jurasek, Richard. "Evaluation of the Marymount College Tarrytown U.S. Department of Education Project: 'Strengthening the Foreign Language and Cultural Component of the International Studies Curriculum.'" Unpublished report, 1986:1-8.

Kramsch, Claire. "New Directions in the Study of Foreign Languages." *ADFL Bulletin* 21,1 (1989):4-11. Examines the challenges arising from a broadening definition of language study and recent developments in research, pedagogy, and teaching. Calls for foreign language education programs that assist teachers in integrating the theory and practice of intercultural communication.

Lange, Dale L. "A Blueprint for a Teacher Development Program," in Jack C. Richards and David Nunan, eds. *Second Language Teacher Education.* Cambridge: Cambridge University Press, 1990:245-268.

Pesola, Carol Ann, and Helena Anderson Curtain. "Elementary School Foreign Languages: Obstacles and Opportunities," in Helen S. Lepke, ed., *Shaping the Future: Challenges and Opportunities.* Middlebury, Vermont: Northeast Conference, 1989:41-59. Cites limited availability of inservice opportunities for professional development as a serious obstacle to improving foreign language instruction in the elementary schools.

Phillips, June K. "Teacher Education: The Target of Reform," in Helen S. Lepke, ed., *Shaping the Future: Challenges and Opportunities.* Middlebury, Vermont: Northeast Conference, 1989:11-39. Advocates that foreign language teachers take responsibility for professionalism. Valuable contribution to the discussion of reform in the field of foreign language education.

Rich, Adrienne. "When We Dead Awaken (1971)" in *On Lies, Secrets and Silence: Selected Prose 1966-1978.* New York: W.W. Norton and Company, 1979.

Richards, Jack C. *The Language Teaching Matrix.* Cambridge: Cambridge University Press, 1990. Uses the metaphor of a matrix to describe the interaction of teacher, learner, curriculum materials, and methodology. Encourages language teachers to use regular self-monitoring as an important dimension of professional development (Ch. 7).

Richards, Jack C., and David Nunan, eds. *Second Language Teacher Education.* Cambridge: Cambridge University Press, 1990. Provides a comprehensive overview of current issues in second language teacher education. Emphasizes the central role teachers themselves must play in professional decision-making. Presents four case studies (Part IV) that argue for a broad view of professional development.

Silber, Ellen S. "Academic Alliances in Foreign Languages and Literatures: A Collaborative Vision for Our Future." *The French Review* 63,6 (1990): 987-995. Describes Academic Alliances in Foreign Languages and Literatures as an important model for faculty development. Discusses accomplishments of individual groups and summarizes an evaluation of Alliances' impact on foreign language faculty in schools and colleges.

Spinelli, Emily. "Beyond the Traditional Classroom," in Helen S. Lepke, ed. *Shaping the Future: Challenges and Opportunities.* Middlebury, Vermont: Northeast Conference, 1989.

Strasheim, Lorraine A. "Preservice and Inservice Teacher Education in the Nineties: The Issue is Instructional Validity." Unpublished manuscript, 1989. Considers a teaching career as "a continuum of self-development" and insists on professional- ism that empowers teachers to make their own decisions about growth. Suggests a variety of formats for inservice education for foreign language teachers.

Widdowson, Henry G. *Aspects of Language Training*. Oxford: Oxford University Press, 1990. Views language teachers as mediators between theory and practice and develops a model of "pragmatic mediation" in Part One, Chapter 4 on "Pedagogic research and teacher education."

Index